Politics and Governance in the Middle East

Also by Vincent Durac and Francesco Cavatorta

**Civil Society and Democratisation in the Arab World:
The Dynamics of Activism**

**The Foreign Policies of the EU and the US in North Africa:
Converging or Diverging Dynamics?** *(co-editors)*

Politics and Governance in the Middle East

Vincent Durac
and
Francesco Cavatorta

First published 2015 by
PALGRAVE

Palgrave in the UK is an imprint of Macmillan Publishers Limited,
registered in England, company number 785998, of 4 Crinan Street,
London, N1 9XW.

Palgrave Macmillan in the US is a division of St Martin's Press LLC,
175 Fifth Avenue, New York, NY 10010.

Palgrave is a global imprint of the above companies and is represented throughout the world.

Palgrave® and Macmillan® are registered trademarks in the United States,
the United Kingdom, Europe and other countries.
ISBN 978-0-230-36133-1   ISBN 978-1-137-52127-9 (eBook)
DOI 10.1007/978-1-137-52127-9

This book is printed on paper suitable for recycling and made from fully
managed and sustained forest sources. Logging, pulping and manufacturing
processes are expected to conform to the environmental regulations of the
country of origin.

A catalogue record for this book is available from the British Library.

A catalog record for this book is available from the Library of Congress.

Contents

List of Illustrative Material

Map

Boxes

Figures

Acknowledgements

Having worked together on a number of different research projects, we decided to write a textbook on Middle East politics and governance that would serve the needs of students interested in the topic. We have tried to offer students a book that does justice to the complexity of Middle East politics, while remaining accessible. When reading about the Middle East, students are very often confronted with either incredibly simplistic accounts, or highly sophisticated scholarly ones. In the first instance, students are not challenged to think deeply about how politics functions in the region, and what are the connections that can and should be made with how politics is conducted elsewhere. In addition, they are encouraged to think of Middle East politics as 'exceptional', which can lead to simplistic characterizations that have very little basis in reality. In the second instance, students who might not intend to pursue further research on the region find themselves lost, having to deal with articles or books that assume vast prior knowledge of Middle East politics. We have tried to make this volume both sophisticated and accessible. The sophistication lies in the extensive research that was undertaken, both theoretical and empirical, to provide a picture of politics and governance that integrates local and global dynamics. The accessibility lies in the linkage between research findings and the broader 'story' of the region, which we tell to account for its most significant events and political phenomena. It is this combination of complexity and accessibility that makes this textbook novel, and we hope that this volume provides valuable insights into, and information about, an often-misunderstood region.

The book naturally draws on our previous research work on different aspects of Middle East Politics, but it should be emphasized that the combination of theoretical frameworks employed in this textbook to describe and explain Middle East politics is an innovation in our work of which we are particularly proud. The chapter on civil society relies on research material that was published in our co-authored volume *Civil Society and Democratization in the Arab World* (Routledge, 2010), but we have expanded our previous categorizations further – in the process, challenging our previous assumptions. For the chapter on social activism, the textbook also draws from Francesco Cavatorta's book *Civil Society Activism under Authoritarian Rule* (Routledge, 2013) and from the volume co-edited by Paul Aarts and Francesco Cavatorta *Civil Society*

Activism in Syria and Iran (Lynne Rienner, 2013). The chapter on gender and politics has benefited from the input of Emanuela Dalmasso, with whom Francesco Cavatorta co-wrote the paper 'The Role of Women in Islamist Movements in Morocco and Tunisia: Negotiating New Gender Roles?' presented at ECPR Joint Sessions held in Antwerp, Belgium, in April 2012. Chapter 10 develops themes explored in Francesco Cavorta, 'International Politics of the Middle East', in Ellen Lust (ed.), *The Middle East* (CQ Press, 2013). Beyond these, we have drawn extensively on the work of other scholars, as the list of references makes clear. No work of this kind is possible without the input of countless others. Any errors, as usual, are entirely our responsibility.

We acknowledge the contribution that the three external referees made to this project. Their comments were extremely valuable in improving the book and we are deeply grateful for their input. The editorial team at Palgrave have been tremendously patient with us and guided us smoothly through the publication process. We would like to acknowledge, in particular, the support and precious insights of Stephen Wenham, who has been unwavering in his support and attention, and unaccountably patient. Vincent Durac would like to thank Colm and Marjorie for ongoing support (and for Schull!), as well as colleagues in the School of Politics and International Relations at University College Dublin. He would also like to acknowledge the love, support and patience of Alexander and Amelia, and the apparently inexhaustible supply of the same from Denise, without whom, once more, his contribution to this project would not have been possible. Francesco Cavatorta would like to thank his former colleagues in the School of Law and Government at Dublin City University and his current colleagues in the Department of Political Science at Université Laval, for their encouragement and support.

VINCENT DURAC
FRANCESCO CAVATORTA

The authors and publishers would like to thank the World Economic Forum for kindly giving permission to reproduce Figure 4.1.

List of Abbreviations

AKP	Party of Justice and Development
ASU	Arab Socialist Union
BMENA	Broader Middle East and North Africa Initiative
CIA	Central Intelligence Agency (United States of America)
DP	Democratic Party
EFU	Egyptian Feminist Union
EMP	Euro-Mediterranean Partnership
ENP	European Neighbourhood Policy
EU	European Union
FDI	Foreign Direct Investment
FFS	*Front des Forces Socialistes* (Socialist Forces Front)
FIS	*Front Islamique du Salut* (Islamic Salvation Front)
FLANGO	First Lady Non-Governmental Organization
FLN	*Front de Liberation Nationale* (National Liberation Front)
GCC	Gulf Cooperation Council
GDP	Gross Domestic Product
GNP	Gross National Product
GONGO	Government Organized Non-Governmental Organization
IAF	Islamic Action Front
IMF	International Monetary Fund
IS (Isis)	Islamic State
JMP	Joint Meeting Parties
JP	Justice Party
MENA	Middle East and North Africa
MENAP	Middle East, North Africa, Afghanistan and Pakistan
MEPI	Middle East Partnership Initiative
NATO	North Atlantic Treaty Organization
NDP	National Democratic Party
NGO	Non-Governmental Organization
NRP	National Religious Party
ODA	Official Development Assistance
PDRY	People's Democratic Republic of Yemen
PJD	*Parti de la Justice et du Developpement* (Party of Justice and Development)
QUANGO	Quazi-Autonomous Non-Governmental Organization

PLO	Palestinian Liberation Organization
RCD	Democratic Constitutional Rally
RONGO	Royal Non-Governmental Organization
RP	Refah Party (Welfare Party)
RPP	Republican People's Party
SCAF	Supreme Council of the Army Forces
UAE	United Arab Emirates
UAR	United Arab Republic
UGTT	*Union Générale Travailleurs Tunisiens* (General Union of Tunisian Workers)
UM	Union for the Mediterranean
UNDP	United Nations Development Programme

Map of the Middle East

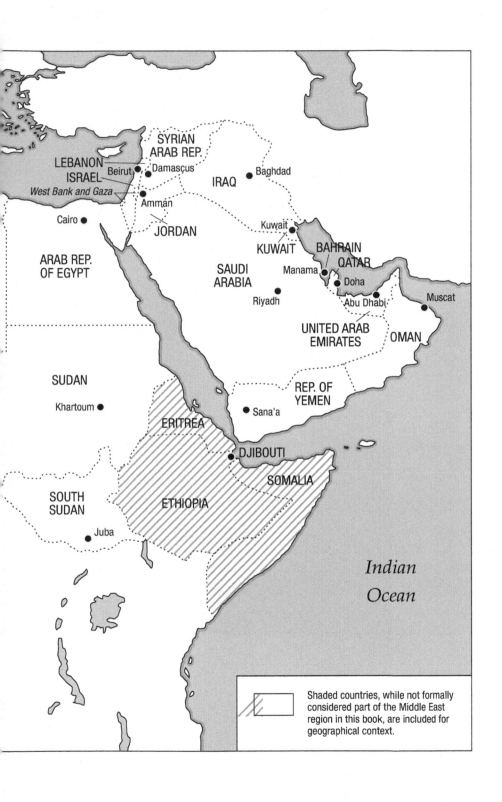

Introduction

Few regions of the world have attracted as much attention in recent decades as the Middle East and North Africa (MENA). Clearly, this is a consequence of the importance of the region for world affairs and for comparative politics. Some of those who have written about the MENA have focused almost exclusively on the politics of individual countries in the region, while others have focused more broadly on region-wide political dynamics. This text adopts an entirely thematic approach to the politics of the region. Rather than opting for an in-depth analysis of the historic, political, social and economic particularities of individual countries, we have chosen to examine the region as whole, highlighting some of its shared issues, traits and challenges.

The MENA, for the purposes of this book, comprises the countries of North Africa from Morocco to Egypt, and those of the Arabian Peninsula: Algeria, Bahrain, Egypt, Iran, Iraq, Israel, Jordan, Kuwait, Lebanon, Libya, Morocco, Oman, the Palestinian Territories, Qatar, Saudi Arabia, Syria, Tunisia, Turkey, the United Arab Emirates, and Yemen. For background information on the countries of the region, see *The World Factbook* at https://www.cia.gov/library/publications/the-world-factbook/. The area includes the formerly British- and French-controlled states of Jordan, Iraq, Lebanon and Syria. Finally, since neither the historic experience nor the contemporary politics of the region would be entirely explicable without reference to them, we also include the non-Arab states of Turkey, Iran and Israel.

In adopting a thematic approach to the region, we are certainly not proposing that its profound diversity and heterogeneity should be ignored. There are enormous differences, for instance, between the historical experiences of parts of North Africa and the countries in the Arabian Peninsula, just as there are significant differences in the way they are governed. While Islam is the dominant religion across the MENA, there is a variety of sects, interpretations and practices of it, in addition to the presence of other major religions such as Christianity and Judaism. Similarly, Arabic is the language most widely spoken, but in a variety of accents and dialects that are not necessarily mutually understandable. Other languages are also spoken, such as Turkish, Persian, Hebrew, Kurdish and Amazigh. In short, we are aware of the complexity and heterogeneity of the region but we believe, nonetheless, that there are processes and trends within

1

which considerable commonalities exist. This volume seeks to strike a balance between similarities and differences. It is also for this reason that the textbook contains 'information boxes', where we link a general theme to a specific historical event, or to a particularly important figure, or to a concept. The boxes have the objective of highlighting the significance of individual details and how they connect to a more general 'story' of the region.

The book is structured around two interconnected frameworks that, we believe, help to explain political, social and economic developments in the region. One is the dynamic interaction between international and domestic variables. The other stems from the ongoing academic debate regarding the tension between processes of democratization and the persistence of authoritarian rule. In relation to the first, rather than simply looking at the history of the MENA in chronological order or dividing the volume into key issues disconnected from each other, the book examines not only the historical context, but also the major themes in the politics of the region through a focus on the impact of international factors on the region and how, in turn, local developments have affected the perception and the policies of external actors towards the MENA over time. This approach avoids telling the story of the region in ways that marginalize the international dimension. Following recent work which built on Putnam's (1988) notion of a two-level game to explore how the interaction between domestic and international factors helps explain political, social and economic outcomes (Haynes, 2003; Yilmaz, 2002; Yom and al-Momani, 2008), this volume locates external variables as central to key developments and events in the MENA, such as state formation, post-colonial political patterns, ideological radicalism, failed processes of democratic transition and the Arab uprisings of 2011. Putnam's work focused specifically on how the negotiating positions of states on the international stage develop through the interaction of international pressures and domestic bargaining among crucial actors. But, the interaction between the 'domestic' and the 'international' can be expanded much further. In this volume, we extend this approach to the understanding of the politics of the region as a whole. Other scholars, including Owen (2004), introduced the international dimension into their discussions of MENA politics. The novelty of the approach adopted here is that we do so systematically for all the themes in the book. This does not mean that local and country-specific events and developments are irrelevant: quite the contrary. The focus on the international dimension in the volume should not be seen as minimizing the agency of local actors, or as an exercise in Eurocentrism but, rather, as a device that illustrates the many linkages and mutual influences – both positive and negative – that have characterized the relationship between the wider international system and the region. In our volume, we treat the two levels as mutually influencing each other in what might be seen as a continuous feedback loop. The interplay of domestic and international factors provides a more complex and, we believe, better picture of MENA politics, which is often misrepresented and 'essentialized', as Edward Said (1978) and others have pointed out (for example, Mitchell, 1991; Abu-Lughod, 2001). The examination of this interplay is all the more important when one considers the influence of the more recent process of globalization on the MENA. The increasingly rapid process of connectivity between societies – which allows for the movement of goods, people and ideas – has transformed the region in different ways, ranging from the import of new political ideas to the transformation of both urban and rural spaces, and from the impact of economic exchanges to the ability to communicate much more quickly through new technologies (Henry and Springborg, 2010). The relevance of the influence of globalizing trends is demonstrated in the numerous books that deal with how globalization has impacted on different aspects of political, social, cultural and economic life in the region. For example, Cohen and Jaidi (2006) examined the consequence of globalization in Morocco, highlighting the deepening confrontation between Western-oriented and traditional visions of how society should be organized. Also, Mohammadi (2003) analyzed in detail the encounter between globalization and Iranian theocracy, and how this has affected both politics and society, providing the regime with both opportunities for and challenges to legitimation. What should also be highlighted is that events in the region and ideas and/or methods of mobilization have had a global influence. We attempt to demonstrate that the forces of globalization not only flow into the region, but also flow out of it, as the case of the Arab Awakening demonstrates. The slogans, organizational characteristics and political messages of the 'Arab Spring' have influenced social actors across the developed world, from the Occupy movement in the United States to the '*indignados*' in Spain. In turn, it is possible to see a profound connection between the 2009 protests in Iran and the 2011 Arab uprisings, which suggests that there are feedback loops at play.

In relation to the second framework, we connect domestic-international dynamics to the theoretical debate between those who frame the region in terms of transition to democracy/democratization and those who emphasize the survival of authoritarianism, in the context of what has been termed 'post-democratization' (Valbjørn and Bank, 2012). The volume proposes an innovative approach to the treatment of well-known material, insofar as it examines an asserted 'paradigm shift' that has taken place in the academic literature regarding Middle East politics. This paradigm shift consists in the claim that the lens of democratization may no longer be useful to explain politics in the MENA and should be replaced by the lens of authoritarian persistence. The argument for such a paradigm shift has not gone uncontested: one of the key aspects of the book is that it examines not only the extent to which each of these approaches may help to explain politics in the region, but also whether, in some cases, it may be necessary to go beyond the rigidity of both paradigms (Pace and Cavatorta, 2012) to allow them to 'converse' in order to highlight what might be both continuities and change in Middle Eastern affairs (Rivetti, 2013). It is, in part, for this reason that the book begins with the analysis of the origins of the Arab Awakening.

There is little doubt that, irrespective of its ultimate outcome, the Arab Awakening (also known as the Arab Spring or the Arab Uprisings) constitutes a significant watershed in the politics of the region and best exemplifies the way in which the two analytical frames we adopt interact with each other. First, the Arab Awakening is central to the debate on authoritarian resilience and democratization in the region. Authoritarianism has been severely challenged in the midst of widespread popular protests whose slogans focused on accountability, political change and improved standards of living. Walls of fear have come down in the most unexpected of countries (such as Tunisia and Syria), while long-established rulers, such as Muammar al-Qadhafi (from this point onwards, we use the more common citation 'Gaddafi'), have either perished during the revolutionary struggle or, like Ben Ali of Tunisia or Saleh of Yemen, have been forced out of power. This has generated renewed interest in processes of democratic transition (Stepan, 2012). At the same time, however, authoritarianism has, somewhat paradoxically, also been reinforced, because of the difficulties that processes of popular contestation have encountered and because of the capacity of authoritarian leaders to learn from the mistakes of their dictatorial peers elsewhere (Heydemann and Leenders, 2011). The vast majority of rulers in the MENA have been able to remain in power and, where change has taken place, there has been a noticeable return to authoritarian practices, as the case of Egypt powerfully demonstrates. Second, the Arab Awakening is crucial in highlighting the connections and linkages that exist between countries in the region. It clearly represents a profound moment of 'transnationalism at work' with issues of 'revolutionary contagion' – and how to avoid it – becoming central to the politics of the region, highlighting the importance of international factors. At the same time, however, the significance of the international dimension of the Awakening is tempered by the specific national environments within which the desire for political change emerged, which affected the way in which different social and political actors perceive such change. Thus, Chapter 1 examines the factors which promoted revolutionary challenge to what appeared to be entrenched and 'upgraded' authoritarian regimes (Heydemann, 2007), breaking a very thick wall of fear in the process. What emerges from this analysis of the origins of the Arab Awakening is that a genuine understanding of it and the forces that shaped it are impossible without a clear picture of the social, political and economic conditions that preceded it. Chapters 2–10 are therefore dedicated to exploring the different aspects of Middle East politics and governance through specific themes. Later, Chapter 11 discusses the legacy of the Awakening.

In Chapter 2, which focuses on the historical and political context within which the modern Middle East has emerged, the two theoretical frames are employed to explain the importance of the colonial experience in 'dragging' the region into global patterns of interaction, while, at the same time, sowing the seeds of post-colonial authoritarianism, as well as intellectual and political efforts to establish political pluralism. The impact of globalization in recent decades further underpins the importance of these two frames of analysis. On the one hand, the region is firmly entrenched in patterns of global integration. On the other, debate about the survival of authoritarianism abounds when placed in the context of democratic norms advancing globally (Camau, 2006).

As we suggest in Chapter 3, external factors, together with authoritarian forms of political rule, have also been instrumental in transforming the region's social reality since independence, although the way in which these factors operated varied significantly from country to country – which underlines, once again, how local agency and factors determine outcomes. This chapter explores social development in the region with a particular – although not exclusive – focus on the impact of external influences.

Chapter 3 links closely with Chapter 4, which examines the region's political economy. While, as we make clear, the political economy of the Middle East and North Africa is not simply and exclusively about natural resources, there is no doubt that their presence plays a considerable role in influencing the ways in which regional economies are structured, as well as having a profound impact on political institutions (Achcar, 2013). An examination of the role of energy resources allows us to link foreign meddling in the region with the persistence of authoritarian rule, while it also leads us to look at how decisions taken in

individual oil and gas exporting countries can trigger significant political and economic consequences across the globe. In addition, we look
at the way in which economic diversification, together with increased
global trade linkages, might disrupt authoritarian rule by creating
new 'democracy-seeking' social classes. Similarly, we examine how
declining income from the energy resources of oil and gas exporting
countries might help to undermine the unwritten pact between rulers and
ruled in rentier states, where the distribution of income derived from the
exploitation and sale of hydrocarbons greatly impacts on economic and
political development.

Chapter 5 briefly addresses the institutional set-up of Arab countries,
which differ on a number of counts. While most have remained solidly
authoritarian, they have done so in different ways. Thus, monarchies
and republics find legitimacy in specific institutions and have developed
radically diverse mechanisms of survival over time. The imperative of
the survival of ruling elites has led to attempts to rejuvenate political
systems. As pressures from below and from the outside to conform to
international norms of democracy and liberal governance increased,
traditional institutions were overhauled to provide a more modern
picture; parliaments were revived, electoral competition introduced, and
independent authorities created. While this did not substantially change
the nature of the regimes, it provided the opportunity for them to be
attuned, if only superficially, to international standards and to engage
with global norms. In particular, the chapter focuses on party politics,
electoral behaviour and elections. These are often neglected topics in
the literature on Middle East Politics, but they have acquired growing
relevance in recent years. While it would be mistaken to claim that political parties and formal electoral politics play a crucial role in the politics of Arab countries, they nevertheless contribute to understanding the
ways in which authoritarian regimes seek to survive and how unintended
consequences of the manipulation of both institutions can be set off. In
addition, the chapter explores party politics and electoral mechanisms in
the democratic states (such as Israel and Turkey) and 'quasi-democratic'
states (such as Lebanon and Iran).

Chapter 6 examines what has often been seen as one of the distinctive
traits of the whole region – namely, the relationship between politics and
religion. For some time, the region was believed to be unique in deviating
from the classic modernization paradigm that envisaged, among other
things, the inevitable relegation of religion to the private sphere. Long
before the Iranian revolution of 1979, the MENA region had seen the
rise of political movements, characterized by different degrees of radicalism and employing different methods of activism, but imbued with

religious principles, as the foundation of the Muslim Brotherhood in 1928 in Egypt illustrates. Rather than progressively becoming a private matter, religion in the MENA assumed an intensely public expression, with many citizens and political movements striving for the adoption of religiously oriented public policies. But it is worth noting that the MENA region is not unique in this respect since religion plays an increasingly important role across a number of countries and continents, from India to the United States, and from Russia to Latin America (Ozzano, 2013). A particular novelty of Chapter 6 is that we do not confine our analysis of the relationship between religion and politics to Islam. We also note that the politicized role of religion is characteristic of both Judaism (no analysis of party politics in Israel would be complete without a discussion of Jewish religious parties) and Christianity (again, a discussion of the politics – indeed, the social characteristics – of countries such as Egypt, Syria, Jordan and Lebanon that did not include reference to the ways in which Christian communities operate politically would obscure much of what takes place).

Chapter 7 is focused on civil society activism, deepening the discussion on the relationship between religion and politics through an examination of the dynamics that influence civic life across the region. Recent decades have witnessed an international drive to stimulate the growth of civil society in the MENA in order to foster democratization and political change. However, we describe how such an externally-driven stimulus can be counterproductive because it projects a vision and an ideal of civil activism that tends to marginalize the very local actors that genuinely 'do' civil activism – namely, faith-based groups. Thus, we examine the paradox of a Western-sponsored secular civil society that has limited impact in terms of political change and that, paradoxically, might end up as a pillar of authoritarian rule (Cook, 2005), while actors that Western countries find inherently illiberal and undemocratic, but that might ultimately be agents of change, are largely neglected. Civil society activism is a crucial topic in discussions on the Middle East and North Africa, and requires to be examined in detail. The authoritarian nature of the vast majority of political regimes has marginalized political parties for a long time (Willis, 2002) and, although their importance has been somewhat revived as detailed in Chapter 5, civil activism has been one of the very few spheres where meaningful political debate could, and still can, take place. It is in this sphere that many political activists still tend to operate. The realm of civil society is also where different and conflicting visions of society emerge and where 'culture wars' are fought out. This is true not only in regimes where the political system is closed off and parties are either absent or marginalized, but is also true in the few democratic systems in the region. Following a global trend, political participation through parties and trust in them is diminishing, rendering civil society the space where a great deal of 'politics' is conducted. The huge demonstrations against the AKP-led government in Turkey in the summer of 2013, as well as the street protests in Israel in 2011 against the high costs of living, are an indication of the capacity of society to mobilize outside formal institutional channels. Given the asserted, if problematic, connection between civil society activism, democracy and democratization, it is important to describe, analyze and understand the dynamics of civil society in the region.

Chapter 8 examines gender relations, one of the most hotly debated themes in Middle East studies. There is little doubt that, to this day, the Western image of the Middle Eastern woman is invariably linked to ideas of inequality and oppression, with a particular obsession with dressing practices that are seen as the embodiment of women's exclusion from the public sphere. Without ignoring the many forms of exclusion that women do face across the region, the chapter challenges the validity of this view as uniform across both time and space. That this patently is not the case is manifested in the way in which women in the region have often been the protagonists of both political and social life. In any case, gender relations and gender politics once again illustrate the relevance of domestic-international interactions, insofar as many ordinary women harnessed imported ideologies such as feminism and secularism to mobilize politically and socially in favour of change. But such ideologies were also either 'indigenized' or, in some instances, completely rejected in order to revisit local traditions linked to Islam or other religions that might also serve as tools of mobilization for social and political change. Discussion of this is linked, inevitably, to the debate on democratization and the persistence of authoritarian rule because, paradoxically, it is often assumed that the rights of women and their progressive emancipation can only be protected by authoritarian leaders through 'state feminism', while the advent of more democratic mechanisms would lead ultimately to the implementation of regressive anti-woman politics.

Chapter 9 shifts the attention away from civil society activism and institutional politics to concentrate, instead, on what Eva Bellin (2004) has described as the main explanation for the authoritarianism that has characterized regimes in the region: the security apparatus. The colonial enterprise left a legacy of state weakness that, all too often, led the military in newly independent countries to take a leading political role. As Owen (2004: 217) correctly observes: 'given the problems faced by most Middle Eastern states after independence, it is easy to see why regimes felt that they needed to create a substantial military force to enhance both internal and external legitimacy'. The grip of the military on regimes strengthened over time in a number of Arab countries, and where the military was not the protagonist of political life and the 'repressor-in-chief' of domestic dissent, security services and the police took over that role, as the case of Tunisia under Ben Ali powerfully illustrates. The discussion of the security apparatus across the region links clearly to that on democratization and the persistence of authoritarianism, which, in turn, is inextricably tied to the costs of dissent. In addition, an analysis of the security apparatus links necessarily to the issue of international support for both military and police forces in the region. This enabled the repression of dissent, but also increased expenditure on arms and, on occasion, generated local conflicts. This pattern was seen very clearly during the Cold War when both superpowers had privileged clients in the region. But it continued in the aftermath of the end of the Cold War and the collapse of the Soviet Union.

Chapter 10 extends the discussion of the role of external actors in the MENA region and, in turn, the impact of events in the region on political life at the international level. The focus is largely on the United States and the European Union, but there is consideration also of the emerging powers of China and Russia. Through the analysis of their foreign policies towards the region, we emphasize once again how such international actors have the power and the means to have great influence on domestic politics in the region, but also how regional events can fundamentally shape those very same foreign policies. This 'loop' has its most significant impact on the nature of domestic political arrangements and the ways in which competing local interests and actors interact with each other.

Finally, Chapter 11 returns to the Arab Awakening and attempts to make sense of political dynamics in the region since the uprisings. It does not predict how events will turn out. But it is reasonable to conclude that, no matter what institutional outcomes are arrived at, in countries such as Tunisia, Egypt, Syria, Yemen, Libya and Bahrain, little will remain the same. New dynamics are at play, new social and political actors have emerged, or returned to the fore, and even those rulers who managed to survive the winds of change are unlikely to govern in the same way as they did in the past. The Arab Awakening has radically altered long-held assumptions about the entrenchment of authoritarianism, but also challenged many of the tenets of the democratization paradigm. It makes sense, therefore, to assess its implications, even though we are far from the conclusion of what are ongoing events. What the Awakening has also done is to reinforce the validity of an analytical approach to the region based on the interplay of domestic and international factors, insofar as both contagion, and efforts to prevent it, demonstrate the powerful nature of internal–external dynamics at regional and global levels.

Chapter 1

The Arab Awakening

By the middle of the first decade of the twenty-first century, the political order in much of the MENA region appeared to be remarkably stable. Despite a series of challenges, political and economic, leaders and regimes in the region were long-lived. In particular, the leaderships of almost all Arab states enjoyed remarkable security in their enjoyment of office. In Egypt, Husni Mubarak succeeded to the presidency in 1981; Tunisia's Zine El-Abidine Ben Ali first came to power in 1987; in Yemen, Ali Abdallah Saleh had occupied the presidency since the country came into existence in 1990, having been the leader of the Republic of Yemen for a further 12 years before that; in Libya, Muammar Gaddafi dominated political life after the 1969 coup which overthrew the monarchy in that country. Meanwhile, in Syria, Bashar al-Asad became Syrian president in 2000 following the death of his father, who had, in turn, ruled the country since 1970 and, in Algeria, the rule of president Bouteflika, foreign minister between 1963 until 1979 and in power since 1999, seemed so secure that his supporters called for him to seek a fourth mandate in 2014, which he indeed obtained. Elsewhere, unelected monarchies of various kinds ensured the maintenance of 'family' rule in Morocco, Jordan, Saudi Arabia and the other Gulf states. Since 1979, Iran had known only two genuine power holders – Khomeini and Khamenei – and, despite the 2009 protests, the clerical regime stood firm and unchanged. With the exceptions of Lebanon and the non-Arab states of Israel and Turkey, nowhere was power transferred through the ballot box. It is no wonder then that a consensus began to emerge among some scholars regarding the enduring capacity of Arab and Iranian rulers to resist pressures, both internal and external, to liberalize their political systems, let alone democratize them.

Democratization or authoritarian 'upgrading'?

Writing in 2007, Oliver Schlumberger noted a number of 'signals' of political change across the Middle East. These included the emergence of new political protest movements mobilizing for change, a degree of realization on the part of incumbent regimes that some political reform was necessary, and, on the international level, a new emphasis on the promotion of 'good governance' by external players. Despite all this, he concluded

that the Arab world remained unique in its lack of freedom: 'The star-
tling fact is that in the Middle East none of the mentioned initiatives and
dynamics have produced a structurally enhanced quality of governance (in
the sense of guaranteed basic freedoms that Arab citizens enjoy), let alone
any instances of democratization. In this respect, the world's most unfree
region is indeed unique' (2007: 5).

Schlumberger was far from being the only scholar suggesting that Arab
authoritarianism was unique in a world where liberalization and democratization were dominant paradigms (Camau, 2006). By the mid-2000s, a
growing number of scholars began to argue that the expectation implicit in
the 'democratization' paradigm – namely, that, sooner or later, democracy
would come to the MENA, just as it was supposed to have done to every
other region of the world – was profoundly misplaced. Eberhard Kienle,
among others, noted that political liberalization is easily reversible and
wrote at book length about the political 'deliberalization' of Egypt (2001).
Daniel Brumberg (2003) argued that instead of liberalizing proto-democ-
racies, what were found typically in the region were 'liberalized autocracies', suggesting that Arab countries had introduced a number of liberal
and democratic reforms – creation of parliaments, regular elections, multiparty politics and human rights legislation – but genuine political power
and its exercise remained in the hands of unelected and unaccountable
institutions. What all of these approaches had in common was the view
that Middle Eastern regimes were not serious about democratizing but,
rather, had evolved sophisticated mechanisms to persuade international
patrons and global financial institutions that some liberalization was on the
political agenda while the real objective was the maintenance of regime
control. In turn, the Western international community pretended to believe
that such liberalizing moves were genuine.

In his study of 'upgraded authoritarianism' (see Box 1.1 for a detailed
discussion of the concept), Steven Heydemann (2007) put forth the most
comprehensive analysis of how political power was exercised in the Arab
world and described a new model of authoritarian governance in which
regimes, through a process of trial and error, adapted to domestic and
international pressures for political reform by developing strategies to
contain and manage demands to democratize. Authoritarian upgrading
consists not of closing Arab societies off from globalization and other
forces of political, economic and social change. Neither is it based simply
on the willingness of regimes to repress their opponents through the use
of widespread coercion. Instead, it involves reconfiguring authoritarian
governance to accommodate and manage changing political, economic
and social conditions, embracing the opportunities that globalization – in
its economic, social and technological aspects – provided to re-invigorate

Box 1.1 Authoritarian upgrading

In what is probably the most coherent theoretical attempt to make sense of the persistence of authoritarian rule in the Arab world, Steven Heydemann argues that authoritarian rulers in the Arab world, over time, have become very adept at creating more flexible, and therefore enduring, forms of authoritarianism. This has occurred despite a global trend towards democratization, and despite the democracy promoting policies of the international community in the region, or local efforts aimed at regime change. Heydemann's argument is based on the exploration of an interesting paradox. By pretending to liberalize their political and economic systems under the pressure and, at times, the guidance, of inter-national actors – the European Union, for example – authoritarian regimes have been able to utilize the reforms they undertook to render their system of govern-ance more flexible, but certainly not more accountable. Heydemann identifies five different characteristics that, in different combinations, all Arab regimes displayed in their authoritarian upgrading.

First, they were able to appropriate civil society activism. Rather than permit-ting genuine pro-democratic and/or liberal activism, they flooded the realm of civil society with government-organized non-governmental organizations (NGOs), allowing those close to the regime to operate, and setting significant 'technical' obstacles for more critical organizations.

Second, they 'managed political contestation' by introducing a number of polit-ical reforms – the introduction of multiparty elections, for instance – to give the impression of liberalization, while relying on informal networks to remain unaccountable to ordinary citizens and depriving the newly created institutions of any meaningful influence.

Third, they liberalized the economy selectively and made sure that key markets were accessed and their benefits captured by a network of 'clients' that were bound to the regime through political, family, kin or clan linkages to secure loyalty and prevent the generation of political dissent among an economic inde-pendent middle-class.

Fourth, they permitted the arrival and widespread use of new technologies to boost economic growth and 'enter modernity' while ensuring, at the same time, that such new technologies were kept under the strict control of the state in order to monitor dissent.

Finally, they seized the opportunities the international system provided by 'shopping around' for alternative sources of patronage and support away from Western countries increasingly interested in democratization.

Source: Steven Heydemann (2007). 'Upgrading authoritarianism in the Arab world,' The Brookings Institution, Analysis Paper, 13: 1–37, available at http://www.brookings.edu/./media/Files/rc/papers/2007/10arabworld/10arabworld.pdf.

authoritarian practices of governance. The concept implies taking advan-tage of the opportunities a domestic and international environment have to offer to avoid genuine change.

Thus, the effective conclusion that many scholars arrived at was that, far from being in transition to democracy, the MENA region was, instead, characterized by the persistence of authoritarianism. This meant that a significant number of studies of authoritarian countries in the region focused on detailing the ways in which authoritarian upgrading worked. This emerging consensus, and its accompanying academic literature, were badly shaken by the remarkable sequence of events that unfolded across the region over the course of just a few months in 2011. It is at this stage that the emphasis on democratization and the transition to a democracy paradigm were revived, stimulating a heated debate about the future direction of the Arab world.

Enter the Arab Awakening

Political unrest in Tunisia, Egypt, Libya and Yemen marked the onset of the Arab Awakening.

The end of four dictatorships

Towards the very end of 2010, protests broke out in the town of Sidi Bouzid in the centre of Tunisia, following the death by self-immolation of a young man named Mohammed Bouazizi. Bouazizi was a 26 year-old street vendor, who supported his family of seven by selling fruit and vegetables. For years, he had complained about having to pay bribes to corrupt local officials. On 17 December, he was accused of failure to pay a fine by local inspectors and had all of his goods confiscated. He complained to the municipal authorities but to no avail. At 11.30 am, he doused himself in paint thinner and immolated himself in front of the governorate building (De Soto, 2011). He died several weeks later. It is worth noting, as Julia Clancy (2012) has pointed out, that Bouazizi's 'sacrificial act of self-immolation' in December 2010 was not the first case of political suicide in Tunisia. A number of young people had killed themselves before 2010 in order to draw attention to the plight of youth, poverty and a lack of opportunities. Clancy writes of a 'culture of suicide' that had developed among the country's marginalized youth (2012: 16). The spontaneous protests, which broke out in Sidi Bouzid, spread within weeks from the Tunisian periphery to major urban centres. The unorganized and leaderless protest movement had at its core young people who mobilized online through social media, but also through informal personal networks usually linked to immigration patterns from the countryside to the cities. This protest movement grew as local trade unionists, lawyers and others disaffected by the regime became involved. However, initially, at least, the established opposition political parties and the leadership of the officially recognized *Union Générale Travailleurs Tunisiens* (General Union of Tunisian

Workers – UGTT) trade union federation were reluctant or unwilling to have anything to do with the protesters. Nevertheless, by 13 January, the situation was serious enough for Ben Ali to order the Chief of Staff of the Armed Forces, Rachid Ammar, to shoot protesters. Ammar refused and was placed under house arrest. But, with his refusal, the extent to which the president had lost key supports had become apparent, and within 24 hours he had departed into exile in Saudi Arabia. While the circumstances surrounding Ben Ali's departure remain mysterious, it seemed to be a last-ditch attempt by members of the ruling élite to stave off more significant threats to their position. Ben Ali's departure, however, strengthened the willingness of protesters who believed that they could achieve much more meaningful changes that the 'simple' departure of the dictator.

Ben Ali's resignation and departure sent shockwaves across the MENA region because it took comparatively little to force Ben Ali out of Tunisia, which, together with Syria, was considered by most analysts to be one of the most resilient and stable authoritarian countries in the Arab world thanks to the effective police-state that he had built to secure his rule. In addition, the strategy of economic development that the regime had adopted had seemed successful in raising living standards, especially when compared with its North African neighbours. The most immediate impact of Ben Ali's departure was in Egypt where an anti-regime protest movement had hitherto made limited inroads. By late January, inspired by events in Tunisia, thousands of people were taking to the streets in cities across the country, echoing the demands of the Tunisian protesters. As in Tunisia, the protests were initially driven by young people, often previously apolitical and, again, mobilizing online and relying on social media to organize and communicate. Also, as in Tunisia, the legally recognized opposition political parties and the leadership of the Muslim Brotherhood were reluctant to take an active role. However, the persistence of the protests and their increasing scale ultimately forced Mubarak's resignation on 11 February 2011 and the hand-over of power to the Supreme Council of the Army Forces (SCAF), which undertook to oversee a transition to civilian rule. Again, forcing Mubarak out can be interpreted as the attempt by the ruling élites to hold on to power by sacrificing the leader, thereby placating the protestors. But, once Mubarak left office, all sorts of outcomes appeared possible for opponents of the regime, including a rapid process of democratization.

Events in Tunisia and Egypt had ramifications elsewhere. The arrest on 15 February of human rights activist Fethi Tarbel provoked protests by 6,000 people in Libya's second city, Benghazi, as well as riots that were suppressed by security forces using water cannon and tear gas. Tarbel represented the families of more than 1,200 political prisoners in the notorious Abu Salim prison who were massacred by the regime in 1996 after they had protested prison conditions. Anti-regime forces in Libya designated 17 February 2011 a 'Day of Rage', during which major demonstrations took place in a number of cities, particularly in the eastern part of the country. By 20 February, anti-government forces had taken control of Benghazi and the central coastal town of Misrata. But, unlike its North African neighbours, Libya was plunged into prolonged, violent conflict, as the regime mustered its forces in an attempt to hold on to power. Gaddafi and his family, counting on the support of loyalist troops and mercenaries, and having witnessed the way in which the Tunisian and Egyptian leaders were dismissed, decided that violent repression would solve the problem. However, Gaddafi did not take into account the strength of the opposition to his rule and, crucially, the support that such opposition would receive from the international community. The leading European powers, notably France and the United Kingdom, as well as the United States, had been caught by surprise by the uprisings in Tunisia and Egypt and were not sure whether to back traditional and loyal allies, or side with the protestors' demands for change and democratic reform. In order to make up for this indecisiveness, but also out of genuine interest in the possibility of ridding the region of 'mad dog' Gaddafi, France, the UK and the United States decided to back the Libyan rebels militarily. The support of the Arab League strengthened their hand, making the Libyan conflict unique for the level of involvement of the international community. On 17 March, the United Nations Security Council authorized a no-fly zone over the country and military action to protect civilians who were believed to be at risk from Gaddafi's forces. This, in turn, led to the involvement of NATO in the effort to remove Gaddafi from power. Despite the forces arrayed against the regime, Gaddafi held out until 20 October 2011, when he was killed in the last major battle of the conflict.

The fourth country to witness the departure of a long-standing autocrat in 2011 was Yemen, where Ali Abdullah Saleh had dominated political life since 1990. As in Libya, the uprising against Saleh was a protracted affair and was also marked by significant external involvement. However, although regime repression of the protest movement did result in significant loss of life, this was not on the scale of Libya (or, later, Syria). The pattern of events in Yemen in many ways resembled those of Tunisia and Egypt. An initially small group of protesters in the capital, Sana'a, was emboldened by events elsewhere, as the protest movement spread across the country, growing in scale until it constituted a major challenge to the regime. On 15 January 2011, the day after Ben Ali had fled Tunisia, a small group of students, civil society and opposition activists attended a rally in Sana'a. The protesters received a boost when Mubarak resigned the presidency in Egypt as thousands of people took to the streets in cities across the country demanding similar change in Yemen. As elsewhere, the protests were led initially by a core of people who were largely previously apolitical, while established opposition political parties were slow to become involved. By March 2011, however, the Joint Meeting Parties (JMP) – a coalition of opposition parties including leftists, Islamists and others – had joined the anti-regime movement. The deaths of dozens of protesters at the hands of security forces on 17 March led to cracks in the regime, as half of the country's ambassadors resigned and a senior military commander, and former key ally of the president, defected to the opposition. Yemen's influential neighbour Saudi Arabia grew alarmed at instability on its southern border and spearheaded an initiative that ultimately led to Saleh's departure from office on 23 November, the transfer of his powers to his vice-president and the establishment of a power-sharing government between the ruling party and the JMP.

Unrest was not limited to these four countries. However, elsewhere outcomes were very different. In North Africa, while Tunisia, Libya and Egypt were convulsed with unrest, the cases of Algeria and Morocco followed a different path. Protests broke out in Algeria in early 2011 but failed to gain any real traction. In January 2011, there were at least four cases of self-immolation by young men in apparent imitation of Mohamed Bouazizi. But, while protests broke out in a number of towns, these did not spread throughout the country and there appeared to be little popular will to challenge the government to the extent that was happening in neighbouring countries (Volpi, 2013). This was due to a number of factors. First, many of the protests were localized and were about local issues, while those involved were unable to create the necessary linkages to make their struggles meaningful on a national level and generate support for them outside core constituencies. Second, the legacy of the civil war of the 1990s played a powerful role in reminding both ordinary citizens and the authorities what had happened in the past when change came too swiftly to the country. Finally, President Bouteflika seized the political initiative by lifting the emergency law, promising constitutional modifications that would democratize the system, and announcing an economic package to deal with unemployment and rising living costs, which were perceived to be the real drivers of the protests in the region.

The pattern was varied, too, in the monarchies of the region. In Morocco, a more substantial protest movement, the February 20 movement, did emerge, and seemed for a time to constitute a powerful challenge to the rule of Mohammad VI – largely because it brought together opposition actors of very different ideological persuasions, united in a common demand for significant political change. But the movement largely failed to achieve its objectives because of the passivity of the political class and the ability of the King to outmanoeuvre them. Seizing the political initiative, the King acknowledged the legitimacy of some of the demands being made and proposed a new more democratic constitution to be voted on in a referendum. While the constitutional changes appeared to be significant, on closer scrutiny they simply confirmed the primacy of the unelected and unaccountable monarchy in the political system (Benchemsi, 2012; Dalmasso, 2012). The opposition eventually ran out of steam, its different components began to drift apart and the Moroccan Spring petered out. The major political parties refrained from putting pressure on the monarchy and deferred to its efforts to make the changes necessary to appease the population. While remaining loyal to the monarchy provided them with the benefits of office, they missed the opportunity to become central players in Moroccan politics and their credibility further suffered.

In Jordan, protests broke out in January 2011. The demonstrations brought together a range of actors from youth-organized protests to coalitions of opposition parties protesting against endemic corruption and demanding increased political participation, greater accountability and a move towards a more constitutional *monarchy*. But, they did not demand the overthrow of King Abdallah or the monarchy more generally, much like their Moroccan counterparts. It was the prime minister, and not the King, who was the focal point of the protesters' demands. Influenced by events in the region, the King dismissed the unpopular prime minister and his government in February 2011, and then promised a series of reforms and a national dialogue on electoral and constitutional reforms (Ryan, 2012: 156–7).

Elsewhere in the Gulf, the typical response to unrest came in the form of economic inducement, although repression and sectarian rhetoric were also employed (Matthiesen, 2013). In Kuwait, the government announced a grant of US$3,500 for every person in the country along with a year's worth of staple goods such as cooking oil, sugar and milk. In February, the Saudi government embarked on the spending of US$80 billion on public sector wage increases, unemployment benefits and low-income housing. In September, Qatar spent US$8 billion on increased public sector salaries and pensions, while Oman promised additional jobs for unemployed youth (Brownlee *et al.*, 2013: 33; Kamrava, 2011: 97–8). The most significant challenge to an incumbent regime in the Gulf came in Bahrain where, in February 2011, non-violent demonstrators set up a local equivalent to Cairo's Tahrir Square in the Pearl Roundabout in the capital Manama. In a country where a Sunni monarchy rules over a Shiite majority, the regime insisted that the protesters were all Shiite and influenced by Iran, despite the presence of Sunnis among the demonstrators from the start. The introduction of the sectarian card, in order to paper over underlying governance problems, was problematic for two reasons. First, Shiite minorities across the peninsula felt targeted. Second, it increased international tensions in the region. Building on the alarmist argument of a 'Shia crescent' that threatened to undermine the stability of the region, Sunni political and religious leaders in the Gulf played the sectarian card to undermine any demand for change as a plot conceived in Iran. This, in turn, helped to stoke sectarian tensions in Syria even further, as the civil war took on increasingly sectarian undertones that had been largely missing from the initial peaceful protests against the regime. In many ways, the instrumental use of sectarian divisions has become a self-fulfilling prophecy. While such divisions were not central to any political demand initially made, either in the Gulf or in Syria, the very fact of evoking them as significant has made them so. In any case, in March 2011, Bahraini security forces joined by 5,000 troops sent by Saudi Arabia and the United Arab Emirates (UAE) dispersed the protesters and restored government control (Tetreault, 2011: 632). Again, this external intervention, sanctioned in Western capitals, was significant because it began to expose the way in which strategic geopolitical games were being played behind the scenes. The demands of the Bahraini protesters were not so different from those expressed elsewhere across the region, but were perceived and interpreted as very different insofar as instability in the Gulf would further escalate tensions with Iran and antagonize the Saudi monarchy.

Finally, in Syria, the arrest and torture in March 2011 of a group of schoolboys, between 10 and 15 years of age, who painted anti-regime graffiti on a wall in the town of Deraa, sparked off a protest which was violently suppressed by security forces. Just a few days before the protests began, President Bashar al-Asad had given an interview to the *Wall Street Journal* in which he claimed that his rule was secure because he was the leader of 'resistance' to Israel and imperialism, and because he had undertaken economic and political reforms during his rule that were meeting people's expectations. He was highly critical of both Ben Ali and Mubarak, implying that they had not seen the uprising coming because they had been too long in power to know what ordinary citizens wanted from their leaders. Many analysts did, indeed, believe that Syria would not face strong domestic dissent, if only because of the penetration of the police state in every aspect of life in the country. Thus, while al-Asad did not expect domestic opposition because he was doing a good job as leader, others thought his rule was secure because of the unrelenting repression the opposition had faced for decades, which had left it weak and disorganized. The surprise generated by the March 2011 protests in Deraa was enormous (see Box 1.2, for a discussion of how Bashar al-

Asad analysed the uprisings and what impact they would have on Syria). When the protesters were met with extreme violence, it seemed, for a moment, that the old reflex of fear would play itself out once again in Syria. But times had changed and the wall of fear had been breached. Peaceful protests spread across the country and were increasingly met with more regime repression. Eventually, faced with state-sanctioned violence, peaceful protests ended and the opposition began to mount armed resistance to the regime, leading to the start of a violent conflict which, ever since, has gripped the country in a spiral of violence which has assumed an increasingly sectarian character. As mentioned earlier, unlike the case of Libya, leading Western powers have refused to intervene militarily in Syria to aid the rebel groups and facilitate the military defeat of the regime, because of the complexity of its geopolitical and strategic location, the opposition of Russia and other international actors, and, to an increasing extent, fear of what a post-Asad government in Syria might look like. Non-Western powers such as Turkey, Saudi Arabia, Qatar and Iran are all sponsoring different parties in the conflict, but their aid is financial, political and diplomatic, rather than troops on the ground, although all parties supply weapons and intelligence to either the insurgents or the regime. In addition, there are reports of Iranian paramilitaries directly engaged in the conflict in Syria.

The origins of the uprisings

Such extraordinary events in so many settings, and over such a short period, called out for explanation. This was particularly so given the prior consensus on the essential stability of political order in the region. Taking a cue from earlier historic moments, early in 2011 the US academic Marc Lynch revived the term 'Arab Spring', which had first been used to describe Arab political mobilization across a range of countries in 2005. The term, of course, recalled earlier historic moments. The European Revolutions of 1848 were known as the 'Spring of Nations', while 120 years later, the 1968 uprising in Czechoslovakia, which inaugurated a brief period of political liberalization, became the 'Prague Spring'. It became commonplace to see these events in terms of revolutionary change. Hugh Roberts (2013) noted that, 'what the media called the "Arab spring" was a succession of revolutions became orthodoxy very quickly'. This echoed the language of many of those involved because the main slogans, far from expressing religious radicalism or leftist utopianism, were about political pluralism, accountability, socioeconomic rights, and an end to arbitrary rule and corruption. In the eyes of many of the protesters, the Arab world was ready to join other modern nations by finally ridding itself of authoritarian rule. The

Box 1.2   Bashar al-Asad on Syria and the Uprisings

In his interview with the *Wall Street Journal* on 31 January 2011, less than two months before protests broke out in the country, Syrian president, Bashar al-Asad expressed confidence that Syria was 'different' from Tunisia and Egypt and therefore not vulnerable to popular protest in the same way. In the interview, he was very critical of the presidents of Egypt and Tunisia. He accused them of not having sufficiently reformed their countries to meet the expectations – notably, ideological – of ordinary citizens and argued that a revolt was an almost natural consequence. In addition, he made the point that the countries where uprisings occurred had all been steadfast allies of imperialist Western policies with which their respective citizens did not agree. For al-Asad, the ideological disconnect between citizens and rulers was crucial in understanding the uprisings. Where the disconnect existed, uprisings were more likely; where it did not, they would not take place. From this, he argued that Syria would not follow the same path as Egypt and Tunisia because the beliefs of the leadership were not out of kilter with those of ordinary Syrians.

In passing, he also mentioned that Egypt and Tunisia might have had a stronger economy and greater material benefits in addition to enjoying US financial support, but that the state of economy was not necessarily the priority of Syrians insofar as they were satisfied with the way in which the leadership was committed to the cause of Arab nationalism. If the price to pay for that was a smaller economy and only partial integration into the global economic system, then Syrians were reasonably happy to pay it. As it turned out, al-Asad's beliefs and assumptions were entirely misplaced and revealed, in fact, that the profound disconnect he had seen in Tunisia and Egypt between rulers and ordinary citizens affected Syria, too.

Source: *Wall Street Journal* (2011). 'Interview with Syrian President Bashar al-Asad', available at http://online.wsj.com/news/articles/SB10001424052748703833204576114712441122894.

terminology of 'spring' was speedily adopted precisely because one could make an easy linkage between the events taking place, the goals of the protests and the outcome. To many European and American observers, in particular, what was happening suggested a '1989 moment', when communism in Eastern Europe collapsed under the pressure of ordinary citizens' demonstrations.

Beyond such labelling, analysts sought to understand what factors might explain such seemingly revolutionary and completely unexpected events. For many, the answer was to be found in a combination of socio-economic and political factors. Throughout the Arab world, and particularly in middle- and lower-income countries such as Egypt, Tunisia, Morocco, Jordan and Yemen, the end of colonialism was accompanied by the emergence of an informal 'social contract' in terms of which regimes undertook to provide for the socioeconomic wellbeing of their citizens in return for political quiescence. However, from the 1990s onwards, and even earlier in certain cases such as Morocco and Tunisia, the adoption of neo-liberal economic reforms across the region, under the auspices of the World Bank and the International Monetary Fund began the process of erosion of this social contract. Measures to liberalize foreign trade, the lifting of import restrictions, changing tariff protection and removing barriers against exports were all enforced, while state intervention in the economy was scaled back. Government subsidies were reduced, as was employment in the state sector (Sika, 2012: 9). But these had been essential to the maintenance of the living standards of the lower- and middle-classes. As a result, the reforms prompted widespread unease.

However, while neo-liberal reforms had a huge impact on the region's economies, they had far less impact on underlying authoritarian political structures, which remained largely unchanged, with the effect that there were few venues (if any) for citizens to express their grievances. While the rhetoric of neo-liberal economic reform envisages the enhancement of the rule of law and 'good governance', Arab regimes adopted such reforms in order to deepen authoritarian systems of control. Indeed, as we have seen, economic liberalization saw the development of 'crony capitalist' systems in which élites tied to the regime derived disproportionate benefit. A similar pattern could be detected in Iran, also. Post-colonial governments had enjoyed a significant degree of popular support because of state intervention in the economy, providing infrastructure, basic services, subsidies for primary foodstuffs, and jobs. Those with ample oil resources initially invested in productive industries, attempting to create a local industrial base – as in Algeria, for example. When this type of economic development ended and neo-liberal reforms were introduced without corresponding changes to political structures, a deadly combination of economic de-development and arbitrary political rule alienated many from the regimes in power. In addition, the picture of growth that was projected internationally, however unequal it might have been, was often the outcome of highly dubious statistics and bookkeeping (Hibou, 2011). Ultimately, as we will see in more detail in Chapter 9, these regimes increasingly relied on the military and security services to stave off growing dissent, and became even less representative of their populations in the process. In the long run, this did not prove politically sustainable for many of them. Despite encouraging macroeconomic growth rates, the positive effects of neo-liberalism and globalization were not shared – wealth was not trickling down in any meaningful way. The uprisings are a testimony in large part to the failed economic policies of the last decades and it is not a coincidence that it was in Tunisia, held to be a model of neo-liberal economic governance by international financial institutions – and the European Union, in particular – that the uprisings began.

All this was exacerbated by demographic patterns in a region where the proportion of young people in the overall population is particularly high – 60 per cent of the region's people are aged under 30, twice the rate of North America. Of the population, 30 per cent is between 14 and 24 years of age. Unemployment is rampant and, among young people, the rate is four times as high as for the rest of the population (Hoffman and Jamal, 2012: 169–70). As Haas and Lesch point out, this youth bulge creates a 'highly combustible' social and political environment, since young people are more likely to act on their grievances to try to rectify them, even if this means large-scale protests or violence (2012: 3). But, as neoliberal reforms generated widespread economic distress, especially for the younger cohort of the population, the closed nature of regimes permitted few outlets for the expression of dissent or for the articulation of any alternatives. Achcar (2013) makes a similar argument, but he makes the crucial point that it is not so much the youth bulge that is relevant for the uprisings; similar percentages of youth in relation to the total population exist in other areas of the globe as well, notably South East Asia and sub-Saharan Africa. What matters, Achcar argues, is the combustible combination of youth and high unemployment, which is unique to the Arab world. All this, combined with the 'demonstration' or contagion effect of the initial uprising in Tunisia, where the course of events proved that a seemingly unalterable status quo could be undone, resulted in political upheaval across the region.

The uprisings in Tunisia, Egypt, Yemen and Libya

In Tunisia, the first country to witness unrest, between 1987 and 2005 around 19 per cent of gross domestic product (GDP) was spent on social provision annually while government spending on health, education and social welfare doubled. But, in the 2000s, there was a marked deterioration in socioeconomic conditions as the Ben Ali regime adopted a number of neo-liberal reforms which brought serious economic difficulties to much of the population. Household debt grew rapidly from the mid-190s onwards, while many families became more dependent on remittances from abroad. The economic status of the middle-class became more financially unstable at a time when society was opening up to a consumerist Western culture which promoted conspicuous consumption and the desire to emulate the lifestyle of the Tunisian super-rich élite. This led to a further disenfranchisement of the poor who did not have access to loans from financial institutions, particularly in the more remote regions of the interior (Kaboub, 2013: 14). Although the overall level of unemployment declined, among undergraduates unemployment rose from 8.6 per cent in 1999 to 44.4 per cent in 2009. There was also a strong regional aspect to socioeconomic distress in Tunisia. Of national production, 80 per cent was concentrated in the coastal areas of the north and north-west of the country and these saw significant drops in poverty levels. But, the south and south-west – including Sidi Bouzid, with 40 per cent of the population – had only 20 per cent of GDP, poverty levels remained unchanged and unemployment levels were well above the national average. Meanwhile, there was a widespread perception of corruption at the heart of the regime associated, in particular, with the families of the president and of his wife, Leila Trabelsi. Leaked US diplomatic cables from 2006 observed that 'good connections' were vital for business success in Tunisia, while the president's extended family (siblings, in-laws and distant relatives) carved out domains in virtually every important sector of the economy. The leaked documents go on to note the widespread fear that the 'conspicuous consumption' of the Ben Ali and Trabelsi families was 'sucking the life-blood' out of Tunisia. Even the development fund – the Caisse 20/20 – that the regime had set up to offset the costs of opening up the economy in the early 1990s was raided in the early 2000s by members of the president's entourage to fund the private takeover of rival businesses (Tsourapas, 2013). This fund had permitted villages and deprived areas of Tunisia to benefit from a modicum of state investment in infrastructures and jobs to offset, in part, the more disadvantageous consequences of opening up the economy through free trade. But this investment dried up once the Trabelsi family began to use the fund for its own private economic activities.

There were few outlets for the expression of socioeconomic distress or criticism of the course of direction of the regime, although, as Box 1.3 suggests, some spaces of dissent did exist. Since the short-lived experiment with a more open political system in the late 1980s, Ben Ali and his party, the RCD, dominated political life, although a facade multiparty system had been permitted to exist. Ben Ali was elected president on five successive occasions. For the first two presidential elections in 1989 and 1994, he was the only candidate and won 99 per cent of the vote. In 1999, he also received 99 per cent but this time was 'challenged' by two minor politicians who were allowed to contest the election, but who spent their airtime during the campaign extolling the virtues of the president. In subsequent elections in 2004 and 2009, his support 'dropped' to 94.5 per cent and 89.6 per cent, respectively. The regime maintained its control though repression of all forms of political dissent, placing controls on basic freedoms, severe limitations on civil society, and the harassing and imprisoning of political opponents. Newspapers were owned by members of the president's family, while the regime developed sophisticated mechanisms for internet censorship working in addition, to infiltrate and eventually emasculate the journalists' union. Under Ben Ali, Tunisia was one of the

---

Box 1.3   Spaces of expression and contestation

As the Tunisian revolution was ongoing, Laryssa Chomiak and John Entelis set
out an analysis which suggested that the open contestation against the Ben Ali
regime witnessed in late December 2010 had not come from nowhere. Contrary
to mainstream interpretations of Tunisian society and politics under Ben Ali,
which emphasized the stability of the regime and the notable absence of dissent
– either because of police repression, or because of genuine admiration for the
achievements of the leadership – Chomiak and Entelis highlighted the small but
significant spaces of contestation that existed throughout the country and in all
sectors of society. They proposed that the public space in Tunisia, which was
believed to be entirely dominated by the authorities, was actually more contested
than at first it appeared. A number of examples – such as rioting against the
police at football matches, or strikes in the countryside to demand better working
conditions – are used to argue that the Tunisian uprising was built on the activism
of many individuals and groups, but to which very few scholars, and virtually no
policy-makers, had paid attention.

In turn, these findings alert us to some of the problematic assumptions of
authoritarian upgrading. While there is much that is valid in Heydemann's argument about the way in which authoritarian regimes in the Arab world adopted
more flexible ways to remain unaccountable through sham 'liberal' reforms in a
number of sectors, the study by Chomiak and Entelis indicates that there may be
also unforeseen consequences that flow from the launching of such reforms. In
essence, the state was unable to control everything, and the reforms undertaken
provided the opportunity for a number of 'unusual' actors to find spaces and
places of dissent, thereby contributing to the erosion of the regime's legitimacy.

Source: Laryssa Chomiak and John Entelis (2013). 'Contesting order in Tunisia: crafting political
identity' in Francesco Cavatorta (ed.), *Civil Society Activism under Authoritarian Rule*, London:
Routledge.

most heavily policed countries in the world with 130,000 police officers
for a population of 10.4 million.

But, it would be unfair to many Tunisians to suggest that no challenge
to the regime existed before the winter of 2010. There were a number of
social and political protests in Tunisia from the mid-2000s onwards, the
most notable being in the mining basin of Gafsa in 2008 (Allal, 2010).
The problem was that the grievances at issue were perceived to be local
in nature, and the regime was able to isolate and deal with them, while
mainstream media and the international community were not interested.
As Chomiak and Entelis (2011) observe, the 2010 self-immolation of
Bouazizi was simply another event in the long list of public demonstrations of dissatisfaction with the regime and its policies. There was, therefore, however limited, a history of dissent in the country, suggesting that
the eruption of the uprising should at least have been considered possible
in the academic and policy-making literature.

As in Tunisia, an informal social contract had existed in Egypt from the time of the 1952 revolution which brought the Free Officers to power, under the terms of which Egyptians ceded the political arena to the ruling party in exchange for material prosperity and security. By the early 1980s, the public sector was producing 50 per cent of GDP and consuming 80 per cent of domestic fixed investment. The state underwrote an extensive network of subsidies that provided food, electricity, gasoline, public transportation, medical care and a host of other services. However, this set of arrangements was undermined by unprecedented levels of population growth, and the inability of the state-centred economy to meet the demands that this posed. Economic reforms were undertaken which led to respectable levels of economic growth in the mid-2000s of 6–7 per cent per annum. Egyptians with the right skills and connections did well out of this, but public sector workers, civil servants and pensioners saw their incomes stagnate as inflation rose. The problem with neo-liberal economic reform in Egypt is that they widened the gap between the rich and the poor, who could no longer rely on the state for a safety net (Joya, 2013). By early 2011, more than 40 per cent of population was below the poverty line and the social contract of the Nasser era was long dead. As elsewhere in the region, young Egyptians were hit particularly hard by the regime's economic performance. In 2006, according to the World Bank, 80 per cent of those unemployed in Egypt were below 30 years of age, while 82 per cent of the unemployed had never worked (Roudi, 2011).

As the economic condition of many Egyptians deteriorated, the political system became even less responsive to their needs. Instead, a corrupt and ineffective state served the interests of a small élite consisting of the ruling party, businessmen with ties to the regime, and Mubarak's family and confidants. Corruption became visible on all levels in the last decade of Mubarak's rule with increasingly close ties between the political and business élites. The perception of corruption among Egyptians went beyond the daily reality of bribery, and the awareness of fraudulent business dealings, to a more generalized sense that incentives and rewards were unfair – that successful business people were part of a closed élite with ties to the government and thus benefited from favourable treatment (Kinninmont, 2012: 5). While Egypt had had a multi-party system since the 1970s, it was one in which the dominance of the ruling National Democratic Party was unquestioned and unquestionable. Most opposition parties were politically irrelevant, the clear exception being the Muslim Brotherhood. However, the Brotherhood remained a proscribed organization whose political participation was tolerated only within strict limits. In the elections of 2005, the opposition won 22 per cent of the seats with most going to the Muslim Brotherhood – enough to lend some credibility to the parliament and provide a forum for venting public anger, but also signaling to Mubarak's allies that they needed to stand by him to avoid the Brothers coming to power. In the 2010 elections, the regime managed the elections to produce a lopsided victory for the ruling party, which won 93 per cent of the seats, while the Brotherhood retained one seat. As elsewhere in the region, civil society was tightly controlled and regulated by the state. This political order was maintained by an increasingly brutal security apparatus. Thus, while the public was being pushed closer to 'economic desperation', peaceful venues for venting anger were closed off (Rutherford, 2013: 39). As in the Tunisian case, this does not mean that demonstrations and protests had not occurred prior to February 2011. From workers' strikes to students' protests and from civil-society based campaigns to individual stances against the arbitrariness of the authorities, Egypt was also the locus of many forms of social and political dissent in the 2000s. The most notable of these, the *Kifaya* ('Enough') movement, attracted cross-ideological support, with its calls for political reform. But, as in the Tunisian case, many of these protests remained localized and disconnected from a wider struggle for regime change, due to class and ideological divisions. However, in February 2011, even the middle-class seemed to have had enough of the regime and decided to march against it, linking its struggle to that of unionized workers and marginalized youth in a historic moment (Kandil, 2012).

In Yemen, where the reach of the central state has never been complete, a Tunisian-style social contract did not exist. Nonetheless, a similar pattern of economic crisis in the context of an unrepresentative and authoritarian political system were at play in the uprising there, while other issues were also significant – in particular, regional grievances. By the mid-1990s, economic problems forced the government to turn to the International Monetary Fund (IMF) for assistance in reducing its debt burden in return for reforms, including discharging thousands of government employees, reducing subsidies and beginning a privatization programme. However, while macroeconomic indicators showed signs of improvement, the general welfare of most Yemenis did not, as unemployment and poverty levels rose alarmingly (Colton, 2010: 417–18).

By 2010, on the eve of the uprising, long-standing structural weaknesses in the country's economy led to situation where life expectancy at birth was 63 years, 43 per cent of the population was living on US$2 or less per day, while the population was growing at 2.9 per cent per annum. The official unemployment rate rose from 7.7 per cent in 1998 to 25 per cent. But, in a country where nearly 75 per cent of the population is under 25 years of age, it is young people who were most likely to be out of work

– the youth unemployment rate in Yemen in early 2011 was estimated at 53 per cent.

Meanwhile, the regime was able to ensure that the opportunities created by the economic liberalization process remained under its control, as were the oil and gas sectors on which Yemen disproportionately depends. Prior to the uprising, oil revenues comprised 90 per cent of the country's export earnings and 75 per cent of central government's budget. (Longley-Alley, 2010: 389). A number of different élite groups were favoured with access to key sectors of the economy, including import and export licences, control of oil concessions, oil distribution rights and lucrative licences to provide mobile phone and internet services. These core élites included elements in the security services (largely dominated by the president's family), tribal groups, and politicians both from the ruling party and the opposition coalition, the Joint Meeting Parties, as well as Yemen's small, traditional merchant élite, many of whom also have close personal ties to the president (Salisbury, 2011: 10–11). As a result, Yemenis saw almost all business activity as being corrupt in some way. The country was ranked 148th out of 178 countries in Transparency International's 2010 International Corruption Index.

However, as was the case elsewhere in the region, there were few opportunities for ordinary Yemenis to influence the course of government policy. While Yemen has had a multiparty political system since the creation of the state in 1990, the grip of the ruling General People's Congress Party was largely unchallenged. Until 2011, the party was the dominant force in the country's parliament, which, in any case, was widely seen as ineffective and remote from the needs of ordinary people. Real power lay with the president, his immediate family and a host of informal political actors who sometimes crossed party lines. For instance, Saleh was re-elected to the presidency in 2006 by a substantial margin in the face of a challenge from a candidate ostensibly supported by all the major opposition parties. Despite this, Saleh secured the support of the leader of the Islamist *Islah* party, the most significant opposition force, because of tribal ties between the party leader and the president.

Libya, the fourth country in the region to witness the demise of a long-standing autocratic regime, shared some similarities with the other cases but was different in important respects, also. While economic factors were significant elsewhere, they were less so in Libya, which had enjoyed a decade of annual growth rates of 5–6 per cent annually. Unemployment, too, was low relative to the rest of the region. Following the relaxation in 2006 of international sanctions against the Gaddafi regime, investors poured into the country and the services and construction sectors experienced significant growth creating jobs for young people in every field.

However, Libya shared with other countries in the region the widespread perception on the part of many people that not only was the political system oppressive, but also that the level of corruption meant that the country's wealth was concentrated at the top (Deeb, 2012: 68). Libya enjoyed vast revenues from the sales of its hydrocarbon resources, and, with a small population, it seemed odd to many of its citizens that they did not have a much higher standard of living, notwithstanding the international sanctions regime that had been in place for over a decade. According to Martinez (2012), one of the principal reasons has to do with the squandering of oil wealth, and the mafia-style manner in which it was controlled and distributed. For instance, significant amounts of money were employed to buy weaponry, to finance terrorism abroad and to conduct military operations in neighbouring countries such as Chad. All of this contributed not only to wasting resources, but also to alienating Libya in the eyes of the majority of the international community. Gaddafi propagated the concept of government by 'the masses', but the reality was that his immediate family and an inner circle of advisers, many of whom were drawn from the security services, dominated the political system, while opposition was ruthlessly suppressed.

Countries that did not experience regime change, or were a genuine threat to the survival of the ruling élites did not materialize, have had to contend with popular demands for change originating from very similar shortcomings. In the case of Syria, for instance, more than a decade of slow but profound liberal economic reforms meant that the traditional social classes that the Baathist regime had always looked after, and from which it derived both legitimacy and support, were progressively marginalized and impoverished, to the benefit of a small urban merchant class with close ties to an increasingly corrupt inner circle around the president and his family (Haddad, 2011). The working class in urban centres, and the vast peasant class in the countryside, found their livelihoods threatened by these reforms, while the *Baath* party was hollowed out so that Bashar al-Asad could find support from a 'civil society' heavily controlled and largely sponsored by the regime itself (Aarts and Cavatorta, 2013).

Despite its oil wealth, and the regularity with which the regime injects money into the economy, Algeria also faces considerable challenges in terms of unemployment, corruption and decreasing living standards for large sectors of the population. While Bouteflika has brought about national reconciliation, following a decade of internal strife, not much seems to have changed from the 1970s and 1980s, when the squandering of the oil wealth and widespread corruption led to the upheaval of October 1988 and the botched liberalization which followed. The opacity of the redistribution of oil revenues, in addition to the corrupt networks of patronage that are at the heart of foreign trade and investment in the country, still characterize Algerian governance.

Moroccan protesters, building on nearly a decade of localized struggles in factories, mines and towns away from the main urban centres, also focused their demands on unemployment, increasing living costs and corruption (Hoffmann and König, 2013). Morocco scores very low on the human development index, suggesting that more than two decades of economic liberalization have not closed the gap between the few haves and the many haves-not. In addition, almost two decades of slow-paced political liberalization did very little to mobilize ordinary citizens to participate in decision-making, given that, ultimately, all important decisions are taken by the monarchy, leaving many with a feeling of disempowerment as a result.

Despite their oil wealth, Gulf countries have also had to face dissent based both on poor economic governance and authoritarianism. The Dubai model (Hvidt, 2009) might be secure for the moment, but it may not enjoy the stability that many believe it to possess (Davidson, 2012). Saudi Arabia appears to be particularly vulnerable because of growing disenchantment with the strict moral order regulating society, and increasing poverty and unemployment, despite the policy of national preference put in place by the authorities. At the moment, oil money is a powerful stabilizing factor, but painful decisions about diversification – both economic and political – will have to be made eventually.

Finally, it is worth mention that the Arab Uprisings had an important regional predecessor – namely, the stand-off between the regime and the opposition 'Green Movement' in Iran in the summer of 2009. While it is still difficult to identify whether Arab protesters found inspiration in the widespread demonstrations that took place in Iran in 2009 in a dispute over the outcome of the presidential elections, it is impossible to deny its importance. The events in Iran over the course of the summer of 2009 shook the entire region and were a powerful reminder that popular mobilization, even in strongly authoritarian settings, could come close to bringing down a regime that was believed to be secure and benefiting from the depoliticization of ordinary citizens. When the results of the presidential election were released, giving a significant majority to the incumbent Mahmoud Ahmadinejad, enormous crowds gathered in most major cities, as they believed with good reason, that the election had been rigged. The reaction of the regime was particularly violent, but the protests did not end immediately, threatening to become revolutionary in their character and demands. Ultimately, repression won out, and the Green Movement was broken up, but its legacy of mobilization through social media, of occupation of city centres, and of peaceful protest found a potent echo in the Arab

Awakening. The 2013 presidential elections in Iran began to restore some of the faith of ordinary citizens in the political system, as the surprise victory of the reformist candidate Hassan Rouhani did not generate a significant conservative backlash, even though some of his appointments have been considered too 'progressive.'

Whether regimes fell or managed to remain in power in the face of the Arab Uprisings, they generally had to face dissent rooted in very similar causes. This is significant because it suggests that irrespective of regime type, degree of economic success and integration in the global economy, international alliances and social make-up, all of the countries concerned shared similar weaknesses, chief of which is a toxic mix of authoritarianism and misguided and selectively implemented neo-liberal economic reforms, that brought about the marginalization of large sectors of society. The factors mentioned above matter when it comes to the success of the survival strategies adopted once dissent publicly exploded.

Fawaz Gerges (2014: 1) is correct when he argues that 'a psychological and epistemological rupture has occurred in the Arab Middle East that has shaken the authoritarian order to its very foundations and introduced a new language and a new era of contentious politics and revolutions' whose effects are likely to be long-lasting. The Arab Awakening constitutes a powerful rupture in the politics and governance of the region, but it is not the first; neither is it unique in its introduction of a new language with which politics is conducted. The following chapters capture and link historical political, social, economic and ideological developments to the Arab Uprisings. Without an understanding of such developments, it is impossible to make sense of the uprisings and their aftermath.

Key questions

- Were the Arab Uprisings of 2011 motivated by political or economic factors?
- Why did Syrian President Bashar al-Asad believe that his country was invulnerable to popular protest in 2011?
- What factors did Tunisia, Egypt, Libya and Yemen have in common on the eve of the uprisings?
- Why did uprisings fail (or fail to gather momentum) elsewhere?

Further reading

Bogaert, Koenraad (2013). 'Contextualising the Arab revolts: the politics behind three decades of neo-liberalism in the Arab world', *Middle East Critique*, 22(3): 213–34.

Filiu, Jean-Pierre (2011). *The Arab Revolution*, London: Hurst.

Haddad, Bassam, Rosie Bsheer and Ziad Abu-Rish (2012). *The Dawn of the Arab Uprisings*, London: Pluto Press.

Kandil, Hazem (2013). *Soldiers, Spies and Statesmen. Egypt's Road to Revolt*, London: Verso.

Lynch, Marc (2013). *The Arab Uprising: The Unfinished Revolutions of the New Middle East*, New York: Public Affairs.

McMurray, David and Amanda Ufheil-Somers (2013). *The Arab Revolts. Dispatches on Militant Democracy in the Middle East*, Bloomington: Indiana University Press.

Online resources

BBC (2013). 'Arab uprisings three years on', available at http://www.bbc.co.uk/news/world-middle-east-12813859.

Heydemann, Steven (2007). 'Upgrading authoritarianism in the Arab world,' Brookings Institution, *Analysis Paper*, 13: 1–37. Available at http://www.brookings.edu/,/media/Files/rc/papers/2007/10arabworld/10arabworld.pdf.

Tahrir Squared (a 'one stop shop' for information about the Arab Uprisings). Available at http://tahrirsquared.com/.

The Arab Awakening (a series of films on Al Jazeera which explore the roots of the uprisings and ask 'what next'? Available at http://www.aljazeera.com/programmes/general/2011/04/20114483425914466.html.

Chapter 2

The Historical and Political Context

This chapter will explore the evolving relationship between the Middle East and the West from the late nineteenth century onwards. It will describe the ways in which European power came to dominate the MENA region and local responses to this domination. Next, it will outline the emergence of the modern state system in the Middle East in the aftermath of World War I and the coming of independence. The chapter will conclude with a discussion of patterns in post-colonial political development, with a particular focus on the trend towards authoritarian forms of rule, the rise and decline of pan-Arab nationalism, and the impact of the Cold War and its aftermath.

The modern Middle East cannot be fully understood unless we take its centuries-old interaction with the West into account. While the region we now know as the Middle East has enjoyed a complex relationship with Western Europe for hundreds of years, the nature of that relationship underwent very significant change at the beginning of the modern era. As the power of European states grew, that of Middle Eastern states and empires weakened. Indeed, it was the increasing power and reach of Europe over the region that, in many ways, gave rise to the modern states and state system of the Middle East.

The Middle East and the West in historical perspective

The rapid expansion of Muslim empires from the earliest decades of Islam brought competition and challenge to rulers in Europe. Armies under Muslim leadership swept across North Africa and southern Europe to be stopped only outside Paris at the Battle of Tours in 732 CE. Parts of today's Spain and Portugal remained under Muslim control until 1492 when the final expulsion of Spain's Moorish population took place following the reunification of the country under the Catholic monarchs, Ferdinand and Isabella. The Muslim Ottoman Empire, which emerged in what is now Turkey in the fourteenth century, ruled over much of Central and Eastern Europe until well into the nineteenth century and continued to expand its European territories until 1683. The empire at its height stretched from present-day Saudi Arabia to Tunisia. It also included Greece, Malta, Cyprus and the Balkans. On two separate occasions Ottoman forces besieged Vienna, the second and failed attempt being in 1683 (leaving behind, according to the legend, the beans that spawned Europe's obsession with coffee!). During this period, the Ottomans posed a serious threat to European powers such as Austria and Russia, and Ottoman rulers were significant players in European power politics entering into alliances with some European rulers as they challenged others (Akhavi, 2003: 551). However, after 1683, a succession of military defeats led to the loss of territory in Central Europe, the Balkans and beyond. In 1798, France launched an invasion of Egypt, then under Ottoman control. Although French occupation of Egypt came to an end under pressure from Britain a mere three years later, it is seen by many as having inaugurated the modern period in Arab history.

The decline of Muslim power

Throughout the nineteenth century, the power and influence of European states over the territories of the Ottoman Empire increased. Britain, France and Russia were the most important actors. However, others, including Germany, Italy and Spain, were also significant. In the early decades of the century, the Empire lost control of some of its most important European territories. In 1808, the Serbs revolted and the revolt was quickly enmeshed in European power politics. The ultimate result was the establishment in 1830 of an independent Serbian state. In 1822, the Greeks, who had been under Ottoman rule for centuries, also rebelled. As in the case of Serbia, the intervention of Europe was crucial to the outcome. In 1827, Britain, France and Russia sent naval fleets in support of the Greeks, defeating the Ottoman forces and leading to the establishment of an independent Greek state in 1832.

In North Africa, Algeria came under European control in 1830 when the French began the colonization of the country. In neighbouring Tunisia, the ruler, Ahmad Bey, played on French concerns to keep the Turks as far away as possible, in order to maintain his country's effective autonomy from the Ottomans. Libya enjoyed a period of relative autonomy until 1835 when concern at the near independence of Egypt under Muhammad Ali, and also at the French presence in Algeria, prompted the Ottoman Sultan to overthrow the ruling Karamanli dynasty and institute direct rule. These events demonstrate that Ottoman control was also beginning to slip due to centrifugal forces from within the Empire, which at times used the European powers to balance against the re-assertive policies of the imperial centre. For instance, in Egypt the young army officer Muhammad Ali was appointed governor by the Sultan in 1805. Although it was Ottoman policy not to allow a governor to stay in any one place for more than one year, he remained in his position until 1848 and Egypt under his rule enjoyed effective autonomy within the Empire. Muhammad Ali's successors ruled Egypt until 1952. Developments later in the century further eroded Ottoman power. The 1878 Congress of Berlin brought independence to Romania and Bulgaria, while France acquired control over Tunisia, Britain over Cyprus and Austria took control of Bosnia. In 1882, Britain occupied Egypt and brought that country under its effective control. European expansion into North Africa was completed with the Italian occupation of Libya in 1911 and the French declaration of a protectorate in Morocco the following year.

In the Arabian Gulf, Britain extended its sway throughout the nineteenth century through a series of treaties with local rulers which legitimized its exclusion of Ottoman, French and German influence from Eastern Arabia and offered greater protection to British interests in India. Treaties were signed with the rulers of the Trucial States (the present day United Arab Emirates) in 1835, Bahrain in 1861, Kuwait in 1899 and Qatar in 1916 (Onley, 2009).

Responses to European encroachment

The push of European countries in the Middle East and North Africa did not go uncontested or unchallenged despite the disparity of means. Local responses took different forms, but the encroachment of European powers left a legacy of what can be termed 'anti-imperialism', which, as we will see, would become a crucial trait of many countries in the region on achieving independence.

Resistance

The increased penetration of the region by Europe throughout the nineteenth century did not go without local responses, as Box 2.1 makes clear in telling the story of resistance in Algeria against French expansion. These responses took a number of different forms. In the first instance, there was violent resistance to the extension of European control. The French invaders of Egypt in 1798 overcame a Mamluk army just outside Cairo in the 'Battle of the Pyramids' before they could occupy the city. However, in what was to become a recurring pattern, the Mamluk javelins, sabres, axes and muskets were no match for the superior weaponry and advanced military tactics of the French, and the engagement is reported to have

---

Box 2.1 Resistance – 'Abd al-Qadir al-Djazairi (1808–83)

'Abd al-Qadir al-Djazairi was the son of the head of a leading Algerian Sufi order and claimed descent from the prophet Muhammad. For a time, he ruled over a virtually independent state with its capital in the interior and extending from the west into the eastern part of the country. As a consequence, he came into conflict with the French, who were expanding their sphere of influence from the east. 'Abd al-Qadir led resistance to French power for 15 years but the superiority of the French forces ultimately prevailed and, in 1847, he surrendered and was sent into exile. He spent his final years in Damascus, where he was much respected and was on good terms with the representatives of the European powers, including France. In the course of defeating 'Abd al-Qadir, the French presence in Algeria was extended to the Sahara, paving the way for large-scale European immigration to the country and the dispossession of local cultivators. By 1870, there were nearly 250,000 French settlers in the country and it was formally annexed to France.

Source: Albert Hourani (1991). *A History of the Arab Peoples*, London: Faber & Faber.

---

lasted no more than forty-five minutes (Tignor, 1997: 7–8; Rogan, 2010: 76). Rather more long-lived was the revolt against the French presence in Algeria following its occupation in 1830 which was led by the legendary figure of 'Abd al-Qadir al-Djazairi.

In Tunisia, the extension of French control in 1881 prompted a violent uprising across the country which saw tens of thousands of tribal warriors join 'Ali ibn Khalifa, a tribal leader from the south-east, in the resistance effort. The rebellion was crushed by French reinforcements and more than 100,000 tribesmen and their families took refuge in the neighbouring Libyan province of Tripolitania (Perkins, 2004: 37). The Italian colonization of Libya in 1911 was also followed by a prolonged movement of resistance led by senior tribal leaders, including Sidi Umar al-Mukhtar. The Italian response was brutal. More than 110,000 people, men, women and children were held in large concentration camps, wells were blocked and livestock slaughtered. According to St John (2011), as many as 70,000 people may have died of disease, malnutrition or starvation. When Al-Mukhtar was finally captured and hanged in 1931, the Italians gathered 20,000 Libyans to witness his execution (St John, 2011: 19).

Defensive developmentalism

Although prolonged in some places, violent resistance was ultimately doomed because of the superiority of the means available to the European powers. In a more sophisticated attempt to resist European encroachment, many rulers embarked on what has been termed 'defensive developmentalism': the adoption of European technologies and practices in the fields of military reform, education, the public service and economic planning was undertaken in order to strengthen local rulers in the face of new challenges and to make governments more efficient in managing their populations and resources. Such policies were adopted in the Turkish heartland of the Ottoman Empire, as well as by semi-autonomous rulers from Egypt to Tunisia and the Qajar Shahs who ruled over Persia. Gelvin (2008) has outlined the key features of defensive developmentalism. The first step was military reform: rulers realized that they could only assert their power internally and defend their territories in the face of external threat if they borrowed strategies from Europe to modernize their armies. However, this required an expansion of the sources of revenue available to rulers and greater control over the activities of the population in the best interests of the state. To achieve these objectives, expanded access to education, legal reforms and centralized economic planning became necessary (Gelvin, 2008: 74). In the Ottoman Empire, major changes took place, particularly in the period from 1839 to 1876. This period of reform, known as the *Tanzimat* (from the Turkish word for 'organizations', but generally understood as 'reordering' or 'reform'), saw major changes in both central and local government, taxation, education (where state schools began to supplant the previously dominant Islamic schools), legal reforms which provided a more secure environment for trade and investment, and major innovations in the fields of communications and transport. The telegraph was extended after 1854 and postal services expanded, while the first railways were built, mostly by European firms. The *Tanzimat* period was inaugurated by a statement from the Sultan in 1839 (the 'Edict of Gulhane') in which he guaranteed that his subjects had rights to life, honour and fortune, and that their property was inviolate. This was the first time that the ruler had conceded that his subjects had secular rights and that these extended to non-Muslims, as well as Muslims (Fieldhouse, 2006: 8–10). Similar reform projects were embarked upon elsewhere. In Egypt, Muhammad Ali began a sustained effort to train doctors, engineers and officials in new schools and by missions to Europe. The taxation system was reformed, agriculture was modernized and the cultivation of cotton encouraged, while modern irrigation methods were introduced. In Tunisia, Ahmad Bey embarked on a series of reforms during the course of his reign (1837–55). His military forces were modernized with equipment from Europe. A military school was established with European instructors. Conscription of the peasantry was introduced to supply manpower, while the resources for his plans were to come from new taxes and increased levies (Perkins, 2004: 15).

However, defensive developmentalism had significant negative impacts on the Middle East. In the first place, although reforms such as those of the Ottoman Sultan greatly improved the status of Christians and Jews in the Empire as they brought a measure of secularization, the emulation of Western state models resulted in a more centralized and authoritarian state, which did not always benefit a majority of Ottoman citizens (Pappé, 2005: 20). Reforms also brought into existence a new class of professional soldiers, intellectuals and bureaucrats who were shaped by their exposure to new ideas coming from Europe. These frequently had little access to political power despite their modern education. The result, as Gelvin (2008: 75) points out, was their involvement in a series of revolts, in the Ottoman Empire, Persia and Egypt in the late nineteenth and early twentieth centuries, in an attempt to gain power. Indeed, defensive developmentalism proved, ultimately, to be counterproductive. The cost of such policies in direct and indirect terms, combined with the further penetration of European ideas and technologies into the Muslim world, had the unintended effect much of the time of creating dependency, rather than strengthening the grip on power of local rulers. The modernization project came with significant costs. Local rulers invariably were unable to support these costs through domestic taxation alone and turned to European sources for loans. Their difficulties were exacerbated by the fact that their economies were increasingly being integrated into a global economic order on unequal terms. The example of Egypt is instructive. The Egyptian ruler, Muhammad Ali, promoted the cultivation of cotton as a cash crop in the early decades of the nineteenth century and for a time income from cotton production grew enormously. The volume of cotton exports rose more than tenfold between 1838 and 1865, while the value of those exports grew even faster. Greater trade with Europe was accompanied by a significant growth in the numbers of European nationals living in the country. By 1881, this figure had increased to 90,000 from around 8,000 some fifty years earlier. Thanks to the reforms introduced by Ottoman rulers, European nationals could be taxed only with the greatest difficulty. Ismail Pasha, grandson of Muhammad Ali, embarked on a series of projects that led to indebtedness to European banks, including the expansion of irrigation canals, and the construction of roads, railways and bridges to speed the export of raw materials. In 1869, the Suez Canal was opened, the construction of which, it has been suggested, cost more than 100,000 Egyptian lives (Marsot, 2007: 79). However, income from cotton production declined rapidly when the American civil war came to an end, and the reforms instituted by Ismail were costly. By 1876, he had run up debts of £100 million – these had stood at £3 million when he had taken office. In 1875, Ismail sold his shares in the Suez Canal to Britain for

£4 million. Nonetheless, European fears that Egypt would default on its debts led to the imposition of a 'European Debt Commission' in 1876 to safeguard foreign interests. The increasing influence of Britain and France over economic and financial matters provoked a revolt led by an army officer called Ahmad 'Urabi. 'Urabi's opposition to European interference in Egyptian affairs was popular. The British, fearful of losing influence in Egypt, intervened militarily in 1882, when, following riots in which 50 Christians were killed, they bombarded Alexandria, and defeated 'Urabi and the first Egyptian nationalist movement at the battle of Tel El-Kebir. The invasion was justified as an attempt to save the Egyptian people from a military dictatorship. Egypt thus became, effectively, part of the British Empire although it was never officially a colony.

The Ottoman Empire was not the only power in the nineteenth-century Middle East. The Qajar dynasty, which had taken control of Persia in the late eighteenth century, also became subject to the increased penetration of its political and economic life by Europe. In Persia (which was never part of the Ottoman Empire), Britain and Russia vied for influence and, between them, came to dominate the political and economic landscape. Britain first became involved in Iranian affairs at the beginning of the nineteenth century to forestall Napoleonic ambitions in south Asia and, in particular, to deter any French attempt to invade India (this was also the motivation for intervention in Egypt). Persia's relationship with Russia arose out of their shared borders. The rivalry between the two for influence and territory had twice led to war in the first 26 years of the nineteenth century alone. There was also a war with Britain in 1856 for control of the city of Herat, which the Persians lost. British and Russian influence persisted throughout the nineteenth century. Persian interaction with the West was on unequal terms and brought negative consequences. The costs of wars and the import of luxury items were high, traditional patterns of manufacturing and agriculture were disrupted. While the country was modernizing and some were growing more prosperous, the income distribution gap increased. There was growing dependence on a few Western countries and a failure on the part of its rulers – the Qajar dynasty, which had been in power since the sixteenth century – to initiate effective reforms to strengthen Iran's economy in relation to the West.

The level of dependence on outside actors was characterized by the grant, from the 1850s onwards, of a series of concessions to European interests to engage in various economic activities. The most far reaching of these came in 1872, when Shah Nasr al-Din granted to Baron Julius de Reuter exclusive rights for railroad and streetcar construction, all mineral extraction rights, all unexploited irrigation works, and a national bank. According to Abrahamian (1982), de Reuter purchased the concession for

£40,000 and 60 per cent of the profits. The concession was ultimately watered down as a result of opposition not only within Persia, but also by the Russians, who were themselves extracting concessions for the north of the country. An even more important concession was granted in 1901 to William Knox D'Arcy by Shah Mozaffar al-Din. D'Arcy was granted exclusive rights to prospect for oil for 60 years in most of Persia in exchange for £20,000, an equal amount in shares in D'Arcy's company and a promise of 16 per cent of future profits. Despite occasional clerical agitation and the existence of a strong movement in favour of more representative government, the pattern of political life in Persia in the nineteenth century was one of effective impotence in the face of foreign domination.

Early nationalist responses

The deepening interrelationship between the Middle East and Europe was characterized not only by the penetration of European political and economic power, but also by increased engagement with European political discourse. One of the critical responses to foreign encroachment on the region towards the end of the nineteenth century was the adoption of nationalist ideas, originating in Europe, as a means of fending off that encroachment. This was to be seen clearly in 'Urabi's adoption of the slogan 'Egypt for the Egyptians', which Pappé characterizes as the first expression of 'pure Arab patriotism' in history (2005: 22) Throughout the decades that followed, nationalist ideas, expressed in a variety of guises, assumed extraordinary significance in the political life of the Middle East.

Arab nationalism emerged from a number of strands in nineteenth-century Arab and Ottoman political thought in the form of Islamic reformists, Christian Arab reformists, and those advocating a broader Arab identity. Muslim reformers and activists preached the need for a regeneration of the religion of Islam in order to remedy the deplorable situation in which the Muslim world found itself. Arab unity was necessary to defend the faith, to force the Ottoman rulers to govern properly, and to fend off the increasing encroachment of the European powers. Islam was the essential bond of union between Muslims and, if this bond could be strengthened, then it would be possible to create and maintain a strong and stable state. In contrast, Christian Arabs within the Ottoman Empire articulated different demands. Some sought an independent state in Lebanon under European protection, which would be the centre of a free Christian life. Others, more conscious of the ties of language and culture that bound all Arabs together, despite differences in religious belief, wanted to see the establishment of an independent Arab state, although they were often hazy as to how this state might work. As early as 1859, the Syro-Lebanese Butrus Bustani was writing of 'the Arabs' and something called 'Arab culture' to which he felt he belonged. Later in the century, the Syrian 'Abd al-Rahman al-Kawakibi was imprisoned and then exiled for suggesting that the Ottomans were corrupting Islamic identity and that Arabs should overthrow the Turks.

Inside the Ottoman Empire also, different trends were at play. Under the oppressive rule of Abdulhamid, the Sultan in Istanbul from 1876 to 1918, the Young Turk movement struggled for constitutional reform. Their organization, the Committee for Union and Progress, forced the Sultan to restore the constitution he had suspended 30 years earlier. But, this constitutional movement eventually split into two groups: those who stood for nationalism based on Ottoman identity and the strengthening of the empire, and those liberals who favoured decentralization of power. The gap between Turks and non-Turks in the Ottoman Empire grew. A group of Turkish nationalist officers seized power in 1913 and the movement towards an exclusively Turkish nationalism was strengthened. A policy of forced Turkification alienated Arabs further, as did the repressive regime of Jemal Pasha, the Ottoman governor of Syria.

In reaction to this, Arab writers and activists moved further in the direction of an exclusive Arab nationalism based on the Arabic language and culture. In the years before World War I, Arab agitation against the Young Turk government became explicit. Movements calling for various forms of autonomy emerged in Cairo, Mesopotamia and Beirut, and in Istanbul itself. In 1912, a group of Syrian Arabs formed the Decentralization Party in Cairo. The following year, they held the first Arab Congress in Paris, despite the efforts of the Ottoman rulers to prevent it from taking place. Nevertheless, Arab nationalism remained undefined. As Sylvia Haim expresses it:

> The absence of a specific ideology of Arab nationalism until the end of the First World War is indeed noteworthy. It was not until the 1930s that a serious attempt was made to define the meaning of Arab nationalism and what constitutes the Arab nation. (1962: 35)

In this respect, it is worth noting that the absence of a coherent nationalist ideology at the time placed Palestinians at a disadvantage when making competing claims over the territory of Palestine with the Zionist movement. Zionists were largely united in their demands, which drew on a far more fluent nationalist discourse, whereas Palestinians had internally conflicting allegiances. This rendered their struggle more difficult from the beginning.

Islamic responses

While Muslim reformers influenced the development of nationalist ideas, Islamic reformism was not a nationalist discourse within the strict meaning of the term. However, among the responses to European influence that emerged in the nineteenth century, few have had such lasting significance. There had been Islamic responses to the West before – many of those who took up arms against colonialism did so in the name of religion. However, the analysis of Muslim society proposed by nineteenth-century reformists, and their prescribed remedies, were far more sophisticated and, ultimately, much more influential. Islamic reformism emerged as a set of responses to the domination of Muslim societies by Europe and the perceived failure – indeed, inability – of Islamic institutions, in particular the traditional scholars, to respond effectively to this domination. Military defeats had occurred in the past without any perception of decline but, in the nineteenth century, many Muslims began to see their societies as being in a state of steep decline compared with European countries. One of the leading reformists, Jamal al-Din al-Afghani put it thus: the Europeans had 'put their hands on every part of the world'. The notion of decline became a recurrent theme in the discourse of Islamic reformists. In its essence, Islamic reformism proposed that Muslim society was sick and its 'salvation' lay in Islam. This sickness manifested itself inwardly in loss of faith and outwardly in political disintegration. According to the reformists, the problem lay not in Islam but, rather, in Muslims. Reformism focused on the task of returning Muslim society to true Islam, which was as valid as ever. It was the Muslims understanding of it which was wrong. Above all, the reformists sought to formulate a rational response to the challenge of the West which transcended the 'formalism and inertia' of the traditional scholars (*ulama*), and accommodated modern civilization.

Al-Afghani (see Box 2.2, for a detailed discussion of his anti-imperialism) consistently opposed European influence in the Muslim world. He opposed all forms of political, military or economic intervention by foreign powers in Muslim countries, and accused those who did not combat colonialism of being traitors. He called not only for political, but also for doctrinal unity among Muslims, and had a special concern for the Arabic language because it is the language of the Qur'an. For al-Afghani, it was treason to cooperate with the Western enemy, or even to adopt a compromising attitude towards it. In order to respond to the threat from Europe, al-Afghani promoted the idea of pan-Islamism. He transformed the idea of the nation by declaring that all Muslims were members of one nation, regardless of ethnic, linguistic and cultural differences. Muslims, in al-Afghani's view, needed to band together to combat European encroachment and, in this enterprise, Islam was the only factor which united them.

Box 2.2   An Islamic anti-imperialist: Jamal al-Din al-Afghani (1839–97)

Sayyed Jamal al-Din al-Afghani was a remarkable globe-trotting proponent of Islamic reformism throughout the second half of the nineteenth century. He was born in 1839 into a family of Shiite *sayyeds* (descendants of the Prophet Muhammad) in Persia and was educated in that country and in the Shiite holy cities of Iraq. But, for much of his life, he claimed to be of Afghan origin in order to have more influence on the Sunni world. In 1857–58, he travelled to India where he developed a lifelong hatred for British imperialism. He then spent time in Afghanistan where he was adopted as an adviser by the Amir. After Afghanistan, he moved to Istanbul where he became involved in *Tanzimat* circles and became a member of the reformist Council of Education. However, he aroused the hostility of leading Ottoman *ulama* (traditional religious scholars) and left for Egypt where he spent eight years. He was given a monthly stipend by the Egyptian government and became a highly influential figure, becoming involved in Egyptian nationalist and anti-British politics and gaining a mass following. As a result, he was expelled from Egypt to India in 1879. He next moved to Paris, editing the anti-British, pan-Islamic journal *al-'Urwa al-Wuthqa* (*The Indissoluble Bond*) with Muhammad Abduh. He next spent some time in London, subsequently departing for the Persian port of Bushehr. He was invited to Tehran by the Shah but soon fell out with him over his anti-British stance. Al-Afghani then spent two years in Russia (1887–9) attempting to promote a war between Russia and Britain which he hoped would lead to Muslim uprisings. He returned to Persia in late 1889. The following year, he was linked to the publication of a leaflet criticizing the regime for concessions to foreigners and was taken by forced march to the Iraqi border in midwinter. From Iraq, and later London, he continued to criticize the Shah. Al-Afghani had been attempting to establish relations with the Ottoman Sultan, Abdulhamid, from 1885 onwards. In late 1892, he went to Istanbul as the Sultan's guest. While there, he met and encouraged a former disciple who returned to Iran and, on 1 May 1896, assassinated the Persian Shah. The Sultan refused to extradite Al-Afghani but, in his later years, he was not allowed to publish and his influence declined. He died of cancer in 1897, although unfounded rumours circulated for years that he had been poisoned by the Sultan.

Source: Nikki Keddie (1981). *Roots of Revolution: An Interpretive History of Modern Iran*, New Haven and London: Yale University Press.

If this bond could be strengthened, then a strong and stable state, or union of Muslim states, could be created and maintained.

The Egyptian scholar Muhammad Abduh (1849–1905), al-Afghani's greatest disciple, ended his days, by contrast with his mentor, in high office. Abduh had joined al-Afghani in Paris, having been exiled in 1882 by the Egyptian authorities for his support for the 'Urabi revolt. However, in 1888 he returned to Egypt, implicitly recognizing British authority there. He was made a judge and became State Mufti, head of the whole system of religious law in the country. Al-Afghani and Abduh located the cause of the malaise of Muslim society in the nineteenth century in the fossilised version of Islam which was propounded by the *ulama*. The *ulama* had discredited the search for scientific truth in the belief that they were defending the Islamic religion but, in doing so, had become enemies of that religion. Abduh wrote of an age in which the torrent of science had engulfed the entire globe and drowned the unsuspecting *ulama* in the process. For the reformists, accommodating the insights and discoveries of modern science was the key to revitalizing Islam and Muslim society. Al-Afghani advocated a synthesis of Islam and science on the basis that there was no incompatibility between science, knowledge and the foundations of the Islamic faith. The ideas propagated by Al-Afghani and Abduh were enormously influential and still retain a contemporary echo.

World War I and the making of the modern Middle East

By 1914, the Ottoman Empire had lost most of its European territories and was generally seen to be in serious decline. Fieldhouse (2006) argues, however, that not least because of the reforms undertaken, and with significant assistance from Germany, the Empire was, in fact, beginning a new phase of reconstruction. Arab nationalism was an élite affair and the great majority of the Empire's Arab subjects remained loyal to it. Therefore, it was entry into World War I and the aftermath of this, rather than an inexorable process of decline or the strength of Arab nationalism, that determined the end of the Empire. The decision to enter the War on the German side was fraught with consequences. So, the question arises as to why the Ottoman leadership took the decision to do so. The Ottomans had drawn closer to Germany in the preceding years and feared Russian designs on their territory. Entering the War on the Allied side held out the possibility that Russian ambitions might be constrained. However, an alliance with Germany could not only forestall the Russians, but also provide support for the Ottoman ambition of regaining territory lost in the Balkans where the Germans had no traditional interests. Furthermore, Germany had been providing assistance in the reorganization of the Ottoman military since the 1880s and was investing heavily in the Empire, including a railway line that was to run from Berlin to Baghdad, and then to Basra and the Gulf (Fieldhouse, 2006; McMeekin, 2011).

Defeat in the War had catastrophic consequences for the Ottomans. It led ultimately to the break-up of the Empire and the assertion of near total European control over its Arab territories. Thus, the War was also pivotal in the emergence of the modern Middle East. From the beginning of the twentieth century, the possible future partition of the Empire had been a feature of European power politics. In 1904, the formation of the Anglo-French Entente was predicated, in part, on the understanding that France had a special claim to Syria in return for its acceptance of the pre-eminent British position in Egypt. At the beginning of the War, Russian objectives were also clear and included control over the Turkish Straits and Istanbul, as well as the eastern section of Anatolia with its Armenian population (Fieldhouse, 2006: 45–6). The need to accommodate Russian concerns led to a set of negotiations between Britain and France which were initiated in 1915 and concluded the following year. The Sykes–Picot Agreement (named after its two key negotiators) constituted a plan to divide the Arab territories into British, French and Russian spheres of influence after the War. The Sykes–Picot Agreement constituted one of three conflicting undertakings on the part of the Allied powers during the course of the War. It was to come into effect only if a second, parallel set of negotiations between Britain and an Arab leader, Sharif Hussein, came to fruition. Hussein came from a family which for centuries had been hereditary guardians of the two most holy places in Islam, Mecca and Medina. In the early years of the War, he entered into discussion with the British on the terms under which he would join with them and fight against the Ottomans. His dealings with General Sir Henry McMahon, the British High Commissioner for Egypt (the McMahon–Hussein Correspondence) led to a British promise of support for the establishment of an independent Arab state under the control of his family. On 5 June 1916, the Arab Revolt began and the Sykes–Picot Agreement was secretly ratified 10 days later.

There is almost as much debate about the extent of the promises made by the British concerning a future independent Arab state as there is about the nature and significance of the Arab Revolt. In relation to the former, the McMahon–Hussein Correspondence is ambiguous. In relation to the latter, while some have seen the Arab Revolt as an early and impor-tant assertion of pan-Arab nationalism, others see it as no more than an expression of the political ambitions of Sharif Hussein and his family (Al-Azmeh, 1995). What is clear, however, is that the British and the French, in negotiating the Sykes–Picot Agreement, assumed the impossibility of the Arabs governing themselves independently. Secret as it may have been, the Agreement became public knowledge following the Bolshevik Revolution in Russia, when the new leadership seized the opportunity to embarrass their former allies and published the details in November 1917. The revelation, unsurprisingly, caused great distrust between the Arabs and the British, coming as it did a mere three weeks after the British government issued the Balfour Declaration, in which Britain undertook to support the creation of a Jewish homeland in Palestine.

His Majesty's Government view with favour the establishment in Palestine of a national home for the Jewish people, and will use their best endeavors to facilitate the achievement of this object, it being clearly understood that nothing shall be done which may prejudice the civil and religious rights of existing non-Jewish communities in Palestine, or the rights and political status enjoyed by Jews in any other country.

British support for the creation of a Jewish state in Palestine has its roots in the Christian Zionist movement of the mid-nineteenth century, which called for the return of the Jews to the Holy Land in order to accelerate the second coming of the Lord. There were also more prosaic *realpolitik* reasons, such as maintaining a presence in the region through a proxy strategic asset. Finally, the lobbying effort on the part of Jewish Zionists should not be discounted.

Versailles and after

The Balfour Declaration deepened Arab fears that their interests were destined to be disregarded in any postwar settlement. In 1919, the victorious allies assembled at Versailles to hammer out the terms of such a settlement. Over the course of four years, 'a new political cartography of the Middle East emerged' (Pappé, 2005: 24). The disregard for Arab concerns was clearly evident when, in November 1918, a committee of 14 Egyptian nationalist leaders, led by Saad Zaghloul, approached the British authorities with a view to leading a delegation to put the Egyptian case for independence to the conference at Versailles. The British refused and, instead, in March 1919 deported Zaghloul and his colleagues to Malta. Egypt rose up in a revolt which spread throughout the country. Rail and communication lines were cut and Cairo was isolated from the rest of the country for weeks. The revolt was only suppressed by a show of superior force. Tens of thousands of British troops were sent into the countryside and air power was deployed to control an essentially unarmed population (Goldberg, 1992: 261). The British finally relented and arranged for Zaghloul to address the conference. However, on the day that the Egyptian delegation arrived in Paris, the American delegation issued a statement recognizing Britain's protectorate over Egypt, effectively dashing Egyptian hopes of self-determination.

In the summer of 1919, Woodrow Wilson, the US president, sent a commission of enquiry to Syria and Palestine to investigate the wishes of their inhabitants. This was done at the suggestion of Sharif Hussein's son, Faisal, who had had become de facto ruler of Syria after the War and tried to use the Versailles conference to consolidate his position. In January

1919, Faisal wrote a memo stating that 'the aim of the Arab nationalist movements ... is to unite the Arabs eventually into one nation'. He sought immediate and full independence for Greater Syria and the western province of Hijaz, while accepting foreign intervention in Palestine and in Mesopotamia/Iraq. The King–Crane Commission found overwhelming popular opposition to the proposed European control of Syria and Palestine. However, their report was ignored by Britain and France. The US, on the verge of 20 years of isolationism, did little to support its findings (Mansfield, 1992: 180–1).

In the aftermath of the War, only four independent states remained in the region. Two of these, Saudi Arabia and North Yemen, were conservative monarchies in the Arabian Peninsula which the Ottomans had effectively abandoned and where no colonial power asserted an interest. The others were the non-Arab states of Turkey and Iran. These escaped European domination partly because of their size and because there was consensus on the need to establish buffers around the emergent Soviet Union. Both countries also saw significant resistance to European encroachment. Much of Persia had been occupied during the war by Britain and Russia. However, after the War, popular mobilization forced Britain to abandon a plan to turn the country into a protectorate and, in 1921, Reza Khan (an officer in the Cossack Brigades) came to power in a military coup. Four years later, he declared himself King (*Shah* in Persian). From 1935 onwards, the country became known by its Persian name, Iran. In Turkey, a military officer named Mustapha Kemal (later known as Ataturk or 'Father of the Turks') led a series of military and, later, political initiatives to repel occupiers and, in the process, established the modern state of Turkey,

The remaining Arab states came under European control. Halliday (1995) offers a useful tripartite division. The states of North Africa, had, as we have seen, come under European control before the war. In the Arabian Peninsula, Britain controlled six territories on the coast – Kuwait, Bahrain, Qatar, the Trucial States (now the United Arab Emirates), Oman and Aden. In the third Arab region, Ottoman territory was taken and divided between Britain and France into five new entities (Halliday, 1995: 26). The Ottoman province of Syria was carved up into four mini-states – Syria, Lebanon, Transjordan (later Jordan) and Palestine – and a fifth new state of Iraq was created out of the Ottoman provinces of Baghdad, Basra and Mosul. Syria and Lebanon came under French control, while Transjordan, Palestine and Iraq were allocated to Britain. As a sop to the promises made to Sharif Hussein during the War, his sons were set in place as kings of Iraq and the new state of Transjordan. The legal mechanism through which much of this was done was the newly-invented 'mandate'. In formal acknowledgment of the principle of self-determination, the charter of the League of

Nations specified that the wellbeing and development of states 'inhabited by peoples not yet able to stand by themselves under the strenuous conditions of the modern world' should be entrusted to 'advanced nations who by reason of their resources, their experience, or their geographic position can best undertake this responsibility'. But, for many in the region, the new mandate resembled nothing so much as the old colony and the creation of new borders seemed particularly contentious, as Box 2.3 details.

As had happened before, the extension of European control did not go unopposed. There were continuing revolts and other forms of nationalist resistance to foreign military occupation. Morocco witnessed a series of rebellions, the most notable of which was led by Abd el-Krim which culminated in 1925 and required a French force of 325,000 troops, backed by tanks and planes and supported by 100,000 Spanish soldiers, to defeat it. In Egypt, the 1919 revolt was followed by guerrilla attacks on British forces stationed in the Canal Zone until their final departure in 1956. There was also strong resistance to British advances in Iraq and Palestine by Ottoman armies composed largely of Arab conscripts, as well as by nationalist forces after Britain had seized control. Two years after the occupation of Baghdad, an Iraqi national revolt enabled the Iraqis to take control of large parts of the country in 1920. The rebellion was suppressed through the deployment of overwhelming force. The number of British troops in the country was raised from 60,000 in July 1920 to over 100,000 in October of that year – the action including the use of heavy artillery and aerial bombardment (Rogan, 2010: 113–14). In Palestine, there were several serious disturbances which culminated in a major revolt against British rule between 1936 and 1939 which was suppressed by the deployment of tens of thousands of British troops. In Syria, the French faced a massive revolt in 1925–6 which was put down by the liberal use of aerial bombardment against villages and cities. Having had to fight their way into Damascus at the outset of their rule in 1920, the French lost control of much of the city and adjoining countryside in 1925, and responded with repeated bombardment of the Syrian capital using artillery and planes.

The coming of independence

Military resistance was doomed to failure. Independence, when it finally came, was the result of a number of factors. In general terms, the adoption of nationalist discourse as a tool of self-determination was highly significant and anti-colonial nationalism, as elsewhere in the colonized world, proved critical in securing an end to direct foreign control. Some states in the region negotiated their independence under the terms of the mandates

Box 2.3   The problematic nature of new borders

Despite the problems that the new Middle Eastern states encountered after their creation at the hands of colonial and mandate powers, they managed, over time, to develop a strong sense of national belonging among the peoples inhabiting the new states. Linguistic, sectarian and religious differences remained significant across the Levant and presented a challenge for the ruling elites but, gradually, a common national identity began to take hold, becoming a legitimating tool for rulers capable of managing the new states. The borders that the colonial powers had created began to be perceived as legitimate and countries in the Levant started operating according to them, although a degree of conflict remained with territorial claims being made periodically. For example, Syria felt amputated of Lebanon, while Iraq had claims on Kuwait. Irrespective of the problematic nature of the new borders, with the passage of time they were less contested and increasingly accepted and acceptable.

The invasions of Iraq in 1991 and 2003, together with the Syrian civil war, have however placed the issues of national borders back at the top of the agenda, and their problematic nature has come back to haunt the international community. The creation of a separate and separatist Kurdish entity in Iraq functions as a pull factor for the territorial disaggregation of both Turkey and Syria. The rise of non-state actors – such as the Islamic State of Syria and Iraq – has led to the virtual disappearance of the border between the two countries, while sectarian tensions in Lebanon, and across the Gulf, threaten the sovereignty and the political stability of these countries. In some respects, there is a powerful popular and, on occasion, well-articulated critique of the borders imposed by colonial powers after the collapse of the caliphate and this is an aspect of post-colonial politics that deserves some attention. The contestation of post-colonial borders is only contingently rooted in post-Arab Awakening volatility; it speaks, in fact, to a much deeper and never fully resolved problem of state legitimacy and nation-building.

Source: Nikki Keddie (1981). *Roots of Revolution: An Interpretive History of Modern Iran*, New Haven and London: Yale University Press.

set up after World War I. But, it was the course and consequences of World War II that proved to be crucial to the end of European rule in the Middle East and North Africa. Although Britain and France emerged from the War on the winning side, both were left economically devastated and dependent on economic support from the United States. France had also experienced occupation at home and in its foreign territories, which significantly eroded the notion of military superiority that had attached to colonial powers in the past. In addition, the French relied very heavily on its '*indigenes*' to secure its liberation and ultimate victory against Germany. A significant number of soldiers were, in fact, from the colonies and the vast majority of them had never seen France – their supposed motherland. They were sent to fight, and fight they did, but some of them saw the War as an opportunity to at least claim equal citizenship rights, given that the were sacrificing their lives for the liberation of the country. When their contribution was belittled or marginalized in the aftermath of victory, this sparked protests and increased politicization, which would ultimately result in demands for independence. On the other hand, the United States emerged from the War as the dominant global power in economic, technological and military terms. The Soviet Union, while it had suffered enormous losses during the War, was also poised to assume a much greater role in international politics. Neither of the emergent superpowers had an interest in assisting the Europeans to maintain their grip on their colonial empires.

After the Iraqi revolt of 1920, Faisal was installed as king. In 1924, a constituent assembly was elected and a treaty regulating relations with Britain was signed. The 1930 Anglo-Iraqi Treaty provided for a 25-year alliance on the basis of which the two countries would consult each other on matters of foreign policy, while Britain would retain use of certain airbases and provide training for the Iraqi army. In 1932, Iraq became independent and joined the League of Nations. Jordan was the only other state to negotiate the end of its mandate. In Jordan, opposition to a much lighter British presence was limited and King Abdullah enjoyed wide support. Jordan became independent in 1946. In the other mandate territories, the situation was more complex. Lebanese political leaders began to prepare for self-rule during World War II as French influence began to wane. This culminated in the 1943 National Pact in which Maronite Christian and Sunni Muslim leaders agreed to share power in a future Lebanese state which would adopt a neutral foreign policy orientation. General elections were held the same year under the terms of the mandate. The new parliament abolished the mandate without reference to the French whose reaction, predictably, was to imprison the Lebanese leadership. This provoked a revolt which crossed sectarian lines. Under international pressure, the French released the prisoners and conceded Lebanese independence. The last of the French forces left the country in 1946. In Syria, French policy was more conciliatory following the revolt of 1925 which continued sporadically for another two years. In 1928, elections to a constituent assembly led to victory for nationalist forces. In 1930, the French High Commissioner promulgated a new constitution, which made Syria a parliamentary republic with France retaining control over foreign affairs and security. In 1936, a new left-wing government in France agreed on Syrian independence with continued Franco-Syrian consultation on foreign policy and the retention of two military bases by France. But, the agreement was never ratified and another change of government in France led to a reversal of policy. It was the War that finally brought about change. Elections in 1943 brought victory for Syrian nationalists and the

---

Box 2.4 The Lebanese National Pact of 1943

In 1943, Lebanon was not an independent state. Its French rulers interpreted its role as mandatory power to suspend the Constitution, shut down the House of Deputies, and dismiss the Cabinet and the elected President. That year, Bechara al-Khouri, the Maronite Christian President, and Riad al-Solh, the Sunni Muslim Prime Minister, entered into an informal agreement to end the French mandate. Their agreement became known as *al mithaq al-watani* (the National Pact). To understand the significance of the Pact, it is necessary to go back to the origins of the state. The new state of Lebanon, as created in the aftermath of World War I, consisted of the historical Ottoman Province of Mount Lebanon, inhabited mainly by Christians and Druze, and of several districts of other provinces inhabited mainly by Sunnis and Shiites. The central problem confronting the new state was the lack of consensus among its inhabitants about their national identity. Most Muslims identified themselves as Arabs and favoured unification with Syria. Most Christians saw themselves as Lebanese and were concerned to maintain a close relationship with the West – and with France, in particular.

The two leaders saw the resolution of this identity crisis, on terms acceptable to both Christians and Muslims, as essential to ending the mandate. Their solution was a compromise in terms of which Christians would accept their Arab identity and dependence on the West for protection, while Muslims would accept their Lebanese identity and give up their aspiration to be a part of a larger Arab state. In a ministerial declaration to the House of Deputies on 7 October 1943, Riad al-Solh stated that Lebanon had an 'Arab face', would seek constitutional amendments to end the mandate, and would establish close relations with the other Arab states to protest its independence, sovereignty and territorial boundaries. In November 1943, the House of Deputies adopted the amendments and eliminated all references to the mandate, thus initiating the country's transition to independence from France.

Source: US Library of Congress (2012).'Lebanon constitutional law and the political rights of religious communities', available at http://www.loc.gov/law/help/lebanon-constitutional- law.php.

French began, reluctantly, to transfer power to the Syrian government. Finally, under pressure from Britain, the French withdrew from Syria, which, together with Lebanon, whose domestic political arrangements were imposed by the French (see Box 2.4), joined the United Nations in 1946.

The path to independence in the fourth mandate country took a very different and complicated course, the legacy of which still affects regional and, even, global politics. In Palestine, shifts in mandate policy, particularly in relation to Jewish immigration and the increasing affirmation of Zionism in Europe (see Box 2.5), saw the British authorities alienate both the Palestinian and the increasingly Jewish population of the territory. Rising anti-Semitism in Europe, especially after the accession of the Nazis to power in Germany in 1933, led to increased Jewish settle-

Box 2.5   Zionism

The Zionist project emerged in the midst of European nation and state building in late nineteenth-century Europe. It was conceived as a traditional national liberation project whose central aim was the creation of a nation-state in which Jews could live as a majority. Zionism delineated Jews not according to religion, but as a people who had the right to have their own nation-state and govern themselves, crucially, away from the societies within which Jews had lived for centuries. In that respect, Zionism was not simply a national liberation movement, but also a political project aimed at solving the problem of anti-Semitism in Europe. For centuries, Jews had been marginalized, discriminated against and periodically attacked in violent pogroms. When European nation-states were being built, Jews were increasingly suspected of having divided loyalties and were therefore often victimized. Theodor Herzl, the founder of Zionism, proposed to solve the problem of anti-Semitism by getting Jews out of the states in which they lived and, instead, creating a state for them on the land of Palestine, with which Jews had a historical and religious connection. The departure of the Jews was seen as a way to address anti-Semitism and, at the same time, allow European societies to get on with their nationalist state-building project without worrying about how to integrate Jews in it.

ment in Palestine. When Zionist ideas began circulating among the Jews of Europe, very few of them were supportive of resettling in Palestine to create an independent state for the Jews. Many European Jews simply wanted to integrate even further in the societies in which they had lived in for centuries, while the more religious sectors of European Jewry were opposed to Zionism on doctrinal grounds. However, the wave of right-wing nationalism with its corollary of anti-Semitism that hit Europe in the 1930s began to focus the attention of many Jews on the problematic nature of their integration into societies that seemed to reject them. Inevitably, and in keeping with a long-standing European tradition, Jews were believed not to belong to the 'real' nations that were affirming themselves across the continent. Jews were the 'internal' enemy and therefore their integration was not simply impossible, but would be deleterious for the strength of the nation. This worrying trend across Europe intensified the emigration of Jews out of the continent, with some of them electing to go to Palestine. It is no surprise that the rising numbers of the Jewish population, from 16 per cent of the overall population to 28 per cent five years later, was a key factor in the Palestinian revolt which broke out in 1936 and lasted for three years. As an increasing number of Jews decided to leave Europe, the Palestinians began to see the potential threat to their claims and revolted against the British authorities, which they accused of favouring Jewish immigration.

Having suppressed the revolt, the mandate authorities reconsidered their policies and, in 1939, introduced strict limits on future Jewish immigration and land purchases which, in turn, provoked Jewish opposition. This was a very understandable reaction on the part of the Jewish community because, by then, the anti-Semitism of many European societies was in full swing, heightening the need for Jews to leave. The problem was now that those who wanted to go to Palestine would be prevented from doing so by the British, who were accused of willfully ignoring what was taking place in continental Europe. By the end of the War, this culminated in the emergence of minority paramilitary groups such as the Stern Gang and the Irgun, whose methods included the kidnapping and murder of British personnel, attacks on trains and train stations, and the bombing of the British headquarters in the King David Hotel in Jerusalem in 1946 which killed 91 people. In spite of these later acts of hostility against the British, throughout the period from the Arab Revolt onwards the Zionist leadership had continued to govern mandate Palestine with the British, and helped them to quell the revolt of the Palestinians. In turn, the adoption of repressive measures seriously weakened the Palestinian leadership and further highlighted its failure in contrast to the Zionist project (Khalidi, 1996). This low-intensity three-way civil war undermined the validity and effectiveness of the British mandate and, in 1947, under American pressure, and with the mandate increasingly unpopular at home, Britain announced its intention to withdraw from Palestine and to hand the matter over to the recently formed United Nations. The UN, in turn, proposed a partition plan on terms rather favourable to the Jewish population. There were 1,269,000 Arabs and 608,000 Jews living within the mandate territories. The partition plan divided the country in such a way that each state would have the majority of its own population. The territory designated to be the Jewish state was slightly larger than the Palestinian state (56 per cent and 43 per cent of Palestine, respectively). The areas of Jerusalem and Bethlehem were to become an international zone. The plan was approved by the General Assembly of the UN in November 1947 – although Arab members opposed it, as did a discredited Palestinian leadership, which refused to negotiate on a partition plan whose underlying logic they rejected entirely. The wartime attempt by Haj Amin al-Husseini, the Grand Mufti of Jerusalem, to secure the support of Nazi Germany was detrimental to the Palestinian cause in the aftermath of World War II and the Zionist movement played on this to portray Palestinian claims as illegitimate. On 14 May 1948, Britain finally withdrew and the Jewish community declared its independence as the state of Israel.

With the exception of Libya, the countries of North Africa had to wait until later into the 1950s to achieve their independence. Italy's defeat in

World War II was followed by its renunciation of all rights to its African colonial possessions, and the question of Libya's future was handed to the UN General Assembly. Following protracted negotiations, the United Kingdom of Libya was proclaimed in December 1951 under King Idris I. The outcome of the War was also crucial to the course of events in Morocco and Tunisia. The first nationalist party in Tunisia was set up in 1919. A successor, the *Destour* (Constitution) Party was established the following year, with the aim of securing 'the emancipation of the Tunisian country from the bonds of slavery' (Perkins, 2004: 79). By 1934, this party had split and a new one was formed – the *neo-Destour* Party, which favoured more aggressive tactics to secure independence. The nationalist movement in Morocco emerged in the 1920s. Within two decades, the *Istiqlal* (Independence) Party had established relations with Sultan Muhammad V, who began to make demands for the end of the protectorate. The French responded to increased demands for independence in both countries after the War with a combination of repression and offers of limited sovereignty. In 1952, Bourguiba and other leaders of *Istiqlal* were arrested in Tunisia. One year later, the Sultan of Morocco issued a demand for complete sovereignty for his country. He was deposed and exiled along with his family, becoming, in the process, a unifying symbol for most Moroccans. This made matters worse, as the nationalists adopted increasingly violent methods and were met with harsh repression in return. However, events elsewhere proved decisive. More significant French interests in Indochina and Algeria came under threat, which prompted negotiations with both the *neo-Destour* Party in Tunisia and the Sultan of Morocco, who was brought back from exile. As a result, both Morocco and Tunisia became independent in 1956.

The Algerian path to independence was far more violent. The presence in the country of one million Europeans out of a total of 10 million, together with the fact that Algeria was considered not a colony but, rather, an integral part of French territory, ensured the rejection by France of any claim to independence. In 1954, the Algerian *Front de Liberation Nationale* (FLN) was established and the war of independence broke out the same year. The war lasted eight years and cost several hundred thousand lives on the Algerian side, as well as 20,000 French. Algeria finally became independent in 1962.

The last territories to remain under British control came to independence over the ensuing 10 years. These were the kingdoms of the Gulf which had enjoyed close relations with Britain since the mid-nineteenth century. In the late 1960s, this arrangement suited local leaders who felt threatened by more powerful neighbours such as Saudi Arabia and Iran, who asserted claims to some of their territories. However, in 1968 the British government announced its intention to withdraw by the end of 1971. In August 1971, Bahrain declared its independence. This was followed by Qatar one month later. Finally, on 9 December, the remaining kingdoms were admitted to the United Nations as the United Arab Emirates (UAE).

Patterns in post-colonial political development

The enthusiasm that independence generated was, for most countries, short-lived due to the scale of the challenges facing them. Not only the issue of boundaries was contested, generating early inter-state rivalries, but the necessity to rebuild or build anew all sorts of infrastructures placed a heavy burden on the new ruling elites and ordinary citizens.

Challenges at independence

One of the key impacts of colonialism throughout the developing world was a legacy of political instability. In general, colonialism established territories and fixed boundaries with limited reference either to what had gone before, or to the interests of local populations. Second, colonialism established a political order within each state, and an administrative hierarchy to run it, which was ultimately based on force. Third, colonialism introduced a political order that was both centralized and authoritarian in nature. Ultimate authority came from overseas. With the coming of independence, this structure was adapted and indigenized such that the line of authority ran to the capital city. But, as Clapham (1985) has noted, the colonial state became the model for the post-colonial state which was seen largely in the same way by most people – as an alien imposition, to be accepted but to be feared, where possible to be exploited, existing on a plane above the people whom it governed, and beyond any chance of control.

The MENA region was no exception to this. However, the post-colonial politics of the region were further complicated by the persistence of outside strategic interests in transit routes, oil and the state of Israel, as well as the regional instability that flowed from the fragmentation of the region into 'a multitude of small states that were bound to be politically and militarily weak' (Hinnebusch, 2003: 19). This was not least because the newly created states were seen as artificial by their inhabitants, whose primary loyalties were to small groups such as tribe, sect or village, or to pan-national identities such as religion. As we shall see in later chapters, the contestation of post-colonial borders has re-appeared as crucial after the Arab Awakening. The virtual disappearance of the border between Syria and Iraq since the spring of 2014 illustrates how the borders bequeathed by colonialism are still problematic. In any case, the result of the artificial nature of some of the new states was an initial period of political instability as the multiparty systems put in place by European powers floundered and gave way to centralized – and, ultimately, authoritarian – political systems.

The post-colonial states of the Middle East and North Africa were dominated by élites who often owed their positions of power to the fact that they had close relationships with the departed colonial power. Under colonialism, a new ruling class of urban notables and tribal chiefs had emerged. But, the new rulers faced a series of deep-rooted challenges. The first of these was the challenge of legitimacy, as states, and the institutions within them, were seen by many as alien impositions, reflecting European interests, rather than expressing local political realities, or the desires of indigenous populations. It was one thing to create an anti-colonial nationalist coalition but quite another to command the allegiance of all citizens. In countries such as Lebanon (where at least six different religious minorities were brought together in a centralized state for the first time), or the new state of Iraq (which included substantial Sunni, Shia and Kurdish populations), this challenge played a major role in post-colonial political life. Syria was no different, with its substantial Christian, Alawite and other minorities.

Newly independent states in the Middle East, as with those elsewhere in the developing world, also faced major socioeconomic challenges, including high levels of poverty and illiteracy, as well as religious and social divisions that had been accentuated during European colonization due to the 'divide and rule' policies on which colonial powers had relied to govern more effectively. In many new states, there was a limited lead-in time to independence and poor preparation for the challenges of governing an independent state. The cases of Egypt or Tunisia, for example, where an educated class of administrators existed at independence, can be contrasted with Libya, where Italian colonial policy destroyed the bureaucracy as well as the military and financial establishment, leaving Libya at independence with no experienced local bureaucrats and little by way of a state (Anderson, 1987: 5). Algeria faced similar problems, insofar as the departure of the European settlers and the legacy of an eight-year conflict left the country deprived of administrative cadres and infrastructure. Meeting popular expectations of independence was also a significant challenge. As with other post-colonial regions, the countries of the MENA suffered from the consequences of their mal-integration into the global economy. The new states of the region exported primary products to the industrialized world and imported expensive manufactured goods, as states of the region had done since the nineteenth century.

Finally, the outcome of the 1948 war between the newly declared state of Israel and its Arab neighbours greatly contributed to political instability in the region. The declaration of Israeli independence was followed by the entry into the territory of the new state of military units from Syria, Transjordan, Iraq and Egypt, ostensibly in the defence of Arab interests. However, there was no effective cooperation between them and their military capacity failed to reflect the numerical balance between the two sides (40 million Arabs as opposed to 600,000 Jews). The War of Independence, as it is known in Israel, or *Nakba* (catastrophe), as it is termed by Arabs, ended with a greatly expanded territory under Israeli control, while Arab East Jerusalem was controlled by Transjordan, and the Gaza Strip by Egypt. The political significance of the Arab defeat was great. The incompetence and rivalry, which characterized the Arab war effort, radicalized public opinion and directly contributed to the first military coup in the region which took place in Syria in 1949. It further radicalized the group of Egyptian army officers who overthrew the monarchy in that country three years later. The inability of the Arab rulers of newly independent states to deal effectively with Israel undermined much of their already shaky credibility.

The trend towards authoritarianism

The inability of either the leaders or the institutions of the states of the region to contain pressure from those who increasingly sought their share of the political and economic power from which they were excluded culminated in a series of challenges to the position of those leaders. The first successful military coup in the region took place in Syria in 1949 and was followed by a period of instability, in the course of which the country moved towards the left and Arab nationalists grew in influence. In Egypt, the 'Free Officers' coup of 1952 ended the monarchical line founded by Muhammad Ali at the beginning of the nineteenth century. The military officers who now took charge of Egypt had no developed ideological position to begin with but, by the mid-1950s, under the charismatic leadership of Gamal Abdel Nasser, they were espousing Arab socialism and pan-Arab nationalism as the solution to the ills of the region. Six years after the coup in Egypt, the monarchy in Iraq was overthrown by the military. In contrast to the bloodless coup in Egypt, the King, Faisal II, and all but one member of the royal family were murdered. The new republic of Iraq aligned itself closely with Egypt. In North Africa, post-colonial political life was dominated, at least in the cases of Tunisia and Algeria, by political parties associated with anti-colonial nationalist movements.

Across the region, as elsewhere in the post-colonial world, there was a significant increase in the power and pervasiveness of the state. The growth in the power of the state was linked to broader trends in regional and international political life. Many of the states of the region were beginning to adopt the rhetoric of socialism in the context of the emerging Cold War rivalry between the United States and its allies and the Soviet bloc. But, this was not the only factor – mainstream thinking in the new academic discipline of development economics envisaged a major role for the state, which was in any case often the only possible agent of development.

A number of other factors, many of which were characteristic of other post-colonial states, were also important. These included the need to maintain security after the departure of the colonial power, the drive to establish control over the whole of the new national territory and the desire to use the state to promote large programmes of economic development and social welfare. Other factors, more specific to the Middle East, were the implementation of land reform programmes in a number of countries in the 1950s, the apparent failure of the private sector to meet the challenge of development, and the sudden departure following independence of thousands of foreign officials, businessmen and agriculturalists. Finally, the expansion of the state was driven by the Arab nationalist quest for union, as well as increased oil wealth in the region (Owen, 2004: 22).

The escalation in state power was accompanied by a huge increase in the power of those who controlled the institutions of the state. Across the region, the role of political parties diminished, replicating a pattern seen elsewhere in the post-colonial world. There were a number of reasons for this. Many felt that multiparty competition was a luxury that could not be afforded by states facing enormous developmental challenges, and the argument that democracy encourages divisiveness prevailed. In Egypt, one of the first acts of the new Free Officers movement was to ban pre-revolutionary parties. In Tunisia, the *neo-Destour* Party, under the leadership of Habib Bourguiba, quickly assumed a dominant position and undertook a series of secularizing reforms of a kind not seen anywhere else in the Arab world. In Algeria, following the end of the war of independence, the *Front de Liberation Nationale* (FLN or National Liberation Front), the political wing of the Algerian independence movement, became the dominant force.

By the 1960s, Syrian and Iraqi politics were also dominated by a single party – the *Baath* (or Renaissance) Party, as the belief that one party could represent the interests of the whole of the country spread. The drift towards single party rule was often accompanied by a huge increase in the power of the state president and the executive in general. As a rule, the state president was the head of state, the commander in chief of the armed forces and party chairman as well. Typically, he took most key decisions on his own in the light of his understanding of the national interest. Writing in

1991, Ayubi noted that the Egyptian President, Husni Mubarak, held the following posts: President of the Republic, Supreme Commander of the Armed Forces, Higher Chief of the Police Forces, Higher Chief of the Judiciary, Head of the ruling National Democratic Party and Commissioner on all military and economic matters and accords touching on national security. All executive authority was vested in the President who appointed the cabinet and was the chief policy-maker in matters of security, diplomacy and the economy (Ayubi adds that Mubarak's favourite title was, nonetheless, 'Elder of the Egyptian Family') (Ayubi, 1991: 227).

The rise of pan Arab nationalism

The increased centrality of the state to political life was linked to the resurgence of pan-Arab nationalist ideology throughout the 1950s. The drive to independence saw the emergence of a system of sovereign states in the region, but, paradoxically, the countervailing trend towards pan-Arab unity grew in influence. At the heart of pan-Arabism lay the belief that all Arabs constitute a single nation and, as such, have the right to self-determination in a single Arab state. Therefore, pan-Arab nationalism explicitly rejected the state system that had emerged in the Middle East and North Africa under the influence of European colonialism and advocated its replacement. The rise to prominence of pan-Arab ideology during this period is inextricably linked to the emergence of two Arab nationalist movements in the 1940s and 1950s – Baathism and Nasserism. The translation of the ideas which underpinned these movements into political practice and their ultimate abandonment reflect the history of the pan-Arab ideal, which could not resolve the contradiction between the desire for unity and the progressive embedding of specific nationalisms in the region, as the new states consolidated their control over the territory inherited at independence. It is also for this reason that different states came to see their specific nationalism as embodying pan-Arabism, leading to competing views and understandings of it, which ultimately undermined the pan-Arab vision of all Arabs living under the same political authority.

In 1940, two Syrians – Michel Aflaq, a Christian, and Salah al-Din al-Bitar, a Sunni Muslim – established a small political and cultural study group, which became the nucleus of the *Baath* Party. The party was officially established in 1947, with its own daily newspaper, and held its first congress the following year. In the mid-1950s, the *Baath* Party amalgamated with a more explicitly socialist party and expanded its influence to almost every Arab country. It became especially strong in Syria, Iraq, Jordan, Lebanon, and among exiled Palestinians. Membership was largely composed of the urban middle to lower-middleclasses. Minority groups

and sects such as Alawis, Druzes, Shiis and Christians were strongly represented because they believed that pan-Arabism would allow minorities to
be seamlessly subsumed into a wider political project with no Islamic religious overtones. By 1954, members of the *Baath* Party held key cabinet
positions in Syria, sharing power on and off with the Communist Party.
In 1963, the party had come to power through a military coup. However,
years of infighting ensued until Hafez al-Asad seized control in 1970. The
Baath Party also became a powerful force in Iraqi politics. The Iraqi *Baath*
came to power initially through a coup d'état in 1963 but lost power later
the same year. However, by 1968 the party was once more the dominant
force in Iraqi politics following another coup.

Baathist ideology was centred on the concept of cultural renaissance
(or *Baath*) which would transform Arab civilization in all of its aspects
and make a unique contribution to humanity and world civilization. The
groundwork for this renaissance would lie in the transformation of Arab
society towards the goals of unity, liberty and socialism. 'Unity, liberty
and socialism', indeed, became the slogan of the party. Progress for the
Arab nation meant revolution, great individual sacrifice, commitment and
burning faith.

Hourani suggests that Baathism was 'an ideology that became a political force', whereas Nasserism was 'a regime which developed quickly a
system of ideas in terms of which it claimed to be legitimate' (Hourani,
1991: 405). As mentioned previously, in the early days of the Egyptian
revolution, the Free Officers expressed no precise plans. Their ideology
was unclear except for the stated goals of ending 'autocracy, imperialism
and feudalism'. The situation rapidly changed as Nasser assumed the leadership of the new regime. By 1956, he had adopted a revolutionary Arab
nationalism similar in many ways to that of the *Baath*.

Nasser's ideology contained a number of elements which possessed
popular appeal. It employed the language of Islam in appeals to the masses,
but this was a reformist vision of Islam which did not oppose secularizing
and modernizing change. Nasser appealed also to Arab nationalism and
unity. Egyptian leadership could lead the Arab world towards social revolution. Social reform was justified in terms of Arab socialism, which was
conceived as a system that was halfway between capitalism and Marxism.
In Arab socialism everyone rallied around the government which, in turn,
pursued the interests of all.

Nasser's version of Arab socialism required public ownership of
communications, banking, heavy and medium industry, and foreign trade,
as well as equality of opportunity, health care and education for both men
and women. Land reform, price and rent controls, food subsidies and
taxation policies were introduced in an attempt to redress the inequitable

distribution of wealth. However, in promising the Arabs freedom, Nasser was not offering personal freedom and liberty but freedom from Western domination. Arab nationalism did not require democratic rule, especially since political parties would never subordinate their own interests to the general good.

The decline of European power

By the 1950s the once dominant position of Britain and France in Europe had been superseded by the United States. US involvement in the region, which had begun in the 1920s with contacts between oil companies and the Saudi regime, depended considerably on the extension to Iran of the guarantees of the Truman Doctrine of March 1947, which had initially offered aid to Greece and Turkey, in order to prevent them falling within the Soviet sphere of influence.

The rise in American influence, at the expense of Britain, was further evident when, in 1953, the government of Mohammed Mossadeq was overthrown in a coup (see Box 2.6) orchestrated by the US Central Intelligence Agency (CIA). Mossadeq, the elected Prime Minister of Iran, was threatening to nationalize the Anglo-Iranian Oil Company (which was a forerunner to British Petroleum) a position which enjoyed considerable support within the country. His plan alarmed the British government and plans for his removal were made. The then British Ambassador in Tehran is reported as saying:

> it is so important to prevent the Persians from destroying their main source of revenue ... by trying to run it for themselves. (Curtis, 2003: 305)

However, the British lacked the means to carry out their plans and the US drafted plans for Mossdeq's overthrow, which were carried out in August 1953.

The clearest expression of the decline of European power and the corresponding increase in superpower influence in the region came three years later with the Suez Crisis – or Tripartite Aggression, as it is known to many in the region. The souring of relations between Egypt and Britain culminated in Nasser's announcement on the fourth anniversary of the Free Officer's coup in 1956 that he intended to nationalize the Suez Canal and to create an Egyptian authority to run it. The proposed move was massively popular in Egypt and beyond, and it fitted with Nasser's anti-imperialist rhetoric. However, it was deeply opposed by Britain, which was prepared to use force to reverse this position. The British and French governments entered into a secret agreement with Israel for a joint inva-

---

Box 2.6　Operation TPAJAX: the 1953 overthrow of Mohammed Mossadeq

In August 2013, the CIA disclosed documents which made clear for the first time its key role in the 1953 coup which overthrew Iran's democratically elected Prime Minister, Mohammed Mossadeq. The role of the US in the coup had been acknowledged both by then Secretary of State, Madeleine Albright in 2000, and, nine years later by President Barack Obama in a speech in Cairo. However, the intelligence services had always formally denied their involvement. In the documents, which were released to the independent National Security Archive, the coup was justified in the following terms by one of its planners, Donald Wilber:

> By the end of 1952, it had become clear that the Mossadeq government in Iran was incapable of reaching an oil settlement with interested Western countries ... was motivated mainly by Mossadeq's desire for personal power; was governed by irresponsible policies based on emotion; had weakened the Shah and the Iranian Army to a dangerous degree; and had cooperated closely with the Tudeh (Communist) Party of Iran.
>
> In view of these factors, it was estimated that Iran was in real danger of falling behind the Iron Curtain; if that happened it would mean a victory for the Soviets in the Cold War and a major setback for the West in the Middle East. No remedial action other than the covert action plan set forth below could be found to improve the existing state of affairs.

Source: National Security Archive (2013). 'CIA confirms role in 1953 Iran coup', available at http://www2.gwu.edu/~nsarchiv/NSAEBB/NSAEBB435/#_ftn1.

---

sion of Egypt. On 29 October 1956 Israeli troops entered Sinai. The following day, Britain and France issued an 'ultimatum' calling on Egypt and Israel to cease fighting and to withdraw their forces 10 miles from the Canal. Nasser refused to comply. When the ultimatum expired, Egyptian airfields were bombed by British and French planes. On 5 November, Anglo-French invasion forces seized Port Said and began to move south along the Canal. However, the tripartite action against Egypt aroused international hostility at a time when de-colonization was high on the agenda. The Soviet Union threatened the use of force against Britain, France and Israel, while the United States threatened to withhold financial support from Britain. On 6 November, Britain and France were forced to accept a UN ceasefire and to begin to withdraw their forces. The sequence of events expressed Britain's miscalculation of the popularity of the new regime in Egypt. It also marked the decline of European influence in the region after a century of domination and the ascendancy of new international actors, which were now going to 'use' the region in the global Cold War.

The Middle East and the Cold War

The increasingly radicalized character of Arab politics, together with the espousal of socialist ideals implicit in pan-Arab nationalism, drew the region into the Cold War struggle between the United States and the Soviet Union, which came to dominate global politics from the late 1940s onwards. For the Soviet Union, its Arab allies were part of a broader 'non-capitalist' bloc that was emerging in the post-colonial world, which had the potential to strengthen the camp of those opposed to the West (Halliday, 2005: 125). The emergence of socialist-oriented regimes espousing what were seen as radical pan-Arabist aspirations represented a threat to the US on two levels. First, there was concern at the possibility of Soviet 'gains' in the region, as states such as Egypt and Syria appeared to be moving closer to the Soviet Union. Second, the objective of a single, Arab state, which rejected foreign influence and was inspired by socialist principles, threatened the grip on power of the remaining monarchies of the region, which had become staunch allies of the West. The US was initially uncertain about British plans for the overthrow of Mossadeq in Iran. However, when he responded to a boycott of the Iranian oil industry by British and other Western oil companies by threatening to turn to the Soviet Union, the US was prompted to take action. In Egypt in 1956, American actions were motivated by concern that the Soviets might exploit the Suez Crisis to expand their influence in the country. As a result, the Americans opposed Western intervention and supported the efforts of the UN to resolve the crisis.

Following Suez, the Soviet Union undertook a concerted effort to expand its sphere of influence in the region, in particular by aligning itself with anti-western Arab nationalism. However, Nasser had no interest in substituting dependence on the Soviet Union for dependence on the West and was distinctly hostile towards communism. Following the 1958 coup in Iraq, the leaders of which proclaimed their alignment with the Soviet Union, he ordered the arrest of hundreds of Egyptian communists.

The same year saw the US dispatched troops to Lebanon fearing a coup against its pro-Western president. The events of 1958 in Lebanon and Iraq led to the formulation of the 'Eisenhower Doctrine' in which the then US president asserted that the power vacuum in the Middle East which was left by the departure of the British and French should be filled by the US before it was exploited by the Soviets.

The impact of the Cold War on post-colonial politics in the Middle East was played out not merely in terms of the alignment or otherwise of individual states to particular superpowers, but also in regional political dynamics. The Cold War had a distinctly 'Arab' dimension in the Middle East as two different blocs emerged within the region. One group, including conservative pro-Western monarchies such as Jordan, the Kingdom of Saudi Arabia and Iraq (until 1958) saw Arab nationalism in terms of interstate cooperation between sovereign states within a framework of brotherhood, solidarity and coordination. A rival group, the radical Arab republics of Egypt, Syria and Iraq (after 1958), followed the pan-Arab view that the interests of the Arab people as a whole should take precedence over those of individual Arab states. Their ultimate goal (if only rhetorically) was the establishment of a single Arab nation-state encompassing all Arabic speaking territory, including Palestine (Valbjørn and Bank, 2012: 11). This radical vision was deeply threatening to the monarchies and their Western allies.

The decline of pan-Arab nationalism

The high point of pan-Arab nationalism came in 1958 – the year of the Iraqi coup and the US intervention in Lebanon when the Syrian Baath party leadership persuaded Nasser to accept the unification of Egypt and Syria under his leadership. The Syrian Baathists were fearful both of a CIA plot and a communist coup. Although the unification proposal represented the first step on the road to pan-Arab unity, Nasser had serious doubts about it, but allowed himself to be persuaded. On 1 February 1958, the United Arab Republic (UAR) was born. However, the union was short-lived as the Syrian politicians who had engineered it were edged out of power. In 1961, the UAR broke up following another coup in Syria. Nasser decided not to oppose Syrian secession from the union and Syria was reborn (Humphreys, 1999: 72). Although there were a number of other Arab unification experiments in subsequent years, none had the substance of the UAR, the demise of which was a severe blow to Nasser's prestige and to pan-Arabism as a practical political project. The outcome of war in 1967 between Israel and its Arab neighbours dealt a further and fatal blow to pan-Arab hopes. Throughout the 1960s, both Egypt and Syria had built up an expensive military capacity with support from the Soviet Union, as tensions between them and Israel had been a constant feature of regional politics. However, when war came, it was in the form a series of pre-emptive air strikes by Israeli forces, which destroyed Arab air forces on the ground – a total of 338 Egyptian aircraft were destroyed in the first wave of attacks. The Syrian air force also suffered huge losses. The war was effectively concluded in six days (June 5–10 1967). By its close, Israel had taken control of Sinai from the Egyptians; the West Bank of the Jordan, including East Jerusalem, from the Jordanians; and the Golan Heights from the Syrians. The outcome of the war had enormous ramifications for the Israeli-Palestinian conflict. It also transformed regional politics. The disastrous result, from an Arab perspective, dealt a fatal blow to the claims of radical, secular nationalist regimes that they would 'liberate' Palestine and restore Arab unity, from which pan-Arabism never recovered. The war eased the threat posed by the radical states to the conservative monarchies of the region and initiated the rise to regional significance of Saudi Arabia, in particular. Finally, the war strengthened Israel and was followed by a deepening of the Israeli relationship with the United States, which subsequently, more than ever, was the dominant international actor in the region.

The ascent to power of Hafez al-Asad in Syria and Saddam Hussein in Iraq in different ways deepened the decline of pan-Arab nationalism. In November 1970, the then Syrian Minister for Defence, Hafez al-Asad, seized power in a bloodless coup. Under al-Asad, the Baathist regime in Syria became little more than a vehicle for the aspirations of the Alawite sect to which he belonged. In 1979, Saddam Hussein pushed the Iraqi president, Ahmad Hassan Bakr, into retirement and secured control of government through a series of violent purges. Under his leadership, which lasted until the US-led invasion of country in 2003, the Iraqi *Baath* Party functioned as an expression of the personalistic interests of Hussein and those close to him, his inner circle dominated by those related to him by blood or marriage.

The MENA after the Cold War

The period that followed the end of the Cold War will be explored in much greater detail in the later chapters in this book. However, it may be useful to offer a summary of overall trends. The demise of the Soviet Union saw the rise to unparalleled power of the US in the new global order. This was expressed perhaps most clearly when, in 1990, Iraqi armed forces under the leadership of Saddam Hussein occupied neighbouring Kuwait. The US quickly assembled a coalition of international allies – including friendly Arab states, such as Egypt, but also the hitherto hostile state of Syria – and, with the support of the United Nations Security Council, expelled the Iraqis from Kuwait. There followed a serious attempt, sponsored by the US to resolve the Palestinian problem and the broader Arab–Israeli conflict. American power appeared to be without rival, not merely in the MENA, but also in a broader, unipolar world.

The end of the Cold War was accompanied on a global level by what many characterized as a new wave of democratization. The demise of military dictatorship, as the standard form of rule in Latin America, was followed by large-scale, if often superficial, processes of political liberalization in sub-Saharan Africa. Increasingly, it was expected that the MENA would follow a now globalized trend towards democratization. This assumption was embedded in the emerging foreign policy of the European Union (EU). The end of the Cold War witnessed the emergence of the first attempts on the part of the EU to develop a coherent common foreign and security policy. For the EU, the pursuit of a 'normative' foreign policy based on 'soft power' led to a focus on democracy promotion, trade and dialogue with its partners in the MENA. It was also increasingly central to academic study of the region, as well as a great deal of policy-making. The democratization paradigm became the preferred lens through which many analyzed political dynamics in the MENA.

However, while the two decades that followed the end of the Cold War witnessed processes of political liberalization across the region, of varying degrees of intensity, it was clear by the mid-2000s that the MENA simply was not democratizing. Significant experiments with political liberalization were reversed in Algeria, Egypt and elsewhere, while facade reforms were the order of the day in much of the region. At the same time, a combination of factors led to a dilution of the enthusiasm of international actors for the promotion of democracy. The near-accession to power of the Islamist *Front Islamique du Salut* (FIS) (Islamic Salvation Front) in openly contested elections in Algeria in 1991 caused significant disquiet in the US and in Europe, particularly in the country's former colonial power, France. The fear that democratic reform would pave the way for a permanent end to democracy was expressed by US diplomat Edward Djerejian in the phrase: 'one person, one vote, one time'. The same international actors were silent, if not relieved, when the Algerian military intervened in January 1992 to annul the electoral process. The subsequent civil war in the country saw the loss of over 100,000 lives.

Fear that democratic reforms would unseat friendly incumbent regimes and bring unfriendly Islamists to power animated Western policy – in particular, after the September 11 attacks on the US in 2001. For a brief period, there was an acknowledgment that supporting authoritarian regimes in the region was a root cause of political instability and, hence, a threat to Western interests. However, this was quickly replaced by a pragmatic realization that, problematic as authoritarian incumbents might be, they were more reliable allies that whatever might issue from democratic political processes.

The result was that, on the eve of the Arab uprisings of 2011, the MENA region (or, specifically, its Arab component states) was dominated by unrepresentative, long-lived regimes in which alternation of power was virtually unkown, and which seemed destined to remain in power, in one form or another, indefinitely. Egypt, Tunisia and Yemen all had presidents who had been in power, in one form or another for decades. The Libyan leader, Gaddafi, assumed power in 1969, while in Syria, the al-Asad family (father and son) had held the presidency since 1970. Elsewhere in the region, unelected monarchs held sway. The non-Arab states of Turkey and Israel, along with Lebanon to a limited extent, were the exceptions to the rule that power did not transfer through the ballot box.

Scholars of the region responded to the apparent strength of authoritarianism in the MENA in a variety of ways. Middle Eastern regimes were 'deliberalized' (Kienle, 2001), 'liberalized autocracies' (Brumberg, 2003) or 'pluralized authoritarian systems' (Phillips, 2008). Above all, their leaders were not serious about democratic reform. As was mentioned in Chapter 2, in 2007, Heydeman argued that a new model of governance characterized the region – 'upgraded authoritarianism' – as regimes adapted to pressures for political reform by developing strategies to contain and manage demands to democratize.

The tension between analyses of the region in terms of incipient democratization versus authoritarian upgrading has assumed enormous significance in the context of the recent Arab uprisings and their aftermath. In the later chapters of this book (in particular, Chapter 11), all of these debates and developments will be explored in much more detail.

Key questions

- Why did 'Muslim' power decline relative to Europe in the nineteenth century?
- What was 'defensive developmentalism'?
- How did the modern Middle East state system come about?
- What were the key patterns in post-colonial political development in the MENA region?
- Why did pan-Arab nationalist ideology gain such influence in the 1950s and 1960s and what explains its decline?
- How did the Cold War impact on political life in the region?

Further reading

Al-Husri, Sati' (1962). 'Muslim unity and Arab unity', in Sylvia Haim (ed.), *Arab Nationalism: An Anthology*, Berkeley, Los Angeles: University of California Press.

Dawisha, Adeed (2003). *Arab Nationalism in the Twentieth Century: From Triumph to Despair*, Princeton: Princeton University Press

Gelvin, James (2008). *The Modern Middle East: A History*, Oxford: Oxford University Press.

Landen, Robert G. (2006). 'Kamal Ataturk on the abolition of the Ottoman Caliphate, 3 March 1924', in Camron Michael Amin, Benjamin C. Fortna and Elizabeth B. Frierson (eds), *The Modern Middle East: A Sourcebook for History*, Oxford: Oxford University Press

Rogan, Eugene (2010). *The Arabs: A History*, London: Penguin Books.

Tignor, Robert (1997). 'Introduction' in *Al-Jabarti's Chronicle of the French Occupation, 1798*, Princeton: Markus Wiener.

Online resources

Avalon Project (2008). 'The Middle East 1916–2001: a documentary record', available at http://avalon.law.yale.edu/subject_menus/mideast.asp.

Council on Foreign Relations (nd). *McMahon Hussein Correspondence, 1915–1916*, available at http://www.cfr.org/egypt/mcmahon-hussein-correspondence-1915-1916/p13762.

Nassar, Galal (2009). 'Pan-Arabism in context', *Al-Ahram Weekly*, 10–16 December, available at http://weekly.ahram.org.eg/2009/976/op6.htm.

National Security Archive (2013). 'CIA confirms role in 1953 Iran coup', available at http://www2.gwu.edu/~nsarchiv/NSAEBB/NSAEBB435/#_ftn1.

Chapter 3

Social Structures and Social Development

The MENA, as did other regions of the non-Western world, underwent a dramatic transformation in the course of the nineteenth and early twentieth centuries, not least as a result of the interaction with the outside world described in Chapter 2. Dramatic changes took place in the sphere of economic production, especially in the rural settings in which the majority of the population lived. These changes, generated by both internal and external factors, in turn stimulated processes of urbanization and class formation which brought with them revolutionary changes in education and literacy, as well as having significant impacts on gender roles and relations. This chapter will examine each of these in turn.

The concept of modernization is crucial to the analysis of the changes which took place in the region over this period. Theories of modernization have their roots in classical evolutionary theories of social change. Social evolutionist paradigms – which imply that societies progress through stages and, for example, that development means a movement from 'tradition' to 'modernity' – have existed in various forms for centuries. John McKay suggests that debate about development, its nature and how to achieve it, is *the* central issue in the whole of Western social science. The Enlightenment 'was fundamentally concerned with progress towards an ideal society, and how the harnessing of rational thoughts, policies and actions might allow the realization of this goal' (McKay 2012: 55). From the eighteenth century onwards, writers such as Condorcet, Spencer, Comte, Durkheim and Marx were all involved in different ways in trying to explain the transition from pre-industrial to industrial society and, from them, twentieth-century modernization theory took the key concept of a transition from 'traditional' to 'modern' society. For example, in the preface to Volume One of *Capital* Marx states that 'the country that is more developed industrially only shows to the less developed the image of its own future'.

Perhaps unsurprisingly then for many social scientists, the role of the West is seen as crucial in promoting modernization. In his classic text, *The Passing of Traditional Society: Modernizing the Middle East*, Lerner proposes that the 'stimuli' that undermined 'traditional society' in the Middle East came from the West: 'What the West is, in this sense, the Middle East seeks to become' (1958: 47).

Or, as Pappé puts it, the West had the magic wand – with Westernization came enlightenment and progress. According to this perspective, Western territorial expansion was central to the modernization of non-Western societies including those of the MENA region. The social, economic and political changes brought about by its intervention, although seen as inevitable, could be hastened by Western educational systems, secularized political institutions and reform in the economic sphere aimed at capitalizing agriculture. The changes were 'cemented' with European political and moral thought (Pappé, 2005: 2–3). Pappé points out that the modernization framework has been pervasive in studies of the Middle East, even if the region continues to be seen as 'stuck' between tradition and modernity. But, he argues, in practice in the developing world, the process of modernization has not been the straightforward and linear process that its adherents have proposed. Instead, the features of change appeared in a 'kaleidoscopic' manner and not in the structured, chronological fashion that is supposed to have characterized modernization in Western development. In particular, assumptions drawn from Western experience regarding industrialization and secularization have proven to be less well-founded in practice in the MENA region.

In response to this, Pappé proposes a less rigid and more open-ended view of development that pays attention to internal actors, both élite and non-élite, as well as the impact of external forces. In this perspective, the history of ordinary people is as important as that of élites, while the non-Westernized past is not dismissed as part of 'traditional' society and hence doomed to irrelevance as that society modernizes. Furthermore, this requires acknowledging that change sometimes strengthened traditional modes of behaviour even if, at other times, it disrupted them. A major factor in this rethink of modernization (see Box 3.1) is that the West comes to be seen as just one factor of change among others. In this way, change is seen as a process that is universal, but with local characteristics, in contrast to the modernization-as-Westernization approach. The 'evolving drama of change' is not always caused by the West and does not necessarily tell a story of becoming 'Western' but, rather, one of 'changing the known and safe world of the past' (2005: 11).

The transformation of rural life

What is undoubtedly clear is that, over the course of the late nineteenth and early twentieth centuries, the MENA region underwent transformative change in many spheres. Amongst the most far-reaching, in terms of their impact, were the changes that took place in the rural areas in which

Box 3.1 Modernization defined

Modernization has traditionally been identified with the way in which Western countries developed from a social, political and economic point of view. The underlying pillars of Western modernization were rational thought and the scientific approach. From an economic point of view, modernization 'implies industrialization and urbanization and the technological transformation of agriculture'. From a political point of view, it implied that countries would over time 'rationalise authority' and develop a bureaucracy. Eventually, the notion of a liberal-democratic system began to be associated with modernity, with this political arrangement becoming the peak of the process of political modernization. In social terms, modernization meant the abandonment of traditional ties – kin, tribe or family – in favour of individualism. In this sense, the marginalization of religion was essential to modernization, as secularism would become the dominant trait of society. In short, to be modern meant to be Western. Over time, this Euro-centric view of modernization began to be contested in favour of multiple paths and understandings of modernity.

Source: Barbara Ingham (1993). 'The meaning of development: interactions between '"new" and "old" ideas', *World Development*, 21 (11).

the majority of the population lived and where agricultural practices had remained largely unchanged for centuries. In the past, people lived close to where water was accessible, grew what they needed for living, managed their herds and generally produced enough for their own consumption. This subsistence economy was based on a land tenure system where the land was owned by the state, while those who cultivated it had the right of 'usufruct' – that is, the right to enjoy the use of the property without damaging or destroying it. In the rural economy, land was held in common by village communities not individuals. Crops were cultivated for local consumption and rural communities were virtually self-sufficient. Villages could sell their surplus to city residents but usually any surplus was removed in the form of tax rather than in trade. Agricultural products that could not be transported far were grown in or near urban settlements. According to Costello (1976: 23), more than half the population of Cairo was engaged in agriculture in the mid-nineteenth century.

In the later decades of the nineteenth century, this situation began to undergo significant change, partly as a result of changes within the Ottoman Empire, and partly in response to the increasing penetration of the region, both politically and economically, by the European powers. But the process of integrating the rural economy into the international economy had begun earlier in some places. In the eighteenth century, French merchants were shipping cotton and silk to Marseilles via the major ports of the eastern Mediterranean. However, it was only in the nineteenth century that Ottoman rulers began to see agriculture as a viable commodity and a potentially valuable source of tax income. This led to a new emphasis on improving land use and cultivation, which led to highly significant changes in the legal infrastructure governing land use, ownership and registration. Under the terms of a new legal code enacted in 1858, ownership of land which had usually been cultivated according to custom and tradition was now defined according to five categories: full private ownership, lands owned by the state, religious endowments, land for public service and uncultivated land.

In part, too, these developments were stimulated by the increased pervasiveness of Europe. From the 1830s, the region was first penetrated by modern transport in the form of steamships. In the second half of the century, the building of telegraphs, railways and ports as well as the inflow of significant amounts of capital from Europe, prompted the emergence of a rudimentary financial system geared to foreign trade. The gross domestic product of most parts of the MENA region increased several times over as it was integrated ever more closely into the global economic order. The import of manufactured goods from Europe led to a decline in traditional handicrafts, and both industry and mining were slow to develop. Instead, the expansion of production was concentrated in the agricultural sector as the cultivation of crops for export expanded. Farmers responded to increased demand by increasing production and exporting any surplus. Initially, many produced cash crops for the market while also growing for their own needs. However, over time, some switched entirely to cash crops, buying their own food from adjacent regions or importing from abroad (Issawi, 1982: 1–3).

The development of a modern economy

These changes in agriculture were linked to significant developments in other sectors of society and the economy. The shift from communal land to private ownership led to the marketization of agricultural property, a process which was exacerbated by the practice of selling land to pay off bad debts. Legal changes introduced in the mid-1850s permitted the sale and purchase of land, both by Europeans and by Muslims. State policy, typically, was to back tribal sheikhs eager to own previously communal land, particularly in Iraq and Syria. In Egypt, Muhammad Ali made possible the emergence of a large landlord class while, in North Africa, European settlers acquired a great deal of the land. In turn, this led to an increasingly significant differentiation between landed and landless classes (Costello, 1976: 24; Issawi, 1982: 4). A crucial element in this was the introduction of a new system for registration of land. This led to the abolition of the special status of tax collectors, and the introduction of clerks who were given responsibility for tax collection and acted as mediators between peasant and state (Pappé, 2005: 66). A further consequence of the transformation of the agrarian sphere was the monetization of the economy. Money became the universal medium of exchange for the first time which, in turn, saw the emergence of organized banking. Foreign-owned commercial banks were first established in the region in the late 1840s. The first bank to operate in the Ottoman Empire was the Commercial Bank of Smyrna which was established in London in 1844 to meet the growing needs of European and other merchants in the Izmir region. The first bank to be established in the empire was the Banque de Constantinople which was founded in 1847 to provide short-term loans to the government and to stabilize the exchange rate of the Ottoman paper currency (Pamuk, 2000: 212). The earliest banks typically concentrated on supporting export and import trade but also made loans to consumers, while smaller private banks owned by members of minorities also played a role. In later decades, mortgage banks, which dealt with large landowners, followed, as did European insurance companies. In addition, this period saw the development of import-export firms to handle the outward flow of agricultural products and the inward flow of manufactured goods. These were almost all owned by Europeans (Issawi, 1982: 7).

In support of the emerging export-oriented economies of the region, major changes took place in the transportation infrastructure. Before World War I, paved roads were uncommon in the MENA region. Most traffic was on carts drawn by horses, donkeys, camels or mules (Pappé: 2005: 66). In this area, too, dramatic change began to emerge from the middle of the nineteenth century onwards. The ports of Alexandria and Algiers were improved from around 1860, while steam navigation penetrated where rivers were navigable. For the most part, however, it was the internal road and railway system that saw the greatest level of change. Lebanon saw the development of its road system between 1859 and 1945, while Egypt began to improve its agricultural roads from the late nineteenth century onwards. The rail network was more significant. The first railway in Egypt was constructed in 1851 before Sweden or central Poland and, by 1914, the network covered the whole country. Trade with Europe was also a major factor in the construction of the Suez Canal, which opened in 1869. Railway-building began in Turkey in 1857, in Algeria one year later, and spread across the rest of the region. Nonetheless, the relative absence of roads meant that thousands of villages across the MENA were largely unaffected by these developments (Issawi, 1982: 5–6).

Finally, population movement of different kinds was directly linked to changes in the economic order in the countryside. Over the course of the nineteenth century, hundreds of thousands of Frenchmen, Italians and Spaniards migrated to Algeria and Tunisia, while tens of thousands of Europeans of various nationalities settled in Egypt. Later, during the interwar period, there was significant French settlement in Morocco, Italian settlement in Libya and Jewish migration to Palestine. Internally, within the region, the combination of improved 'efficiencies' in the agricultural sector, together with innovations in health care, which lowered mortality rates, led to the emergence of an impoverished landless cohort which began to swell urban populations.

By 1914, to use Issawi's expression, Europeans held 'all of the commanding heights' of the economy except for land ownership, and minority groups occupied the 'lower slopes' (1982: 9). However, as we saw in Chapter 2, the period from the end of World War I onwards saw the gradual reversal of European control of the region. The 'capitulations' which, for hundreds of years, had given foreigners and their protected subjects extraterritorial jurisdiction and protection from taxes, were abolished by Turkey at the beginning of the War, re-imposed at the armistice and finally abolished by Ataturk's government in 1923. Iraq did likewise in 1922, followed by Iran in 1928 and Egypt in 1937. This not only gave those governments greater control over resident foreigners, but also allowed them to extend taxes to them. The abolition of the capitulations was followed by the lapse of commercial treaties which had severely restricted the freedom of governments in the region in relation to fiscal and developmental policies. From the late 1920s, most countries regained the right to set their own tariffs to produce revenue and to encourage different sectors of the economy. Another important development in this period was the establishment or strengthening of national banks to provide credit to sectors that had been neglected by foreign-owned commercial banks. The interwar years also witnessed the attempts by governments to improve inadequate infrastructure. Turkey doubled its rail network; Iraq and Morocco greatly extended theirs. Iran built its first major railroads. This continued after World War II, when there was further development of the rail network in Iran, Saudi Arabia, Israel and Syria. In addition, between the 1920s and the 1960s, many governments took control of foreign-owned or controlled utilities, either by expropriation or purchase. In this way, railways, streetcars, ports, gas, water and electrical companies came under state control. The takeover of the oil industry over the course of the second half of the twentieth century (which is discussed in more detail in Chapter 4) completed this process (Issawi, 1982: 12–15).

Box 3.2 The resilience of the traditional economic sector in the MENA

While a great deal of attention has been focused on the modernization of the economy in the region, Rodney Wilson points out that this by no means represents the demise of the traditional economic sector which continues to exist and, indeed, to thrive in places. Subsistence agriculture, handicrafts and what Wilson terms 'informal economic intermediation' have existed for thousands of years and remain among the region's economic strengths. In absolute terms, traditional economic activities continue to expand and, in some cases, are proving to be more resilient than modern industries established at great cost. Wilson offers the example of Iran under the Shah, in which new manufacturing industries were protected from international competition and generously subsidized by the state, while the traditional bazaar merchants came under stringent controls. Yet, the traditional sector supplied most of Iran's non-oil exports, while the modern industries struggled to produce goods of sufficient quality to be acceptable to the domestic market.

In the Gulf States, by contrast, the oil boom years were the best period for the traditional economic sector. Government expenditure helped to stimulate traditional economic activities and, while imports flowed in, these were new goods for distribution and sale. They did not replace domestically produced goods as was the case in Iran. Modern industries were created but these were in areas such as petrochemicals and therefore did not impinge on traditional economic activity.

As a result, as Wilson points out, it is not at all clear that the traditional economic sector will be replaced by the modern economy, even in the longer-term.

Source: Rodney Wilson (2013). *Economic Development in the Middle East*, London: Routledge.

Urbanization

These dramatic changes in the economies of the region were accompanied by the increased urbanization of its population. As we have seen, this began with the drift of the newly landless unemployed to urban centres at the end of the nineteenth and the beginning of the twentieth centuries.

Towns and cities had always been important in the history of the MENA. The urban population was usually concentrated in 'intensively cultivated nuclei' which performed a number of important functions. As well as being market centres, they were sites of religious practices and administration. Locations such as Aleppo, Ankara and Tabriz also sometimes had a defence role while, in the past, small groups often seized power and ruled from urban bases (Costello, 1976: 5). In addition, the major religions of the region have close associations with particular urban centres. The cities of Jerusalem, Mecca, Qom and Karbala are virtually synonymous with their religious significance and functions. Finally, the great 'caravan' cities of Cairo, Istanbul and Baghdad have had the most extensive contacts with the outside world and in the past have had populations in the hundreds of thousands.

Nonetheless, at the beginning of the twentieth century, most people in the MENA region still lived in the countryside close to water and arable land. But the emergence of a domestic market in the region led to the revival of provincial towns and the emergence of new ones, along with a growth in the size and significance of many ports. Provincial towns began to act as wholesale markets for their hinterlands and as centres of administration for governments that were anxious to maintain and extend their control over growing economic areas. In Egypt and elsewhere, administrative structures changed with shifts in the economic sphere. The traditional sheikhs of the urban centres were deprived of their fiscal and policing functions, which became the responsibility of centralized government departments.

Urban growth came slowly at first. The 22 largest towns of Egypt had a total population of just 400,000 in 1821. This rose to over 1.5 million by the turn of the twentieth century but their share of the population overall only rose from 9.5 per cent to 14.3 per cent. Syria was highly urbanized long before the twentieth century with nearly 25 per cent of its population living in towns of more than 10,000 people. A similar proportion of the population of Iraq lived in towns, a figure which remained unchanged until 1932 (Costello, 1976: 24–5).

The process of urbanization gathered pace from the 1920s onwards, as political and economic change took hold. An 'army of landless workers', who lost out during the economic transformation of the countryside, moved to the cities (Pappé, 2005: 67). Costello identifies four other factors that promoted urban growth in this period. The first of these is political centralization. The newly emerging states of the region required a network of regional urban administrative centres to carry out new policies. Second, urban growth was exacerbated by internal political strife. In the years after 1914, 50,000 Armenians moved to Aleppo as refugees from massacres taking place in modern day Turkey. Nearly one million Palestinians fled their homes as a result of the conflict that preceded the establishment of the state of Israel in 1948. Many of these took refuge in urban centres – Amman, Kuwait, Beirut and Riyadh, as well as elsewhere. Third, changes in foreign trade patterns and relations prompted urban development as the region's geographical position at the crossroads of three continents – Europe, Africa and Asia – was confirmed. Other changes such as the departure of large numbers of foreigners created opportunities for local enterprise. Finally, the development of the oil industry contributed to urban growth, creating employment opportunities and generating capital for economic development (Costello, 1976: 29–30).

Box 3.3   Urbanization: the environmental cost

The rapid increase in the rate of urbanization in the MENA and the consequent increase in population of towns and cities has obvious environmental costs. Dona Stewart has itemized some of these in a survey of research on urban studies in the region. 'Heat islands' have been identified as a cause of global warming in Turkey. In Egypt, there is considerable concern over the loss of agricultural land to urbanization in the Nile Delta. According to one estimate, 12 per cent of total agricultural land has been lost in this way. In addition, the cumulative growth rate of small villages – often overlooked in studies of urbanization – was 77 per cent over the period from 1972 to 1990.

Atmospheric pollution abounds in the region, not least due to the ready availability of leaded petrol, large numbers of older cars and high levels of 'particulate' matter (e.g. sand) in the atmosphere.

Finally, urbanization together with industrialization places obvious demands on water resources. According to recent research, demand for water in Saudi Arabia is expected to increase from 60 per cent in 1995 to more than 80 per cent in 2025.

Source: Dona J. Stewart (2002). 'Middle East urban studies II: growth, environment and economic development', *Urban Studies*, 23 (4): 388–94.

As a result, there were significant increases in the size of major urban centres (with associated costs as Box 3.3 highlights) such that, after Latin America, the region is now the most urbanized in the developing world. Between 1950 and 1965, the urban population of Turkey grew by 135 per cent. Between 1950 and 1980, the urban population of Saudi Arabia, Oman, Libya and the United Arab Emirates doubled, as it did in Iran and Iraq over roughly the same period. The slowest rate of urban growth was in Egypt where 43 per cent of the population lived in urban centres in 2005 compared with 32 per cent in 1950. Yemen is the least urbanized country in the region – in 2010, 69 per cent of the population still lived in rural areas. By contrast, Kuwait, Qatar and Bahrain are 'virtually city-states' (Moghadam, 2010: 19). The process of rapid urbanization has had a host of significant consequences as the economic crisis of the 1980s, in particular, put an end to the hopes of integration into the workforce for a significant portion of the population. Social mobility stagnated and it is in the growing shantytowns around major urban centres in cities such as Casablanca, Cairo, Tunis or Algiers that the social work of Islamists began to resonate powerfully.

The emergence of new social classes

Changes in the economic sphere and increased levels of urbanization had dramatic impacts on the class structure of the MENA region (see Box

3.4 for the specific case of Egypt). However, there is considerable divergence of opinion on the subject of class, especially in the early decades of the twentieth century. El-Ghoneimy (1998) suggests that the changes that took place led to the creation of two distinct classes – the very rich and the landless workers. The very rich consisted of large landlords, wealthy merchants, tribal sheikhs and collaborators with the colonial rulers. These wealthy élites included the sheikhs of Al-Azhar, the pre-eminent Islamic university in Egypt, the rich Coptic Christians of Upper Egypt, the Maronites of Lebanon, city merchants and 'grainlords' of Syria, as well as former tax collectors, the Ottoman élite, family members of ruling élites, and foreign landowners and bankers. At the other extreme were those who lost out as a result of economic transformation – landless workers, sharecroppers, nomads and city peddlers. El-Ghoneimy suggests that, in between these extremes of the very rich and the very poor, were an amalgamation of several groups that did not constitute a distinct class. This looser category included bureaucrats, members of the military establishment, the few trained professionals, some Muslim learned men, urban artisans and private moneylender (El-Ghoneimy, 1998: 36).

Others, such as Farsoun and Pappé, propose that a more complex set of arrangements emerged. Pappé (2005) notes the development not only of a class of workers and clerks – 'busy most of the time in surviving rather than seeking meaning or comfort in life', but also of a middle class – indistinct at first but with clearer identity after World War II. This middle class emerged from the urban notables of the nineteenth century and became politicized under colonial rule. The French and British resisted the mobilization of the new élite of young professionals – known as *effendiyya* – who were united in their objective to end foreign presence in the region. Instead, they preferred to deal with the old élites – the *pashas* – of the Ottoman period who were more amenable to cooperation. By the end of World War II, the *pashas* seemed to be resigned to a semi-independent Egypt, which would tolerate a continued British presence. Popular opinion, however, supported the *effendiyya*. In Syria, the shift from the collaboration of the *pashas* with French power to opposition to foreign influence came in the 1920s when the *effendiyya* formed the National Bloc, a political organization that subsequently led the country to independence (Pappé, 2005: 138–41).

Farsoun (1988) contributes a further layer to this analysis. He notes the significance of the migration overseas of large numbers of people, particularly to the countries of the Gulf, as their oil sectors developed (this will be discussed in more detail in Chapter 4), which had major consequences for social development. Some workers on their return became members of the petit bourgeoisie, while an even smaller number who had become

Box 3.4 The emergence of a class structure in Egypt

Owen and Pamuk (1998) suggest that the social structure of Egypt during the interwar years can be conceived as 'a very flat pyramid with an extremely broad base'. At the apex, were the 2,750 or so families that owned over 100 acres of land. This group, in turn, was dominated by an even smaller group of 282 families, including the king and some members of the royal household, who owned over 500 acres. These families dominated rural life on the basis not only of the control of land, but also their occupancy of the most important posts in local administration, from village mayor to provincial governor. They were also in a position to use their influence on the government in Cairo. The large landowners were connected with the political parties and had a strong presence in the parliament. According to one estimate, they constituted an average of 58.5 per cent of the membership of all parliamentary committees between 1924 and 1952.

Below this lay a growing stratum of professionals, some 53,000 persons in 1937 and 88,000 in 1947. The majority were teachers in schools and universities. The rest were engineers, doctors, dentists and lawyers. These formed the top layer of a larger urban middle class of some 500,000 (6 per cent of Egypt's labour force in 1947).

Finally, at the base of the pyramid were the workers, the peasants and the unemployed. Owen and Pamuk note that a central feature of Egypt's system of social stratification was 'the minimal opportunities it offered for upward mobility'. By 1940, only 6.9 per cent of the population was attending state schools and only 8,500 were in higher education.

Source: Roger Owen and Sevket Pamuk (1998). *A History of Middle East Economies in the Twentieth Century*. London: I. B. Tauris.

quite wealthy joined a rapidly expanding bourgeoisie, the scope of which had expanded with the later adoption of economic liberalization policies in many non-oil producing states. In the oil producers themselves, a bourgeoisie emerged that was composed of middlemen, merchants, brokers and agents of Western economic interests who were allowed, or even encouraged, to enrich themselves.

Farsoun points out that these changes had two major consequences for Arab societies. The first was a steady rise in incomes and in living standards. This also led to a homogenization of Arab consumer lifestyle with an imitation of many aspects of Western lifestyles in both consumer goods and behaviour. The second major consequence was 'the reproduction and expansion of inequalities', in spite of the rise in living standards. Inequalities within and between countries also contributed to the fragmentation and heterogeneity of Arab society (Farsoun, 1988: 17–18).

The increased social fragmentation of society is reflected in the emergence of the third group identified by Pappé – the unemployed – as the numbers of those living on the margins of cities grew. Shantytowns and slums developed near urban centres full of immigrants who were underemployed or could not find jobs (Pappé, 2005: 160) and who were closed off from a network of support that was failing employed and unionized workers too. The increasing proximity of trade unions, or at least the central leadership of such unions, to the ruling authorities left workers exposed to the market-oriented reforms that many countries in the region began to adopt in the 1980s under the direct or indirect guidance of international financial institutions. It would, however, be erroneous to believe that the decreasing relevance of unions is simply due to the 1980s market reforms, insofar as newly assertive authoritarian regimes (see Box 3.5, on trade unionism in Egypt) attempted to limit independent and autonomous activism in the name of national unity. The effort to achieve socio-economic development, as conceived by the political leadership, should involve all members of society and should not tolerate dissent in the name of sectional interests such as those that trade unions defended and promoted.

The domination of authoritarian rulers over trade unions that had a history of strong activism and political dissent seemed to signal the end of unionism across the Arab world, in particular. With some notable exceptions, not much scholarship was dedicated, for instance, to the analysis of unions from the 1970s onwards. In some respects, this was understandable because unions played a minor role in Arab politics and tended to act as a broker favourable to the regime at times of social conflicts. However, and to the surprise of many, trade union activists re-emerged as powerful players during the Arab uprisings, notably in Tunisia and Egypt. As we will explain in greater detail in Chapter 11, local trade unionists helped in organising protests – providing a 'class' dimension to the uprisings. In part, this combative attitude dervived from their experiences at the coal face of social protests in Egypt and Tunisia in the mid-2000s. It should be further highlighted that this activism took place against the wishes of the central leadership of the unions still committed to operate through the mechanisms the ruling elites had in place. Not all unions and not all local leaders 'rode' the protests of the Arab uprisings to the extent of endorsing regime change, but the protests were nevertheless useful for unions across the region to try to reassert their autonomy and negotiating power.

Education, literacy and mass media

Prior to the advent of colonial rule and for some time after, education in the MENA was largely limited to schools established by Islamic institutions and individuals in order to teach children the Qur'an, as well as some knowledge of Arabic and arithmetic. These indigenous schools played a valuable role in promoting a basic level of literacy, in the face of

Box 3.5 The rise and fall of Egyptian trade unionism

The emergence of a working class in the MENA region is contemporaneous with the first signs of workers organizing and the rise of trade unionism. Even before World War I, this process had begun – not long after similar movements had emerged for the first time in the West. Workers in Egypt were in the forefront of this process. In 1913, workers had begun to organize themselves within unions. One year later, the Cairo railway workers union succeeded in organizing a strike which the population at large saw as an important part of the anti-colonial revolution. This was because industrial action inflicted losses on foreign investors who had a stake in the national railway company and the tram network. As a result, the workers were party to subsequent negotiations with both the government and the foreign companies.

After World War II, it was Egyptian textile workers who led the Egyptian trade union movement – comprising, as they did, 37 per cent of the country's industrial workers. In alliance with workers in other sectors, they engaged in strikes and other industrial actions several times between 1945 and 1952. However, the situation changed with the success of the Free Officers' Revolution, after which the trade union movement was integrated into the Nasserite state and lost much of its bargaining function on behalf of its members.

Nasser often spoke of an alliance between the army, workers, peasants and 'national' capitalists. Improving the living standards of the labouring masses was proclaimed to be a national goal. Workers were encouraged to join trade unions and labour federations close to the regime. The members of trade union federations received a range of benefits – job security, higher wages, lower working hours, health care, unemployment insurance, pensions and access to consumer cooperatives – in exchange for their integration into the apparatus of the revolutionary state. For the most part, strikes disappeared as an expression of protest and those that did take place were suppressed by the regime. The very first act of the Free Officers in the realm of economic and social policy was to suppress the strike of textile workers at Kafr al-Dawwar in August 1952 and to hang two of its leaders.

Sources: Joel Beinin (1999).'The working class and peasantry in the Middle East: from economic nationalism to neoliberalism', *Middle East Report*, Spring: 18–22; Ilan Pappé (2005). *The Modern Middle East*, London: Routledge: 128–9.

colonial indifference or even hostility to the idea of educating Muslims. But, by the late nineteenth century, a new kind of school was emerging in the Ottoman Empire. To begin with, and in response to awareness of the growing strength of Europe, specialized institutions were established to train government officials, doctors and engineers in the major cities of Istanbul, Cairo and Tunis. This system grew and, by the end of the century, boys could attend primary and secondary schools in the major provincial centres of the empire and then go on to attend higher institutions of learning in Istanbul, prior to entering the imperial government. Other educational institutions also emerged. In Tunisia, there were some

Franco-Arab schools while, in Algeria, elementary schools spread slowly across the country from the 1890s onwards. Besides government schools, others were established by foreign missions. In Lebanon, Syria and Egypt, schools were established for Christian communities. American Protestant missions provided education not only for a small Protestant community in the region, but also for other Christians and, later, for some Muslims also (Hourani, 1991: 302–4).

In the interwar period, modern education was very much restricted to those who could afford it. It was further limited by two factors. The first was the reluctance of largely Muslim populations to send their children to be educated in schools which were often under the control of European or American religious or cultural missions, and which would alienate them from their families and tradition. The second was the unwillingness of rulers to educate them. In some instances, education of the rural poor was 'actively discouraged', as in the case of Egypt's Farouk monarchy. Elsewhere, Arab and Berber children were either entirely excluded from education or channelled into segregated schools under colonial rule (Richards and Waterbury, 1991: 114). Nonetheless, over the decades the provision of modern education expanded, if only to a relatively limited sector of the population. By 1939, the numbers of holders of secondary school certificates in Algeria were still in the hundreds, with even fewer university graduates. By contrast, in Egypt the numbers in secondary schools rose from 10,000 in 1913–14 to more than 60,000 some 30 years later. In 1925, a small private university, which had been established 18 years previously, was taken over by the state, becoming the government financed Egyptian University, with schools of arts and science, law, medicine, engineering and commerce.

Despite the expansion of education, by the time of independence in the early 1960s, the rate of adult illiteracy was extremely high across the region ranging from 70 per cent in Syria and Tunisia to 85 per cent in Algeria, Libya and Iraq. The lowest rates were in Kuwait (53 per cent) and Lebanon (45 per cent), and the highest were in Sudan (90 per cent) and Mauritania (95 per cent).

Given these less than propitious circumstances, the post-independence countries of the MENA region made extraordinary progress in the field of education. In 1960, the average number of years of schooling among those over the age of 15 ranged from a low of 0.61 in Tunisia to a high of 2.9 in Kuwait. As a result, the region had the lowest level of educational attainment in the world. Remarkably, by 2000 almost all countries had managed to bridge this gap in performance – the Middle East was averaging 5.3 years of schooling, far ahead of South Asia and sub-Saharan Africa, and only a little more than one year behind East Asia and Latin

America. Between 1980 and 2000, the educational attainment of the adult population increased by more than 150 per cent, more rapid than in any other region or income group in the world (Yousef, 2004: 101). Higher education also expanded. In 1970, enrolment in tertiary institutions was under 10 per cent for most of the region. By 2005, Libya's level of tertiary enrolment was 56 per cent, surpassing all other states in the region. The lowest levels of tertiary enrolment are to be found in Morocco and Yemen at 11 per cent and nine per cent, respectively

This turnaround was largely due to changing government priorities in the field of social policy. Beginning in the 1960s, governments began to spend large amounts of money on health and education, although some have expressed concern that the expansion of education has come at the expense of its quality (Karshenas and Moghadam, 2009: 55).

The extension of educational provision across the region utterly transformed the reading habits of the population. One impact of Europe, as noted by Hourani, was the development of a generation 'accustomed to reading'. Many of these read in foreign languages and were often bilingual. Printing in the Arabic language spread throughout the century, especially in Cairo and Beirut. Newspapers and periodicals began to play a major role over the second half of the nineteenth century (Hourani, 1991: 304). The first newspaper 'published by Arabs for Arabs', *Jurnal al-Iraq* (*The Iraqi Newspaper*) first appeared in 1816 in Baghdad in both Arabic and Turkish. The Egyptian government published two newspapers in Alexandria in the 1820s and an official newspaper, *al-Mubashir* (*The Herald*) appeared in Algeria in 1847. Newspapers were subsequently published in countries across the region. The most famous, *Al-Ahram* (*The Pyramids*), was founded in Cairo in 1875 by the Taqla family from Lebanon. By 1913, Egypt alone had 283 newspapers, although only a few survived. By 1974, there were 95 daily newspapers across the Arab world (Pappé, 2005: 189–90).

However, Pappé points out that the flourishing of newspapers was accompanied by restrictions on freedom of speech and of expression, both under colonial governments and their successors. In Tunisia, the government established an independent press agency on the day that independence was declared. On the same day, two government newspapers were established: one in Arabic and one in French. In neighbouring Algeria, freedom of the press was proclaimed as one of the goals of the post-colonial constitution. However, within three years there was a clampdown on dissident reporting, and independent newspapers were shut down (Pappé, 2005: 203).

Social change, gender and the family

Among the most significant impacts of processes of modernization in the
MENA region have been in the spheres of gender and the family (this will
be discussed in greater detail in Chapter 8). The past century has witnessed
a complex set of changes that include those in marriage, the economic
role of women, their social role and their ability to act as public figures.
This has not come without opposition due to the influence of conservative interpretation of Qur'anic injunctions on women, together with resistance on the part of some Muslim men to changes that concerned what
they felt was the last sphere over which they exercised any control, once
sovereignty and much of the economy had come to be dominated by the
West. Despite such opposition, social and economic change prompted the
emergence of forces in favour of change in the position of women. To
begin with, modernizing liberals tended to come from the higher social
classes, while the petty bourgeois and bazaar traders tended to support
traditional ways (Keddie, 1991: 13–14). Reform movements began to look
for changes in family law in the areas of marriage, divorce, polygamy,
child custody and inheritance. The Ottoman Law of Family Rights of 1917
was the first attempt at codification of Islamic family law (Moghadam,
2004: 146). This was abolished in 1926 by Ataturk, who took the unique
decision to adopt Western legal codes that abolished polygamy and
provided for substantial legal equality for women. The next most radical
set of reforms were enacted in Tunisia in 1956 in the form of the Personal
Status Code which, as in Turkey, outlawed polygamy and created substantial legal equality for women while retaining some Islamic features. In
the late 1960s, the government of Marxist South Yemen adopted a largely
egalitarian family law and encouraged women's organizations to carry
out propaganda and education, although the practice of polygamy was
permitted in exceptional circumstances (see Box 3.6 for social reforms in
family law in socialist Yemen). Less thoroughgoing reforms were adopted
elsewhere. In Egypt under Nasser, women made some gains but family
law retained male privilege. Other countries, including Jordan, Morocco
and Saudi Arabia, adopted family laws that were much more controlling
of women, reflecting tribal custom and the most patriarchal interpretations
of Islamic law (Keddie, 1991: 16; Moghadam, 2004: 146).

These developments took place in the context of dramatic change in
the sphere of women's education. As late as 1970, female illiteracy rates
were as high as 79 per cent (on average) across the region. By 2010, these
rates had declined dramatically in most countries. While 60 per cent of
Moroccan and Yemeni women are illiterate, the figure is only 10 per
cent for Qatar and the UAE. Women's enrolment rates in education have

Box 3.6 Family law in a socialist Arab state: the case of the People's Democratic Republic of Yemen

Following the British withdrawal from south Yemen in 1967, the new government of the People's Democratic Republic of Yemen (PDRY) adopted 'scientific socialism' as the basis of its policies. The first, and only, Marxist-Leninist state in the Arab world promulgated a new constitution in 1970 in which state legitimacy was based not on religion but, rather, on 'the people' – particularly, 'the interests of the working class' as expressed by the dominant Yemeni Socialist Party. Under this framework, the equality of women and men was enshrined in several articles of the constitution.

The Family Law of 1974 took this further. The principle of free choice in marriage was set out, a minimum age for marriage was established (16 years for girls; 18 years for boys) and polygamy was generally prohibited, with very limited exceptions. The most controversial changes related to the area of divorce. Men no longer enjoyed the automatic right to divorce their wives – all divorces were required to go through the courts. Also, men no longer enjoyed automatic custody of children in the event of divorce. Male children would normally remain with their mother until they were 10 years of age; female children until they were 15. The courts retained the right to make decisions in terms of the best interests of the child.

The new law resembled the radical legislation previously introduced in Tunisia and Syria. Indeed, legal experts from each of these countries were involved in the drafting process. However, as Molyneux points out, the changes in the PDRY were introduced in the context of the most far-reaching progamme of socialist modernization undertaken anywhere in the Arab world and were very much an instrument of regime ambition to alter social relations. When the two Yemens (the Yemen Arab Republic in the north and the PDRY in the south) unified in 1990, as the Cold War drew to a close, the social and political context changed dramatically. In the newly-established Republic of Yemen, many of the reforms adopted by the PDRY in the area of women's rights were effectively abandoned.

Source: Maxine Molyneux (1995). 'Women's rights and political contingency: the case of Yemen 1990–1994', *Middle East Journal*, 49(3): 418–31.

increased significantly in recent decades and currently stand at 85–95 per cent of male rates and, in some cases, exceeds that of men. At a third level, women's enrolment rates now exceed that of men in most countries.

Wider provision of education to women is positively correlated with lower fertility rates. In the late twentieth century, fertility levels began to fall, especially among young educated women in urban areas. Overall, across the region, fertility rates fell from an average of seven children per woman in the 1950s to 4.8 in 1990 and 3.6 in 2001. While some governments, notably those of Iran and Egypt, have actively pursued policies relating to population concerns, urbanization and education have also accelerated this process. Moghadam cites evidence drawn from a number of countries in the region which supports the thesis that education, socio-economic status and urban/rural residence determined the number of children, as well as the health of mother and child (Moghadam, 2010: 23).

Changes in education, employment patterns and the opening up of public space to women have had major impacts on traditional family and gender roles. The extended family has increasingly been replaced by the nuclear family, while early marriage has become rare, as levels of educational attainment increase and young men and women interact with one another in universities, workplaces and other public settings typical of the urban environment. Before the 1970s, women were usually married in their teens and early twenties. Today, the average age of first marriage has risen to the mid-twenties for women and is three to five years older for men. This, too, is influenced by urbanization – urban youth marry later in all countries. It is unsurprising then that the lowest age of marriage is for girls in the poorest countries and in rural areas. More than 15 per cent of women marry before the age of 20 in Yemen, Oman and predominantly rural areas of Egypt and in Gaza (Moghadam, 2010: 29).

Key questions

- How relevant are theories of modernization to the MENA region?
- What is the significance of the transformation of rural life over the course of the past 150 years?
- Why has the process of urbanization been so important in promoting social change in the MENA region?
- In what ways is the concept of class useful in understanding social change in the MENA region?
- What impact have increased levels of educational attainment had on the position of women?

Further reading

Issawi, Charles (1982). *An Economic History of the Middle East and North Africa*, New York: Columbia University Press.

Keddie, Nikki R. (1991). 'Introduction: deciphering Middle Eastern women's history' in Keddie, Nikki R. and B. Baron (eds), *Women in Middle Eastern History*, New Haven and London: Yale University Press.

Landen, Robert G., (2006). 'Economic change: Muhammad Ali's development schemes in Egypt and Syria, 1834 and 1837', in Camron Michael Amin, Benjamin C. Fortna and Elizabeth B. Frierson (eds), *The Modern Middle East: A Sourcebook for History*, Oxford: Oxford University Press.

Islamfiche Project (2006). 'Journalism in Egypt in the 1920s and 1930s: from *The Education of Salama Musa* 1947', in Camron Michael Amin, Benjamin C. Fortna and Elizabeth B. Frierson (eds) *The Modern Middle East: A Sourcebook for History*, Oxford: Oxford University Press.

Moghadam, Valentine (2010). 'Urbanization and women's citizenship in the Middle East'. *Brown Journal of World Affairs*, 17(1): 19–34.

Pappé, Ilan (2005). *The Modern Middle East*, London: Routledge.

Online resources

United Nations Development Programme. 'Arab Human Development Reports', available at: http://arab-hdr.org/.

World Bank, 'Arab World Education Performance Indicators', available at: http://data.worldbank.org/data-catalog/arab-world-education-indicators.

Kharoufi, Mostafa (1996). 'Urbanization and urban research in the Arab World', UNESCO, available at http://www.unesco.org/most/khareng.htm#introduction.

Chapter 4

Political Economy

In their classic text on the subject, Richards and Waterbury (1991) note that the political economy of the Middle East is dominated by 'three simple facts': little rain, much oil and a rapidly growing – and hence young – population. Although tending towards the simplistic, there is a great deal of truth in their observation. Much of the MENA region is in the arid zone of the Eastern Hemisphere, a zone that stretches from Morocco to Mongolia and receives less than 20 inches of rain per year. As King Hassan II of Morocco was fond of reminding his foreign visitors, to govern with success is to have abundant rainfall. Because of its low rainfall and limited agricultural potential, the area has a low overall population density. While the MENA covers 11–12 per cent of the world's land area, its population (in 2012) of 339.6 million is roughly 7 per cent of the global total (World Bank, 2014). For many observers, the political economy of the MENA is synonymous with oil. The reasons for this are unsurprising. Around two thirds of known global reserves of crude oil are to be found in the region and the dependence of the global economy on the continued flow of Middle Eastern oil is clear. Nonetheless, oil is by no means the only factor in the political economy of the region. Although it is, by far, the most important natural resource, it is certainly not the only one. Iran has the world's largest proven reserves of natural gas (around 15 per cent of the world's total), while Algeria, Morocco, Tunisia, Jordan and Syria account for around 35 per cent of the world's phosphate production. Other important natural resources include potash in Iran, Israel and Jordan; iron ore in Iran and Mauritania; cotton in Egypt and Sudan; tobacco in Syria; and coffee in Yemen (El-Erian *et al.*, 2006).

Oil is, without a doubt, of enormous significance for the political economy of the MENA region (Achcar, 2013). However, before this significance can be understood it must be placed in context. The states of the MENA region have adopted a range of approaches to the management of their economies as they have faced a variety of important challenges. This chapter will begin with an overview of economic policy-making and the performance of MENA economies since independence before turning to a number of critical challenges that face governments in the region. The chapter will then conclude with a discussion of the impact of oil on the economic and political life of the region.

Patterns in economic policy-making and economic performance

Any examination of the performance of the economies of the MENA region has to begin with a caveat. Roger Owen and Sevket Pamuk (1998) make the important observation that there are real problems with available statistical data on the Middle East, both in terms of how they are collected and, very often, in terms of what is attempted to be measured. This point has been reiterated more recently by Hibou (2011) in her work on the supposed Tunisian economic miracle of the 1990s and 2000s. National income statistics record only activities to which monetary value can be attached and, as a consequence, ignore much of what goes on in the domestic sphere, especially work done by women. The 'black' or informal economy may account for a large part of total economic activity but this goes unreported and unrecorded. Finally, notions such as employment/ unemployment and measures of educational achievement such as literacy/ illiteracy are notoriously difficult to measure (Owen and Pamuk: 1998: xvi).

State-led economic development

The economic development strategies adopted by post-colonial states in the MENA region varied considerably. They ranged from the socialism espoused at various points by Egypt, Algeria, Iraq, Syria, Tunisia and Yemen to the free market economic system that prevailed in Lebanon. However, what almost every country in the region had in common was a high level of reliance on the state as the engine of economic development. This was by no means exclusive to the region; it was characteristic of the broader post-colonial world. Indeed, as Tony Judt points out in *Postwar: A History of Europe Since 1945*, on a global level, there was

> a great faith in the ability ... of the state to solve large-scale problems by mobilizing and directing people and resources to collectively useful ends. (Judt, 2010: 68)

Turkey provided the template for state-driven economic development policies even before World War II. In the aftermath of the 'Great Depression' of 1929, the Turkish government, in 1932, embarked upon a new economic strategy of *étatisme* (statism). This promoted the state as a leading producer and investor. By the end of the 1930s, the state played a significant role in production in a wide range of sectors, such as iron and steel, textiles, sugar, glassworks, cement, utilities and mining. The Turkish example proved to be very influential on economic policy in the postwar MENA region, as the state assumed ever-greater significance (Owen and Pamuk, 1998: 18). In impoverished post-colonial settings, the state was believed to be the only actor capable of efficiently mobilizing the few resources available.

In the case of Egypt, this began after the military coup of 1952 which overthrew the monarchy. The new regime embarked on major industrialization projects such as the construction (with Soviet assistance) of a new dam at Aswan in the south of the country, and major coal and steel works at Helwan on the outskirts of Cairo. The new regime also put in place a series of land reform laws between 1952 and 1960 which, by the late 1960s, saw the redistribution of nearly 800,000 acres, nearly 8 per cent of the cultivable total, to peasant farmers. Following the Suez Crisis/Tripartite Aggression of 1956, the military regime initiated a wave of nationalizations of companies identified with British, French or Jewish interests. These included banks, insurance companies and factories. A further round of nationalization of Egyptian-owned property began in 1960. By 1964, the state controlled much of the banking and insurance sectors, and 42 of its 'largest industrial and commercial concerns' (Owen and Pamuk, 1998: 130–1). One result of all of this was a huge increase in the numbers of those employed by the state, which, by the mid-1960s, was three times greater than it had been before the 1952 coup, a period during which the overall population of the country grew by half.

Similar policies were undertaken in both Syria and Iraq from the late 1950s onwards. In Syria, following the short-lived union with Egypt from 1958 to 1961, the leaders of the UAR embarked on an 'outspokenly socialist' course, launching a wave of nationalizations. While this was temporarily halted by a conservative coup in 1961, a further coup in 1963 restored Syria to the socialist path. The new leaders nationalized a large number of industrial and commercial concerns, and embarked on an ambitious land reform process in which eight times more land than was sequestered in Egypt was subjected to nationalization. By 1973, with the apparatus of the state now under the control of Hafez al-Asad, the Syrian government controlled a substantial part of agricultural and industrial production and a rapidly growing public sector and public administration (Perthes, 1995: 3). In Iraq, following the overthrow of the monarchy in 1958, the new regime of 'Abd al-Karim Qasim embarked on an ambitious land reform initiative which targeted an area 11 times greater than that of the Egyptian reforms. As with Syria, the aspiration for pan-Arab unity provided further stimulus for government policy – in 1964, in order to meet one of the requirements laid down by Nasser for a proposed union between Egypt and Iraq, many large industrial conglomerates were nationalized, along with the major banks and insurance companies. The reforms left the state in control of one third of overall manufacturing output. Qasim also proposed the nationalization of Iraq's increasingly significant oil sector. In 1960, when an earlier initiative to share ownership and profits with the state was rejected by the Anglo-American owned Iraqi Petroleum Company, the new government proposed to establish a national Iraqi oil company. The proposal drew widespread opposition, especially outside the country. In 1963, Qasim was removed from power in a Baathist coup, which it is widely believed had the blessing of Britain and the US. According to the American historian Douglas Little, the CIA was closely involved in the planning and aftermath of the coup, in the course of which Qasim and thousands of his followers were captured and executed 'by Baathist death squads' (Little, 2004: 696).

The prominence of the state in economic life was not, however, confined to the emerging 'socialist' countries of the MENA. While Morocco never aspired to socialist ideals, the increasing intervention of the state in the economy resulted in state ownership of some 700 enterprises by the late 1970s in which a state-dependent élite was employed. The King, Hassan II, became the most important businessman in the state. He enjoyed a majority share in the holding company, Omnium Nord Africain, which in turn owned shares in 50 of Morocco's most significant private businesses (Sater, 2010: 9–10). In relation to the prominent role the monarchy has in the economy, little has changed since the arrival of Mohamamed VI to power in 1999. For critics of the monarchy, the accumulation of both economic and political power in the hands of the king is a considerable source of corruption, clientelism and, ultimately, authoritarian rule (Graciet and Laurent, 2012). In neighbouring Tunisia, the new government, which took power in 1956, expressly sought to maintain the liberal economy of the French protectorate era. Thus, the state provided land for peasant farmers, not by infringing on private property rights, but by redistributing land vacated by Europeans and those of European descent who left the country at independence. However, as the difficulty of meeting the needs and aspirations of a growing population became increasingly apparent, the government moved from a vague nationalist policy to a more interventionist role for the state and the espousal of 'Neo-Destour socialism'. A Ten-Year Plan (1962–71) was set out with ambitious targets which required increased state involvement in industry, bringing foreign-owned enterprises under Tunisian control and establishing a network of agricultural cooperatives (Perkins, 2004: 145–7).

In the Gulf States, the discovery and exploitation of vast oil resources transformed political and economic life (this is discussed in greater detail later in this chapter) and the role of the state was more limited than elsewhere. Most governments did at least begin to make plans for economic diversification beyond the oil sector – in Saudi Arabia, the Saudi Industrial Development Fund was established in 1974 to encourage the development of an industrial sector, while the production of wheat and other cereals was subsidized in the name of food security, although this was both extremely costly and depleted scarce water resources (Owen and Pamuk, 1998: 212–13). Nevertheless, Hvidt (2013) concludes a study of economic diversification in the Gulf by noting that, while important steps had been taken to move away from dependence on oil and gas, the oil sector continues to dominate, and few of the industries and services established would survive in a post-oil era.

In the non-Arab states of Iran and Israel, there was also extensive state involvement in political life. In Israel, economic life after the 1948 Declaration of Independence was dominated by institutions and organizations established by the Jewish community while, under the British mandate in Palestine, especially the *Histradut* (the General Federation of Israeli Labour). Under a series of Labour party governments, Histradut enterprises assumed a significant role in economic life and accounted for 20 per cent of net domestic product between 1957 and 1960. Economic management was characterized by extensive state intervention and the private sector was 'kept severely in check', although it was necessary to preserve the image of a mixed economy in order to attract foreign investment, especially from the US (Owen and Pamuk, 1998: 180).

Under the Shah, the Iranian government embarked on a major reform programme in the early 1960s, one outcome of which was to entrench the position of the state in economic life. The so-called 'White Revolution' inaugurated a major land reform programme which saw the transfer of between 50 per cent and 60 per cent of agricultural land to occupant share-croppers and tenant farmers. The public sector also grew rapidly. During the 1960s and 1970s, employment in the bureaucracy rose from one fifth of the economically active labour force in 1956 to more than one third some 20 years later. By the mid-1970s, the public sector was responsible for more than 50 per cent of GDP, while much of the balance came from state expenditure of oil revenues (Ashraf, 1996: 27–31).

Economic liberalization

The 1970s has been described as a 'golden period' for the MENA region. GDP growth across the region was 6 per cent per annum on average, while the region as a whole enjoyed substantial flows of aid. However, the decline of oil prices in the 1980s exposed structural weaknesses in MENA economies, especially the extent of over-reliance on oil. The drop in oil revenues led to a drop in migrant remittances and reduced aid from the Gulf states to their poorer neighbours. This coincided with recession in the West which led to a decline in aid from Western countries. GDP in the MENA decreased on average by 1 per cent per annum in the 1980s, a rate worse than any other region in the developing world, apart from sub-Saharan Africa (Harrigan and El-Said, 2010: 2; Harrigan *et al.*, 2005: 253). Across the region, governments began to engage with the IMF and the World Bank in processes of liberalization that were designed to reform their economies and restore growth. This began with Morocco in 1983, followed by Tunisia (1986), Jordan (1989), Egypt (1991) and Algeria (1994), although Tunisia, Morocco and Egypt had undergone earlier, if unsuccessful, attempts at reform which prompted social unrest. For instance, in 1977 in Egypt, 80 people were killed in two days of protests, which followed the removal of subsidies for flour, cooking oil and other staples at the suggestion of the IMF and World Bank. In Tunisia, seven years later, the IMF and World Bank demanded the lifting of subsidies on bread and other basic foodstuffs. The price of some foodstuffs instantly doubled, leading to two weeks of rioting across the country and the questioning of the way in which the father of Tunisian independence, Habib Bourguiba, governed. The same year in Morocco, up to 100 people were killed in protests, which followed the announcement of a rise in the price of basic foodstuffs, again at the insistence of the international financial institutions. Such violent responses to the adoption of liberalizing measures in the economy cautioned governments across the region against moving too quickly, with the result that it is characteristic of reform processes that they have been halting and incomplete. In Algeria, a dramatic decline in living conditions in the late 1980s, which saw GDP per capita drop from US$2,572 in 1987 to US$1,607 just four years later, led the government to enter an agreement with the IMF to implement a series of reforms in return for just under US$2 billion in credit. Public enterprises were targeted, loss-making and non-viable enterprises were liquidated, while some companies simply had their assets transferred to their employees (Corm, 1993). Nevertheless, according to one commentator:

> By and large, more than a decade after the introduction of the World Bank and IMF-sponsored reforms, the case is still not one of strong and prolonged economic recovery. (Aghrout, 2008: 42)

The requirement to follow the 'one size fits all' of the World Bank and the IMF led to disastrous results in relation to inequality. The removal of subsidies, privatization, and the closure of loss-making enterprises, however patchy and selective, were meant to be the stepping-stone towards better economic management and greater growth, which, in the medium term, would be beneficial to all sectors of society. The basic principle was that a certain amount of pain needed to be inflicted, but that the pain would be short-lived because economic reforms would eventually work. The reality has been very different. Inequality has increased significantly since the introduction of the structural adjustment programmes. As we can see in the chapters dealing with the Arab Awakening, economic and social inequalities were central to the uprisings and to the street protests that occurred not only in the Arab world, but also in Israel. At the heart of the protests are the highly contentious legacies of the neoliberal economic reforms advocated by both the World Bank and the IMF.

In addition to the inherent problems that structural adjustments brought, it is also necessary to take into account the fact that such reforms took place in a context of political authoritarianism, which compounded the problem of inequality, without generating economic efficiencies in the long term. Writing in 2002, Dillman argued that the partial nature of reforms in the region reflected the preferences of state élites to maximize the economic resources available to them and to avoid potential threats to their political power through the creation of a loyal set of 'economic winners'. Therefore, despite some devaluation, debt-rescheduling, gradual tariff reductions and a freeing of prices, there was no far-reaching banking reform, public sector restructuring or privatization. Partial reform, while not ideal from the perspective of the economy, was preferred because it avoided the perceived risks associated with more thorough-going economic liberaliza-tion – higher social costs, divisions within regime members and the crea-tion of autonomous sources of economic power (Dillman, 2002: 69–71). Thus, liberalization was implemented in a selective fashion – bureaucrats, regime members, families of heads of state, leaders of political parties and the upper echelon of the military established private businesses in the pursuit of quick profits. But, while members of ruling élites and their clients have benefited disproportionately from liberalization, the cost of reform, as mentioned, has been borne by the poor majority of the popula-tion in the form of rising unemployment, the removal of food subsidies and the erosion of other supports (Schlumberger, 2000: 258).

Partial or incomplete reform processes are one of the reasons why the economic performance of the MENA region as a whole continues to lag behind much of the rest of the world to the present day (Achcar, 2013). Combined with over-reliance on oil-derived income and the challenge of meeting the needs of rapidly growing populations, the inability or unwill-ingness of regimes in the MENA to reform their economies effectively has made for a very uneven economic performance on the part of Arab states. Between 1980 and 2004, per capita economic growth increased by less

Box 4.1   Geopolitics and economic liberalization in the MENA

The political components of economic reform are not limited to the domestic sphere. A number of writers have noted the extent to which international political allegiances have impacted on reform process. The case of Egypt is an apt example of this. Since concluding a peace deal with Israel in 1978, it has received substantial aid from the United States in spite of a poor human rights record. It has received programme loans from the World Bank and IMF despite the very uneven pace of economic liberalization in the country. Perhaps, the clearest indication of the importance of its international political allegiances came in the aftermath of the first Gulf War in 1990/91, when Egypt supported the US-led attack on the Iraqi invasion force in Kuwait. After the war ended, Egypt received substantial loans from the IMF and the World Bank, More importantly, it also received a write-off of debt worth US$15 billion – the highest level of debt forgiveness in the history of the MENA. Other countries have also bene-fited from their geopolitical orientation. Since Jordan signed a peace treaty with Israel in June 1994, it has been one of the largest recipients of American aid in the world. Tunisia and Morocco were long considered as having friendly, pro-Western regimes. Both have received favourable treatment from the European Union, the IMF and the World Bank compared with regimes considered less friendly to the West.

Source: J.R. Harrigan and H. El-Said (2010). 'The economic impact of IMF and World Bank programs in the Middle East and North Africa: a case study of Jordan, Egypt, Morocco and Tunisia, 1983–2004', *Review of Middle East Economies and Finance*, 6(2) 1:26.

than 0.5 per cent annually. In the 1990s, this rose to 1.2 per cent. However, this figure was worse than those for most other regions, and better only than sub-Sahahran Africa and the countries of East and Central Europe, which were at that time making the painful transition from state dominated economies. Trade figures are also unimpressive. World trade rose overall by 8 per cent in the 1990s but MENA trade with the rest of the world grew only by 3 per cent in the same period. The region's trade is overwhelm-ingly dominated by oil. Oil and oil-related products account for about 75 per cent of the region's exports and about 40 per cent of global exports of these products. But non-oil exports have remained at a low 7 per cent of GDP since the 1980s (see Figure 4.1). Total non-oil exports from the region amounted to US$28 billion in 2000. In comparison, Finland with a population of just over 5 million people, had almost twice the level of non-oil exports of the MENA with its population of nearly 400 million (Iqbal and Nabli, 2004).

The figures for foreign direct investment (FDI) are equally discour-aging. FDI is the biggest source of capital for developing countries but, apart from Turkey, the share of the MENA region dropped from 11.6 per

Figure 4.1   *Non-oil exports from the MENA compared*

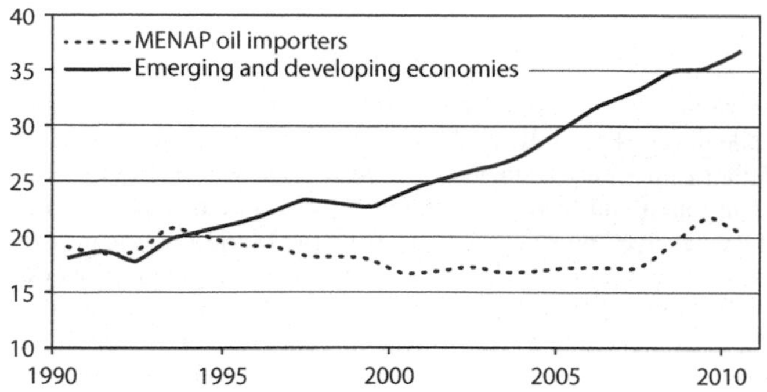

MENAP oil importers include Djibouti, Egypt, Jordan, Lebanon, Mauritania, Morocco, Syria and Tunisia as well as Afghanistan and Pakistan

Sources: World Economic Forum (2010): http://www3.weforum.org/docs/WEF_GCR_ArabWorldReview_2010_EN.pdf.

cent in 1990 to a mere 3.3 per cent seven years later. The MENA region, excluding the oil producing states of the Gulf, received a net inflow of FDI worth US$2.2 billion in 2000, a little more than 1 per cent of the total of US$160 billion to all developing countries, and not greatly exceeding the US$1.633 billion received by the state of Israel alone (Index Mundi, 2014). Three Asian countries – Malaysia, the Philippines and Thailand – together received US$8 billion, four times the total of the entire MENA region, while four Latin American countries – Bolivia, Chile, Mexico and Brazil – received US$50 billion, 22 times that received by the MENA (Iqbal and Nabli, 2004). Outside of the energy sector, multinationals are discouraged from investing in the MENA region not only because of trade and other restrictions, but also because of the lack of transparent economic information. Henry and Springborg note, somewhat bleakly but accurately, that the most visible foreign presence in the region is not FDI in manufacturing but fast food chains such as McDonald's and KFC, which are aimed at local consumers and merely represent a reverse flow of capital to corporate headquarters from the local investors who buy the franchises (2005: 49). It is true that in countries with little in the way of oil and gas reserves, FDIs in manufacturing do exist in part because they are attracted by an extremely favourable tax regime and cheap labour. This is the case with Tunisia, for instance. Under Ben Ali, it developed what can be termed 'special economic zones' to attract European manu-facturers who did, indeed, come in some numbers to the country. In addi-tion to finding reasonably favourable economic conditions, they were also attracted by the political stability of the regime. However, the type

Box 4.2 Islamic economics in the MENA region

Across the MENA region, in parallel with conventional economic practices, an Islamic financial sector has grown in significance. Islamic financial practices are those deemed to be in compliance with Islamic law, most notably the prohibition of interest-based, speculative products. The first Islamic financial institutions were established in the 1950s and 1960s. The Islamic Development Bank was set up by the Organization of the Islamic Conference in 1974. The significance of the sector in individual countries has much to do with the relationship between the state and the Islamic movement more generally. In Egypt, members of the Muslim Brotherhood were involved in the establishment of the first Islamic bank, the Faisal Islamic Bank, in 1979. As relations between the state and the Islamic movement deteriorated, these members were expelled at the request of state security. The only Islamic bank in Tunisia was caught in the hostile relations between the Islamic movement in Tunisia and the regime of former President Ben Ali in the 1990s. By the year 2000, the bank held deposits of a mere 0.2 per cent of the national total, not least because it did not advertise its existence.

Nonetheless, the sector has grown rapidly in recent decades. The Islamic banking sector in the Gulf Cooperation Council (GCC) countries has assets of nearly US$90 billion. Elsewhere, in Yemen, Islamic banking represents 30 per cent of assets and 45 per cent of loans. Jordan's Islamic finance industry is reportedly worth US$5 billion. However, there remains considerable ambiguity as to what precisely constitutes Islamic finance. Critics have argued that Islamic banks do not operate very differently from conventional banks. This is borne out by a fatwa issued by the then Egyptian State Mufti, Sayyid Tantawy, in 1989, when he conferred religious legitimacy on interest taken and dispensed by conventional banks. Later, in 1997, Tantawy stated his opinion that conventional banks were closer to Islam than Islamic banks.

Source: Vincent Durac (2009). 'Globalizing patterns of business, finance and migration in the Middle East and North Africa', *Mediterranean Politics*, 14(2): 255–66.

of manufacturing involved is where marginal profits are minimal, reinvestment low and trickle-down effects non-existent. This, of course, is unlikely to stimulate sustainable growth, and attracting 'better' FDIs is extremely difficult.

The critical difficulty is that MENA countries have relied on oil-led economic growth for decades. However, this has created weak structural foundations in their economies, although Islamic economics attempted to set itself up as a powerful alternative (see Box 4.2, for a detailed account of this) and therefore move slightly away from pure market mechanisms. Arab countries are turning into import-oriented and service-based economies. But, the types of services found in the region contribute little to local knowledge development and lock countries into inferior positions in global markets. This is at the expense of agriculture, manufacturing and industrial production. According to the United Nations Development Programme (UNDP), the Arab world has experienced significant 'deindustrialization' over the last four decades – Arab countries were less industrialized in 2007 than in 1970 (UNDP, 2009: 103). This problem has been exacerbated by economic liberalization programmes. Algeria was praised by the IMF in the mid-1990s for its adoption of economic reforms. But, public sector industry was producing only 69 per cent as much as it had done 10 years earlier, with no sign of private industry taking up the slack (Henry and Springborg, 2005: 118–19).

The economic difficulties experienced by countries in the region in the economic sphere have multifaceted origins. However, two crucial elements in this are high levels of dependence on oil, combined with the challenge of rapidly rising – hence young – populations. The rest of the chapter will discuss these aspects of the political economy of the region.

Population growth and its challenges

Population growth within the MENA region has brought with it various challenges, which this section will now discuss: a gender gap in employment, migration within the MENA retion and also migration to Europe, the need for remittances to support dependants and also the effects of environmental degredation in the area.

Population increase

Demographic patterns constitute one of the major issues in the political economy of the region. For hundreds of years, the population of the MENA hovered at around 30 million. It reached 60 million early in the twentieth century. Since then, the rise in the population level has been dramatic. The total population rose from around 100 million in 1950 to nearly 400 million by the end of the century – an almost fourfold increase in 50 years. According to a census of 1917, Egypt had a population of 12.7 million, fewer than 2 million of whom lived in the major cities of Cairo and Alexandria, or in 13 other towns that had a population of over 20,000. Today, the population of greater Cairo alone is at least 11 million, while the total for Egypt as a whole is estimated at 83 million. In 1924, the population of Turkey was approximately 13 million, slightly more than the 10.3 million estimated to be living in present-day Istanbul. The total Turkish population is now close to 80 million. Other countries in the region have experienced similar growth. Transjordan (later Jordan) had a population of 250,000 in 1922. This had risen to 375,000 some 25 years later. Today, the

Figure 4.2 *Current and projected population levels: 1950–2050*

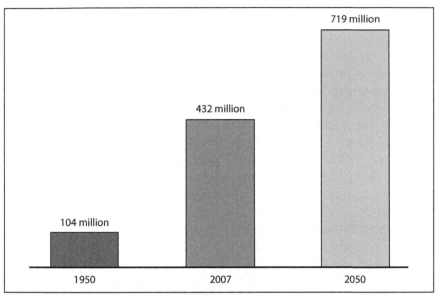

Source: Data from Population Reference Bureau (2001).

population is 6.5 million. The total population of the Arabian Peninsula was estimated at between 6 and 7 million in 1918. The present-day population of Yemen alone is nearly 25 million and is projected to have almost doubled by 2050, while that of neighbouring Saudi Arabia is close to 27 million. A significant feature of demographic growth in the region is increased levels of urbanization. Almost half the population lives in cities. In the year 2000, the region had 16 cities with over 1 million inhabitants.

In light of these figures, it is not surprising that the MENA has experienced the highest rate of population increase of any region in the world in the past century. From 1975–80, the Total Fertility Rate of the region was 6.5 – this meant that the average Arab woman would give birth to six or seven children over the course of her childbearing years. While this rate declined to 3.6 for the period from 2000 to 2005, it was still significantly higher than the population replacement rate of 2.1. While overall population growth rates are declining, the total is projected to grow to 568 million by 2025 and 719 million by 2050. This level of population growth has enormously important consequences for economic and political life in the region. (See Figure 4.2.)

One immediate effect of these demographic patterns is the region's 'youth bulge'. Young people are the fastest growing component of the overall population – around 60 per cent of the total. The average age in the MENA is 22 years compared with a global average of 28. Linked to this is the problem of unemployment. In 2005, the overall average unemployment rate for the Arab world was approximately 14.4 per cent of the labour force, compared with a global average of 6.3 per cent. The overall unemployment rate has increased over the past three decades. In 1980, the rate for non-Gulf countries varied from 16.6 per cent in Algeria to 4.8 per cent in Syria. The average unemployment rate for this group of countries was 10.6 per cent in the 1980s. In the 1990s, the unemployment rate for Algeria rose to 25.3 per cent, followed by Morocco with a rate of 18 per cent. The overall average for Arab countries outside the Gulf rose in the 1990s to 14.5 per cent. The upward (if negative) trend continued into the new century. By 2005, the figure had risen again to 15.5 per cent overall. In addition, there is the considerable problem of under-employment, which means that even those who are employed may not work on a consistent or regular basis. Headline rates also conceal important variations within the overall pattern of unemployment. Given the youth bulge in the population, it is not surprising that unemployment rates for young people are significantly higher than those for the labour force overall. Estimates for the year 2005–6 show unemployment rates for young people ranging from a high of 46 per cent in Algeria to a low of 6.3 per cent in the UAE. Saudi Arabia had a youth unemployment rate of 26 per cent; Kuwait 23 per cent and Bahrain 21 per cent. In Jordan the rate was 39 per cent; in Libya 27 per cent; in Tunisia 27 per cent; and in Egypt 26 per cent.

Dramatic as these figures are, in turn, they mask the extent to which unemployment in the MENA region 'often wears a female face' (UNDP, 2009). Female unemployment rates in the MENA are much higher than are those for their male counterparts. Indeed, they are among the highest in the world. In 2005, the youth unemployment rate for men was 25 per cent of the male labour force. For women, it varied from a high of 59 per cent in Jordan to a low of 5.7 per cent in the UAE. Young and educated women experience discrimination in the labour market across the region and, disproportionately, find employment in the low-waged agricultural sector, or in jobs without social insurance or benefits. The clearest expression of this is to be seen in the fact that the Arab world is the only region in the world where the proportion of women employed in agriculture is increasing (UNDP, 2009: 109–10).

Migration within the MENA region

The combination of high levels of population increase and the incapacity of governments in the region to manage their economies to accommodate the ever-increasing pool of labour has had the effect of rendering the MENA region one characterized by high levels of migration, both within

Figure 4.3 *The gender gap in employment*

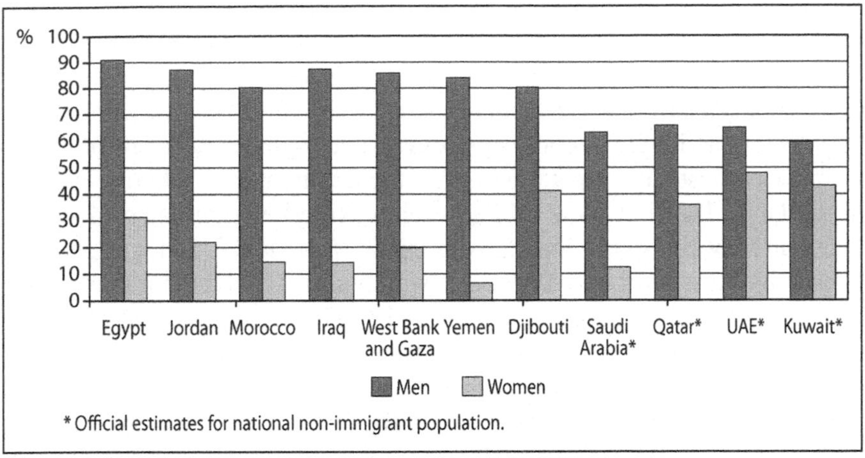

Source: World Bank (2004).

and outside the region. This has had very important consequences for both political and economic life.

The region has always been the site of waves of enforced migration. After World War II, and with decolonization, European settlers began to return to their countries of origin. For instance, an estimated 800,000 people of French descent left Algeria in the years following the end of the War of Independence in 1962. Earlier, the establishment of the state of Israel led to the departure of a similar number of Palestinians seeking refuge in neighbouring Arab states. In turn, the new state attracted up to 1.5 million immigrants from outside the region up until 1990, as well as several hundred thousand from Arab states such as Iraq, Yemen and elsewhere. The Lebanese civil war (1975–90) also saw a significant movement of people from that country, while the Iranian revolution of 1979 led to a large wave of emigration, mainly to North America (Corm, 2008: 2–3). More recently, the 2003 war in Iraq displaced millions of Iraqis fleeing the conflict and subsequent civil war to Syria and Jordan. The civil conflict in Syria that began in March 2011 has led millions of Syrians to cross the borders into neighbouring states, including Jordan, Turkey and Lebanon. Both conflicts have provoked an enormous rise in the numbers of internally displaced people. This number is in addition to the millions internally displaced by conflicts in Sudan and Iraq.

Migration has played a major role in the economic and political life of the region, not least because of the opportunities created by the growth of the oil sector in the region. During the early days of the development of the oil industry, labour shortages in oil-producing states with small populations, such as Kuwait and Saudi Arabia, attracted an inflow of skilled and educated labour from outside. The oil producing states typically had small populations with limited educational provision. For example, there were a mere 650 literate people out of Qatar's total population of 30,000 in 1949. A census eight years later in Kuwait revealed that the country had two doctors and eight accountants (Owen and Pamuk, 1998: 208). Thus, from the earliest days, a pattern of dependence on migrant labour emerged in the Gulf. The first wave of Palestinian skilled workers arrived in the 1950s in Kuwait, Saudi Arabia, Abu Dhabi, and Dubai, and was accompanied by American and European workers associated with the major foreign-owned oil companies. By the 1970s, oil rich states could afford to import labour for a variety of unskilled and menial jobs. Saudi Arabia had a migrant population of more than 1 million, the majority of which were drawn from Yemen, Jordan and Egypt. By 2008, over 65 per cent of the total population of GCC countries comprised foreigners (including both Arab and non-Arab nationals). In Saudi Arabia, the foreign population constituted just over 50 per cent of the total, in Kuwait this rose to 80 per cent, while in Qatar the figure was 92 per cent. Not all of these worked in essential services. In the case of the UAE, 5 per cent of the total population consisted of domestic servants (Winckler, 2011: 11).

The total number of migrants from the MENA region at the end of the twentieth century was estimated at 9.7 million, or just over 3 per cent of the total population. Of these, almost half were in Gulf or other Arab countries, while a further 40 per cent were in Europe; the remainder were to be found in North America or Australia. The countries with the largest number of emigrants were Egypt, Morocco, Palestine, Iraq and Iran. While intra-regional migration continues to be highly significant, the proportion of Arab migrants in the Gulf has declined in recent years because of policy choices made by many Gulf states. Rising unemployment levels have led to a new emphasis on 'job nationalization' in the form of limits on the employment of non-nationals, the introduction of minimum quotas for nationals and the imposition of higher costs for hiring non-nationals (Calandruccio, 2005: 279). In addition, Gulf states increasingly began to replace potentially troublesome Arab workers with migrants from Asia, who were seen as more politically compliant. By the early twenty-first century, there were nearly 7.5 million workers from Bangladesh, India, Indonesia, Pakistan and other Asian countries in GCC states compared with 3.5 million from MENA countries.

The flow of migrants in the region has taken place outside any institutional or legal framework. There are no agreements in place between sending and receiving countries either to regulate the flow of migrants, or to set out their rights (Corm, 2008: 5). In this situation, migrant popula-

---

Box 4.3 Migrant vulnerability: Yemeni migrants in Saudi Arabia during the first Gulf War

Increasing Yemeni migration to neighbouring Saudi Arabia meant that there were around 1 million Yemenis in the country by 1990. The expansion in the size of the Yemeni population had been facilitated by preferential Saudi policies which granted Yemenis privileges that were not enjoyed by other migrants. They could enter the country easily, could work and reside independently without a local sponsor, and were even permitted to own their own businesses – something no other foreign nationals were allowed to do. However, the first Gulf War changed this, illustrating the utter vulnerability of Yemeni migrants, despite their apparently secure situation.

When Iraq invaded Kuwait in August 1990, newly unified Yemen occupied a place on the United Nations Security Council. Yemen refrained from voting on a resolution condemning the invasion of Iraq and very quickly found itself on the wrong side of Saudi Arabia, which vigorously opposed Iraq with the support of the United States and many others. First, Yemeni diplomats were expelled. Then, on 19 September 1990, Yemeni workers in Saudi Arabia were given 30 days to find a Saudi sponsor or guarantor for their business. Effectively, the 1 million Yemenis in Saudi Arabia were forced to leave the country, many leaving their possessions behind. In addition those expelled from Saudi Arabia, the country had to cope with the return of 45,000 Yemenis from Kuwait and Iraq, and some 2,000 from Qatar, Bahrain and the UAE. In the short term, Yemen managed to house returning migrants in refugee camps with basic resources. But there was a devastating impact on an already over-stretched economy. The Gulf States cut their aid of US$200 million per annum, while US aid was cut from US$20.5 million to US$2.9 million. In 1991, inflation rose to 100 per cent and GDP fell by 4.8 per cent. Unemployment reached 35 per cent in 1992. In effect, the poorest country in the Arab world was left with an extra 1 million people to support while drawing on more limited resources.

Source: Gwen Okruhlik and Patrick Conge (1997). 'National autonomy, labour migration and political crisis: Yemen and Saudi Arabia', *Middle East Journal*, 51(4): 554–65.

---

tions have been vulnerable on a number of levels, including their vulnerability to external shock, as Box 4.3 exemplifies.

Migration and Europe

As well as intraregional migration, there has been significant migration to Europe for decades. This is particularly so in relation to the countries of the Maghreb, although not limited to them. Almost 3 million Moroccans, Algerians and Tunisians live in Europe, of whom 1 million have European citizenship. In 2000, there were 2.3 million migrants from the MENA living in France, in Spain the figure was just over 300,000 and, in Italy, just under 300,000. Despite these figures, the share of migrants from

MENA countries in the total number of migrants is rather low in most European countries. Nonetheless, migration occupies a prominent role in relations between the EU and states in the region. European policy focuses on three objectives – reducing migratory pressures through job creation, the fight against illegal migration, and the protection of the rights of legal migrants. However, according to Fargues (2004: 148), it is the impact of migration on security that is of particular concern. One key aspect of this concern relates to the passage of migrants from sub-Saharan Africa and other countries through the MENA to Europe. According to some estimates, between 65,000 and 120,000 sub-Saharan Africans enter North African countries each year, many of whom try to cross the Mediterranean to Europe. Several European countries have reacted by trying to 'externalize' border controls (De Haas, 2006). This has taken the form of putting pressure on North African countries to clamp down on irregular migration and to sign readmission agreements in exchange for development aid, financial support for border controls, military equipment and limited numbers of work permits for immigrants. For one critic at least, this means that the Sahara has been transformed into 'a kind of border outpost with the forced recruitment of North African countries as outpost sentinels' (Bensaad, 2007: 58).

Despite concerns felt by some in Europe regarding inward migration from the MENA, there are good reasons to believe that this phenomenon will continue. One has to do with demographic patterns on both sides of the Mediterranean. In 1950, the total population of what is now the European Union was around 350 million, while that of the 10 Mediterranean countries from Morocco to Lebanon was 70 million. According to UN forecasts, by 2050 both blocs will have a population of 400 million each. However, the profile of the European population has led one commentator to write of 'super-ageing' in the middle decades of the twenty-first century while, in the Mediterranean countries, there will be fewer older people and the relative size of the working age population will be much greater. The logic of this is that migration into the EU from the countries of the Mediterranean will be a large and increasing phenomenon (Wilson, 2007).

Remittances

High levels of migration within and outside the region mean that migrant remittances play a very significant role in the economic life of the MENA region. The importance of remittances is demonstrated by the fact that their value has greatly exceeded the amount of Official Development Assistance (ODA) received by North African countries. For the Maghreb countries alone, remittances were worth 135 per cent of ODA in 1980. By 2003, this had risen to 561 per cent of ODA (Corm, 2008: 13). Remittances, therefore, constitute a significant source of income to states whose citizens have emigrated. In 2009, migrant remittances constituted 22.4 per cent of total GDP in Lebanon; 15.6 per cent of GDP in Jordan and 4–6 per cent of GDP in Morocco, Tunisia, Yemen and Egypt. However, while remittances clearly constitute an important source of income for recipients in MENA countries, studies show that their long-term benefits are questionable. The flow of remittances is vulnerable to shifts in the economic conditions of 'sender' countries, while the available evidence shows that remittances are used primarily for consumption purposes. Therefore, the developmental potential of remittances is questionable (Abdih *et al.*, 2012: 20).

Environmental degradation

The impact of high levels of population growth is not limited to the economic sphere. The environmental implications of demographic patterns in the MENA are increasingly apparent – indeed, alarmingly so in some contexts. One of the clearest examples of this can be seen in declining water stocks in the region. The combination of rising population levels, the climatic conditions of the region and poor resource management make for what some consider an unsustainable situation. Population growth leads to increased demand for food and agricultural products. But the agricultural base of the MENA is poor. Most of the region is desert – the arable and permanent crop area constitutes only 4 per cent of total land. The climate is very hot and dry, and is characterized by low levels of annual rainfall. As a result, the MENA has the worst water scarcity problem of any world region – with 4 per cent of the global population, it has only 1 per cent of its renewable water resources (Mubarak, 1998: 878). In the extreme case of Yemen, it has been predicted that catastrophic water shortages will take place in major urban centres within 10 to 20 years, if current water usage practices and government policy remain unchanged. Indeed, some have raised the spectre of Sana'a becoming the first capital city in the world to run out of water.

Perhaps unsurprisingly, water resources have been seen by some as likely to spark future conflict in the region. In 1990, Boutros Boutros Ghali, then Egyptian Foreign Minister and later Secretary-General of the UN, famously predicted that the next war in the Middle East would be fought over water. Such concerns stem partly from the fact that more than half of the external surface water resources of the MENA are shared between neighbouring countries. The major rivers in the region lie within and beyond the region. The Tigris and the Euphrates are shared by Iraq, Syria and Turkey; the Orontes is shared by Lebanon, Syria and Turkey; the Jordan is shared by Jordan, Palestine, Israel and Syria; and the Nile is shared by nine countries of which only Egypt and Sudan are in the MENA (UNDP, 2009: 37). However, fears of coming water wars have been dismissed as 'groundless'. Selby (2005) points out that, despite the frequent predictions, water did not overtake oil as the dominant source of conflict in the region by 2000. Indeed, as Selby notes, the prediction made by Boutros Ghali came three months before the start of the 1990/91 Gulf War 'an oil conflict if there ever was one'. Water, Selby argues, comes low on the list of national priorities for most MENA regimes, which are dominated by other concerns such as ideological, economic or strategic relations with neighbouring states and outside powers, access to foreign aid and investment and oil revenues and remittances (Selby, 2005: 338–9).

It is important to note that many of these social and economic developments played a significant role in the setting off the Arab Awakening, which will be discussed in more detail later.

Oil and politics in the MENA

While rapid population growth and the challenges associated with this have hindered economic development in the MENA, there is no doubting the significance of the region's dependency on oil. In 2008, 55 per cent of the population of the region lived in its oil-exporting countries. Oil accounted for almost 90 per cent of the exports of those countries and 50 per cent of their GDP (World Bank, 2011b).

The origins of the oil industry and changing patterns of ownership

The MENA region plays a hugely significant role in the international oil industry. Five Gulf states hold 65 per cent of the world's known oil reserves. The Saudi Arabian share of these alone is 25 per cent. The North African states of Egypt, Algeria and Libya have oil reserves which amount to over 4 per cent of the global total. The exploitation of such resources has generated enormous wealth. Thus, it is not surprising that oil has had a huge impact on all aspects of life in the region, while the dependency of the outside world on the region's resources has helped to shape its interactions at the international level (see Box 4.4).

The first place in the MENA where oil was discovered and exploited was Iran. Trial production began as early as 1903. Five years later there was a major discovery at Masjed Suleyman and, within three years, oil was being piped to a refinery near Basra. The Anglo-Persian Oil Company, later to become British Petroleum (BP), which was established in 1909,

> **Box 4.4   The world's top oil producers**
>
> In 2012, only six of the world's leading oil producers were in the MENA region. The top 15 are as follows:
>
> | | | | |
> |---|---|---|---|
> | 1 | Saudi Arabia | 9 | Mexico |
> | 2 | United States | 10 | Kuwait |
> | 3 | Russia | 11 | Brazil |
> | 4 | China | 12 | Nigeria |
> | 5 | Canada | 13 | Venezuela |
> | 6 | Iran | 14 | Qatar |
> | 7 | United Arab Emirates | 15 | Norway |
> | 8 | Iraq | | |
>
> *Source*: US Energy Information Administration (2012), 'Top world oil producers – 2012', available at http://www.eia.gov/countries/index.cfm#.

dominated oil production in the country. In 1911, Winston Churchill, then First Lord of the Admiralty, took the decision to convert Britain's navy to oil for its source of power in place of coal. From this point onwards, a crucial link was established between the strategic interests of outside powers and Middle Eastern oil, a link that has yet to be broken.

Oil was discovered in British-controlled Iraq in 1927 but its exploitation was limited in the early years. The effective monopoly enjoyed by Britain over oil production in Iran forced US companies to look elsewhere. Standard Oil of California discovered oil in Bahrain in 1932. Six years later, CalTex found major reserves in Kuwait. Also in 1938, Standard Oil of California had its first strike in the eastern province of Saudi Arabia, where a consortium of American oil companies, the Arabian-American Oil Company (ARAMCO), was established to exploit oil resources. ARAMCO developed the Ghawar and Safaniya oil fields in the Dhahran area, which were to prove to be the largest and most lucrative in the entire world (Wilson, 2013: 111). There were other discoveries in Kuwait, Qatar, Abu Dhabi, Dubai and Oman.

To begin with, foreign oil companies paid royalties to the government of the host nation and kept the profits for themselves. For local rulers, this was a more than acceptable bargain. Oil-related revenues came without any great effort on their part whereas extracting, transporting and refining oil was a very expensive business, the costs of which were borne by the oil companies. However, once the infrastructure of the oil industry was in place, the returns to the oil companies were enormous and, as early as the 1920s and 1930s, there were conflicts over the share of revenues. ARAMCO enjoyed profits three times greater than the royalties paid to the Saudi government in 1949, and paid more in US taxes than the Saudi share (Rogan, 2010:

448). By 1950, the Saudis had negotiated an equal share of oil revenues with ARAMCO and other Arab states soon followed this example. Libya, where the first significant oil find took place in 1959, set a new precedent for Arab control of oil in 1970 when the Gaddafi regime negotiated a majority 55 per cent share of profits with Occidental Petroleum. A year later Iran, Iraq and Saudi Arabia negotiated similar deals. It was, in Rogan's words:

> the end of the era of the Western oil barons and the beginning of the age of the Arab oil shaykhs. (2010: 454)

But, the termination of the era of overt Western domination of the oil industry in the MENA region did not bring its interest in oil to an end. Indeed, many see that interest as underpinning just about every action the West has undertaken in the Middle East. While this is greatly to over-state the reality, Western dependence on the region's energy resources has undoubtedly shaped policy responses and interventions. As has been noted, Western dependence on Middle Eastern oil dates back to before World War I. The extent to which Western actors would go to secure interest in a stable supply of oil had been vividly exemplified in the overthrow of Iranian Prime Minister Mohammed Mossadeq in 1953. Mossadeq's over-throw further highlights the interaction between domestic and international politics, as the popular will of Iranians and the necessity of securing oil supplies and the profits that came with this collided. The episode remains crucial in the historical narrative of the current Iranian regime in its pursuit of what can be termed 'anti-imperialist' policies. More recently, attention has focused on the role played by oil in the formulation and execution of US policy in the region. A number of examples are frequently cited – the strategic alliance between the USA and Saudi Arabia, the US-led mili-tary effort to expel Iraqi forces from Kuwait in 1991 and, later, the 2003 invasion of Iraq. Not all these examples carry the same weight insofar as 'petropolitics' alone does not explain US policy-making in the region. For instance, the 2003 war in Iraq cannot be understood without refer-ring to the 'September 11' attacks in 2001 on the USA and the immense significance of the event in convincing the Bush administration to attempt reshaping the region. In this respect, oil did not play a major role and certainly not as much as broader geostrategic concerns.

However, the discovery in the 1930s of Saudi Arabia's 'unparalleled' oil resources laid the foundations for that country's relationship with the USA. Pollack (2002: 78) quotes an unnamed US official in 1944 to the effect that: 'The oil in the region is the greatest single prize in all history'.

In the years that followed, close ties developed between the two coun-tries. By 2012, the USA was importing nearly 1.5 million barrels of Saudi oil per day (Krauss, 2012) although it is worth noting that the US imports around the same amount of oil from Mexico. Oil is not the only factor in the US–Saudi alliance. The two countries have a long-standing security relationship. In 1943, US president Roosevelt declared that the defence of Saudi Arabia was vital to the defence of the United States. In 1951, a permanent US military training mission to the Kingdom was established. When in 1990, Iraqi forces under Saddam Hussein invaded neighbouring Kuwait, then US president George H.W. Bush reiterated that 'the security of Saudi Arabia is vital to US interests and ... to the interests of the Western world'. The USA led a coalition of states to expel the invaders and to protect Saudi Arabia from any possible assault. As Pollack pointed out, while large arms sales to the Kingdom kept American defence contractors production lines open, they had done little to lessen its essential dependence on the USA for defence and security (2002: 84). The subsequent stationing of US troops in Saudi Arabia aroused hostility within the Kingdom, and, by 2003, most US forces were withdrawn. The tensions between the two states were seen by some as supplying a partial if not full explanation for the US invasion and occupation of Iraq in 2003. Jhaveri (2004: 8) argued that the invasion was part of a US strategy to diversify from its dependence on Saudi oil and claimed that to be its objective. However, Bromley proposes a more nuanced view of US policy in which it is seen as using its power to promote its preferred model of the global economy – an increasingly open liberal international order in which, as the leading economy, the USA will be able to secure its needs through trade (2005: 254). Others reject the emphasis on 'petro-politics' and focus instead on mutual misperception as key to understanding US–Iraqi relations in the run-up to the conflict. Iraqi president Saddam Hussein perceived a shared interest between Baghdad and Washington that was not reciprocated. He also saw a misleading analogy with Gaddafi's Libya as a guide to how the USA would deal with Iraq, while overestimating the knowledge and competence of the US intelligence services. US policy-makers, for their part, never understood how Saddam saw Iraq, or its place in the region and in history, and failed to recognize that he was more concerned with the threat from Iran than from the USA. As a result, they formed a 'non-falsifiable' enemy image of Iraq that became the sole explanatory construct for everything that Iraq said and did (Duelfer and Dyson, 2011: 27).

The domestic impact of oil

The domestic impact of oil revenues on the region was transformative. Before the discovery of oil, the major source of government revenue in Saudi Arabia was a tax on pilgrims, supplemented by duties levied on trade or on merchants. Government offices were thinly staffed – there were 182 state employees in the Hijaz in 1930 (Owen and Pamuk, 1998: 80). It was oil revenues that enabled the Saudi state to develop, and a similar claim could be made for states such as the UAE, Qatar, Bahrain and Kuwait. For decades, the main exports of Libya were esparto (a type of grass used to make paper for currency bills) and scrap metal from the weaponry abandoned in the country in the course of World War II (Yergin, 1991: 527). Oil revenues transformed this situation. In 1962, the average income of a Saudi was 40 times higher than in 1957. This rose a further fourteenfold by 1970. In Libya, the impact of oil was even greater. El-Ghoneimy (1998: 56–7) suggests that there is no precedent in human history for the growth in affluence seen in Libya in this period. In less than 25 years, Libya had reached an average annual income of US$7,170, a level of gross national product (GNP) per person that had taken the currently rich industrialized countries 220 years to attain.

Beyond the economic sphere, Herb (1999) sets out six ways in which the emergence of what he calls 'petro-states' altered Arab society. The expansion of the central state led to the displacement of the myriad other clans in Arabian societies that had exercised state power and enjoyed an autonomy that, before oil, was predicated on the weakness of the central state. A new educated class emerged to fill the numerous posts in the new petro-states which demanded technical skill, specialized training or, at least, literacy. The rural populations and, particularly, the nomads settled in the urban agglomerations of Arabia. The military potency of the bedouin collapsed in the face of the newly powerful central state – however, the bedouin were recruited into the new praetorian guards in an effort to create forces that would check the revolutionary ambitions of parts of the middle class. Merchants took up state offices in those bureaucracies dealing with matters of business and state contracts, and did not interfere in the dynasties monopoly of political power. Finally, millions of foreigners came to the oil monarchies to work but did not become citizens and remained 'politically inert' (Herb, 1999: 52–3).

Perhaps the most significant claim for the impact of oil revenues on domestic political dynamics in the MENA is that they have acted as a barrier to the emergence of more representative politics and aided autocracy. This is encapsulated in the notion of the rentier state, which Lisa Anderson has described as 'one of the major contributions' of Middle East studies to political science (1987: 9). A rentier economy is one that relies on substantial external rent – rent, here, being understood as a reward for the ownership of natural resources. In a rentier state, only a few are engaged in the generation of this rent. The majority are only involved in its distribution or utilization (Beblawi, 1990: 85–7). The

Arab oil producers are, therefore, classic rentier states, given the dependence of their economies on oil revenues. The essence of the rentier state paradigm is that access to a non-productive source of income, in the form of 'rents' from the exploitation of oil resources, makes the states of the region less reliant on the extraction of wealth from their populations to finance the state. This breaks the link between taxation and representation. But, just as opposition to unfair taxation contributed to democratization in the West, so the absence of an onerous tax burden helps to explain the failure of populations in rentier states to demand participation (Pripstein Posusney, 2004: 129–30). Since rentier states do not need to tax their populations (or tax them much), they are freed from the accountability to their populations that taxation normally brings. Enjoyment of rents has two further crucial impacts on state–society relations. It increases the capacity of the state to buy off and to repress opposition. Oil revenues also prevent the changes in class structure that have historically been associated with the development of democracy (Herb, 2005: 298). The empirical evidence for all of this is to be seen in the absence of political parties, meaningful elections, or genuinely participatory political life from the major oil producing states of the region. In many respects, the resource curse is alive and well across the region, as the abundance of natural resources prevents sustainable economic development and political liberalization from taking place.

However, while the rentier state paradigm has been extremely influential, it has also been questioned by a wide range of scholars. Okruhlik (1999), for instance, rejects the argument that oil incomes preclude the emergence of meaningful opposition. She points out that, in Saudi Arabia, Kuwait and Bahrain, opposition to incumbent regimes has developed, raising a discrepancy between the expectations generated by the rentier state theory and empirical reality. Gurses (2009) notes that a wide and diverse group of countries from Norway to Malaysia have managed to escape the 'resource curse' to translate natural resource wealth into investment and development. He suggests that it is necessary to move beyond a 'categorical denial' of a positive link between oil wealth and democratization. In early-industrialized countries, state–society relations evolved over centuries, whereas most countries with significant natural wealth came into being in the mid-twentieth century. Finally, Haber and Menaldo (2011) argue that it is necessary to invert the causal relationship between possession of oil resources and the nature of the state. Global oil reserves happen to be concentrated in countries with weak state capacity but this weak capacity preceded the discovery of oil. They conclude that oil reliance 'does not promote dictatorship over the long run' – indeed, the opposite may be true (Haber and Menaldo: 2011).

Key questions

- What is meant by the term 'political economy'?
- What non-oil factors are important for the political economy of the MENA?
- How has oil influenced political development in the MENA?
- What is a 'rentier state' and how relevant is this to the MENA?

Further reading

Guazzone, Laura and Daniela Pioppi (2009). *The Arab State and Neo-liberal Globalization. The Restructuring of State Power in the Middle East*, New York: Ithaca Press.

Haddad, Bassam (2011). *Business Networks in Syria: The Political Economy of Authoritarian Resilience*, Stanford: Stanford University Press.

Hertog, Steffan (2011). *Princes, Brokers and Bureaucrats: Oil and the State in Saudi Arabia*, Cornell University Press.

Hvidt, Martin (2009). 'The Dubai model: an outline of key development-process elements in Dubai', *International Journal of Middle East Studies*, 41(3): 397–418.

Peters, Ann Mariel and Peter Moore (2009). 'Beyond boom and bust: external rents, durable authoritarianism and institutional adaptation in the Hashemite Kingdom of Jordan', *Studies in Comparative International Development*, 44(3): 256–85.

Ross, Michael (2012). *The Oil Curse: How Petroleum Wealth Shapes the Development of Nations*, Princeton: Princeton University Press.

Twomey, Michael (2006). 'Statistical tables and comments', in Camron Michael Amin, Benjamin C. Fortna and Elizabeth B. Frierson (eds), *The Modern Middle East: A Sourcebook for History*, Oxford: Oxford University Press.

Online resources

Abdih, Yasser, Adolfo Barajas, Ralph Chami and Christian Ebeke (2012). 'Remittances channel and fiscal impact in the Middle East, North Africa and Central Asia – IMF Working Paper', *International Monetary Fund*, available at www.imf.org/external/pubs/ft/wp/2012/wp12104.pdf.

Corm, Georges (2008). 'Labor migration in the Middle East and North Africa a view from the region', *World Bank*, available at http://siteresources.worldbank.org/INTMENA/Resources/SF_background-3.pdf.

Haber, Stephen and Victor Menaldo (2011). 'Do natural resources fuel authoritarianism? A reappraisal of the resource curse', *American Political Science Review*, 105(1): 1–26.

The Prize – an eight part series adapted from Daniel Yergin's book *The Prize: The Epic Quest for Oil, Money and Power*, available on YouTube.

Chapter 5

Institutions, Parties and Elections

The Arab uprisings in 2011 refocused attention on the importance of the institutional set-up of the countries of the MENA region, particularly when it began to appear that the Arab republics were more vulnerable than monarchies to potential regime change (Gause and Yom, 2012). The institutional differences between republics and monarchies are significant in explaining different national trajectories between countries in the region and this chapter will return to them to underline the influence of institutions on the behaviour of political and social actors. However, these differences have been discussed extensively and satisfactorily elsewhere (for example, Pratt, 2007), including in Chapters 2 and 3 of this volume. Therefore, this chapter will focus more specifically on an understudied area of Middle East politics that is becoming increasingly relevant – namely, party politics and elections. This is not to suggest that political parties have become crucial actors in the politics of the region overnight. But there are at least three factors that should be considered before they are dismissed as irrelevant.

First, one of the strategies authoritarian leaders employed to upgrade their rule to satisfy international pressures consisted of creating – or, in some cases strengthening, however superficially – the role played by political parties in the system. In some cases, such as Morocco or Egypt, political parties had always been active to some extent and functioned as legitimizing tools for regimes. In other cases, multiparty politics was either banned or extremely circumscribed. Upgraded authoritarianism led to a 'rediscovery' of political parties, which were now allowed to operate openly, channel public debates and, crucially, compete in elections. As a consequence, parties emerged or re-emerged during the 1990s and 2000s across the region. It is important to analyze what their return to the scene, even in the context of authoritarian oversight, has meant for both the parties themselves and for society more broadly.

Second, elections have consistently taken place across the region since the 1990s, often characterized by strong party and candidate competition. Ultimately, of course, the vast majority of these elections were considered meaningless because the results were either rigged or irrelevant, in the sense that no meaningful political change issued from them. However, a growing literature on elections under authoritarianism, while acknowledging their limitations, convincingly argues that they were important because of what they had to say about state–society relations, mechanisms of transmission of public debates and the allocation of patronage.

Finally, one should not forget that party politics and elections are genuinely important in the democratic and quasi-democratic systems in the region, as attested by the cases of Israel, Turkey and, to a limited extent, Lebanon and Iran.

Monarchies versus republics

As was outlined in Chapter 2, broadly speaking, the post-colonial order saw the emergence of two distinct types of system of government in countries in the region. Some of the new independent countries became monarchies. The surviving monarchies in the region are Morocco, Jordan, Saudi Arabia, Kuwait, Bahrain, Qatar, Oman and the seven members of the UAE (Abu Dhabi, Dubai, Sharjah, Ajman, Umm al-Qawain, Ras al-Khaimah, Fujairah); others became republics, these including Egypt, Tunisia, Libya, Iraq, Syria and Yemen. The institutions and legitimizing ideology differed markedly between the two distinct types of system, leading to the formation and subsequent evolution of different regime types. But, while the distinction between republics and monarchies is crucial, sub-types exist in both categories.

For example, in relation to monarchies, one can think of the significant differences that exist between Morocco and Jordan on the one hand, and the monarchies of the Gulf on the other. First, the level of religious legitimacy of the monarchs differs sharply and has implications for the institutions of governance. For instance, the Moroccan king enjoys the title of Commander of the Faithful because of his 'lineage' going back to the Prophet and his role as interpreter of Maliki religious precepts. In this respect, the notion of religious legitimacy to rule is hard to challenge, leaving opposition groups with the difficult task of articulating how he might be an illegitimate rule from a doctrinal standpoint. His role as Commander of the Faithful also gives the monarch the opportunity to adjudicate on complex and controversial matters when religious interpretation is required.

Recourse to religious legitimacy on the part of the royal families of the Gulf is quite different. In fact, particularly in Saudi Arabia, there is a mutual legitimacy between the royals (the political rulers) and the religious scholars. As studies of the creation of the Saudi state emphasize, it is the long-standing alliance between the al-Saud family and that of the conservative religious reformer Muhammad Ibn Abd al-Wahhab that constitutes the fundamental pillar of legitimacy of the state (Menoret,

2005). This alliance first developed in the mid-eighteenth century and has persisted in various forms. Indeed, Al-Rasheed suggests that Wahhabism provides the raison d'etre of the ruling family (2010: 237). This implies that the al-Saud do not possess religious legitimacy per se but, rather, that it has been bestowed on them by the religious class of scholars who have an interest in seeing their brand of religiosity enforced in the country. The al-Saud are therefore only, and controversially so, the guardians of the holy places. A similar argument can be made for many other smaller Gulf monarchies.

The different bases on which religious legitimacy rests leads to another significant point of divergence within monarchies. The security from effective challenge, which its religious role afforded to the Moroccan monarchy, gave it scope for the development of a partly-free political arena, characterized by a rather lively party system, although pressure from nationalists after independence also played a part in this. In this system, the king plays the role of arbiter and balancer. King Hassan himself described the role as being 'above political parties' such that he could 'judge and sanction' with complete impartiality (Herb, 1999: 223). The Jordanian political system, in which the royal family asserts a claim of direct descent from the prophet Muhammad, is somewhat similar, as political parties compete, under authoritarian constraints, for political office. For the first three decades of his reign, King Hussein of Jordan ruled more or less absolutely but, when threatened by rioting that followed the imposition of IMF-inspired reforms in 1989, he opted for controlled political liberalization. Following elections, the King convened a national conference to draft a pact which would set out 'the rules of the game' – the King would respect political pluralism and multiparty political life while the opposition would acknowledge the pre-eminent place of the King in the political system (Herb, 1999: 226–7). Thus, while both the Moroccan and Jordanian kings retain strong executive powers and assume the role of arbiters of the political system, they also allow for the development of party political life. This is not the case in Saudi Arabia and in the other Gulf monarchies where there are no real political parties to speak of and all decision-making takes place within the 'family' (Herb, 1999). The exception is Kuwait where a constitution and an elected assembly temper monarchical power to some extent (Al-Awadi, 2014).

Thus, it is clear that the monarchies are quite different from one other in the ways in which they function, and allocate duties and rights to citizens. As a result, dynamics of opposition are also different because the formal and informal institutions that characterize regimes influence how they engage in practice. In monarchies that are 'partly' free, where there is a degree of political electoral competition and where constitutions make provision for how the game of politics is to be conducted, genuine opposition politics is permitted, and even encouraged, because it takes place within a framework that does not lend itself to extra-institutional challenges to the regime. In monarchies that are politically closed, the nature of opposition politics is rather different and the pluralism that exists in society is not reflected institutionally, leading to the widespread suppression of such pluralism. However, this exposes 'closed' monarchies to problematic and potentially violent challenges, although the redistribution of rents (as discussed in Chapter 4) and the centrality of informal politics have, so far, prevented this from occurring on a scale that genuinely threatens regimes.

With regard to the republics, there are also several differences worth noting. As we mentioned in Chapter 2, after independence many of the Arab republics saw the military occupy the most prominent political position in driving economic and social development. While presidents became 'civilians', the military remained the most important institution in many MENA countries, although single parties also had a central role, particularly functioning as 'transmissions belts' to society of what the leadership decided behind closed doors. In this respect, it has always been somewhat problematic to categorize Arab republics with precision. Before the Arab Awakening, the original radical socialist republics had already mutated into very different regime types. The progressive retreat of the army from direct involvement in politics, as we will see in greater detail in Chapter 9, together with the need for regimes to present a more pluralistic image abroad, contributed greatly to this mutation. In addition, whereas the early political and economic radicalism of the republics was also a function of the attraction of the Soviet model of development, by the late 1980s this model was completely discredited. In turn, many of the radical republics were effectively obliged to embrace the market economy and subscribe, if only rhetorically and with varying degrees of enthusiasm, to the 'victorious' liberal-democratic model. In any case, military backed and single-party regimes changed their formal institutional set-up quite dramatically in the 1990s and 2000s.

Party politics and elections

Party politics and political parties in the MENA region do not function in the same way as in established democracies. After independence, multi-party politics was seen as detrimental to the goal of development because it was inherently divisive at a time when 'the people' had to be united in their national developmental effort. As discussed, the conservative monarchies of the Gulf did not have political parties, while in the republics they disappeared very quickly once the military took over the political leadership. Nasser wrote in 1955 that political parties had joined in 'despotic rule contrary to the interests of the nation' and therefore it was necessary to dissolve them (Nasser, 1955: 203). This does not mean that parties did not exist; indeed, the opposite is true. A significant number of political parties emerged across the Arab world, but they were for the most part proscribed and persecuted because ruling parties, whether the Tunisian Neo-Destour (later the RCD), the Algerian FLN, the Baath Party in Syria and Iraq, or the NDP in Egypt, monopolized the political system. The marginalization of parties – and, with time, even the single party – was also due to the emergent presidentialism of the republics. Thus, by the late 1980s the region had monarchies with executive monarchs and little or no party politics, and republics with presidents – former military men usually – utilizing the single party of the state in an increasingly personalized manner. By the 2000s, the concepts of hybrid regimes (Diamond, 2002) or liberalized autocracies (Brumberg, 2002b) better captured the institutional reality of most countries in the Arab world where elections – and the participation of political parties – had become routine.

Thus, political parties were an intrinsic part of the political system across the region and, in some cases, highly involved in policy-making, even if, as in most MENA countries, they are not the central actors in the process (Storm, 2013). Broadly speaking, though, the literature on Arab politics has tended to neglect political parties and there are very few detailed studies about how they function, the nature of their specific roles, what kind of anchoring they have in society, their membership and their policy preferences. There are three reasons for this neglect. First, political parties have traditionally been seen as instruments controlled by ruling élites to provide the facade of democratization for external consumption. In this respect, it should be highlighted that party political life, while much freer than in the past, is still very much straitjacketed by authoritarian constraints. A few examples suffice to illustrate this point. On coming to power in 1987, President Ben Ali of Tunisia needed to send the message that he was intent on liberalizing the political system. He opened up competition for parliament to a number of political parties that had been banned under his predecessor. While the Islamist *Ennahda* party was not legalized, its members were permitted to contest elections as independents. In the general election of 1989, *Ennahda* candidates won up to 20 per cent of the vote. However, the nature of the electoral system, combined with regime control of the media and other interference in the electoral process, meant that the ruling RCD party won every seat in parliament. Moreover, the strength of the potential threat to the regime from the organized Islamist opposition led to a crackdown on *Ennahda* and a slide back into authoritarianism for Tunisia (Alexander, 1997). Thereafter, political life was characterized by a tame and controlled multiparty system in which the other parties in the competition simply provided the impression of pluralism. Over time, their participation became routine.

Algeria has followed a similar path since the 1990s, as regular elections in a multiparty system were employed to demonstrate that the country was returning to normality after the military coup of 1992. However, what followed has been described as neither a fully-fledged authoritarian state, nor a viable democracy but a 'facade democracy' in which even procedural democratic rights have not been attained. Instead, political life has been characterized by limitations on freedom of assembly and association, as well as judicial harassment of the media, while elections have been marred by irregularities. Neither do the legal opposition parties enjoy popular credibility. With the suppression of the Islamist FIS (see page 66) and the neutralization of the oldest opposition party, the *Front des Forces Socialistes* (Socialist Forces Front) (FFS) no genuine opposition party remained (Zoubir and Aghrout, 2012).

In Jordan, King Hussein embarked on a process of political liberalization in 1989 that saw the holding of full national legislative elections. Although a ban on political parties remained in place, representatives of 'underground' parties could run as independents, while the Muslim Brotherhood was able to put candidates forward as it was considered a charitable organization and not a party. Despite the efforts of the regime to distort the electoral system in its favour, Islamist and other candidates opposed to the pro-Western foreign policy of the King won a substantial share of the vote. For the subsequent election in 1993, and sensitive to criticism of Jordan's engagement with the US-sponsored 'peace process', the King made substantial changes to the electoral system and the parliament that resulted had a diminished opposition presence (Pripstein Posusney, 2005: 96–7). The succession of Hussein's son, Abdullah, raised hopes of a more democratic party-based political system in the country. However, Hamid has argued that the founding institution of the state – the Hashemite monarchy – is the most significant impediment to democracy, since, for as long as the monarchy retains both its hegemonic position and its many constitutionally guaranteed prerogatives, substantial reform will remain unlikely (2010: 122).

Such top-down constraints on the behaviour of political parties suggested that studying them would provide little insight into political life apart from confirmation that they acted as instruments of authoritarian upgrading.

The second reason for their neglect is the assumption in the literature that they simply serve as clientelistic institutions and compete not for power but for patronage (Lust, 2006). The argument is that while competitive elections do take place, all citizens are aware that parties do not actually hold the real levers of power and have very little influence in policy-making. But, the parties and their elected officials do have access, to varying degrees, to state resources, which can then be redistributed and employed to satisfy the needs of specific constituencies. For example, writing of Yemen, Longley Alley noted that most prominent élites, whether aligned with the ruling party or members of the formal opposition, have access to some form of patronage and therefore have an interest in maintaining the status quo (2010: 393). As clientelistic relations develop, the study of parties and elections allows us to examine how and to whom patronage is distributed. But there is very little of intrinsic value in studying the policy positions of parties or their links to society, because they only serve patronage functions. In part, this explains why a number of parties prefer to run in rigged elections, thereby validating the legitimacy of the system. A clear consequence of this is the fact that opposition parties and parliamentary institutions enjoy little popular confidence. Zoubir and Aghrout (2012: 67) note a poll of 2012 which showed that 75 per cent of Algerians had no trust in parliament, while a recent poll in 12 of Yemen's governorates revealed that roughly 35 per cent of respondents held parties to be unimportant, and 47 per cent had no confidence in them at all (Yemen Polling Centre, 2010).

The final reason for the relative neglect of political parties in the literature is related to the almost overwhelming focus on Islamist parties, their origins, history, beliefs and, crucially, their potential role in democratization. While there is little doubt that they constitute the most popular parties in the region, the almost exclusive attention paid to them leads, in turn, to the neglect of wider party politics and the absence of analysis of what non-Islamist parties stand for or how they behave. Islamist parties have, of course, participated in elections across the region when the option has been available to them. They have done so to remain relevant and to be ready to play a more meaningful role, should the opportunity arise. However, the same could be said of other political parties, but these are significantly under-examined.

The relative paucity of studies on Arab political parties and how they interact with each other and with the system should not detract from the importance of looking at the institutional rules framing their activities. The problem is that the traditional tools of comparative politics may not be very helpful for this task. Nevertheless, it is important to account for the variety of forms of government and electoral systems because a growing literature suggests that they are crucial in understanding how power is maintained and, by implication, how it could be challenged (Gandhi, 2008).

First and foremost, it should be noted that the vast majority of Arab states have always had a very strong executive, enjoying significant powers. As discussed earlier, in the monarchies such powers are held by the monarch and transmitted through hereditary rule, whereas in the republics it is presidents who have enjoyed a quasi-monopoly of executive power. These powers usually stem from highly centralizing constitutional provisions that allow the executive to hold sway both over the legislature and the judiciary. Thus, the primary and predominant role of the executive was enshrined in law, adding formal powers to the informal powers that presidents and monarchs already enjoyed, whether because of their prior membership of the armed forces, their religious legitimacy, or their ties with key constituencies. It is precisely in the area of executive powers that both monarchs and presidents had to re-invent their roles in order to renew their political legitimacy.

Republics

One of the ways in which this renewal of legitimacy was achieved was the transformation of some systems from presidential systems to semi-presidential ones (Box 5.1 analyses Tunisian reforms in detail). In established democracies, the president and the legislature play a complex game of checks and balances, which largely depends on the way in which the party system is structured. In the Arab world, presidential forms of government entrenched authoritarianism. In order to promote increased contestation, a number of countries introduced constitutional reforms to make the system more semi-presidential. This entailed the creation of the post of prime minister and a degree of power sharing with the president – as occurred, for instance, in Tunisia and Palestine. The problem, as can immediately be seen, is that in authoritarian systems where there is either a single party – or, at the very least a dominant party – such reforms do not make much difference.

In Egypt, the accession to the presidency of Anwar al-Sadat in 1970 was followed, in 1976, by the splitting of the Arab Socialist Union (ASU) into three platforms reflecting the ideological orientations of left, right and centre. The following year, Sadat established the National Democratic Party (NDP) and, prior to the 2011 uprising, there was a proliferation of political parties. However, power remained with the NDP and the president. Elections were conducted to ensure large parliamentary majorities for the ruling party, while the activities of other parties remained circumscribed. These parties operated under severe restrictions and were relegated to a playing ground 'demarcated by the regime' and insulated from decision-making 'with an efficiency that can hardly have been found else-

Box 5.1   Tunisia's institutional reforms before the uprising

Tunisia is paradigmatic of the ways in which the presidential system mutated into a semi-presidential one without any genuine impact on where power resided. From 1957 until 1969, Tunisia was a nominal presidential system with the 'father of the country' Habib Bourguiba holding sway over the whole political system. The president enjoyed legislative initiative, prepared the budget, appointed all sorts of officials and had wide-ranging powers of decree. In 1969, the constitution was changed in order to create the post of prime minister. But the substance of governance did not change because the legislature remained subordinate to presidential powers. In many ways, this did not create a problem because the legislature was dominated by the single-party system. When multiparty politics was reintroduced in 1987, the single party simply became the dominant party. The other parties in the system could not compete fairly with it because the president, and leader of the dominant party, controlled the state machine and therefore ensured that electoral results were always favourable to him. Thus, the succession from Bourguiba to Ben Ali did not alter the fundamentals of the system, although the institutions – constitution, electoral system and creation of a senate – did change substantially.

Source: Sujit Choudhry and Richard Stacey (2013). 'Semi-presidentialism as a form of government: lessons for Tunisia', Center for Constitutional Transitions. Available at: http://www.yemenintransition. com/YetraCpanl/artImge/Semi-Presidentialism%20as%20a%20Form%20of%20Government%20-% 20Lessons%20for%20Tunisia.pdf.

where in the world' (Kienle, 1998: 220). In 2005, the Egyptian parliament, under pressure from an emerging domestic movement for political reform, as well as from outside actors such as the United States and the European Union, passed a number of laws relating to political participation. These included a constitutional amendment that provided for the direct election of the president. For the first time, opposition parties could, under certain circumstances, put an alternative candidate on the ballot paper. In elections held in September 2005 under the newly reformed system, Mubarak comfortably won with 89 per cent of votes cast against 8 per cent for his nearest rival, Ayman Nour of the *Ghad* (Tomorrow) Party. However, any expectations of a genuine political opening were dashed when, in December 2005, Nour was jailed for five years having been convicted of forging signatures to register his political party. The charge was widely believed to have been trumped up by the regime in order to discredit the only candidate to offer a genuine challenge to Mubarak's grip on the presidential office (Durac, 2009: 80).

The presidentialization of politics has, therefore, helped to marginalize political parties even further across the Arab world. But it should be noted that in Algeria in 1991, in Palestine in 2006, and in Egypt (see

Box 5.2, for a detailed account of the elections in 2011–12) and Tunisia in 2011, we have had free and fair elections in which parties of all ideological persuasions participated and in which citizens also took part in significant numbers, which suggests that the removal of authoritarian constraints provides a crucial incentive for both parties and citizens to become involved in electoral politics. In such circumstances, the parties do carry out the functions for which they are established. The outcome of such elections has been quite clear: Islamist parties are by far the most popular and enjoy widespread support in all sectors of the population. The holding of genuinely competitive elections constitutes a significant event and electoral results can provide major insights into party politics and society, even in cases where such elections are simply a one-off, as in Algeria and Egypt. In the Algerian case of 1991–2, it became apparent, for instance, that the ruling party (the FLN) had lost most of its credibility, particularly among those who were young enough not to be swayed by the claim of historical legitimacy the party had for its role in securing the country's independence. The massive loss of support for the ruling party, far more than FLN leaders were willing to contemplate, provides the first insight of elections of this type – namely, the wide disconnect between rulers – and what they think their popular support is – and the ruled. A similar insight could be derived from the 2006 Palestinian elections, which saw voters punish the ruling Fatah in favour of Hamas. A second insight that can be drawn from the open electoral contests is that voters rewarding Islamist parties with their preference might do so more out of programmatic promises regarding the economy than for reasons based in religion. The economic aspect of voting for the Brotherhood in Egypt in the 2011–12 elections is, for instance, highlighted by Tarek Masoud (2014) in his work to explain the outcome of the elections. This emerges also in the context of the Algerian elections of 1991–2, when the FIS enjoyed the 'benefit of the doubt' in terms of its ability to better manage the economy, which the FLN had dealt with badly. Even in Palestine, where the national question remains central, Hamas tended to play down its religisosity to focus instead on their ability to manage public funds and public institutions. A third insight is that political parties in the Arab world operating in a free environment are more than capable of running well-oiled and organized electoral campaigns, putting to rest the notion that party politics is somehow alien to the region.

Monarchies

In the monarchies of Jordan, Morocco and Kuwait also, constitutional reforms have been undertaken over time with the specific objective of

Box 5.2   The 2011–12 parliamentary elections in Egypt

Despite the contested narrative of the parliamentary elections – either the highest point of the revolution and the beginning of the construction of a new system, or a ruse to demobilize protestors and facilitate the army's takeover – it is beyond doubt that all sorts of political parties and candidates took such elections seriously, although a number of parties opted for a boycott. The results of the elections saw the success of the coalition called Democratic Alliance for Egypt, whose pillar was the Freedom and Justice Party created ad hoc by the Muslim Brotherhood. The alliance took 37.5 per cent of the votes and 235 seats out of 508. The Islamist Bloc, led by the newly created al-Nour party, came in second place with 27.8 per cent of the votes and took 123 seats. The liberal party al-Wafd came in third with 9.2 per cent of the votes and took 38 seats, closely followed by the Egyptian Bloc with 34 seats. The victory of the two rival Islamist alliances was particularly problematic for a set of domestic and international actors, but seemed to reflect the genuine will of ordinary Egyptians. It is interesting to note that Parliament is composed of 508 seats, 498 elected and 10 appointed. The 498 seats up for grabs were allocated in part through a system of proportional representation (two thirds of the total), and in part through individual candidacy races (one third of the total).

Source: Hesham Sellam (ed.) (2013). *Egypt's Parliamentary Elections. 2011–2012: A Critical Guide to a Changing Political Arena*, Washington: DC: Tadween Publishing.

turning the monarchs into arbiters of a game where parties would nominally exercise power while, in reality, beholden to monarchical sanction. In these settings, there is a degree of competition between political parties that accept the primacy of the monarchy and its pre-eminent role in the political system. Elections are usually reasonably fair, not least because participants agree to work within the system and implicitly agree not to challenge the monarchy.

For example, Jordan, formally speaking, is a constitutional monarchy. There is a bicameral parliament – a 40-member House of Notables, appointed by the king, and an 80-member House of Deputies, elected by universal suffrage. However, real power resides with the king, who is constitutionally empowered to appoint the prime minister and may dismiss him. The king also appoints and may dismiss ministers, and can dissolve both houses of parliament. He can issue royal decrees that are not subject to parliamentary oversight and can issue legislation through the cabinet if the parliament is not sitting or has been dissolved. Political parties are virtually non-existent and the Islamic Action Front (IAF) is the only viable opposition force. Legislation on political parties in 2007 transferred oversight of party political activities to the Ministry of the Interior. The result of all of this, according to former Jordanian Foreign Minister Marwan Muasher (2011), is that parliaments have been weak and unrepresentative. Muasher argues that the election law has been structurally designed to prevent the development of a strong parliament that is capable of exercising oversight.

A similar situation prevails in Morocco and Kuwait. Morocco is technically a constitutional monarchy in which the king has the right to appoint the prime minister and to appoint and remove members of the cabinet. While the constitution provides for political parties to participate in the representation of the country's citizens, they do not have any special functions. They can build coalitions but ultimate power remains with the king. Kuwait, likewise, is a constitutional monarchy with a parliamentary system but one in which the monarch enjoys a privileged position. The emir appoints the prime minister and approves the cabinet, which is appointed by the prime minister. The formation of political parties is proscribed but there are a number of political groups that act as de facto parties and several voting blocs in the Assembly, for example, tribal groups, Shiite activists and secular liberals. Kuwait was the first country in the Gulf to have an elected parliament. However, while parliament enjoys greater powers than other elected bodies in the Gulf, ultimate power resides with the ruling family and parliament has been dissolved five times since 2006.

Thus, even in the reformed monarchies, the monarch retains significant executive powers and can dictate policy guidelines for the government, which is therefore quite constrained in what it can and cannot do. These constraints permit the monarch to remain aloof from the political squabbles that characterize legislative politics. Second, political parties are nominally in charge but, with very few real powers available to them, they are exposed to public criticism for whatever problems follow from the policies that they pursue. The monarch, on the other hand, can legitimately claim that he appointed the prime minister, on the basis of election results, and therefore is not responsible for the government's failings.

The question arises then as to why political parties would accept participating in such systems; the answers vary from party to party. Some are 'royal creations' and are simply used as props by the monarch to do his bidding in the legislature and in government. Others genuinely believe that they can have a degree of influence in specific policy sectors. For instance, some Islamist parties consider that their presence in the legislature can either block liberal legislation with which they do not agree or promote conservative laws about which they care deeply. Other parties do not wish to fade into complete irrelevance and hold the hope that, in the event of radical political change, their political experience might place them in a privileged position. However, as we have seen, irrespective of the reasons why many political parties seem to legitimate authoritarian or semi-authoritarian regimes, their standing in society is low, as is trust in them on the part of ordinary citizens.

Institutions, parties and elections in the MENA democracies and quasi-democracies

Even with the enactment of reforms in recent decades, parties and elections have continued to play a circumscribed role in much of the MENA region, at least prior to the uprisings of 2011. The situation is very different in four countries where electoral politics has played, and continues to play, a highly significant role. Israel and Turkey are the only two states that have a claim to being fully functioning democracies in the region. In two others, Lebanon and Iran, democratic institutions are important despite the fact that significant (if different in each case) qualifications attach to any claim of truly democratic legitimacy.

Israel has what is generally considered the most democratic political system in the MENA. However, it has been argued that the asserted 'Jewish and democratic' nature of the state constitutes a diminution of its claim to being a full democracy. Certainly, the country has a functioning democratic multiparty system in which the parliament, the Knesset, plays a vastly more significant role than in any of the Arab states. Israel has adopted a proportional electoral system. Voters cast their ballots for party lists rather than for individual candidates. Before elections, parties hold internal elections, which determine the order in which candidates will occupy any seats the party might win. For example, if a party won 110 seats, then the first 10 names on the list would take up those seats in parliament. The Knesset appoints the prime minister and also has the power to remove the president. The system is highly proportional – parties that gain more than 2 per cent of the overall vote gain representation in the Knesset (in Turkey, by contrast, the threshold for representation in parliament is 10 per cent). No party has ever secured a majority of seats and governments have consisted of coalitions of parties. As a result, critics argue that smaller parties have tended to enjoy a disproportionate influence in political life (Kaplan and Friedman, 2009).

In the three decades that followed the establishment of the state of Israel in 1948, political life was dominated by the socialist party, Mapai, and later the Labour Party, into which Mapai merged. All prime ministers and senior ministers came from these parties. However, in the 1977 elections the government suffered a humiliating defeat, as its representation in the Knesset fell by 19 seats and Likud, a coalition of different components, emerged as the largest party and its leader, Menachem Begin, became prime minister. Likud retained power in elections four years later. However, elections in 1984, following the government's loss of a vote of confidence in the Knesset, led to no clear winner. Eventually, Labour and Likud agreed on a government of national unity, which featured a rotation of the office of prime minister between Labour's Shimon Peres and Likud's Yitzhak Shamir. A further national unity government in January 1989 lasted just over one year. Likud and Labour continued to dominate political life until the emergence of a third major force in Israeli politics. Divisions within his Likud party prompted its leader, Ariel Sharon, to leave and establish the Kadima ('Forward') party. The party entered power in coalition with Labour in 2006. However, in recent years, Likud has once more emerged as the strongest party in Israeli politics. Its current leader, Benjamin Netanyahu, has been prime minister since 2009 and secured re-election in 2013 with the support of a number of smaller parties. As in other established democracies, Israel has also seen the rise of increasingly populist political parties that enjoy significant support in specific constituencies, as the case of Shas detailed in Box 5.3 explains. In addition, it should be highlighted that religious parties also play a crucial role in Israeli politics and are often necessary in the formation of government coalitions.

However, while Israel is broadly acknowledged as having the most consolidated democracy in the MENA, it has been argued that democracy in Israel 'falls short of the major Western civic democracies' (Smooha, 2002: 478). Smooha focuses on Israel's characterization as a 'Jewish and democratic' state. Although its Arab citizens are granted both individual and collective rights, nonetheless, Arab rights are incomplete and not properly protected. Arab Israelis are regarded as potentially disloyal to the state, and are placed under security and political control. They are exempted from military service and excluded from other security forces, although exceptions are made for the small Druze and Bedouin populations. The state retains 'unlimited powers to suspend civil rights in order to detect and prevent security infractions' and denies Arab cultural autonomy for fear it may be misused to organize against the state (Smooha, 2002: 489). Smooha concludes that Israel, is, as a result, best considered as an ethic democracy, based on Jewish and Zionist hegemony and on structural subordination of its Arab minority (Smooha, 2002: 497). However, it should also be underlined that the Arab minority in Israel enjoys full political rights and a number of Arab political parties are represented in the Knesset. Moreover, securing the support of Arab voters has been crucial for Israeli politicians in the past, as was the case with former Prime Minister Ehud Barak.

Box 5.3   Shas and elections in Israel

One of the most interesting aspects of electoral politics in Israel is the presence of overtly religious parties participating in democratic politics. Far from being an exclusive trait of Arab political regimes, religion plays a prominent role in Israeli politics and very few parties can claim to have been as influential as Shas over the last three decades. As a response to the growing dissatisfaction of religious Sephardic Jews with the political and social system in Israel, which seemed to be dominated by Askhenazi Jews of European extraction, Chief Rabbi Rav Ovadiah Yosef set up a political party in 1984 with the objectives of introducing religious laws as the foundation of the state of Israel, and of ending discrimination and the social exclusion of Sephardic Jews. The party has been a prominent political actor since its foundation and was part of numerous government coalitions, as it often was the king-maker of Israeli politics with the power to decide which way to ally itself and secure as many policy concessions as possible. While the party never had more than 17 seats in Parliament – in the 2013 elections, it obtained 11 seats and currently sits in opposition – it can claim to have achieved considerable successes during its time in power, although it never managed to see the intro- duction of religious law as the legal framework of the country. Its hard stance on the conflict with the Palestinians has been evident, as are its usually successful attempts to deliver better socio-economic services to its constituency of refer- ence, the ultra-orthodox Sephardic Jews.

Concerns have also been expressed about the militarization of Israeli politics. Since 1955, retired military officers have served as ministers and, since the 1970s, the rate of membership of retired officers in government remained at around 15 per cent between the 1960s and the early 2000s. Four retired officers – Yitzhak Rabin, Ehud Barak, Ariel Sharon and Benjamin Netanyahu – have served as prime minister. However, as Goldberg notes, while this has raised fears of the development of a 'military' democracy, in Israel retired officers who enter politics tend to do so as individuals and do not behave in an organized manner, as has been the case elsewhere in the region. Generals in the same party do not necessarily cooperate with one another and, sometimes, compete. Goldberg (2006: 392) gives the example of the 1977 government of Menachem Begin in which Ariel Sharon and Ezer Weizman, both retired officers, held ministerial positions. Weizman moved increasingly in favour of peace with Egypt, while Sharon was one of the leaders of the hawkish bloc in government.

The situation in Israel may be contrasted with that of Turkey where the army, as an institution (as opposed to individual officers), has played a persistent and influential role in political life. The military intervened to remove elected civilian governments in 1960, 1971 and 1980, while it also engineered the so-called soft coup of 1997 against the Islamist party that had won the elections. However, each time the military intervened, there was a relatively swift transition to democracy, suggesting that there was no intent to create a lasting military regime as has happened in many states in the MENA. Turkey has experienced what Ulusoy (2014: 181) has described as a 'long transition' to democratic rule where democratic practice, pluralistic party politics and authoritarianism have gone hand-in-hand since the end of World War II. In the 1930s, the political system was consolidated as a single party regime which recognized only one form of identity: Turkish. After a shift to multiparty rule, the first truly competitive elections took place in July 1946. The elections were won by the Republican People's Party (RPP), which was associated with the founding father of modern Turkey, Kemal Ataturk. The RPP won 396 seats in parliament as opposed to the 62 won by the opposition Democratic Party (DP). Independents won some 7 seats. However, the political landscape remained controlled. While inter-élite competition was permitted, certain groups were excluded from the political arena – communists, socialists, minorities and religious parties (Ulusoy, 2014: 186). Following changes to the electoral system, the DP won parliamentary elections in 1950, 1954 and 1957.

Ulusoy suggests that, after the introduction of multiparty politics in the mid-1940s, the civil and military bureaucracy maintained supremacy through military interventions whenever they believed that political élites were deviating from the founding principles of the state. The military coup of 1960 followed this logic, as it was seen as an attempt to restore Kemalist hegemony in response to the persistent success of the DP in the 1950s. The coup produced what many see as the country's most liberal constitution, but it also saw a crackdown on political activism (Park, 2012: 59). In 1961, the leadership of the DP, including Adnan Menderes, who had held the office of prime minister from 1950 to 1960, was tried on a variety of charges, including criminal behaviour, corruption and violations of the constitution. Hundreds were convicted and three, including Menderes, were executed in September.

Despite the attempt to crack down on the DP, the elections that followed the coup saw a strong showing for the Justice Party (JP), led by Suleyman Demirel and a successor to the DP, which entered into coalition with the Kemalist RPP. Demirel, in turn, was forced from power by the military coup of 1971. The 1970s saw a number of coalition governments, not least because a system based on proportional representation had been introduced after the 1960 coup.

A significant feature of Turkish politics in the 1970s was the emergence of Islamic political parties although Islamic political ideology, and Islamist actors had been incorporated into the system previously through the DP and the JP. The National Order Party was the first Islamist party, established by Necmettin Erbakan, in 1970. It was banned in 1971. Erbakan went on to found the National Salvation Party, which won 48 seats in the 550 seat parliament in the elections of 1973 and subsequently entered into coalition government with the RPP. This proved short-lived but the party was part of coalition governments again in 1975 and 1977. Increasing levels of political violence in the country, particularly between left- and right-wing forces brought the military back into political life. The 1980 coup saw a crackdown on leftists, extreme nationalists and Islamists. After the coup all existing parties were banned. The electoral law was then changed so that the largest parties received large bonuses in terms of representation in parliament. The Motherland Party, under the leadership of Turgut Ozal, emerged as the dominant party. Ozal propagated a 'Turkish-Islamic' synthesis as the new ideological framework of the state. This synthesis represented an attempt to merge Sunni Islam with Turkish nationalism. A return to multiparty politics saw the re-emergence of Islamist representation, as well as other political actors. The *Refah* or Welfare Party (RP) under the leadership of Erbakan emerged as a significant force. It won local elections in Ankara and Istanbul in 1994 and then won 21.8 per cent of the vote in general elections the next year. The party entered government in coalition with the True Path Party (led by Demirel) and Erbakan became Turkey's first Islamist prime minister.

The rise of Islamist forces drew a response from secularist elements in the armed forces. This resulted in the so-called 'postmodern' coup of 28 February 1997 when, at a meeting of the National Security Council, a group of Kemalist generals presented Erbakan with an 18-point programme designed to counter 'radical' Islam. Erbakan was forced to resign; his party was forced out of government and subsequently banned by the Constitutional Court. In anticipation of the ban, leading figures in the RP established the Virtue Party but this, too, was banned in 2001. However, repeat attempts to prevent Islamist parties from gaining power in Turkey had limited success. When another coalition government collapsed in 2002 over the question of reforms required by the European Union of Turkey in relation to the process of seeking membership, a new party, the Party of Justice and Development (AKP) came to power. The new party, led by a former leading member of the Welfare Party, Recep Tayip Erdogan, characterized itself as a conservative and democratic organization, rather than Islamist. It won 34.3 per cent of the vote which, under the Turkish electoral system, gave it 363 seats out of 550 in parliament. The AKP has dominated Turkish political life since 2002. In the elections of 2006, it increased its share of the vote to 46.7 per cent, which increased further in the elections of 2011 when the AKP won just under 50 per cent of the vote. Erdogan became the first Turkish prime minister to win three general elections in a row. These elections were generally considered free and fair by international standards. More recently, however, concerns have been expressed about an 'illiberal' turn in Turkish political life, as signified by proposed constitutional amendments that would give the government the power to 'pack' the courts with judges more favourable to the ruling party, and interference with an official investigation of a corruption scandal, as well as the suppression of public protest (Cook, 2014).

As in Turkey, Lebanon has also had a multiparty political system since the end of World War II. Following independence in 1946, Lebanon adopted a set of political structures that appeared to conform to the essential characteristics of a Western liberal-democratic state. It had a president, prime minister, cabinet and an elected parliament. There were regular elections contested by a range of parties, an independent judiciary and alternation of power (Najem, 2012: 14). However, as a number of authors have observed, the reality of Lebanese politics is far from the Western liberal-democratic ideal. The division of Lebanese society along religious lines that predate independence was reflected in a sectarian system that was institutionalized in a pre-war consociational power-sharing agreement – the 1943 National Pact, an unwritten agreement between the Maronite Christian president and the Sunni Muslim prime minister (Salloukh, 2010: 135). Salloukh suggests that the system ensured that the balance of power rested with the presidency, which dominated the state's political, security, financial and judicial institutions. However, Najem argues that confessional divisions – and, more specifically, the unwritten arrangements negotiated by sectarian leaders – ensured that no single group could dominate the national agenda (2012: 17–18). Under the terms of these arrangements, the presidency was reserved for a Maronite Christian, and the prime minister would be a representative of the Sunni Muslim community, while the speaker of the parliament would come from the Shia community. In parliament, to allay Christian fears of domination, the ratio of Christians to Muslims was designated as 6:5. This delicate balance of power ensured that the Lebanese system, while far from a liberal democracy, never descended into authoritarianism. However, by the mid-1970s this system had become dysfunctional in a number of important respects. First, the Lebanese state had become too weak to deal with the challenge of changing internal and external circumstances. Second, pre-existing sectarian divisions were deepened by the fact that the power-sharing arrangements put in place at independence did not take significant demographic changes into account. Third, the penetration of the Lebanese system by foreign elements, especially the Palestinian Liberation Organisation, exacerbated sectarian tensions and drew the traditionally neutral country into the Arab–Israeli conflict. In 1975, Lebanon descended into a vicious civil war, which lasted for 15 years. The war was finally brought to a close by the Taif Accords, signed in 1990. The Taif Accords modified the arrangements issued from the 1943 National Accord. It shifted the balance of power away from the presidency, vesting it in the cabinet. In consequence, this empowered the Sunni prime minister, while the powers of the Shia speaker of parliament were increased in relation both to the cabinet and the parliamentary assembly.

However, transition to democracy was obstructed by the 'unprecedented penetration of post-civil war Lebanon by neighbouring Syria (Najem, 2012: 55). From 1990 until the final withdrawal of its troops in 2005, Syria played a preponderant role in Lebanese political life and effectively rendered any claim to genuinely democratic status meaningless. Rather than sponsoring the kind of consociational democracy envisaged by the Taif Accords, Damascus ruled the country with a heavy, if indirect, hand through its intelligence apparatus and with the cooperation of some Lebanese forces. Syria also imposed bilateral treaties upon the country – the 'Treaty of Brotherhood, Cooperation and Coordination' of May 1991 and the 'Defence and Security Agreement' of 1991 which, in Salloukh's phrase, reduced Lebanon to the status of 'a Syrian protectorate' (2010: 137).

Parliamentary elections were held in 1992, 1996 and 2000 but merely served to create a political class subservient to Syria. El-Khazen (2003: 624) observed that Lebanese political parties sought only to maintain the status quo regardless of its damaging impact on political pluralism and the democratic process. However, after the fall of Baghdad in 2003, following the US-led invasion, the position of Syria in Lebanon became increasingly untenable. US pressure culminated in a UN Security Council Resolution, which called for the withdrawal of all foreign forces and the holding of free and fair elections. When Syria was widely believed to be implicated in the assassination of Lebanese Prime Minister Rafiq Hariri, a combination of domestic, regional and international pressure finally forced a Syrian withdrawal.

However, the parliamentary elections that followed merely saw the return of confessional politics, as four broad confessional communities emerged – the Shia, the Sunnis, the Druze and the Maronites – leading Salloukh to conclude that post-Syria Lebanon inherited the same contradictions as the post-civil war state: a paralyzed state, penetrated by external actors, besieged by political crises and divided by sectarian leaders into neo-patrimonial fiefdoms (2010: 143).

As in Lebanon, Iran also has many of the trappings of a functioning democracy. However, also as in Lebanon, the extent to which democracy exists in the country is heavily qualified by some of the unique characteristics of the Iranian political system. Nonetheless, while it is not a democracy in any Western understanding of the term, there are undoubtedly democratic elements in the system to an extent that surpasses many of Iran's Arab neighbours.

As we have already pointed out in Chapter 1, since 1979 Iran has had what Ali Abootalebi (2011) has described as 'complex cleric-dominated but popularly driven political system' that embraces both popular participation and a balance of power within the ruling élite circle. Under the terms of the Iranian constitution, which was overwhelmingly approved in a referendum on October 24 1979, the form of government of Iran is that of an 'Islamic Republic'. This concept – that of an Islamic Republic – is another of the novel contributions of the Iranian Islamic revolution, inserting as it does, however uncomfortably, the Western notion of the republic into an overarching Islamic framework. The dominant institution of the new republic is that of the Supreme Leader, who, according to the constitution, is charged with the leadership of the *umma* (the entire Muslim community). The Supreme Leader is appointed by the popularly elected Assembly of Experts, which has the constitutional right to dismiss him if it decides he has abused his authority. He is expected not to interfere in the day-to-day running of the government, although he is the commander-in-chief of the armed forces and has the power to dismiss the president and to appoint the heads of the judiciary, the revolutionary guards, the heads of state-owned media and the military. The Guardian Council is comprised of religious lawyers appointed by the Supreme Leader and of lay lawyers elected by parliament. Its role is to ensure that all legislation conforms to Islamic law.

Since 1988, the Expediency Council has been in charge of resolving the conflicts that often arise between the Guardian Council and parliament. The reshaping of the Expediency Council, in the weeks prior to the departure from office of then President Rafsanjani in 1997, resulted in an increase in the power and prestige of the Council, which the Supreme Leader now heads (Abootalebi, 2001: 20–37).

Zaccara (2014) characterizes the system as a 'hybrid-regime'. He proposes three reasons for this. The first is the combination of religious and democratic legitimacy within its institutions. Article 5 of the 1979 constitution established the principle of *velayet-e-faqih* – rule by Islamic religio-legal experts, together with the principle of popular sovereignty in the form of regular elections of parliament, the president the Assembly of Experts and local councils. The second reason is that the constitution establishes three independent branches of power – executive, legislative and judicial – while giving ultimate power to the Supreme Leader. Finally, although the Supreme Leader is the ultimate power-holder, his selection, confirmation and dismissal are in the hands of the Assembly of Experts, which consists of 86 religious scholars and jurists who are elected directly every eight years by Iranian citizens. Therefore, the legitimacy of the leader is based indirectly on popularly sovereignty. In practice, however, there are strict limitations on the power of the Assembly of Experts in relation to the Supreme Leader. It has rarely exercised any of its powers in relation to the Supreme Leader. This may be linked to the fact that candidates for the Assembly are vetted by the Council of Guardians – half of whose members are appointed directly by the Supreme Leader in the first place (2014: 153–5).

The hybrid nature of the system means that while the Iranian political system is a long way from being democratic, its electoral system provides channels of political participation that regulate limited political competition and pluralism, albeit within set boundaries. Thus, while elections take place under authoritarian constraints, surprises can occur illustrating that results are not predetermined, as has been the case in much of the Arab world since independence. The election to the presidency of Mohammed Khatami (in 1997 and 2001) and of Mahmoud Ahmadinejad (in 2005 and 2009) are examples of such electoral 'surprises' and represented the elections of heads of state that were regarded with hostility by the Supreme Leader and a significant part of the religious-political establishment (Zaccara, 2014: 157–8).

Key questions

- What explains the illusion of significance of political parties in the Arab world?
- What are the reasons for the neglect of political parties in the literature on Arab politics?
- What are the advantages and disadvantages of the Lebanese consociational system?
- Why is the Iranian political system considered a hybrid regime?

Further reading

Albrecht, Holger (2005). 'How can opposition support authoritarianism? Lessons from Egypt', *Democratization*, 12(3): 378–97.

Garcia-Rivero, Carlos and Hennie Kotze (2007). 'Electoral support for Islamic parties in the Middle East and North Africa', *Party Politics*, 13(5): 611–36.

Pellicer, Miquel and Eva Wegner (2012). 'Socio-economic voter profile and motives for Islamist support in Morocco', *Party Politics*, 20(1): 116–33.

Online resources

Muasher, Marwan (2013). 'The path to sustainable political parties in the Arab World', *Policy Outlook*, Carnegie Endowment for International Peace. Available at: http://carnegieendowment.org/files/sustainable_arab_polit_parties.pdf.

The Center for Constitutional Transitions at NYU Law (2014). 'Political party finance regulation: constitutional reform after the Arab Spring', Institute for Democracy and Electoral Assistance. Available at: http://www.idea.int/publications/political-party-finance-regulation/loader.cfm?csModule=security/getfile&pageID=64580.

Chapter 6

Religion and Politics

Few phenomena in the politics of the modern Middle East have received more attention in recent decades – whether from scholars and the media, or policy-makers and politicians – than the impact of religion on political life. Much of the focus is on Islamic politics, the impact of which has been felt in every country in the region (and many beyond it). However, the intertwining of religion and politics is not confined to Islam: both Christianity and Judaism also play significant roles in the political life of the region. This chapter will first provide a brief, but important discussion of the terminology currently employed to define the relationship between Islam and politics. Then the chapter will place the rise of Islamism in context and provide an account of what can be described as the resurgence of religion in politics in the Middle East. Finally, the chapter will examine in detail how the three monotheistic religions present in the region each influence, and are influenced by, political developments.

Terminology: fundamentalism, Islamism, political Islam

Before it is possible to discuss Islamic politics in the MENA region, it is important to say something about the language we use to deal with this phenomenon. A number of terms have been relied on in recent years to encompass what some see as the resurgence in Islamic politics globally, the most common of these being 'fundamentalism', 'Islamism' and 'political Islam'. Does it matter which one we use? Are the terms unproblematic and interchangeable, or are there significant distinctions to be made between them? Many writers and commentators have come to the conclusion that the term 'fundamentalism' is more problematic than useful in shedding light on the phenomenon it purports to describe. This is for a number of reasons. In the first place, it has been pointed out that our understanding of 'fundamentalism' originates in the study of Protestant Christianity, with particular reference to those sects which call for a return to the foundational or fundamental beliefs of their religion. There are obvious problems in transposing a term which originates in the study of one religion to the study of another, completely different religion. Since belief in the Qur'an as the literal word of God is a core tenet of the religion of Islam, it is arguable that all Muslims are 'fundamentalist' in this sense. This would seem to empty the term of any analytic force in the context of a study of Islam because it does not permit us to distinguish between the very varied, and even conflicting, interpretations and practices of the faith that are displayed by ordinary Muslims. If all Muslims are 'fundamentalist', then the term tells us nothing (Shehata, 2012: 3).

It has also been strongly argued that use of the term 'fundamentalism' is associated with views intrinsically hostile to Islam. From this persepctive, 'fundamentalism' is associated with the view that Islam and the West are on a collision course, with Islam representing the 'fundamentally' unreasonable threat. In the words of American scholar John Esposito, Islam is seen to represent 'a triple threat: political, civilizational, and demographic' (2003: 89). This view has been expressed perhaps most infamously in Samuel Huntington's 'clash of civilizations' thesis, although views similar to those expressed by Huntington have also been articulated by others such as Bernard Lewis in his 1990 essay 'The Roots of Muslim Rage'. Huntington expressed the view that the interests of the Islamic world and those of Western 'civilization' were intrinsically opposed. He suggested that the current antagonism between the West and the Muslim world was exemplary of a conflict the origins and history of which had subsisted for the past 1,300 years (Huntington, 1993a: 30–2).

Finally, as Shehata argues, the term 'fundamentalism' implies a homogeneity that is at variance with the reality of Islamist politics:

> Islamist movements differ in terms of ideology, mobilization strategies, views about formal political participation, the use of violence, acceptance of the nation-state as the basis for political community, as well as on many other dimensions. (2012: 4)

Arising out of these arguments, many writers have sought to avoid the term 'fundamentalism' completely in order to avoid the difficulties associated with it, preferring instead to speak of 'Islamism' and 'political Islam'. Here, Islamism indicates the conscious choice of an Islamic doctrine in political action, suggesting that religious precepts and personal religiosity should be a guide for policy-making. Graham Fuller, in his book, *The Future of Political Islam*, defines an Islamist simply as:

> one who believes that Islam has something important to say about how politics and society should be ordered in the contemporary Muslim world. (2004: xi)

He suggests that the related term 'political Islam' should be neutral in character, 'neither pejorative nor judgmental in itself'. This approach, he argues, captures the full spectrum of Islamist expression that ranges 'from radical to moderate, violent to peaceful, democratic to authoritarian, traditionalist to modernist' (2004: xii).

The diversity one finds in Islam (see Box 6.1) matches the diversity one finds in the political expressions of Islamism and must be borne in mind when discussing the relationship between Islam and politics.

A global Islamic resurgence?

Regardless of terminology, it is clear that in recent decades Islam has come to be seen as a prominent factor in the political life of the Muslim world. From a Western perspective, this was an unexpected development which both academic and journalistic commentary were ill-equipped to explain. This was partly due to the expectations generated by theories of political development in the post-colonial world and, in particular, the widely held view that increasing modernization, industrialization and 'development' would lead to a reduction in the significance of religion in the developing world. This was believed to be inevitable because it was the same process that was presumed to have happened in the West. This assumption of inevitable progressive secularization has been thrown into question by the experience of the Muslim world, but it is now also clear that religion plays a more prominent public role globally and across cultures.

In spite of the expectation that religion would be relegated to the private sphere, or even wither away altogether, in the wake of continuing modernization, Islam (or, more correctly, particular interpretations of Islam) has increasingly influenced political life across the Muslim world from the 1970s onwards. However, a focus on the renewed significance of religion and politics in recent decades should not obscure the fact that Islam has been a persistent force in the politics of the region, at least since the initial impact of colonialism. In a number of countries, the struggle against the colonial powers was conducted through the use of religious categories adapted to politics. In Egypt, where the largest Islamist mass movement in the region, the Muslim Brotherhood, was formed as far back as 1928, the resurgence of Islam was especially visible under the presidency of Anwar al-Sadat, who succeeded Nasser in 1970. But two events in 1979 gave dramatic expression to the increased prominence of Islam in political life in the MENA, signalling to the rest of the world that religion still had a significant role to play in determining and influencing political outcomes. In February 1979, the 77 year-old Ayatollah Ruhollah Khomeini returned to Iran after 14 years in exile, to lead the revolution which overthrew the Shah and culminated in the establish-

Box 6.1   Diversity within Islam

Sunni/Shia Islam

The majority of the world's Muslims are adherents of Sunni Islam. Shia Muslims constitute a majority of the population in Iran, Iraq and Bahrain. In Lebanon, where the population is more evenly split between Christians and Muslims, there is a more even balance between Sunni and Shia Muslims (although in the absence of census data exact figures are not available). Elsewhere in the Muslim world, Sunni Muslims predominate, although there are significant Shia minorities in a number of states. A key difference between the two groups concerns the Shiite doctrine of the Imamate, as opposed to the Sunni Caliphate. For Sunnis, the Caliph was the elected or selected successor to the Prophet Muhammad's political and military, but not religious authority. By contrast, for the Shia, leadership vests in the Imam who, although not a prophet, is a divinely inspired and infallible leader of the community. The line of Imams came to an end in 874 CE when the Twelfth Imam 'disappeared'. Shiite doctrine holds that he went into 'occultation' but that he is mysteriously present as the Imam al Zaman (the 'hidden Imam'). The hidden Imam will return as the 'Mahdi' (the 'awaited one') at the appointed time to bring salvation.

Kharijites/Ibadiyyah

The Kharijites ('those who went out') have been described as the earliest dissenters in Islam. They emerged initially as a result of a dispute over leadership of the early Muslim community between Ali, the prophet Muhammad's son-in-law and Mu'awiyya, governor of Syria and cousin of the third Caliph, Uthman. The Kharijites broke with Ali when he accepted arbitration of the dispute believing that he was the rightful head of the community and was obliged to wage war on his challenger. The Kharijites were eventually destroyed but a non-violent group which stemmed from the Kharijites, the Ibadiyya, founded Ibadi imamates in East Africa, Yemen and Oman. Their descendants still exist in small numbers in North Africa and Oman, where Ibadi Islam is still the official religion.

Zaydis

The Zaydis are a Shia sect which split from the main group in the ninth century after the death of the fourth Shia Imam, 'Ali Zain al-Abidin. They recognized his younger son, Zayd ibn Ali, as the fifth Imam, rather than his older brother, Muhammad al-Baqir. They hold that any descendant of Ali can be Imam, unlike most Shias who believe that the Imamate is handed down through a particular

---

ment of an Islamic Republic in Iran, bringing with him the idea that a theocracy could be a modern and viable political system. In November 1979, a group of several hundred Islamist militants seized the Grand Mosque in Mecca and held it for over a week before it was retaken with the assistance of French special forces (Trofimov, 2007). The militants claimed that the ruling Al-Saud family had lost its legitimacy because of its toleration of increased Westernization in the country and called,

line of descendants. A Zaydi state was founded on Tabaristan on the Caspian Sea in 864. Another was established in northern Yemen, where Zaydis were the dominant group until the overthrow of the Zaydi Imamate in 1962.

The Ismailis

In the eighth century, the Shia community split once more in a dispute over whom the sixth Imam had designated as his heir. This led to the emergence of the Ismailis (also known as Seveners). Ismailis believe that the line of Imams ended on the death of Ismail, the designated seventh Imam. The early Ismaili movement was revolutionary: they attacked and killed political and religious leaders, seized power and, at their peak, ruled an area from Egypt to India. One branch established the Fatimid dynasty which ruled North Africa, Egypt, Sicily, Persia, West Arabia and part of India between the tenth and twelfth centuries. Another branch developed into the sect known as the Assassins under the leadership of Hassan al-Sabah. A descendant of Hassan al-Sabah received the title of Aga Khan which has passed to the leader of most Ismailis today.

The Druze

The Druze constitute another offshoot of the Ismailis. They originated in the eleventh century and are followers of the Fatimid Caliph al-Hakim, whom they believe embodied the one true God. They possess their own scripture, the 'Book of Wisdom' and believe in the transmigration of souls until perfected souls ascend to the stars. They are regarded as heretics by both Sunni and Shia Muslims. The Druze survive today in Syria, Israel and Lebanon, and number several hundred thousand.

The Alawis

The Alawis (also known as Nusairis) are another Shia sect which emerged in the ninth century. They believe that manifestations of God occur cyclically in three persons. They, too, believe in the transmigration of souls and the eventual return of the soul to its primordial state as stars, and are regarded as heretical by mainstream Muslims. Alawis constitute around 12 per cent of the population of Syria. However, they occupy a predominant place in the political life of the country. The family of the president, Bashar al-Asad, belongs to the Alawite community which constitutes a crucial support base for the regime.

Sources: J. Esposito (1998). *Islam: The Straight Path*, Oxford: Oxford University Press; M. Ruthven (2006), *Islam in the World*, Oxford: Oxford University Press.

instead, for a return to the original principles of Islam. These two events shocked the outside world as well as many within the region and seemed to herald a much broader resurgence of religion in politics across the Muslim world – and the MENA, in particular. Two years later, Egyptian President Anwar al-Sadat was assassinated by radical Islamists in Egypt bent on stimulating the revolutionary conditions for the creation of an Islamic state. In Lebanon, around the same time, two Shiite groups came to prominence during that country's prolonged civil war from 1975 to 1990. The Movement for the Dispossessed, originally founded in 1974, later became known as the *Amal* movement and constituted an important Shia militia group during the civil war. In the early 1980s, another Shia group, *Hizbullah* (literally 'Party of God') emerged in response to the Israeli invasion of southern Lebanon in 1982 and has since become one of the most significant, if controversial, actors in the political life of the region. Both movements – and, in particular, *Hizbullah* – have a distinct religious character and appeal, largely to a specific religious constituency.

Islamist movements were prominent elsewhere. The Egyptian Muslim Brotherhood, although still banned, was permitted to contest parliamentary elections in 1984 and 1987, in coalition with recognized opposition parties under Sadat's successor, Hosni Mubarak, winning significant support. In Syria, the al-Asad regime repressed an Islamist rebellion in the 1980s. A military coup in Sudan in 1989 brought Islamists to power and two years later, in 1991–2, the Algerian Islamist *Front Islamique du Salut* was poised to win the first free and fair legislative elections held in the country, only to be denied access to power by a military coup. Beyond the MENA region, in the 1990s the Islamist Taliban movement took control of most of Afghanistan and instituted a theocratic rule of the most conservative and discriminatory nature, leading many to equate Islam and Islamism with backwardness, authoritarianism and illiberal practices.

The pattern of increased Islamist involvement in political life continued over the following decades. In Tunisia, a brief period of political liberalization saw the Islamist *Ennahda* ('Renaissance') party take part in elections in 1989 winning between 10 per cent and 17 per cent of the vote nationally by putting forth candidates who were nominally running as independents but, in reality, were linked to the movement. In 2006, the Palestinian Hamas won control of the Palestinian Legislative Council through free and fair competitive elections. Their electoral victory also symbolized the increasing split among Palestinians between the more secular Fatah – committed to the peace process with Israel - and the Islamic movement, which rejected the Oslo accords and supported violent resistance against Israel.

The image conjured up by these events was frightening and alien to many in the rest of the world. Islamists were typically, although not always, seen as anti-modern and anti-Western, and analyses of Islamism frequently focused on the issue of violence. However, this fails to do justice to the complexity and variety of Islamic movements and actors across the MENA region and in the broader Muslim world. Many Islamic organizations that emerged at this time were not overtly political and were more concerned with the provision of welfare and attempting to Islamize society from below. For instance, for decades the Palestinian Hamas, an offshoot of the Muslim Brotherhood, enjoyed the covert support of Israel because it was perceived as a potential rival to the Palestinian Liberation Organization (PLO). Initially, Hamas did not become involved in politics and focused its efforts on charity; this political quietism was beneficial to Israel. When Hamas politicized, it became a powerful enemy for the state of Israel (Milton-Edwards and Farrell, 2010). Islamic non-govern-mental organizations were, and remain, prominent in the development sector in almost every country, delivering health, welfare, educational and other services to the population, often filling gaps left by over-extended or incompetent states, particularly in the aftermath of neo-liberal reforms that had reduced the welfare provision capacities of Arab states.

Islamist movements have continued to participate in electoral politics across the region where and when the opportunity arose (Brown, 2012). Throughout the past two decades, Islamist political parties have contested elections in Morocco, Algeria, Jordan, Lebanon, Yemen, Kuwait, Israel and elsewhere. Perhaps the most successful entry into electoral politics on the part of an Islamist party has been in Turkey where the AKP (*Adalat ve Kalkinmi Partisi* – Justice and Development Party) won an overwhelming victory in the parliamentary elections of 2002 (see p. 129). The party remains the most popular in the country by far, its support having increased in successive elections. The pivotal role played by Islamist parties in the formal politics of the MENA has been reinforced by developments across the region in the aftermath of the Arab uprisings of 2011. In the most free elections ever held in both Tunisia and Egypt, Islamist parties received the largest share of the vote. In Tunisia in 2011, *Ennahda* won over 41 per cent of the vote in elections to a new constituent assembly, while in Egypt, in the same year, the Freedom and Justice Party, linked to the Muslim Brotherhood, won 47 per cent of the vote in the first post-Mubarak parlia-mentary elections. In 2012 in Egypt, the Muslim Brotherhood's candidate, Muhammad Mursi, won presidential elections, allowing the movement to reach the heights of institutional power, before his removal from office one year later by the military. However, the picture is more complex than this. Both within and across the countries of the region, newly reformed political systems have seen the entrance of a range of political actors relying on competing understandings of Islam. These come from different ideological and political backgrounds. Fifteen Islamist parties emerged in Egypt after Mubarak's resignation in 2011. While the Freedom and Justice Party was the largest in the new Egyptian parliament, it competed with the Salafi *Hizb al-Nour* (the Party of Light) which won 111 seats, as well as smaller Salafi parties such *Al-Bina w'al Tanmiya* (Construction and

Development) and *Hizb al-Asala* (the Party of Authenticity). Salafi parties also emerged in Tunisia, Libya and Yemen. Nothing in the post-uprising MENA region better underscores the diversity of political Islam than the emergence of these new actors, active both at the institutional and social level. Obviously, this does not mean that there are not Islamic groups determined to reach their political goals through violence and terrorism. The most notorious are the al-Qaeda franchises in the Arabian Peninsula, in North Africa and in Syria and Iraq, all committed to the creation of an Islamic state. The Lebanese Hizbullah and the Palestinian Hamas have also employed violence throughout their history, but cannot solely be considered terrorist organizations, as both movements are also involved in institutional politics and civil society activism (Coffman-Wittes, 2008). Furthermore, from their perspective, the use of violence is dictated by the national liberation struggle in which they perceive themselves to be engaged. Violent Islamist groups do exist in a number of countries and operate both nationally and internationally, but, they constitute a minority of Islamist activity in the region.

Islamic 'resurgence': origins and causes

It is probably futile to try to identify a comprehensive set of factors which explain the rise in significance of political Islam in the MENA region over the last forty or so years as so much depends on the specific contexts within which particular Islamist actors operate. Nonetheless, Islamic political activism has generated a great deal of analysis by both academics and policy-makers and, while it is safe to say that no single set of explanatory factors will suffice to make sense of this phenomenon, the answer may lie in a combination of approaches. In the next section, analyses that focus on political, socioeconomic and ideological factors will be considered.

Political factors

For many scholars, political Islam can be explained in terms of a set of responses to changed political circumstances in the region. The impact of the Arab defeat in the 1967 war with Israel, the dramatic changes initiated by Anwar al-Sadat when he became president of Egypt in 1970, the revolution in Iran in 1989 which quickly assumed an Islamic orientation are all seen as key to analysis of Islamic politics subsequently, as is the broad context of authoritarian political structures and systems.

The 1967 Arab–Israeli War ('the Six Day War')

It is commonly asserted that the key to the emergence of Islamism in recent decades in the Middle East was the defeat of the Arab states in the 1967 war with Israel – the war in which the forces of Egypt and her allies were devastated over the course of a mere six days (Kepel, 2003). Although, as we have seen, the most significant Islamist movement of the contemporary era, the Muslim Brotherhood, was founded in 1928, Islamism was neither a political nor a social force to be greatly reckoned with until the late 1960s, mainly because the post-colonial West-inspired modernization project undertaken by ruling regimes in the region was perceived at first to be both successful and legitimate. Defeat in the Six Day War had three major consequences. First, it represented the death of the dream of pan-Arab nationalism. The 1950s and 1960s had seen the rise of Arab nationalist ideology, with Nasserism and Baathism promising Arab unity based on the concept of a single Arab nation. The defeat of the Arab states by Israel revealed just how weak and disunited Arab regimes were and how two decades of independence had failed to create solid, successful nation-states. Second, defeat was seen as emblematic of the failure of all imported ideologies in the Middle East: Arab governments had promised not only Arab unity but Arab socialism, economic development, non-alignment and independence from the West. In the aftermath of devastating defeat in 1967, these promises were seen as empty and the ideologies which underlay them seen as failures. In response, there was a return to the indigenous or 'authentic' ideology of Islam as a source of values. Third, it is argued that the 1967 war not only discredited the secular Arab nationalist governments – such as Egypt, Iraq and Syria – but, in turn, increased the influence of Saudi Arabia in the region. This influence was exacerbated greatly by the oil crisis which followed the 1973 war with Israel (and which led to a huge increase in the revenues of oil-producing states). According to this view, Saudi influence and funding had a large role in the resurgence of Islamic activism that followed. Saudi Arabia and the smaller Gulf states were suspicious – and, in part, afraid – of pan-Arab nationalism and took the opportunity presented by the 1967 defeat to project a more assertive regional role based on the ideological tenets of a conservative form of Islamism, which was quietist with respect to the governing élites, but vocal in the Islamisation of individual and collective social behaviour.

Sadat and the 'Islamization' of Egypt

Although many commentators take 1967 as the key starting point for the recent resurgence of Islam, Beinin and Stork point also to the significance of the policies pursued by Anwar Sadat with respect to the Islamic movement, when he succeeded Gamal Abdel Nasser to the Egyptian presidency in 1971 (1997: 8). Nasser had savagely repressed Islamic opposition on two occasions in the 1950s and 1960s. It is, indeed, during Nasser's years in power that one of the most important intellectuals of political Islam, Sayyd Qutb, was executed. However, when he came to power, Sadat sought to co-opt the Islamic sector to counter the threat from other forces in the country who were opposed to his reversal of key Nasserist policies, notably economic reform and alignment with the West. Sadat encouraged the mainstream Muslim Brotherhood to engage in political activity once more. In elections to the People's Assembly in 1976, six members of the Muslim Brotherhood stood as candidates for the ruling party. Numerous Islamic societies, which had sprung up in Egyptian universities, were given encouragement and support to purge campuses of leftist and Nasserist forces. The number of religious publications increased, as did religious programming on television. Religion became a compulsory subject in schools and the construction of mosques took place 'in every corner and in every small street' (Hanafi, 1982: 65–7). This particular tactic of supporting Islamist movements and groups in the face of the rise of a revolutionary left, particularly active on university campuses, was not limited to Egypt. Both in monarchies such as Jordan or Morocco, and republics such as Algeria and Tunisia, the ruling élites sponsored Islamization as an antidote to the growth of Marxist and socialist movements that sought to exploit the weakness of the state in the aftermath of the 1967 defeat to create genuine socialist republics that would be truly modernizing, redistributive and secular. The state-driven encouragement for Islamist activism was welcomed in Western policy-making circles because it was employed against revolutionary leftist activists at a time when the socialist left – broadly understood – was the global rival.

The Islamic Revolution in Iran

While the 1979 revolution in Iran, which overthrew the Shah and ultimately led to the installation of an Islamic regime under the leadership of Ayatollah Khomeini, was rooted in Iranian history and Shiite Islam, it had reverberations throughout the broader Muslim world. In specific terms, it gave impetus to Shiite activism in the MENA region (and beyond), including *Amal* and *Hizbullah* in Lebanon, and opposition groups in the Arabian Gulf states. But, beyond its Iranian and Shiite character, its consequences were global. Before 1979, few believed that it was possible to overthrow an existing regime in the name of Islam and to establish a revolutionary new order (Hardy, 2010: 39–40). The success of the Iranian revolution in replacing a powerful, Western-backed regime with an 'Islamic' order had implications that travelled well beyond the world of Shiite Islam. Here was a powerful example of how an unjust and authoritarian ruler could be overthrown. It was an example that could serve for the purpose of anti-regime mobilization across the entire region. Furthermore, the 'Islamic' outcome of the Iranian revolution galvanized Islamists across the region regardless of the Shiite character of its origins.

Authoritarianism and Islamic resurgence

There is considerable debate as to how the largely undemocratic and unrepresentative political systems of the MENA have impacted on Islamist activism. The initial response of many states in the region to the renewed popularity of Islamist movements has been to exclude them from political participation often accompanied by outright repression. This has been a recurring feature of political life in the region. Governmental repression of Islamist movements had taken place in Egypt in the 1950s, 1960s and 1990s. The Islamist opposition in Tunisia was subjected to proscription and repression with the exception of brief interludes, under Bourguiba – when the latter was under threat from the far left, and, later, under Ben Ali – when he was still attempting to solidify his rule in the late 1980s. So, too, was the Algerian Islamist opposition movement, the *Front Islamique du Salut* (or Islamic Salvation Front) after it came close to winning national elections which had been held during a short-lived phase of political openness at around the same time. The Moroccan monarchy did not accept any political role for Islamists until the late 1990s, and then did so only when Islamists accepted the political and religious primacy of the monarchy. For those Islamists who refused to acknowledge such primacy, repression and marginalization continued. In Jordan, the Muslim Brotherhood had historically found a reasonably friendly environment and enjoyed good relations with the monarchy. However, its opposition to the 1994 peace treaty with Israel and its sustained criticism of the domestic and international policies of the King ushered in an era of repression and political marginalization.

The key questions here concern whether exclusion from the political system, and the experience of repression, make Islamist movements more prone to adopting violent methods and whether, as a corollary, political participation encourages them to pursue their objectives through peaceful means. The evidence on these points is ambiguous. Regime repression can have the effect of radicalizing Islamist opposition, as happened in Algeria after the cancellation of elections in 1992 (Hafez, 2003). In neighbouring Tunisia, however, it appears that repression and exclusion had a moderating

Box 6.2   The Islamic Movement in Turkey before the AKP

The Islamic movement in Turkey has followed a very different trajectory to that of its counterparts in the Arab world. But, although mainstream Islamic activism has been more consistently integrated into the political system than its equivalent in Egypt, for example, the forces of Turkish Islamism have also consistently attracted the opposition of powerful opponents in the military and political establishments.

Organized Islamic political activity resumed in the nominally secular Turkish state in the 1960s. A variety of Islamist parties – the National Order Party, the National Salvation Party and the *Refah* (or Welfare) Party – operated in succession under the leadership of Necmettin Erkaban. *Refah* increased its popular support from the 1970s to the 1990s, culminating in its success in elections in 1994 and 1995. In the local elections of March 1994, *Refah* won 28 mayorships throughout the country, including Ankara and Istanbul, as well as leadership of 327 local governments. It received 19 per cent of the vote. In national elections the following year, it garnered 21 per cent. The party became the largest in parliament, by a small margin, but was excluded from power at first, as Turkey's two traditionally dominant (and traditionally rival) parties entered coalition. When this unlikely coalition broke down, *Refah* became the first Islamist party to enter government in Europe, in coalition with the True Path party of Tansu Ciller, and Erkaban became the first Islamist Prime Minister. This coalition did not last long. Disputes between the two partners over legislation were intensified by a crisis created by the anti-secular rhetoric and activities of some party officials, which antagonized secular public opinion. The party's commitment to democracy was also called into question. Its support for constitutional changes made some worry that it was trying to dilute the secular state. Women worried

effect and led not to a violent Islamist response but, rather, to the growing moderation of *Ennahda*'s positions on democracy, the rights of women and minorities (Cavatorta and Merone, 2013). The Turkish example is also ambiguous. The AKP party, which has been in government since 2002, represents the outcome of both political participation and repression. It is the latest in a line of Islamist parties in Turkey whose predecessors participated in political life at various points in the recent past but were excluded when it was deemed that they represented a threat to the secular values of the state. Before the AKP (as we have seen in Chapter 5 and as we further highlight in Box 6.2), all five previous Islamist parties in Turkey had been shut down either by military intervention or rulings by the constitutional court (Taspinar, 2012). Thus, it is unclear 'whether Turkish Islamism would have become the moderate force it is today merely by being allowed to participate in the democratic process or whether it was coerced into becoming so by an authoritarian state' (Dalacoura, 2006: 522). The issue of moderation is particularly significant in the aftermath about the reduction of their rights. Finally, there were allegations that the *Refah* Party had connections with militant Islamist groups.

The party was brought to court in May 1997 and the coalition with the True Path party broke down; Erbakan was banned from politics and the party was outlawed in January 1998 by the Constitutional Court, on the grounds that it violated the principles of secularism and the law of the political parties.

However, the Islamists did not go away. Not for the first time in recent Turkish history, the forces of political Islam regrouped and a new party was established – the Virtue Party under the leadership of Recai Kutan on 17 December 1997. At that time, it had 144 seats in the parliament, which it had obtained as a result of the switchover of Refah deputies. The new party was split between its conservative wing, which was controlled by Erbakan, and a reformist wing, led by then-Istanbul Mayor Recep Tayip Erdogan. The new Virtue Party actively sought to distinguish itself from *Refah*. It recruited a number of highly educated, upper-middle-class modern women and appointed three female members to its central decision-making board. In contrast to *Refah*, the Virtue Party supported Turkey's application for membership of the European Union. Where *Refah* demanded its supporters observe an Islamic dress code, Virtue downplayed the significance of this. The new party espoused of democracy, human rights and personal liberty, and pledged to create a humanitarian state that meets the nation's needs without totally dominating it, a more democratic rather than more authoritarian state. On the Kurdish issue, the new party's leadership spoke in favour of Kurdish cultural rights, including the right to educate and publish in the Kurdish language. In August 2001, a group of MPs and administrators left the Virtue Party to establish what became the AKP, which quickly went on to dominate Turkish political life.

Source: Pinar Tank (2005). 'Political Islam in Turkey: a state of controlled secularity', *Turkish Studies*, 6(1): 3–19.

of the Arab uprisings, as Islamist parties took power, or were poised to take power, in a number of countries and questions are asked about their democratic credentials and credibility.

However, focusing exclusively on the question of whether repression leads to moderation or radicalization is limiting, insofar as it neglects two important factors. First, there have been, and still are, important intellectual and ideological debates taking place within Islamist movements and parties about the relationship between religion, democracy and liberal rights. It is often these internal debates that lead a specific movement in the direction of either radicalization or moderation. Second, the international dimension is very significant here: outside events can affect the ways in which Islamist movements might develop, regardless of what kind of policies a specific regime might be pursuing on the domestic level. Events such as the 1991 Gulf War, or the invasion of Iraq in 2003, have had profound consequences for the methods of action and ideological stances that Islamists across the region take.

Socioeconomic factors

Some of the earliest scholarship on the Islamic 'revival' sought to rationalize Islamist activity in terms of social crisis. Post-independence, Muslim countries experimented with a plethora of socioeconomic systems under a variety of regimes. Yet, many problems remained unresolved. Lack of socioeconomic justice, increasing official corruption and the failure of political élites to mould strong identities produced what Dekmejian characterized as a 'crisis of legitimacy' where the moral bases of authority are called into question (1988: 8–9). This crisis is compounded by political repression, military weakness, oil-generated consumerism and cultural penetration from outside. Added to this, is the failure of states across the region to meet the problems of development. As we saw in Chapter 4, in many states in the region, unsuccessful or partial processes of modernization and rapid economic development have had negative consequences for significant proportions of the population. One of the most important consequences of rapid economic development has been an exodus from rural to urban settings with consequent social and cultural dislocation. Cramped conditions, overcrowding and very limited access to basic services – such as water, sewers and transport – led to growing disenchantment with political systems that did not seem to provide for the basic needs of their citizens. This was compounded by growing levels of education which were not met by an increase in the availability of employment. These difficulties were compounded by the realization on the part of many people that some sectors of the population were enjoying disproportionate access to the fruits of economic development. As a result, there was an increase in feelings of relative material deprivation, as people simultaneously became aware of the promise of consumerism and of their own lack of access to it (Butko, 2004: 33–5). According to some scholars, the failure of 'imported' models of development prompted a 'return' to the authentic, in the form of Islamic ideology. Explanations of Islamic resurgence which focus on socioeconomic factors draw strength from the welfare provision activities of a significant number of Islamist charities, particularly at a time when the state was 'forced' to withdraw or scale down its involvement in economic activity and service-provision due to the constraints of structural adjustments or neo-liberal governance. While the political role of Islamic charities should not be overemphasized, just as its middle-class nature should be noted (Clark, 2004), it is not a coincidence that Islamist charities are often the incubators of Islamist political leadership and provide for the political mobilization of what can be termed the 'dispossessed'.

Ideological factors

While political and socioeconomic factors have clearly shaped the emergence and development of Islamist activism, ideology has also played a key role. Islamist political actors draw on a rich ideological repertoire. However, just as the spectrum of political Islam is diverse so, too, is the range of interpretations of Islamic sources that are relied on to justify activism.

Islamic reformism

In the nineteenth century, as already noted in Chapter 2, Islamic reformists such as Jamal al-Din al-Afghani and Muhammad Abduh proposed a rationalist approach to Islam that would revitalize Muslim society through a synthesis of Islam and science on the basis that there was no incompatibility between science, knowledge and the foundations of the Islamic faith. Al-Afghani consistently opposed European influence in Muslim world. He opposed all forms of political, military or economic intervention by foreign powers in Muslim countries, and accused those who did not combat colonialism of being traitors. Muslims, in al-Afghani's view, needed to band together to combat European encroachment and, in this enterprise, Islam was the only factor which united them.

Hasan al-Banna and the Muslim Brotherhood

Keddie claims that Islamic reformism was the main intellectual trend in the Muslim world from the late nineteenth century until after World War II. (1994: 484). However, despite this undoubted influence, it was not until later in the twentieth century that political Islam found expression in a mass political movement. In March 1928, in the Egyptian town of Ismailiyya, a teacher named Hasan al-Banna established the *Jama'at al-Ikhwan al-Muslimin* (the Society of the Muslim Brotherhood). Over time, it has become the largest and most influential Islamic organization in the Middle East. But, although the Brotherhood has been hugely significant in the development of political Islamist organizations throughout the Muslim world, it was not originally established for purely political objectives. Rather, al-Banna had the grander aim of representing Islam as it should be properly understood, lived and implemented, and of using Egypt as a base from which to reform and unite the entire Islamic *umma*. However, the Brotherhood rapidly developed as an overtly political organization, as well as being a religious organization. The move towards overly political activism on the part of the Brotherhood stemmed from al-Banna's analysis of the social and political situation in Egypt in the 1920s and 1930s. As had al-Afghani and Abduh, he believed that Muslims had lost their way in the face of increasing European cultural and political encroachment. The solution to the dilemma facing Muslims in Egypt, as identified by al-Banna, lay in a return to the core insights of Islam. His views on the nature of Islamic government are expressed in the programme of the Brotherhood, which consisted of two items. These were the internationalization of the movement, in order to facilitate the liberation not only of Egypt, but also of the entire Islamic homeland from foreign control; and the institution in this homeland of:

> a free Islamic government practising the fundamentals of Islam, applying its social system, propounding its solid fundamentals, and transmitting its wise call to the people. (Enayat, 1982: 85)

The programme went on to state that as long as this Islamic government was not established, Muslims were guilty before God of failing to establish it (Enayat, 1982: 85). The transformation of the Muslim Brotherhood into a mass political movement attracted the hostility of both the pre- and post-revolutionary governments in Egypt. The Free Officers who came to power in 1952 quickly moved to suppress the movement and many leading figures were imprisoned. One of these, Sayyid Qutb, became a key inspiration for radical Islamists across the Muslim world.

Sayyid Qutb and Radical Islamism

In the late 1930s, Qutb was a literary essayist whose initial writings were 'anti-Islamic and anti-traditionalist in attitude'. However, by the late 1940s, his attention turned from literature and poetry to Islam and social issues. This, it has been suggested, was in response to his frustration with Western policies towards Arabs and Muslims and, in particular, British and American attitudes towards Palestine. In 1949, Qutb wrote a work entitled *Social Justice in Islam* which reflected his new-found concern with issues of social and economic justice. In his early work, he proposed Islam as an alternative to the ideologies of communism, nationalism, liberalism and secularism. However, a progressive radicalization of his ideas can be seen from the earliest books to his last, *Milestones*, which was first published in 1964. *Milestones*, perhaps the best known of Qutb's writings, comprises excerpts from a 37-volume commentary on the Qur'an, *Fi Zilal al-Qur'an* (*In the Shade of the Qur'an*), which was written while Qutb was serving a 15-year prison sentence following his arrest in 1954. In the last phase of his writings, he rejected all forms of government and held that mere reform of society was no longer enough. The total destruction of the old system was necessary if the kingdom of God was to be established on earth (Haddad, 1983: 69).

Two central concepts lie at the heart of Qutb's mature writings – *jahiliyya* and *hakmiyya*. The concept of *jahiliyya* is used in the Qur'an to refer to the period of ignorance in which the people of Mecca lived prior to the revelation. Qutb extracted it from any historical or geographical context to apply it to all contemporaneous societies. In *Milestones*, from the outset, Qutb makes his position clear. The whole world is steeped in *jahiliyya*. This all-pervasive condition stemmed, in the first instance, from man's denial of the sovereignty of God or *hakmiyya* and the transfer of that sovereignty to man, making some men lords over others. For Qutb, this is an unpardonable sin. Only in the Islamic way of life can men become free from servitude to others and devote themselves to the worship of God alone. For Qutb, *jahiliyya* is everywhere, permeating every aspect of contemporary Muslim life. *Jahili* societies included the communist society, all 'idolatrous' societies (such as those of India, Japan, the Philippines and Africa), and all Jewish and Christian societies, because they have distorted the original beliefs and ascribe certain attributes of God to other beings. Finally, Qutb claims that all so-called 'Muslim' societies are also *jahili* societies – not because they believe in deities other than God or worship anyone other than God, but 'because their way of life is not based on submission to God alone' (Qutb: 1978: 150–2).

Qutb's later works place priority on the destruction of the un-Islamic order and the establishment of a true Islamic society, after which the detailed laws and systems of such a society could be worked out. Qutb's vision of how the Islamic society would be established contained three essential elements. A 'vanguard' must emerge which would emulate the methods of the Prophet Muhammad when he led the first Muslim community from *jahiliyya* to faith in God and in Islam. The members of this vanguard must, in imitation of the Prophet's own example, cut themselves off from today's *jahiliyya* and dedicate themselves to the realization of the Islamic social order. Finally, this vanguard must, if necessary, engage in *jihad* to establish the Islamic society (Qutb: 1978: 17–18).

Qutb's analysis and, in particular, his views on the un-Islamic nature of contemporary Muslim societies and the need to remedy this through *jihad* if necessary, were a major influence on subsequent Islamic activism throughout the MENA region and beyond. In Egypt, as the Muslim Brotherhood increasingly took advantage of limited openings to participate more fully in the political mainstream, more radical, and sometimes violent, groups emerged. Groups such as *Al-Gama'a al-Islamiyya* (the Islamic Group) and *Tanzim al-Jihad* (the Jihad Organization) engaged in anti-regime violence throughout the 1990s.

Box 6.3   Islamic modernism

Graham Fuller notes that while the liberal, modernist mode of thinking about
Islam is not yet the dominant trend among Islamists, the trend is growing in
significance over time – particularly as the need for more creative responses to
the realities and challenges facing the Muslim community grows more evident.

He offers a useful synopsis of the core elements of the modernist argument:

— God bestowed upon mankind the power of intellect, rationality and freedom
of choice, which he clearly intended for humans to employ, even at the risk
of occasional error.
— Each individual must find his/her own way to awareness of God and the
message of Islam. No one can be compelled into belief; neither can the state
impose a religious message. Such compulsion destroys most of the merit of
faith.
— Human understanding of God's message has changed and grown over time
but is never perfect. Just as today's knowledge and understanding of God's
creation and plan is richer than it was in seventh-century Arabia, so mankind
will have better understanding in the future than today.
— No one possesses a full understanding of God's message and purpose. No
one will ever attain perfect understanding. Therefore, no one can claim to
possess a monopoly on understanding God or Islam.
— A democratic state offers maximum opportunities for freedom of study,
discussion, and debate of religion – a process that best enables individuals
and society to understand God's message and its relevance to constructing a
just society.

Source: Graham Fuller (2004). *The Future of Political Islam*, Basingstoke: Palgrave Macmillan.

Islamic Modernism

However, while radical Islamism, and its association with violent means,
has attracted a great deal of media and academic attention, it does not
exhaust the category of contemporary Islamism, as Box 6.3 explains. The
conventional Western focus on radical Islamic movements, organizations
and ideologies often blinds us to the reality that, as Antony Black puts
it:

> most Muslims, intellectuals and community leaders, as well as ordinary
> people, are not fundamentalists. Like members of other religions, they
> adopt a variety of political attitudes. (2001: 338–9)

Contemporary modernist theorists struggle with the need to integrate
the Muslim world with modernity. To them, Islam and Muslims have to
coexist with modernity – the problems of the world are the problems of

Muslims. To such thinkers, radical Islamist ideologies represent misplaced attempts to ignore the conditions created by the modern world. Some modernist thinkers would argue that the modern world has existed in Arab and Muslim society for over 150 years and is not something to be rejected or denied. They want a more open society and look for political solutions which pay heed to human rights, democracy, women's rights and the rights of minorities. Notable among these intellectuals are Rachid Ghannouchi in the Sunni world and Abdelkader Soroush in the Shiite sphere.

Christianity and politics in the MENA

Policy-making and academic commentary has, for the most part, focused on Islamic politics in the MENA region. However, this is to neglect the hugely significant role played by other religions in the politics of the region – notably, Judaism in Israel and Christian denominations of different kinds in several other countries.

Christians constitute an important, if declining, minority in several countries in the MENA, especially Egypt, Lebanon, Syria, Jordan and Palestine. The exception to this trend is Israel, where the size of the Christian community is on the increase (Sharon, 2012). Coptic Christianity, one of the older Christian denominations, has 5–8 million adherents in Egypt and Christians have played a prominent role in political life at different points in the past: there was a Christian prime minister as far back as 1908. However, by the 1930s Christians were increasingly marginalized due to their perceived Western sympathies. Under Nasser, Church properties were nationalized, along with the assets of richer Coptic Christians. Rowe describes how this treatment led to the development of greater political assertiveness amongst Egypt's Copts. By the 1970s, the Coptic Church was active in the defence of the rights of Christians and staging demonstrations against the Islamist direction that the regime was pursuing. The high point of this came in 1980. In May of that year, in protest at the decision of the government to adopt a constitutional provision which enshrined *shari'a* as the source of Egyptian law, the Coptic Pope, Shenouda, cancelled Easter celebrations and the President expressed his suspicion that the Church was conspiring against national unity. Sectarian clashes led to the deaths of 18 people in Cairo and, in September, the Coptic pope was sent into internal exile (Rowe: 2009: 112–15). Relations were restored with Sadat's successor, Hosni Mubarak, and Shenouda subsequently adopted a more low-profile approach in cooperation with the regime, although key Coptic grievances – especially under-representation in public life and restrictions on the building of churches – continued to be voiced.

Christians have also played a major role in Lebanese politics, where they constitute a significant minority of the population. Lebanon is the only member state of the United Nations that has not conducted a population census since the end of World War II. The only census that has taken place was held in 1932 under French rule. According to this, Maronite Christians comprised 28.8 per cent of the population, Sunni Muslims 22.4 per cent and Shiites 19.6 per cent. As a result, the presidency of the republic, the most powerful office in the political system, was allocated to the Maronites; the next most powerful position, that of prime minister, was allocated to the Sunnis; and the position of speaker of parliament was reserved for the Shiites. In recognition of their position as the largest religious denomination, Lebanese Christians were allocated slightly more than half the seats in parliament and a similar proportion of government positions (Faour, 2007: 909–10).

Relations between Christians and Muslims have dominated political life in post-independence Lebanon. While the institutional framework of the state guaranteed the Christian population a privileged and powerful position, the demographic reality was that Muslim population growth was outstripping that of Christians. These tensions fed into the brutal civil war which began in 1975 and cost up to 150,000 lives over the course of 15 years. Although religion was by no means the only factor in the conflict, it was significant – and some church leaders played an important role. Henley points to a document produced by major Christian monastic orders which characterized the war as 'a struggle for all that is Christian, authentically Lebanese and civilized' (Henley, 2008: 354). Indeed, Christian monastic orders played an active part in the war. The superior general of the Permanent Congress of the Lebanese Monastic Orders was one of four leaders of the Lebanese Front coalition formed in 1976, while the monastic orders supported Christian militias fighting in the war with all means available. These included propaganda campaigns regarding the Islamic 'threat' to Christian minorities in the Middle East, and the use of monasteries as bases for fighters and for the storage of weapons, as well as funding. According to Henley, there were even reports of monks wielding Kalashnikovs and holding strategic positions around monasteries (2008: 357).

Maronite Church leaders also played a part in the ending of the civil war, when the Patriarch, backed by Maronite bishops, faced down opposition from Christian political leaders to support the agreement signed in Taif, Saudi Arabia, in 1989 which brought the conflict to a close. The Taif Accords led to a revision of the institutional balance of power arrangements bequeathed by the French authorities. The Maronites retained the presidency but the authority of the office was reduced, while the roles of prime minister and speaker of parliament became more powerful. The ratio of Christians to Muslims in the allocation of public positions was revised to 1:4 (Faour, 2007: 911). The Accords acknowledge the reality of the declining share of Christians in the Lebanese population overall which, some suggest, threatens them with increasing political irrelevance (Baroudi and Tabar, 2009: 228). The sectarian divisions of Lebanese society are being played out once again in the context of the Syrian civil war that began in March 2011.

In Syria, the political participation of Christians has been closely tied, in the views of many observers, to the Baathist regime which first seized power in 1963. Christians comprise around 10 per cent of the total population and are divided into 11 different, officially recognized sects. They have been involved in public life and are to be found in ministerial positions and in the National Assembly. The Syrian regime, dominated by an Alawi minority in a Sunni majority country, has sought to minimize the significance of religious identity, appealing instead to a common Arab national identity – which is attractive to minorities because it allowed them to transcend sectarian division. Nonetheless, while the regime officially promotes 'brotherhood' between Christians and Muslims, it maintains personal status legislation based on religion, rather than citizenship, and plays on Christian fears concerning their status in any Syrian polity ruled by the Sunni Muslim majority (McCallum, 2012: 10–11).

There are two broad interlinked themes that characterize the way in which Christians in the region deal and engage with politics. First, there is the widespread tendency to associate Christian churches and organizations with support for authoritarian political power. Insofar as Christians are minorities in states where they live, they have a stake in supporting – however unwillingly – the authoritarian status quo, for fear of the unknown that regime change might bring. Second, there is the assumption that Christians and Christianity are under threat due to the resurgence of Islamism whereby there is an almost inevitable hostility between Islam and Christianity, given the aggressive and discriminatory nature of the former. The outcome is that authoritarian rule, as mentioned, can be perceived as the bulwark against Islamism and therefore, for Christians, preferable to democracy. The reality on the ground is much more complex than this and many Christians oppose authoritarianism, but the story of Christianity under threat is, at times, of a convenient one for Orientalist readings of Middle East politics (Middle East Report, 2013). However, this should not obscure some of the problematic developments that have occurred since the onset of conflicts with profound sectarian undertones during the 2000s. Both the Iraqi and Syrian civil wars acquired a prominent sectarian dimension within which Christians became targets, leading many to leave their countries and others to 'hunker down' and wait for better times.

Judaism and politics in the State of Israel

Just as Christianity is an important political variable in the region, contemporary Israeli politics cannot be fully understood without reference to the role played by Judaism, or interpretations of Judaism, in political life.

Although the state of Israel identifies itself as a secular democratic state, the separation between religion and politics can be hard to discern. Religion is at the heart of the identity of the state and permeates key laws. The 1948 Declaration of the Establishment of the State of Israel pronounced the establishment of a Jewish state, 'to be known as the State of Israel' while proclaiming its adherence to the precepts of liberty, justice and peace 'as envisaged by the prophets of Israel', as well as setting out commitments to upholding the full social and political equality of all its citizens, without distinction of race, creed or sex, full freedom of conscience, worship, education and culture, safeguards for 'the sanctity and inviolability of the shrines and Holy Places of all religions' and to the principles of the Charter of the United Nations (Israel Ministry of Foreign Affairs, 1948). Despite these commitments to democratic principles in the declaration, a number of authors question whether the Jewish and democratic character of the state can fully co-exist. The democratic character of the state is extremely significant, since Israel hosts a number of religious minorities that enjoy freedom of religion and worship. In addition, all citizens enjoy full political rights. Nonetheless, some argue that the assertion of the Jewish character of Israel prevents non-Jews from feeling fully part of the nation (Avnery, 1998). In addition, as Uri Davis (2003) highlights, the Arab minority is prevented from exercising their rights in full.

The central position of the Jewish religion is enshrined in a series of laws governing citizenship, immigration and personal status, although challenges to them exist, as Box 6.4 highlights. For example, the 1950 Law of Return proclaims that every Jew has the right 'to come to this country' as an immigrant and adopts an ultra-orthodox definition of who is a Jew (i.e. being born of a Jewish mother) as the criterion for this right. The 1953 Rabbinical Courts Jurisdiction (Marriage and Divorce) Law provides that the marriage and divorce of Jews shall take place only according to Jewish law (Haklai, 2007).

Beyond the formal legal sphere, religion has become increasingly significant in recent decades. There has been a substantial increase in the numbers of those who describe themselves as religious Jews – now just under half of the population (Haynes, 2013: 258). This trend is also reflected in the military. According to one source, an estimated 50 per cent of soldiers in officer training colleges are now religious (Press, 2010). This increased religiosity impacts on political life in a number of ways.

Box 6.4   The 'Women of the Wall'

The intersection of the religious and the political has important implications for women in Israel. 'Women of the Wall' (WOW) is a group of mostly religiously observant Israeli women who have campaigned from 1988 for the right to pray at the Western Wall in Jerusalem – one of the holiest sites in Judaism – on the same terms as Israeli men. Since Israel regained control of the Western Wall (sometimes known as the 'Wailing Wall') in 1967, it has been run in accordance with ultra-Orthodox protocol. Only men could sing from the Torah, wear white prayer shawls and wear the black leather *t'filin* straps, which are worn by observant Jews during morning prayers.

WOW was founded in December 1988 during the first International Jewish Feminist Conference in Jerusalem. A group of 100 women who attended the conference went to pray at the Wall where they were disrupted by the physical and verbal assaults of ultra-Orthodox men and women. In 1991, WOW appealed to the Israeli Supreme Court, arguing for the right to worship according to their custom in safety and security. A series of legal manoeuvres and commissions followed. In 2002, the Supreme Court issued a judgement in favour of WOW, granting women the right to wear prayer shawls, to pray aloud and to read from a Torah scroll as part of a prayer service. Four days later, the ultra-Orthodox Shas political party submitted several bills to parliament in an attempt to over-ride the court's decision, including one that would make communal prayer by women punishable by a fine and seven years in prison. In 2005, another court judgement went against the women. In 2013, 10 members of WOW were arrested for illegally wearing prayer shawls. In April of the same year, the Supreme Court finally conceded that the Women of the Wall should be allowed to pray freely at the site, although religious conservatives continue to oppose their claims.

Sources: Sarah Szymkowicz (2013).'Women in Israel – women of the wall', *Jewish Virtual Library*, available at https://www.jewishvirtuallibrary.org/jsource/Judaism/WOW.html; Phoebe Greenwood (2013), 'Victory for Israel's women of the wall after 25 year campaign', *The Guardian*, 9 June.

Religious Jews are central to the project of settlement on territories occupied by Israel following the 1967 war. From 1967 to mid-2011, Israel established 124 'official' settlements in the West Bank In addition, some 100 outposts (settlements built without official authorization but with the support and assistance of government ministries). By 2012, some 350,000 settlers were living on the West Bank. This does not include the 300,000 Jews living across the 1967 border in East Jerusalem. Although many of these settled in the territories due to the financial incentives provided, many others are there out of religious conviction and 'to redeem' the land.

As Haklai notes, much of the literature on Jewish settlers focuses on ideology. The settlers' movement is said to be messianic and guided by the ideology of the 'whole Land of Israel'. That is, it is making a biblical claim to the territory between the Mediterranean and the river Jordan. The movement's followers believe that settling this land, and thereby perpetuating Jewish rule over it, is an essential part of their religious mission. But, he points out the success of the settlement project cannot be explained by ideology alone and the assistance, official and unofficial, of government officials and bodies has been crucial to the enterprise (Haklai, 2007: 721). Given their motivation, it is unsurprising that religious Jews are particularly vocal in their opposition to the policy of conceding parts of 'Biblical' Israel to the Palestinians as part of the peace process. The clearest expression of this came in November 1995, when the then Prime Minister, Yitzhak Rabin, was assassinated by Yigal Amir, a 25-year-old religious Jew, because of Rabin's willingness to negotiate with the Palestine Liberation Organization.

Increased levels of religiosity in Israel have translated into a substantial presence for religious parties in the Knesset, the Israeli parliament. In the first general election after independence, religious parties joined together in a common list and subsequently acted as a bloc in parliament. Some of these went on the establish the National Religious Party (NRP) which was the main religious grouping in the country for a long time, consistently winning between 10 and 12 seats in elections up to 1970, although a number of smaller religious parties also existed. The 1980s saw the emergence of a new ultra-orthodox party, Shas, which became the biggest religious party in the Knesset, winning 17 seats in the 1999 elections (Ismael and Ismael, 2011: 311). In the parliamentary elections of 2013, a total of 39 'religious' members of the Knesset were elected (Kenig, 2013). Since 1967, more extreme religious zealots have organized in various movements such as *Kach* and *Kachane Chai*, often expressing the views of religious settlers that occupied land should not be handed back to non-Jews. Finally, on the ultra-orthodox fringe is a small faction known as *Neturei Karta* (Guardians of the Gate) whose members refuse to recognize the legitimacy of the state and strongly denounce Zionism (Ismael and Ismael, 2011: 311).

Key questions

- What are the most significant factors that have given rise to the phenomenon of Islamism?
- In what ways can the work of Sayyd Qutb be considered crucial for resurgence of Islamism?
- How do Christians in the Middle East advance and defend the interests of their community?
- How does Judaism affect Israeli political life?

Further reading

Ali Abdelkader, Deina (2011). *Islamic Activists. The Anti-enlightenment Democrats*, London: Pluto Press.
Brown, Nathan (2012). *When Victory is not an Option. Islamist Movements in Arab Politics*. Ithaca: Cornell University Press.
El-Ghobashy, Mona (2005). 'The metamorphosis of the Egyptian Muslim Brothers', *International Journal of Middle Eastern Studies*, 37(2): 373–95.
Gleis, Joshua and Benedetta Berti (2012). *Hezbollah and Hamas: A Comparative Study*, Washington, DC: Johns Hopkins University Press.
Meijer, Roel (2009). *Global Salafism*, London: Hurst & Co.
Rosefsky Wickham, Carrie (2013). *The Muslim Brotherhood: Evolution of an Islamist Movement*, Princeton: Princeton University Press.
Shehata, Samer (2012). *Islamist Politics in the Middle East: Movements and Change*, London: Routledge.
Volpi, Frédéric (2011). *Political Islam: A Critical Reader*, London: Routledge.

Online resources

Centre for the Study of Islam and Democracy: https://www.csidonline.org/index.php.
I Knew Bin Laden, Al Jazeera documentary on the life of Usama Bin Laden: http://www.aljazeera.com/programmes/general/2011/05/2011510143387 15787.html.
Ijtihad: Return to Enlightenment: http://www.ijtihad.org/ – a website maintained by US-based scholar Muqtedar Khan.
Islam in Comparative Context – Online Resources://orias.berkeley.edu/islam.html.
Islamic Philosophy Oneline:http://www.muslimphilosophy.com/.
Liberal Islam website: http://www.unc.edu/~kurzman/LiberalIslamLinks.htm.
Princeton University Library Web Sites for Jewish Studies: http://www.princeton.edu/~pressman/jewsub.htm.

Chapter 7

Civil Society and Political Change

This chapter introduces the concept of civil society and discusses its relationship with democracy before turning to the expansion in civil activism in the Middle East in recent decades. It then sets out five ways in which civil society in the Middle East can be analysed and understood before concluding with a short discussion of the role of civil society in the recent Arab Awakening, which will be dealt with in greater detail in Chapter 11.

Middle Eastern and North African countries have often been characterized as having passive and supine societies heavily policed by a 'fierce' state that would only tolerate social mobilization when the state itself was charged with directing it. Spontaneous mobilization was – and, in many cases, still is – perceived to be detrimental to the stability of the state and as undermining the unitary pursuit of national developmental goals. This is the perhaps understandable outcome of what occurred in the region immediately after decolonization. With independence, the need to build a modern nation-state saw many of the civil society organizations that had emerged previously under colonial rule channel their efforts into state-led projects of modernization, despite the authoritarian nature of the regimes in power. The objectives of social and economic modernization on the national level were deemed more important than the advances of a specific social group, as the narrative of a single undivided people, striving for the same objective, took hold. As we saw in Chapter 3, this was the view of independent trade unions which submitted their sectoral interests to the need to advance a national cause. In this respect, there was near consensus that the pursuit of specific demands emanating from particular social groups was too divisive, and that all societal demands should be reconciled, even if in potential and actual conflict with each other. Thus workers, women and other groups that might have had competing interests fell behind the state-led project (Pratt, 2007).

Through the unification of different sectoral demands behind the goal of modernization, the state took control of society itself and gradually suffocated dissenting voices. This was particularly true in republican regimes, where the state, often under the control of the military, directed development according to a unitary narrative and with a unitary purpose. Where militaries run the state, there was also an ingrained habit to punish dissenters, which inhibited the emergence and legitimacy of alternative views and policies to those dictated by the regime.

160

However, a similar trend towards the quashing of demands that deviated from the perceived consensus was also present in the conservative monarchies as well. It should be underlined that, initially, many civil society groups accepted this unitary narrative and willingly accepted that their specific demands be put aside in favour of reaching the national goal of modernization. Neither did the authoritarianism of the political systems seem overly burdensome initially. There was widespread popular support for the view that the nation – and the state – had to pull in the same direction. In this way, authoritarian rule suppressed autonomous civil activism and, as a result, civil society activism has often been identified as the crucial missing ingredient for democratic political change in the region. In many ways, the uprisings of 2011 have challenged the myth of the passivity of Arab societies and signalled the awakening of civil society in the face of political authoritarianism, repeating what occurred in Eastern Europe in 1989. However, any such re-awakening should be examined with a degree of caution, insofar as the civil actors involved in the Arab Uprisings are not those that might have been expected to have a prominent role (Challand, 2011).

This chapter analyses the issue of civil society activism in the MENA in the context of the inter-paradigm debate between democratization and authoritarian resilience, and discusses the ways in which the Arab Awakening, while helping to dispel received notions of Arab societies, raises a number of puzzling points which must be considered in terms of the possible contribution of civil activism to political change.

Civil society: an overview

What is civil society?

Civil society is generally understood as comprising voluntary associations that operate in the zone between those of the individual and the state, but outside family or tribal linkages (Box 7.1 illustrates the debate about the definition of civil society). The dominant understanding of civil society emerged in the later-eighteenth and early-nineteenth centuries, and saw it as a defence against the infringement by the state on newly acquired rights and freedoms. Thus, voluntary associations could curb the power of centralizing institutions, protecting pluralism and nurturing constructive social norms. Civil society was conceived in opposition to the state as a liberal sphere that would keep the authorities in check. In this way, a highly articulated civil society was seen as the foundation of a stable democratic polity, a defence against domination by any one group and a barrier to anti-democratic forces (Edwards, 2004: 7). From this, it follows that an inherently normative character is ascribed to civil society, which is seen as a force for good, resisting the tendency of the state and its institutions to dominate. Civil society therefore functions as a barrier and safeguard against an overbearing state. However, while this is the orthodox view of civil society in Western political thought, it is not the only view. Other approaches – drawing on thinkers such as Hegel, Marx and Gramsci, in particular – focus on the inequality and conflict that characterize civil society. Abdelrahman suggests that those who see voluntary organizations as the primary means of democratic governance fail to recognize 'enduring conflicts' within society and the prospect that the most powerful interests will dominate (2002: 24). The multiple, and often conflicting, definitions of civil society and civil activism have characterized their analysis in the context of the Middle East, providing numerous insights as to the value of these notions.

Civil society and democracy

There is no doubt that the central question when examining the role of civil society and how it operates is about the relationship between civil society and democracy. The mainstream view of this is that civil society and democracy are positively correlated. In other words, the existence of a thriving civil society sector is an indication of, and a precondition for, democracy. Therefore, promoting the existence and activities of civil society organizations is crucial to promoting democracy in any society; so, it is no surprise that the Western international community sees support for civil activism in authoritarian settings as one of the pillars of its democracy-promotion efforts. The view that civil society plays a key role in promoting democracy comes, in part at least, from an analysis of the political transformations that took place in Latin America and Eastern Europe in the late 1980s and early 1990s. In this perspective, a host of voluntary organizations – including civic movements, trade unions, religious associations and student groups – came together to put pressure for change on narrowly based authoritarian groups, achieving considerable success. The independent Polish trade union, Solidarnosc, is often cited as the best example of the success of civil activism under authoritarian constraints. However, some are more cautious in relation to all this and suggest that the fall of authoritarian governments in Latin America and Eastern Europe had more to do with their lack of legitimacy (Tempest, 1997) than the relentless demands emerging from civil society. In any case, the view that civil society was crucial in fostering democratic change prevailed and, for both scholars and decision-makers, the connection between civil activism and democratization is often seen as unproblematic.

Box 7.1 Defining civil society

There is no definition of civil society on which everyone agrees. This is made clear in Michael Edwards's brief survey of theorizing on the subject. Edwards suggests that, in classical tradition, civil society was treated as synonymous with the state – both concepts referred to a type of political association that governed social conflict 'through the imposition of rules that retrained citizens from harming one another'. This tradition was continued in late-medieval thought, which equated civil society with 'politically organized commonwealths'. However, this approach took a different turn between 1750 and 1850. In the Enlightenment tradition, civil society was seen not as indistinguishable from the state but, rather, as a defence against impingement by the state on newly acquired rights and freedoms.

'The dominant theme in this debate was the value of voluntary associations in curbing the power of centralizing institutions, protecting pluralism and nurturing constructive social norms ... A highly articulated civil society with overlapping memberships was seen as the foundation of a stable democratic polity, a defence against domination by any one group, and a barrier to anti-democratic forces' (Edwards, 2004: 7). However, while this has become the dominant view of civil society, it is not the only tradition in political thought. Others have focused on structural obstacles that prevent some groups from articulating their interests within society. This approach has been associated with Hegel, Marx and Gramsci, in particular. Hegel focused on the inequality and conflict that characterized civil society and which required resolution through state intervention. Gramsci's ideas of civil society were subsequently taken up by theorists such as John Dewey and Hannah Arendt in the United States and by Jurgen Habermas in Europe, who developed the idea of the 'public sphere' as an essential component of democracy.

Source: Michael Edwards (2004). *Civil Society*, Cambridge: Polity, 7–9.

The assumption, however, that a simple expansion in the number of civil society organizations will, of itself, engender democratic political change is challenged by Kamrava and Mora (1998). The two authors argued that, to become agents of democratization, civil society oragnizations must themselves operate democratically, complement their own agendas with demands for democracy, and either be sufficiently powerful in their own right, or work with other organizations to promote change. Berman adds another cautionary note, pointing out that under certain circumstances a strong civil society may even weaken a democratic regime. Using the example of inter-war Germany, where voluntary organizations flourished, she argues that civil society can fragment as much as unite a society, accentuating and deepening existing cleavages, if pre-existing political institutions are weak (Berman, 1997: 565). For others, such as Jamal (2007), there is no reason to believe that an inevitable connection exists between civil activism and democracy. There is, thus, a plethora of views regarding the precise relationship between civil society and democratization, and a dominant view which assumes a positive correlation between the two is being increasingly challenged.

Civil society and the Middle East

Regardless of how the relationship between civil society and democracy is conceptualized, it seems clear that there has been a very significant upsurge in civil society activism in the MENA in recent decades. According to Yom, the numbers of civil society organizations in the region grew from around 20,000 in the 1970s to 70,000 by the 1990s (Yom, 2005: 18) and this rise in numbers accelerated during the 2000s (Howe, 2005) – although this growth in numbers varies greatly from country to country, with Morocco at the higher end of the spectrum and Syria at the lower end. It should also be noted that there has always been a very strong tradition of civil activism in Israel and Lebanon, due to the democratic or quasi-democratic nature of their political systems, and the degree of political pluralism in both countries. Similarly, in Turkey, despite periods of direct intervention of the military into politics, civil society activism has been traditionally strong. In any case, there are a number of possible reasons for the growth of civil society in authoritarian settings in the MENA. These include the suppression or co-optation of opposition political parties, which meant that activism moved to the civil sphere; social trends, such as increased levels of urbanization and education; and the encouragement of civil society by international actors; as well as increased consciousness of human rights, environmental and feminist issues (Carapico, 2000). This connection with what can be considered global issues should not be underestimated because these have allowed a number of organizations across the region to build on them to make local claims.

Despite this increased level of activity, theoretical debate continues as to how relevant the concept of civil society is to the MENA region, on the grounds that it is a unique expression of Western political development and, therefore, does not have application in other contexts. In reality, as Browers (2006) argues, it is precisely the many ways in which the concept has been translated, integrated and subsumed into non-Western political theories that allow scholars to utilize it in relation to the Arab world. Civil society entered the academic and political lexicon of Arab social and political actors a long time ago. The lively intellectual debates in the region about the conceptualization and meaning of civil society should not be seen merely in terms of reaction to debates originating from outside. The MENA is the site of an intense intellectual life across the region which makes a rich and autonomous contribution to global debates, and is not merely a passive recipient of ideas from other cultural and political settings. Nonetheless, both the definition and practical relevance of civil society activism remain contested. As highlighted earlier, until the late 1990s the dominant approach to the study of Arab politics drew on theories of democratization, which reflected both Eurocentric experience and the political preoccupations of the international community. Heavily influenced, as we have seen, by analysis of the transitions in Eastern Europe and Latin America, the paradigm of democratization was applied to the MENA, with particular attention being paid to the role of civil society and civil activism. The growth of civil activism was interpreted as a positive development with the potential to pose a strong, challenge to authoritarian élites, since the more autonomy civil society enjoyed from the state, the greater its capability to make strong demands of that state.

From this perspective, there is an inextricable link between civil society, democracy and democratization. However, when considered from the perspective of the paradigm of authoritarian persistence, the same concept takes on a more nuanced characterization. Rather than leading to the promised land of democracy (Kubba, 2000), the growth of civil society may be seen as either ineffective or counter-productive in challenging authoritarianism.

These diverging points of departure have led to the emergence of a number of specific approaches to the relationship between civil society and political change in the region, or the absence thereof. Some of these adopt a normative conceptualization of civil society activism and link it inextricably to political liberalism and democratization. Other approaches rely on a normatively neutral definition of activism de-linking it from the same notions. Depending on the approach, very different analyses of activism in the Arab world are presented. This has profound implications not only for our understanding of the concept itself and its practical application, but also for the policy-making choices of internal and external actors, and the potential impact of these for political change. For instance, supporting increased civil society activism has consistently been identified as a necessary element in challenging Arab authoritarianism (Kubba, 2000). As a result, the Western international community invested significant resources in stimulating such activism, in the hope of generating sufficient momentum for society to 'take on' authoritarian ruling élites. This policy strategy flows from the assumption that civil activism, per se, is capable of 'fighting' against authoritarianism, due to its liberal and democratic character. But what if the concept is stripped of its normative content? Would strengthening activism, then, have any effect on prospects for political change? These questions are not merely theoretical, insofar as the answers to them inform the ways in which policy prescriptions are, and should be, formulated. In the post-Arab Uprisings context, such questions retain their validity.

Civil society activism in MENA: main approaches

From all of this, at least five main approaches can be identified, when civil society activism in the MENA is examined.

Civil society as liberal

The first approach follows the traditional normatively-laden definition of the concept of civil society, anchored in democratic theory and drawing on an exclusively liberal understanding of the concept. It focuses attention on the numerical paucity and limited influence of civil organizations that are 'secular in ideology, civil in their behavior, legally recognized, and supportive of democratic reform' (Yom, 2005). This is the crucial point within this approach, reflecting its Eurocentrism and its inability to conceive of activism outside strict ideological parameters. Rather than examining what groups and associations do or demand in practice, or how they interact with each other and other actors in the same environment, their religious ethos is taken as disqualifying them from being considered legitimate civil society actors. In some ways, this rigidity is understandable insofar as the defence and promotion of individual rights – the very basis of liberal democracy – is perceived to be in inherent conflict with religious injunctions which, by their very nature, constrain the personal choices available to individuals. What emerges is a picture of civil society activism in the MENA region that is inevitably disappointing because democratic and liberal values are not as widespread as would be required to challenge authoritarian rule successfully. The weakness of civil activism is compared with its strength in Eastern Europe and Latin America, where, according to received wisdom, it was able to undermine authoritarianism precisely because of the widespread appeal of the liberal and democratic values which underpinned an autonomous civil society. The liberal approach, while not explicitly denying that the concept of civil society can be exported to the Arab world, proposes that it is extremely difficult for civil society to emerge in what are considered deeply illiberal societies still imprisoned, in a sense, by their religion-inspired conservatism. Therefore, civil activism is the preserve of the very few, usually enlightened, members of an urban middle class who have close contacts with Western societies. The main problem this approach identifies is that dissent from the authoritarian practices embodied in the state does not coalesce around liberal and democratic notions but, rather, around regressive, conservative, undemocratic and illiberal religious fundamentalism. The outcome of this dynamic can only be the reaffirmation of authoritarian practices of governance that are present both at the level of the state, where they are expected, and at the level of society.

Because this approach proposes a conceptualization of civil society as uniquely liberal and democratic in nature, the idea of an Islamist civil society is a contradiction in terms. When the civil society organizations that dominate the field of activism in the Arab world are examined through this liberal definition of civil society, it can only be concluded that they are very weak. In turn, this weakness is seen as a great obstacle to political change (Abootalebi, 1998) and, as long as liberal and democratic values are not prevalent, authoritarianism will persist. It follows that even if incumbent regimes were to collapse, those replacing them would be equally dictatorial, if not more so (Zakaria, 2004). This is a problematic approach, because it is largely de-contextualized from the reality of the Arab world and denies even the possibility of religious values being in kilter with support for pluralistic politics and government accountability. According to a number of studies, the majority of ordinary Arab citizens see democracy in positive terms (Pew Research, 2012; Tessler *et al.*, 2012). Crucially, it also essentializes the European experience and its construction of liberal-democracy. Nonetheless, this approach, despite its problematic ahistoricity, is often the basis on which Western democracy-promotion policies are based.

Civil society as 'neutral'

The second approach builds on the theoretical work of Encarnacion (2006), who conceptualizes civil society in neutral terms and refuses to assume that the concept is necessarily rooted in liberal democratic theory. Encarnacion does not specifically refer to the Arab world, but his argument – that civil society does not necessarily possess a normative liberal-democratic nature – offers a better understanding of the complexity of activism in Arab countries. Whereas the first approach discards the possibility that Islamism might be part of civil society, the second makes no such assumption. This is particularly useful in relation to Arab countries where Islamic activism is by far the most popular form of civil engagement, whether through charitable associations or more openly political groupings, learning societies or cultural movements. What matters in this approach is the individual nature and ethos of the associations that make up civil society and the values to which they subscribe, together with the demands that they make on the authorities. This focus on the values that they promote and defend means that civil society can, potentially, be both strong and 'uncivil' (Kopecky and Mudde, 2003) at the same time. In this respect, activism is the most important element of civil society because its 'civility' does not necessarily coincide with liberal and democratic values, but it is simply an indication that the *civis* is becoming involved in a number of different issues to change the way in which decision-making takes place.

This approach in some ways rediscovers the original definition of civil society, stripped of its normative content, whereby it simply becomes the space between the state and the individual, in which voluntary groups are formed with the intention of pursuing a specific social goal. From this understanding, it follows that Arab civil activism is not as weak as the first approach contends, because significant numbers of groups and associations operating autonomously from the state do exist and have characterized Arab societies for a long time. This approach, in addition, makes clear that both the notion of civil society and its practices pre-date colonial times and are therefore de-linked from the Eurocentrism that often characterizes studies of civil activism in the region. The work that most closely epitomizes this second approach is Berman's study of Egyptian civil society (2003). Her argument is that, contrary to received wisdom, Egyptian civil activism is far from being weak. In fact, it is extremely strong, particularly because the state has retreated from the public sphere and from the delivery of a host of public services, leaving society to self-organize, and to respond to the demands and social needs of different sectors of the population. In Egypt, as elsewhere across the Arab world, the extent of state intervention in society decreased considerably over the last three decades, as Chapter 4 on the political economy discussed in detail, under the combined pressure of privatization and globalization, allowing society to garner significant strength through a process of autonomous self-organization and mobilization. The retreat of the state was intended to improve economic performance, but also, at least from the perspective of international financial institutions, to loosen the political grip of the state, particularly on the middle class. With economic reforms delegating increasing autonomy to the private sector, thus detaching the middle class from state patronage, political demands for democratic change would emerge. This did occur to some extent and, as a result, 'the region is replete with domestic political activism' (Singerman, 2004: 149) based on civil society organizations.

The second approach offers a picture of a strong civil society that enjoys a degree of independence from the state and is able to pursue specific objectives almost unhindered. The problem is that this does not necessarily lead to political change, since this expression of civil society is unsuited to the promotion of democracy and liberal values because Islamist groups and associations dominate the field. Demands for change did, indeed, emerge, but they were not couched in the familiar language of liberalism and, crucially, liberal-democracy. For Berman, as for many other scholars, the problem lies in the *ethos* of Islamist movements that are considered illiberal and undemocratic by definition. The nature of Islamism is particularly problematic because Islamists:

> want to re-articulate the boundary between the public and private itself to propose a less secular and autonomous vision of the good life and governance. (Singerman, 2004: 150)

This re-articulation runs counter to liberal norms and, therefore, constitutes an obstacle to democratic political change. Two specific reasons have been offered for the absence of political change due to the dominance of Islamism in society. First, and quite obviously, the Arab state, despite having retreated from engaging with society, retains strong repressive powers that it displays when faced with a significant threat to its existence. In some ways, the Islamization of society in itself is not necessarily a concern for the ruling élites if such Islamization is confined to social activism and does not threaten the grip of the élites on political power. Indeed, the social work of Islamist organizations can even be useful because, in part, it relieves the state of some of its duties when it comes to the provision of social services. The evidence of this can be found in the toleration, if not outright promotion, of quietist Salafism in countries such as Egypt, Morocco and, since the mid-2000s, Tunisia. Quietist Salafists refrain from entering the political arena and focus their attention on doctrinal matters, religious education and charity work, subscribing to the view that Muslims should accept whatever ruler is in place without questioning him, as long as he allows them to carry out their religious mission. This type of Salafism is beneficial to rulers because its supposedly 'apolitical' stances are, in reality, profoundly political, in the sense that they favour stability and, therefore, the status quo (al-Anani and Malik, 2013). But, when Islamization becomes an open political challenge in the form of an alternative conceptualization of state authority – as represented by the Egyptian Muslim Brotherhood, political Salafists insisting on the application of *shari'a* law or *jihadi* Salafists committed to violence to overthrow the regime – the state reacts through co-optation and/or repression to defuse the danger. The outcome is authoritarian stability despite significant social change. Thus, society can be as Islamized as may be. What matters is that the upper echelons of the state and its authority are not endangered. The second, and some-

Box 7.2　'Civil' versus 'uncivil' society?

The tension between secular and Islamic civil society organizations is clearly to be seen in the campaign to reform family law in Morocco in the late 1990s and early 2000s. The *Moudawana* – the legal code that governs areas of family law such as marriage, divorce, inheritance and child custody – gave few rights to women on its introduction in 1958. It was, in fact, based on a 'pact' whereby the monarch would ensure the continuation of traditional social practices in exchange for the allegiance of tribal groups to defeat the nationalist movement, which wanted to marginalize the monarchy as a powerful political player in independent Morocco. The *Moudawana*, for example, allowed men the right unilaterally to divorce their wives, while women's right to divorce was highly restricted. Women could not marry without the approval of a guardian or tutor, and married women were obliged by law to obey their husbands, whereas men could marry multiple women without the consent of their wives.

Following a campaign by women's rights activists, some limited reforms were enacted in 1993, during the reign of King Hassan II. The Moroccan King enjoys religious legitimacy and he took it upon himself to rule on the issue in order to avoid political dissent between modernists and conservatives. The problem for the King was that the women's rights movement had linked their 'sectoral' issue to the broader question of democratization, which needed to be defused by rewarding women activists with some token reforms of family law. Hassan died in six years later and there was widespread expectation of change when the new King, Muhammad VI, came to power. Predominantly secular and liberal women's rights organizations became involved in lobbying at both national and international levels for more radical reform of the law. However, this was

what more insidious, way in which stability is maintained is through the division that already exists between what are perceived as the few liberal democrats and the supposedly many authoritarian Islamists. This is certainly a crude characterization of Arab societies and many other cross-cutting cleavages exist such as the class or rural–urban divides. However, divisions within society over the fundamental values that should underpin it prevent the articulation of a new post-authoritarian vision (Cavatorta, 2009a). For example, Egyptian political struggles in the aftermath of the departure of Mubarak, or the inability of the Moroccan protest movement of 20 February to secure more thorough changes from the monarch in the spring of 2011, are partly due to the significant divergences between a broadly secular and a religious vision of society that affected political movements in both countries. A similar dynamic characterizes other countries of the region, also. The Turkish context, for instance, can be seen as a powerful reminder of the profound differences that exist in the country when it comes to the issue of the *laicité* of the republic (Cevik and Tas, 2013).

opposed by Islamic scholars, religious organizations and the Islamist *Parti de la Justice et du Developpement* (the Party of Justice and Development – PJD).

On 12 March 2000, what became known as 'the battle of the marches' took place. Several hundred thousand people took to the streets in the capital, Rabat, in support of the reforms. However, this success was eclipsed, as an even greater number marched the same day in Casablanca, in a protest organized by Islamists opposed to the reforms. The Casablanca march demonstrated the extent of popular opposition to reform of the family law code in what was considered a Western imposition of mores and traditions. The impasse was resolved only when the King intervened and used his personal and religious authority to ensure the passage of the reforms through parliament. The opportunity to do this was created by the Casablanca bombings of May 2003 which were carried out by the radical Islamist group, *Salafiya Jihadiya*. The women's movement celebrated victory, while the Islamist opposition, with varying degrees of reluctance, came around to supporting the reforms, because the new law subscribed at least nominally to Islamic values. However, the manner in which the reforms were secured had significant implications for all sectors of civil society. First, a liberal outcome was secured through reliance on inherently undemocratic mechanisms. Second, this had implications for the implementation of reform on the ground – it has been strongly suggested that the reforms are not widely implemented in practice. Third, the manner of the intervention of the King to secure the passage of the reforms suggests that there is no reason why, in the future, liberal reforms might not be reversed in the same way, should the King (or a successor) deem it appropriate to do so.

Source: F. Cavatorta and V. Durac (2010). *Civil Society and Democratization in the Arab World: The Dynamics of Activism*, London: Routledge, 60–5.

One of the most telling examples of how divisions within civil society impair what should be a common struggle against authoritarianism concerns the issue of women's rights. While Chapter 8 is dedicated entirely to gender politics, it is worth exploring this in some detail, in order to see how the secular–religious divide functions in practice. What can be observed is that liberal/secular groups engaged in advancing individual women's rights find it almost impossible to share the terrain with Islamists, because of conflicting visions about the role – and, therefore the legal status and rights – of women in society. This ideological conflict inevitably extends to how these two sectors of society envisage a potential post-authoritarian future. The absence of any consensus on how to proceed, once the regime falls, undermines the possibility of unitary efforts. From Algeria to Morocco and Tunisia to Syria, the question of women's rights is very divisive within civil society, as the numerous struggles over personal status legislation indicate. The politics of post-uprising Tunisia, as will be illustrated later in more detail, has seen the issue of women's rights rise to the top of the political agenda, with the Islamist *Ennahda* party proposing the notion of the 'complementarity' of women to men and the secular parties – as well as civil society organizations – wholly rejecting this in favour of the clear and undisputable notion of equality. While it can be contended that the issue was blown out of proportion, it is still indicative of the rawness of the divergence of views.

From the perspective of this approach, civil society can be both strong and uncivil and, in the Arab world, the role of being 'uncivil' is accorded to the dominant Islamists, who are believed to be a priori illiberal and undemocratic, by virtue of the values they stand for and the policies they wish to implement once in power (see Box 7.2). The resulting interactions between the state, the liberal sector of civil society and Islamists prevent meaningful political change from occurring. Indeed, if it were to occur, as it did in Egypt after the fall of Mubarak in 2011, it would be undesirable in the long term because it would lead not to democracy but, rather, to a different form of authoritarian rule. The implications of this approach inform the ways in which many understand political dynamics in the region after the Arab uprisings – preferring, therefore, authoritarian stability to a democratic uncertainty that might lead, in any case, to the reproduction of authoritarian political and social practices.

Despite being rooted in profoundly different definitions and understandings of civil society, the first two approaches arrive at the same conclusion regarding the relationship between civil activism and political change. They both contend that there are two separate sectors of civil society that simply do not combine in a way that is conducive to the establishment of democracy. The first approach, framed within the democratization literature, contends that only traditional secular and liberal associations are deserving of the label 'civil society'. Given that such groupings are small and constitute only a minority in society, political change through civil activism is deemed impossible. The second approach also builds on the assumption of a neatly divided society where 'good' secular and 'bad' Islamic associations compete. While it acknowledges that civil society, as a whole, possesses significant resources and popular legitimacy, from this perspective also, democratic political change is deemed to be impossible to achieve through activism, because the triumph of civil society would translate into an Islamist takeover, which would simply lead to a different form of authoritarianism. The most important criticism that can be laid at the door of both approaches is precisely the simplistic assumption that they make about the divided nature of society and the normative character that is assigned to its two constitutive parts. The reality is that, when one examines Arab civil society and activism in the region in any detail, what emerges is a much more complex picture where a priori labelling is not particularly helpful in explaining or understanding social and political dynamics.

Certainly, there are associations that have a more secular ethos while others subscribe to a religious ethos. But the differences are not always that stark and, in countries such as Jordan, Morocco, Tunisia or Egypt, there have been instances of cooperation between the two sectors. In addition, a priori labelling is often a superficial characterization that comes from the outside and is not especially helpful in identifying what a specific association stands and works for in all its complexity. Over a decade ago, Brumberg (2002b) highlighted the problem of attempting to identify the essence or nature of political and civil society groups with precision. This is for two reasons. From a theoretical point of view, it is extremely difficult to ascertain the character of an organization in isolation from the surrounding environment. This is because interactions with other groups, with the state and with its own members can conceivably modify its supposed true nature. This does not mean that there are not groupings – such as the Aryan Nation, or the Ku Klux Klan in the United States – whose values cannot be established with precision. But, the exercise becomes complicated when groups simply represent that they have a religious ethos, which can be construed and practised in very different ways. From an empirical point of view, both secular/liberal and Islamist associations have a very mixed record in defending and promoting the values of democracy and liberalism. Islamist associations are frequently accused of being illiberal and undemocratic. But, while some of them have certainly been so in the past and some might remain so today, there is a deal of evidence to substantiate the claim that many have also been engaged in the defence of democratic procedures and key liberal values (Cavatorta, 2006). The struggle of the Moroccan Islamist Justice and Charity Group against the use of torture on the part of the state is but one example. Conversely, secular and liberal organizations have not necessarily been the beacons of liberal-democracy and, at times, have defended undemocratic and illiberal positions in order to gain short-term benefits from incumbent regimes (Cook, 2005). Again, the example of Morocco is particularly telling. Many human rights organizations and activists either supported – tacitly or publicly – or were silent, when widespread human rights abuses were committed by the state's security forces against Salafis throughout the 2000s (Cavatorta and Durac, 2010: 69–70).

Civil society as regime tool

Taking into account the criticisms that the previous approaches have drawn, the third approach relies on empirical data as the starting point for analysis of relations between civil society and political change. It builds on a neutral definition of civil society, which encompasses both Islamist and secular organizations, without a priori judgements as to their nature, to highlight the ways in which Arab civil society has been strengthening over the last two decades, while noting that this led to little political change before the Arab Awakening, which, in any case, did not have at its core traditional civil society activism. As a result, this third approach proposes that civil society has largely been 'created' by incumbent regimes to deflect attention from political authoritarianism, to please the international community, extracting financial benefits in the process, and to get to know their societies better in order to upgrade authoritarian rule (Heydemann, 2007). Thus, the explosion of civil activism is not an indication that the Arab state is losing control of its society. Rather, the state, through the enactment of more liberal legislation regarding freedom of association, has simply enabled society to create more civil society organizations. But these are not wholly autonomous or independent from the state. First, the repressive apparatus of the state monitors them closely, and, when necessary, infiltrates them or constrains their activities. For instance, the Tunisian Union of Journalists was taken over by the members of the intelligence services in mid-2005, after having elected a controversial anti-regime figure as its head. The union continued to exist and operate, but it loyally sided with the Ben Ali regime. In addition, this emerging civil society is fully aware that its work can be quickly brought to an end and is, therefore, careful not to upset the powers-that-be. Finally, members of the ruling élites create associations that cannot be easily distinguished from state-sponsored institutions and that are far from autonomous (Liverani, 2008). Overall, the third approach examines civil society in the Arab world as it if were an artificial creation with limited autonomy of action, at best, and acting as an instrument for ruling élites to pre-empt political opposition and to move controversial debates outside the political system, at worst (Wiktorowicz, 2000). As a consequence, political change does not occur, because there is no intent on the part of the state to reduce its control over society, and society itself is incapable of challenging its own 'creators'. This approach may be criticized for overstating the extent to which civil society organizations are no more than artificial regime creations. Nonetheless, it possesses a great deal of validity, as Wiktorowicz's (2000) analysis of civil society in Jordan makes clear, together with Liverani's study of Algeria (2008). Indeed, this extends to all authoritarian countries in the region. The artificial creation of organizations that are labelled as constituent elements of civil society, but lack all of the meaningful attributes of a civil society organization, is captured by the category of government-organized non-governmental organizations (GONGOs) and similar types of organizations, as Box 7.3 highlights.

GONGOs deserve to be described in some detail because they are an important part of the story of civil activism in the Arab world and they

Box 7.3   GONGOs, RONGOs, QUANGOs and FLANGOs

Attempts by regimes in the region to infiltrate and control the civil society sector have given birth to a range of acronyms in an attempt to capture this phenomenon. These include:

- GONGOs – government-organized non-governmental organizations
- RONGOs – royal non-governmental organizations
- QUANGOs – quasi-autonomous non-governmental organizations
- FLANGOs – First Lady non-governmental organizations

The last has been a particularly prevalent element of civil society activism across the region. Suzanne Mubarak, the long-time First Lady of Egypt, established or chaired a number of CSOs, including the Integrated Care Society, which promoted the provision of public libraries for poorer children; the Egyptian Society for Childhood and Development; the Egyptian Red Crescent; and the Suzanne Mubarak International Women's Movement for Peace, which claimed to be the first 'peace-calling' women's organization in the Middle East.

Leila Trabelsi, wife of former Tunisian president Ben Ali, founded the Basma Association in 2000 to help secure employment for disabled people, as well as SAIDA, which was an initiative to improve cancer treatment in the country. She was also prominently associated with the Union Nationale de la Femme Tunisienne (the National Union of Tunisian Women).

Princess Lalla Salma, wife of the King of Morocco, is closely involved with the Association Lalla Salma Contre Le Cancer.

Queen Rania of Jordan is closely associated with the Jordan River Foundation, which has the protection of the rights and needs of children and the empowerment of individuals and communities as its objectives.

remain crucial actors in Morocco, Jordan and the Gulf States. These organizations are directly set up by regimes, or prominent figures within the regime, to function as civil society actors, although there is a widespread recognition that they emanate directly from the ruling élites, and, more often than not, have powerful patrons with direct links to the ruler. One of the most interesting examples can be found in Syria, where the wife of President Bashar al-Asad is the initiator and patron of the very large association Syria Trust whose work is devoted to promote activism in fields as varied as entrepreneurship, education and the environment. Salam Kawakibi (2012) has examined the workings of the association in great detail. The Syria Trust functions as a large development NGO which purports to promote the values of individualism, freedom and creativity with which civil society activism is usually associated. But the contradiction is quite obvious since the organization is clearly a device through which the regime attempts to re-organize and mobilize society, in order to better integrate it into the modernization path that the regime itself has chosen by way of alternative to the traditional mobilizational role played by the *Baath* party.

The Syria Trust, as in the case of the other GONGOs across the region, has been created for three reasons. First, they fill the vacuum the state has left in providing social services through Victorian-style charity work, which is meant to highlight the concern of the ruling élites for the poor and disenfranchised. It is no coincidence that it is often First Ladies who act as patrons of these associations, as in the Syrian case, and in Jordan, as well as Tunisia under Ben Ali and Egypt under Mubarak. Rather than choosing a path that would genuinely liberate the social and economic resources of their countries and adopting policies that would see meaningful attempts by the state to lift citizens out of poverty, ruling élites display their 'concern' for the less well-off through charitable organizations and bestow patronage in so doing. Second, the creation of GONGOs constitutes an opportunity for the regime to link up with members of emerging social groups by offering both material and moral benefits in a professionally run environment. Finally, GONGOs can attract significant sources of foreign funding because they can offer international partners a smooth implementation of their projects, given the political connections they enjoy.

The presence of GONGOs throughout the region partly vindicates the third approach. However, because it discounts the presence of genuinely autonomous and independent groupings, this approach fails to do justice to the complexity of activism in the Arab world, where many activists have suffered personally for their engagement, and many groups have been forcefully shut down and severely repressed. Thus, this approach may be criticized for its lack of sophistication, insofar as all associations and organizations are considered to be artificial regime creations or easily co-opted – and therefore marginalized politically. This is not the whole reality. If one examines the effectiveness of genuinely autonomous organizations, the record is one of very limited efficacy. Nonetheless, their existence should be beyond dispute, as should their autonomy. As Kubba (2000: 87) points out, 'thousands of private organizations have survived government attempts to thwart their activities and reduce their influence', which suggests that autonomy rather than compliance is what many organizations display. If this were not the case, there would be little need to maintain a large apparatus with responsibility for disrupting the activities of such groups and activists. From those agitating for human rights to Islamist activists, and from trade unionists to cultural intellectual figures, Arab prisons have been filled with genuine regime opponents who attempted to organize grassroots activities with the objective of challenging the hold of regimes on societies.

Civil society and authoritarian constraints

The fourth approach is a more nuanced version of the third one and has been dominant in recent years. It continues to provide an important contribution to the understanding of how civil society works in the Arab world, even in the aftermath of the Arab Uprisings. This approach relies greatly on the theoretical work of Amaney Jamal (2007), who argues convincingly that, rather than looking at the activism of civil society activism and the organizations that make it up, the focus should be on the broader authoritarian context that frames activism and constrains it (as Box 7.4 illustrates), in accounting for the legislative armour states employ to contain activism. According to Jamal, it is these authoritarian constraints that determine the way in which civil society operates so that both liberal and Islamist movements are unable to challenge the authoritarian system and, consequently, perform the function that seems natural to civil society – namely, to strive for democratization. The problem therefore is not the ethos – or the supposed ethos – of individual associations; neither is it the conflict between ideologically divergent sectors of society. The inability of civil society to function as an enabler of democracy has clear origins for Jamal. In order to carry out their work and achieve their stated objectives, associations have to work within the constraints of authoritarian systems when it comes to practical issues such as funding, permits to operate, validity of statutes and so on. This means that they need to acquiesce in many of the practices that characterize authoritarian rule, including reliance on patronage networks, to obtain what they need. If they conform then they can operate, be effective and increase social capital. However, if they refuse to play by the 'corrupt' rules of the game, they can be shut down, ostracized and become ineffective, losing social capital as a consequence. The problem is obvious. On the one hand, if associations work well and are effective, it is because they compromise on the liberal and democratic values that they are supposed to hold as members of civil society. Their effectiveness and practical achievements paradoxically strengthen authoritarian rule, because these depend on the goodwill of the regime, or at least on its neutrality. On the other hand, associations that refuse to embrace the rules of the game, and are determined to fight them in the name of normative values and rights, incur all sorts of practical problems that prevent their effectiveness. This applies equally to secular/liberal organizations, as well as to Islamist organizations.

The fourth approach avoids the pitfalls of the third, insofar as it does not consider all organizations operating in society as artificial creations, or as easily co-opted. It acknowledges that genuine and autonomous groupings may be active, but it also recognizes the fact that they might be extremely ineffective precisely because they decide to challenge the system and its values, rather than playing along. This paradox explains the absence of democratic political change.

However, this is a rather problematic argument because it does not seem to contemplate the possibility of change. While it is beyond dispute that authoritarian constraints structure the ways in which civil society organizations operate and condition the terms of their engagement with authoritarian regimes, Jamal predicates her argument on endless rigidity. Given the structures in place, it becomes impossible for change to occur despite the best intentions of individual groupings. Instead, change can only come about as a concession from the top. But there is no incentive for this to occur because challenges are routinely and easily dealt with. By dismissing the possibility of change, the validity of this approach is undermined, because, when change does take place, we are at a loss to explain it.

Civil society as activated citizenship

While building on Jamal's intuition and acknowledging the impact of authoritarian constraints in shaping civil activism, the fifth approach seeks to incorporate the possibility of change, by broadening the definition of civil society itself and, crucially, by widening the net of actors that are considered to be part of it. The notion of 'activated or activist citizenship' is incorporated within this conceptualization of civil society. This concept allows us to go beyond the examination of activism as the product of formal organizations and structures, as the previous approaches do. Without exception, the four approaches that have been outlined emphasize traditional hierarchical and structured associations as the only actors that can be considered part of civil society. This limited view does not capture the complexity of how society 'expresses' itself, particularly in authoritarian regimes where organizing along the lines of formal associations might be counter-productive, if one wishes to promote liberal-democratic values, or values that are in any way at odds with those of the regime. A structure, a statute, a hierarchy and formality provide an easy target for the repressive apparatus. It follows that other modes of engagement might exist beyond those that feature the 'usual suspects' of civil society as protagonists, including practices of individual dissent that cannot be easily observed. These might range from the individual writings of lone dissenters that are then circulated or 'represented', to mass participation in specific events such as football matches, to open political engagement through social media to individual behaviour that runs against what the state sanctions as legitimate and proper. Thus, it is not only the nature of civil society that is being re-shaped, but also its

Box 7.4   Egypt's laws on civil society

Legislative provision for the operation of civil society organizations in Egypt illustrates the degree to which regimes in the region seek to control and direct the sector. The 1964 Law 32 regulated civil associations in Egypt. Under this law, such associations could not function without first registering with the Ministry of Social Affairs. In order to register, associations had to undertake not to engage in any 'political activities'. The ambiguity of the phrase allowed the ministry to intimidate organizations by threatening to suspend their activities, if and when regime officials deemed it necessary. Furthermore, the authorities had the right under the law to reject an association if its establishment was not 'in accord with security measures', or 'if the environment has no need for the services of another association'.

Law 32 was replaced, first, by Law 153 of 1999, which was deemed unconstitutional on procedural grounds by the Egyptian Constitutional Court in 2000. The regime then adopted Law 84 of 2002. This proved to be even more restrictive in its provisions than its predecessors. The new law required associations to register with the Ministry of Social Affairs and prohibited them from engaging in 'political and union activities' without specifying what the scope of such activities might be. It provided that the Boards of Directors of associations should be approved in advance by the Ministry and banned them from receiving foreign funding without the prior permission of the government. In February 2012, 43 foreign workers with organizations promoting democracy and human rights were sent for trial on charges of involvement in illegal activity and illegal receipt of foreign funds. In June of the same year, all were found guilty and sentenced to between one and five years in prison, although many had already left the country when the verdicts were delivered.

Source: Al-Tawi, Ayat (2013). 'New NGO law strikes fear in Egyptian civil society', *Al-Ahram Weekly*, 24 May, available at http://english.ahram.org.eg/NewsContent/1/64/71987/Egypt/Politics-/New-NGO-draft-law-strikes-fear-in-Egyptian-civil-s.aspx.

actors. The overwhelming focus on classic hierarchical and formal organizations also prevents observers of civil society from engaging with the numerous technological changes that underscore new forms of activism. In his study of Cuba's civil cyber-activism, Hoffman asserts that the distribution of information and ideas through the internet, and particularly the blogosphere, created a more:

self-assertive 'citizenship from below' which demands, and, to some degree enacts, (empowered by digital and web-based technologies), a widening of the public sphere, and a greater degree of citizen autonomy from the state, leading to a different type of civil society activity. (2012: 237)

This has made a tremendous difference when compared with the type of activism previously seen on the island. While the role of social media in the Arab Awakening should not overstated, it should not be dismissed either. This type of activism does not conform to traditional mobilization, rendering it more efficient and less penetrable by the security services. This does not mean that hierarchical associations and organized social movements are no longer relevant, but the broadening of the definition of who is part of civil society allows for acknowledgment that a large part of civil activism might be taking place beyond such hierarchical organizations precisely because, in authoritarian systems, the constraints in place favour operating beyond immediately recognizable forms of activism. In this respect, the notion of non-movement that Asef Bayat proposes is particularly interesting, because it places at the centre of activism the daily acts of resistance that are neither counted nor perceived as such, but that add up over time. It is also significant that the fifth approach refuses to embrace the assumption that civil activism equates to the promotion of liberal and democratic values. Despite integrating forms and actors of activism that are non-traditional, the fifth approach adheres to a neutral definition of civil society, seen as a competitive arena where organizations and activated citizens have different – and, at times, potentially conflicting – objectives. For instance, it is possible that activated citizenship will work to create a space for itself to be heard on a specific issue to the detriment of others, preferring to struggle for voice rather than for choice (Fumagalli, 2012).

The events of the Arab Spring seem to validate the linkage between civil society activism and political change. With the interpretive maps that the five approaches offer, we now turn to examine the connection between civil society and democratic openings in the Arab world.

Civil society, activated citizenship and the Arab Awakening

The arrival of the Arab Awakening has been greeted in some quarters as the '1989' moment for the region, recalling the momentous events of 1989 in Eastern Europe when communism began to crumble, leading to one of the most intense periods of transition to democracy in history, as countries across the globe began to abandon authoritarianism. However, the reference to 1989 also has another meaning which relates to the defeat of the authoritarian state at the hands of civil society. As mentioned, the collapse of communism in Eastern Europe has been hailed as a victory for civil society activism over the state, and the Arab Awakening has been interpreted in the same manner. Notwithstanding the fact that the contribution of civil society activism to the democratization of Eastern Europe might be more a matter of myth than historical reality, a closer reading of the Arab Awakening and its protagonists suggests that the influence of civil society activism on political change in the Arab world might not be as strong as many consider and might not necessarily lead to liberal-democratic governance. In this respect, the fifth approach to the study of civil activism seems to have been vindicated in a number of respects, and can provide an explanation as to why and how wider society confronted authoritarianism, albeit in a manner that was unexpected.

First, the role of traditional formal hierarchical structures and organizations in bringing about change has been extremely limited. Across the region, well-known and long-established politicized associations were notably absent in the early days of the protests. In Morocco, for instance, none of the principal human rights organizations participated in the early pro-democracy demonstrations. The initiative for early protests rested with young members of society, connected through social media and often disconnected from established civil society groups. Such groups were, in fact, reluctant to join the protests and, thereby, commit to a process that, if it failed, would likely lead to their disappearance at the hand of the regime. Both secular/liberal and Islamist groups refrained from embracing demonstrators in the early days. The absence of Islamist civil society groups at the helm of the demonstrations is particularly interesting because they were believed to be the most capable in mobilizing dissent. In Egypt, for instance, it was only under pressure from its younger members that the Muslim Brotherhood decided to join the protests after they had already been organized and carried out by a host of diverse ad hoc groups of young people employing social media to mobilize in the streets. As we will discuss in Chapter 11, their initial reluctance did not prevent them from later becoming the protagonsts of post-authoritarian arrangements in Tunisia, Egypt, Yemen and Libya. In any case, traditional civil society actors were as surprised by the events of 2011 as were regimes and the international community. The Tunisian journalist Béchir Ben Yahmed (2011: 4), writing in the aftermath of the uprising in that country stated that 'no party, no union, no politician gave the impetus for this popular uprising nor were they in any way involved'. This assertion obscures the contribution of explicitly political associations in Bahrain, or local trade unionists in Egypt and Tunisia, as well as human rights groups in Libya. Nonetheless, it captures the point that the root of the protests, their protagonists and the forms through which they occurred, did not conform to what was expected of traditional civil society. As Challand wrote:

> I choose the phrase 'counter-power of civil society' to describe the ongoing developments [in the Arab world] ... because I believe that there is more

to civil society than its organized form. There is more to civil society than NGOs and the developmental approach which imagines that the key to progress is when donors, the UN or rich countries, give aid to boost non-state actors, in particular NGOs, in the developing south. (2011)

The protagonists of the 'Awakening' were not to be found in main-stream civil society. In Tunisia, for example, the apolitical and 'disorgan-ized' youth in disenfranchised neighbourhoods across the country was largely responsible for battling the security forces and demonstrating that the regime was not as strong as it portrayed itself to be. Other sectors of society joined in and the 'Jasmine revolution' became a reality.

Thus, the fifth approach allows us to understand how civil society activism can be found outside the bounds of the mainstream. This suggests that there are multiple modes of engagement beyond formal institutions, including individual dissenters who can mobilize through social media; local activists who, on their own initiative, deviate from the official line of the organization to which they belong; mass events where spontaneous demands are voiced; and individuals who, both on- and off-line, live the reality of activism in their everyday life (Bayat, 2009). All these modes of engagement can then be activated when specific 'triggers', such as the self-immolation of Mohammad Bouazizi in rural Tunisia, are pulled.

The youth factor is extremely significant in this context. The older generation of activists across the region, particularly in the secular sector of society, had become pessimistic and disillusioned with the apparently apolitical character and behaviour of a younger generation, who seemed to be interested in either consumerism or personal religious piety, but not in politics and civil activism. The 'surprise' of older activists, expressed when talking about the youth, is a recurrent element of how the story of the Awakening is told. The view that the youth was either disengaged from politics or, for a minority of young people, interested only in political violence was misplaced. Traditional activists, as with many scholars and regimes, understood activism in terms of traditional notions and modes of engagement usually linked to hierarchical organizations that would seize on an opportunity to mobilize and 'confront' the regime with their demands. In fact, a great deal was happening 'under the radar' and it took forms that had neither been wholly codified, nor understood. Many young people did take an interest in political, social and economic issues, but organized themselves beyond the affiliations of traditional political parties and outside long-established civil society groups. The preference was for mobilizing along non-hierarchical lines, in ad hoc committees, with rotating and variable membership, and on very specific issues that seemed superficially apolitical. In a report on civil activism in Morocco that looked at the changing nature of activism in the country – one where socio-political activism had traditionally flourished despite repression, the magazine *La Jeune Afrique* noted that 'whereas the older generation of militants fought for democracy and political freedoms, [the new generation of militants] fights for the rights of every individual to act according to his/her own free will'. The report read as some sort of accusation against young activists because they had seemingly left 'big' ideas and objectives behind in favour of small and individual-centred struggles.

The tendency of older activists, whether secular or Islamist, to condemn such forms of activism indicates their inability to grasp the changes that activism itself had to go through. On the one hand, young activists shunned traditional activism because, simply put, it had not been successful in achieving what it had set out to do. Meaningful political change – the creation of liberal-democracy, or the creation of an Islamic state or, at the very least, the fall of the regime – had simply not occurred, while traditional forms of activism had been successfully neutralized by the authorities. On the other hand, the connection between individualistic small struggles and a wider objective was missed because it was believed that, once success had been achieved on small issue, de-mobilization would occur. Instead, small successes encouraged others to follow the same strategy and this led to the building of numerous cross-ideological and cross-issue linkages. The suggestion here is not that the new activism was part of a cunning strategy to deceive regimes with the impression of apolitical, non-ideological and individualistic civil engagement, but that this choice became natural in the face of the closure and ineffectiveness of traditional civil activism. As it turned out, the younger generation of activists was then perfectly placed to take advantage of the wavering of regimes at specific moments of crisis. These changes in the nature of civil activism had been taking place over the last ten years and, while they were deemed to be sufficiently apolitical to be tolerated (Haugbølle and Cavatorta, 2012), they profoundly mutated the 'game' of activism, providing three crucial advantages that traditional activism did not have. New activists have no strong political or ideological affiliations. There is no baggage from previous struggles, infighting and failures – leading to greater ideological flexibility which, in turn, translated into organizational flexibility. This allowed for the setting up of effective alliances and coalitions, which could then quickly be disbanded and reorganized along different lines to attract more supporters or to blindside the regime. In this context, the issue of political divisions on how to realize their objectives is deferred until political change is achieved, permitting an almost exclusive focus on the struggle at hand. With no real second-guessing of each other's intention, it was easier to work together and be attractive to large swathes of the population. In this respect, it is also quite easy to see why post-uprising coalition-making has proven so difficult. All social and ideological groups felt represented through the populist slogan of 'freedom, dignity and bread', but when it came to setting up institutional rules, legislating and implementing a specific vision, splits tended to appear quickly. What is also interesting about the forms that new activism took is its diffuse leadership. There is no Martin Luther King-like figure that everyone can point to in order to recognize easily what the struggle and its objectives are about. The absence of hierarchy, together with a high degree of decentralization, means that activism is unlikely to be hijacked by a charismatic leader, as has happened in the past. Again, this proved an advantage against the repressive apparatus, but left post-uprising politics exposed to countless claims to leadership that ended in political infighting. The youth factor is particularly intriguing because it also provides the link between the new type of activism and its means of mobilization. It should be emphasized from the beginning that the Arab uprisings are not 'twitter revolutions'. Street mobilization, face-to-face social networks, the on-the-ground leadership of local activists, and physical confrontation with the security forces as occurred in the poorer neighbourhoods of Tunis, for instance, were crucial means of mobilization, particularly when one takes into account the fact that internet access is not as widespread in the MENA region as it is in other parts of the world. Nevertheless, the importance of online activism should not be underestimated. It is significant because it provides a forum of civil engagement for many people who were isolated in highly repressive environments, but who could, as individuals, try to organize online around different campaigns that were not even necessarily political. Breaking the feeling of loneliness around issues about which an individual felt passionate permitted the linkage not only between individuals, but between causes as well, without the need for such causes to be framed in any specific ideological language – be it liberal-democracy, or the Islamic state. The denial of real space for activism to challenge ruling élites prompted its migration to online social media. There it was possible, despite the heavy policing of the internet, to create linkages that could subsequently be mobilized offline, at the right time. Social media and new technologies provided the perfect means for politically unaffiliated youth to act socially without ever having developed offline social trust.

Finally, the fifth approach is also validated by the unexpected role that trade unions came to play during the Arab Awakening. A neglected aspect of the Arab uprisings is that it has as much to do with economic demands as with political authoritarianism. In fact, according to Aita (2011), Springborg (2012) and Achcar (2013), among others, the social and economic inequalities created by the liberalization of Arab economies are the root causes of the uprisings, and are more important than democratic demands. The revival of trade unionism is important for the relationship between civil activism and political change in two ways. First, it was believed that trade unions, as civil society actors, had been completely marginalized by the state and the security forces, in the sense that their leaderships had been co-opted, in order to guarantee the social peace necessary to implement a programme of economic liberalization. Thus, they were disregarded as potential agents of change. But, the dismissal of trade unionism has proven to be misplaced, at least at the local level. In the face of increasing penury, declining living standards, rising unemployment and worsening work conditions, local trade union activists generated a significant amount of social activism that eventually resulted in the sidelining of their central leadership and the participation of workers to the uprisings. Suddenly, it became apparent that the works stoppages, strikes and demonstrations that had been a feature of Arab politics for several years before the uprisings were an indication of an activism that was to underpin subsequent political contestation. Although it has been seen by some as the manageable and confused reaction of the 'losers' of globalization, and therefore non-threatening to regime stability, the revival of trade union activism demonstrated, once again, that, outside the mainstream, important activism was being carried out (Allal, 2010). Second, the demands made by trade unionism of post-uprising regimes are very much rooted in traditional unionism, having to do with better pay, improved working conditions, and a greater role in the running of both public and private enterprises. This indicates that, while the institutions of democracy are important, they are seen by large sectors of trade unionism more as means to an end, than as ends in themselves. The work stoppages and strikes that have characterized post-Ben Ali Tunisia are an indication of how central economic demands are, because they take place while new democratic institutions are being built.

Conclusion

The five different approaches to the study of civil society activism and political change in the Arab world that have been identified in this chapter share surprisingly little in common aside from the fact that they focus on the mobilization of society outside the bounds of family linkages, the market and the state. Each approach contributes, in part, to a better understanding of activism and its relationship with political change, or the lack thereof, in the region. But, it is only the last approach that offers the neces-

sary tools for an understanding (if incomplete) of the recent Arab uprisings, and the power of civil society to bring about democratic change in
authoritarian contexts.

There are a number of lessons that can be learned from the analysis
provided in this chapter. First, the mobilization of society in the Arab
world is very different from that which characterized Eastern Europe
and Latin America in the 1980s and 1990s, when organized hierarchical
groups, with charismatic leadership, were able over time to develop a
theoretical critique of incumbent regimes and provide a political alternative firmly rooted in liberal-democratic values. This has been absent in the
Arab world. Second, the emphasis on hierarchical organized structures,
such as NGOs, as the protagonists of activism is misplaced. The insight of
the fifth approach is to look beyond such organizations and shed light on
other forms and modes of engagement. This has clear application to the
new type of activism that has characterized the Arab Uprisings.

Finally, it should be emphasized once more that no normative characterization should be attached to the concept of civil society. While political
change following the Arab Awakening may follow the direction of liberal
democracy, this is by no means the only potential scenario.

In conclusion, there is a linkage between civil activism and political
change. But it might not play itself out in a natural and linear path towards
democracy, and might not be brought about according to traditional expectations and canons.

Key questions

- What is meant by 'civil society'?
- Is there a relationship between civil society activism and
  democratization?
- Can Islamist civil society organizations be democratic?
- Does civil society activism in the MENA region challenge or
  strengthen authoritarian regimes?
- How should the role of civil society in the Arab uprisings be
  understood?

Further reading

Abdelrahman, Maha (2002). 'The politics of "un-civil" society in Egypt', *Review of African Political Economy*, 29(91): 21–36.

Berman, Sheri (2003). 'Islamism, revolution and civil society', *Perspectives on Politics*, 1(2): 257–72.

Cavatorta, Francesco (2006). 'Civil society, Islamism and democratisation: the case of Morocco', *Journal of Modern African Studies*, 44(4): 203–22.

Edwards, Michael (2004). *Civil Society*, Cambridge: Polity.

Wiktorowicz, Quintan (2000). 'Civil society as social control. State power in Jordan', *Comparative Politics*, 33(1): 43–61.

Online resources

Carapico, Sheila (2000). 'NGOs, INGOs, GO-NGOs and DO-NGOs: making sense of non-governmental organizations', *Middle East Report*, 214. Available at http://www.merip.org/mer/mer214/ngos-ingos-go-ngos-do-ngos.

Hassan, Kawa (2012). 'Rethinking civic activism in the Middle East: agency without associations'. Available at http://www.hivos.net/Hivos-Knowledge-Programme/Themes/Civil-Society-in-West-Asia/Publications/Policy-Papers/Re-thinking-Civic-Activism-in-the-Middle-East.

International Centre for Not-For-Profit Law: http://www.icnl.org/.

Ottoway, Marina (2004). 'Middle Eastern democracy: is civil society the answer?' *Carnegie Endowment for International Peace*. Available at www.carnegieendowment.org/files/CarnegiePaper44.pdf.

Chapter 8

Gender and Politics

Among the most controversial and frequently misunderstood topics in the study of the MENA is the role of women in society. The realm of women's rights is typically seen as one of the most divisive issues between the Muslim world and the rest of the globe. Specifically, the region is often presented as resistant to the modernizing trends that have taken place in other parts of the world, Western and non-Western, when it comes to women's rights and the participation of women in society. The Western image of the Middle Eastern woman is invariably linked to notions of inequality, and oppression, veiling and seclusion, despite the fact that this does not reflect the reality of many women in the region, above all in Israel, Turkey and, to a lesser extent, Tunisia, Lebanon, Morocco, Jordan or Algeria. Irrespective of the complex and varied reality, there is a widespread opinion that women, as a whole, are subjected to widespread oppression and unequal treatment.

This chapter will outline how this particular view emerged and was utilized for political purposes at the time of colonization – and even after decolonization, as recently as the invasions of Afghanistan and Iraq. The chapter will challenge the validity of this view and will analyze the ways in which women in the region have often been key protagonists of both political and social life. In part, this has been due the phenomenon of state feminism, but also to the capacity of many ordinary women to mobilize, harnessing imported ideologies such as feminism and secularism, or revisiting indigenous traditions linked to Islam. In all of this, it is important not to ignore the history of practical politics that lies behind the struggle in a variety of contexts to assert the rights of women. Crucially, this chapter examines women's activism in Islamist parties and movements in some detail, problematizing the notion of feminism and its political expressions. This is an important part of the story of the political and social engagement of women in the region.

Historical overview

As mentioned, current debates about Muslim women and their role in society find their roots in colonial times. Although European occupying powers initially refrained from interfering in the gender relations of the locals, a binary representation of the indigenous woman quickly established itself (Haddad, 1999), particularly where France was the colonial master. On the one hand, the 'Muslim Woman' was seen as the powerless victim of a patriarchal society where anti-modern religious precepts prevented her from having any meaningful political or social role, leading to her 'disappearance' into the home. On the other hand, the Muslim Woman was portrayed as 'temptress'. In any case, the colonial powers were not interested, at first, in 'liberating' women given that, to a large extent, similar attitudes to women existed in Europe as well. This laissez-faire attitude lasted for a long period of time, until nationalist movements across the Arab world began to grow and to challenge colonialism. But, the status of women in society became a terrain both of confrontation and contestation in the course of attempts to link the maintenance of foreign rule to the benefits of modernization that colonial powers purportedly brought to the region. Thus, the colonial authorities sought to use 'women's rights' to weaken nationalist demands, arguing that the end of Western influence would have negative consequences for the project of modernization – and therefore women's liberation – that they were pursuing. At the same time, nationalist movements across the Arab world began to emphasize the role of women in the liberation struggle, giving them a number of significant roles. In the Algerian national liberation struggle, for instance, women were central actors entrusted with carrying out military operations against the French. However, it should be underlined that the most important role conceived for women within the context of national liberation was that of 'mothers of the country' that would be born out of the struggle. According to Kandiyoti (1997), by virtue of her biological role as creator of life, the 'woman', in nationalist discourse, reproduces ethnic boundaries and passes culture down to her progeny. This was to be problematic later, in the aftermath of independence. As outlined elsewhere:

> there are obviously national differences in the Muslim and Arab world relating to the emergence of the gender question during colonial times, but there is nevertheless a similar trajectory insofar as the Woman, in her social and political role, seems to become the point of contestation for different sets of values. (Dalmasso and Cavatorta, 2009)

This narrative possesses a degree of validity, but it does not exhaust reality and, crucially, denies agency to indigenous women, who should remain central to any analysis of gender dynamics in the region. For instance, from the mid-nineteenth century onwards, a number of social and economic reform movements in the MENA region began to demand a more active role for women. The publication of *Tahrir al-Mar'a* (*The Liberation of Women*) by Egyptian writer and activist Qasim Amin in 1899, and the emergence of Arab journals such as the *al-Fatat* that explored issues of central concern to women as early as the 1890s, have been cited as examples of historical efforts to achieve gender justice led both by women and men in Arab and Muslim regions of the world. At first, demands for reform were articulated by men but, by the end of the century, women were increasingly involved and such demands were, crucially, independent from the efforts of colonial powers to place women at the centre of their modernizing efforts.

It should be also recognized that the role of women in European countries at the time was far from being equal to that of men. Therefore, it is important not to make the mistake of viewing the historical experience of the MENA region from the perspective of the position of women in contemporary Western societies. To do so would risk ignoring the vitality of local experiences at the turn of the century across the Arab world. The earliest women's organizations were active in Turkey and Egypt from the first decade of the twentieth century, demanding education, work opportunities and reform of personal status and family laws governing marriage, child custody, divorce and inheritance. They also campaigned for an end to the strict segregation and seclusion of women as practised by the middle and upper classes. The global flow of ideas about changing traditional patriarchal patterns affected the Arab world and spread across the region. At the same time, regional experiences fed into the global mood of change for women in their respective societies. It is no surprise that those who were involved in the early women's movements were from well-to-do urban families, who were receiving private education at home. Nonetheless, irrespective of social class and family income, this picture of activism, however limited, is in sharp contrast to the prevailing Western stereotype of such 'harem' women as passive, ignorant and subject to male whims.

In Egypt, the women's movement was particularly prominent and was, unsurprisingly, linked to the universality of the message of the nascent liberal feminism that was also sweeping through the West. This activism was inextricably linked with the struggle against colonialism. The participation of Egyptian feminists in the nationalist movement strongly indicated that the values of equality and liberalism coincided with national independence. In Box 8.1, we look in some detail at the life and work of Doria Shafik, a prominent Egyptian scholar and activist in the early part of the twentieth century in Egypt. In fact, by the 1920s, activists such as Huda Sharaawi and Nabawiyya Musa had established contact with the wider, international feminist movement. At the same time, a number of women became involved in anti-British nationalist agitation. When Saad Zaghloul, the leader of the nationalist Wafd Party was arrested and deported to Malta in 1919, his wife took his place in addressing public

Box 8.1   An Egyptian feminist: Doria Shafik (1908–75)

Doria Shafik was born in 1908 into a middle-class Egyptian family. With support from Huda Sha'rawi, founder of the Egyptian Feminist Union, she studied at the Sorbonne in Paris, where she wrote a doctoral dissertation on 'Egyptian Women and Islam'. On her return to Egypt in 1945, she founded the magazine *Bint Al-Nil* (*Daughter of the Nile*). Once the magazine was well-established, she included a new political section, where the serious issues with which she was really concerned were discussed. In 1948, she founded *Ittihad Bint Al-Nil* (the Daughter of the Nile Union), a broadly based, middle-class feminist association focused on female literacy and political rights for women. This was followed in 1953 by the establishment of the Daughter of the Nile political party, which was closed down by the government within one year. Shafik was a militant most of her life. Her most eye-catching action came on 19 February 1951, when she led a group of 1,500 women who broke into parliament and demanded consideration of the demands of Egyptian women. As she set out, she wrote: 'No one will deliver freedom to women, except woman herself'. The event made her a celebrity but also aroused hostility. The King is reported to have told her husband: 'Let your wife know that as long as I am king, women will have no political rights'.

Shafik continued her activities under the new regime which followed Egypt's 1952 revolution and criticized the government for neglecting the issue of women's rights. She described the new constitution of 1956 as a 'catastrophe'. Under the constitution, women would have to apply to vote or run for public office and, in doing so, would have to demonstrate their literacy. These conditions were not applied to men. On February 1957, she entered the Indian embassy resolving to go on hunger strike until her demands were met. Nasser secured her departure from the embassy and, although she was not arrested, placed her under house arrest. This was followed by 18 years of seclusion and her death by suicide in 1975.

Source: Faysa Hassan (2001). 'Speaking for the other half', *Al-Ahram Weekly*, 523. Available at http://weekly.ahram.org.eg/2001/523/sc3.htm.

meetings. The Egyptian Feminist Union (EFU) was founded in 1924. However, a major limitation of the EFU and women's movements elsewhere, such as those of Turkey or Iran, was that their work affected only a small sector of the population and it was extremely difficult to expand activism beyond that. But similar constraints weighed on women's movements across the globe. The majority of women, poor and rurally based, were hardly affected by changes in the legal system, or by new educational and employment opportunities. Nevertheless, it should be pointed out that, for instance, Turkish women got the vote significantly earlier (1930) than their counterparts in France (1944), Italy (1945), or Switzerland (1971).

As mentioned, the development of the women's movement was linked to broader movements for political change and national independence.

Therefore, the association between the promotion of gender equality and Western actors is tenuous at best, because many women activists in the Arab world were able to recognize and work through the contradiction of the colonizers' message about equality. It is for this reason that indigenous sources of inspiration for women's activism have always remained important. The supposed appeal of Western-style feminism running through Muslim societies in the region is a post-colonial construct that is usually employed to justify interventionist policies without much regard for how different societies operate intellectually to work through their own path towards modernity. In Iran and Turkey, women's organizations developed rapidly after the demise of autocratic governments in the first decade of the twentieth century. However, after World War I, and in a pattern that was to be repeated subsequently, authoritarian governments began to co-opt the previously autonomous women's movement in both countries. Women were used as symbols of modernization and secularization and, while reforms were introduced in some areas, women were permitted little autonomous activity. In Turkey, Kemal Ataturk introduced far-reaching reforms of the personal status laws; these were based not on *shari'a* but, rather, on the Swiss civil code, and discouraged the practices of veiling and seclusion. In Iran, Reza Shah introduced more limited reforms. Veiling was abolished and access to education was improved. The Arab Maghreb states of Tunisia, Algeria and Morocco were slower to introduce reforms due to the later achievement of independence. Tunisia was the leader – the Personal Status Code of 1956 is the most progressive in the Arab world, outlawing polygamy and granting expanded rights to divorced women; labour legislation introduced in 1966 provided some protection for working mothers. In Algeria, reform came later and was more modest. Although the state abolished colonial legislation relating to family matters in 1975, it was not until 1984 that a new family code was introduced and this, as with those in other Arab countries, was enacted within the framework of *shari'a*. Morocco was the slowest country in the Maghreb to respond to pressures to reform family law. However, in 2004 reform of the law finally took place. Women were no longer legally obliged to 'obey' their husbands. Both men and women share equal responsibility for the family. Polygamy has been rendered virtually impossible, according to some commentators, and women may retain custody of children even upon remarrying.

This picture suggests that simplistic assumptions and explanations about the way in which women's rights are conceived, fought for and articulated in legislation should be abandoned in favour of a much more complex reading in which the agency of women itself is taken into account. There is however an undisputable point about women's rights activism during the colonial period and in the post-independence period. Whether informed by

Box 8.2   Personal status legislation in Tunisia

A few months after the proclamation of independence in 1956, Tunisia introduced what remains to this day one of the most progressive personal status codes (CPS, in the French acronym) in the MENA. The legislation was a very significant step in reducing gender inequality on matters related to family law and was designed to orient the country fully on the modernizing path. The CPS is one of the clearest expressions of what would later be labelled 'state feminism'. The progressive CPS was not, in fact, the product of pressure from below, or from any mass organized women's movement demanding equality. It was, rather, almost entirely the personal political project of a small section of the ruling élite, who believed that, in order to achieve economic and social progress, the 'backwardness' of religious precepts weighing down society should be eliminated. One way of achieving this was the radical alteration of family and kinship patterns which, until then, had been regulated in *shari'a* courts. In short, the introduction of much greater gender equality was part of a broader modernizing effort whereby Tunisia would soon be on the way to developmental success, both economically and socially.

The paradox of the success of the CPS – and it was, indeed, a success for women's rights and gender equality in the country – is that it rested on the authoritarian nature of the Tunisian political system. The promotion of 'feminism' on the part of the state authorities and its defence against the return of Islamism, with its conservative views and presumed anti-equality agenda, became one of the most important pillars of both the Bourguiba and Ben Ali regimes.

The fall of the regime in 2011 has once again placed the CPS centre-stage, in public and political debate, as there are fears, particularly in liberal and secular circles, that the rising tide of Islamism will undermine past efforts at achieving equality, through the introduction of discriminatory, religion-based legislation.

Source: Amel Grami (2008). 'Gender equality in Tunisia', *British Journal of Middle Eastern Studies*, 35(3): 349–61.

the instrumental motivations of colonial powers, by the modernizing effort of the post-independence Arab republics, or by the bottom-up activism of many women, women's rights and a 'new' role for women in society were typically pursued through traditional liberalism and, since the 1970s, through what can be termed 'liberal feminism'. While this obscures a number of significant local experiences, it 'forces' scholars and activists to contend with this dominant feature. In particular, as post-uprisings politics has made clear in a number of countries, there is a significant degree of political disagreement over the role of women in society. On the one hand, a global liberal model that seems empowering is held to be the only way out of conservatism and towards modernity in a democratic framework. On the other hand, a political drive to return to traditional understandings of women's rights and duties has emerged strongly, precisely as a critique of the liberal model as empowering.

Islam and feminism

The reforms of family law introduced by many post-colonial regimes were intended, at least in part, to counteract the influence of traditional conceptions of gender and gender roles which many associate with religion. The argument is frequently made that religion – and, more specifically, Islam – lies at the heart of the asserted oppression of women in the Middle East and in the Muslim world more generally. In this respect, the strength of Orientalism, which sees Islam at the root of the misogyny that appears to characterize the region, has not diminished over time. This view is not only the product of colonialism. Many, across the MENA, both men and women, also subscribe to the idea that the conservative nature of Islam – indeed, of all religions for that matter – prevents genuine modernization, and with it gender equality. From this perspective, without a thorough marginalization of religion in the public sphere, acceptance of the absolute priority of individual rights, and adherence to traditional liberal feminism, there cannot be meaningful equality in law and in social practices. The struggle of early feminists in the region relied on this dismissive attitude towards religion as a guide for public policy and gender relations in society, because Islam was seen as legitimizing and reinforcing patriarchy. This early feminism found its inspiration in the Western feminist experience and, as we have seen, in some cases (such as that of Tunisia), it found a strong ally and promoter in the state. In the aftermath of colonialism, a number of states in the region identified secularism and, therefore, the pursuit of a degree of gender equality as strategies in order to marginalize social and political actors linked to the old order. 'State' feminism – the imposition from above of legal rules and policies that were designed to weaken patriarchy through the marginalization of Islam – was widespread and, in some cases, successful for a time. The cause of women's rights was thus assimilated to the wider goals of modernization and development. However, the claim that Islam, per se, is to blame for gender inequality and the persistence of patriarchal structures is resisted by many. In turn, 'state' feminism, despite its focus on Islam as the root source of women's oppression, can itself be seen as a manifestation of patriarchy, insofar as it promotes traditional roles and represents men as the protector of women through the power of the state.

In fact, many Muslims, both men and women, argue that Islam is at heart an egalitarian religion and that such gender inequality as exists is the product of a multiplicity of political, social and economic factors that have very little to do with the religion, which has been misread and misrepresented to justify patriarchy, since this serves the interests of specific social and political actors. Proponents of this approach point to the orthodox

Muslim view that the divinely revealed Qur'anic text provided progress in all areas, including the condition of women, which is all the more striking in view of the condition of ignorance and barbarism in which pre-Islamic Arabs lived. They emphasize the improvements in the position of women which were introduced in the Qur'an. Women have a separate and independent legal, economic and religious identity, an inalienable right of inheritance and a negotiated marriage contract. Thus, the Qur'an empowered and continues to empower women, giving them rights in divorce and inheritance, and as mothers of children and widows. Perhaps, more importantly, Islam is one of the few religions that do not single out women as the cause of all evil, placing it therefore in a different light from the other monotheistic religions. Unlike her Christian counterpart, the Muslim Eve is, like Adam, led astray by the serpent. The text of the Qur'an is explicit on this point. Neither was Eve created from the left rib of Adam, as in Christian belief, and thus inferior. In the Qur'an, God has invited women to be the partners and helpmates of men. Furthermore, marriage is not ordained as a once-and-for-all institution. It is founded on a revocable contract. Women are paid a negotiated sum for the consummation of their marriage and it is the woman herself who must consent to the marriage and receive the dowry. The husband is obliged to support his wife and the marriage contract is a legal document, binding in all its stipulations and, while men have the right to divorce their wives at will, women can stipulate the right to themselves. Seen in this light, marriage in Islam has been described as a flexible arrangement between consenting partners who can part whenever they please. Nor are men entitled at any time to take back what they have given to their wives: the Qur'an is quite explicit that the dowry cannot be returned.

However, while such positions found in the sacred texts may have been highly progressive when they first appeared, to many they now seem conservative and out-of-step with the requirements of modernity. Furthermore, critics point to inequalities in the treatment of women in the text that cannot be rationalized away. While the Qur'an was innovative in introducing property rights for women as long ago as the eighth century CE, female inheritance is half that of the male. Likewise, although women enjoyed an independent legal existence, by virtue of the Qur'anic text, centuries before their Western counterparts, the legal testimony of a woman is worth only half that of a man. Men have an unlimited right to divorce and have claimed the right to polygamy, in spite of the Qur'anic injunction that all wives must be treated impartially and that, failing impartial treatment, only one may be taken. More problematic is the dictum that all married women should obey their husbands, who are entitled to beat their disobedient wives. All this is taken as reinforcing the conservative view of the rights of women in Islam, justifying underlying inequalities in the position of men and women.

The debate on the treatment of women in Islam is both practical and ideological. For a period of time, traditional Western liberal feminism constituted the dominant framework through which feminists in the Middle East conceived of their struggle. In that respect, the inequalities inherent in Islam were to be fought against with the instruments of development and modernization, which relied heavily on secularism and the assertion of individual liberal rights, together with the purging of religious precepts from public policies involving personal status legislation. This confrontational attitude toward religion, coupled with the importation of ideological assumptions and frameworks from the colonial West, held little sway in vast sectors of society, and whatever level of gender equality was achieved seemed to be largely the product of an unholy alliance between authoritarian rulers and small constituencies of secular feminists. The widespread conservatism of Middle Eastern societies, together with the resurgence of Islamism, seemed to threaten even the few reforms in favour of gender equality that had been implemented. More significantly, they led to a reframing of how women's rights and gender equality could be pursued. Given the hostile reactions that liberal feminism attracted, and the inability of liberal feminists to reach wider sectors of society with their message, a number of intellectuals began to devise ways in which religious precepts could support and substantiate demands for gender equality. By making references to Islam, feminist demands were transformed from an attempt to impose a Western model into demands aligned with divine intentions, and therefore not only permissible, but necessary. From this attempt to 'Islamize' feminist demands arose the phenomenon of Islamic feminism. For some critics, this is little more than a simple and simplistic attempt to introduce liberal feminism by stealth. Others claim that the only way though which gender equality in the Arab world can be achieved is by re-interpreting the sacred texts in order to rediscover their intrinsically egalitarian nature. While Islamic feminism is an important intellectual development that has had significant practical consequences for the way in which activists struggle for gender equality, some confusion prevails about its specific meaning (more will be said on this later in this chapter). In any case, whether through a liberal critique or through its re-interpretation, Islam is still very much central to discussions about women's rights and gender equality. The view that Islam is the source of women's inequality has been challenged from a number of perspectives (not least by Muslim and Islamist scholars and writers), as has the claim that Islam is the source of women's liberation. However, some scholars propose that it is necessary to move the debate away from religion in order to explore alternative perspectives on gender inequality in the Middle East, allowing us to see commonalities between the MENA region and other parts of the globe. This becomes particularly important if one considers that, even in Israel, with its democratic institutions and recognition of individual rights, there are confrontational debates in society about the 'appropriate' role of women in society and the notion of equal citizenship, as the debate on whether women are permitted to pray at the Western Wall indicates.

Alternative perspectives

One trenchant critic of the predominant focus on Islam, Nikki Keddie (1979: 10), argues that the study of women's history in the Middle East has been flawed by its 'philosophically idealist bias', most notably the assumption that 'the Qur'an, the traditions of the Prophet, and the writings of theologians and jurists were the main determinants of women's position'. Conversely, it can be argued that placing Islam at the centre of the debate on gender equality suffers from a similar problem: essentializing the nature of religion and conflating it with a phenomenon that might have other causes.

Keddie argues that the view that the subordinate position of women is the direct result of what the sacred texts have to say has its roots in Western orientalist tradition. For years, orientalist writers tended to begin their studies with theology, language and literature, and were inclined to give inordinate emphasis to religious and legal works and traditions, taking them to represent reality. Yet, all societies provide numerous examples of the deviations of the followers of religion from their religious books and leaders and also of deviations from the law. However, such 'ideal' sources – the Qur'an and the traditional sayings of Muhammad, jurists and theologians – are, of course, the easiest to find and to put into a coherent picture, which helps to account for their popularity. Nonetheless, other sources, such as contemporary anthropology, sociology and economics exist, and should be drawn on, according to Keddie, in order to counter this 'idealist' bias. In fact, this idealist bias can work in the opposite direction to that taken by Orientalists. There are just as many scholars who are preoccupied with the 'positives' one can find in the sacred texts but, just like the Orientalists, they also over-emphasise religious sources to the detriment of the lived reality of individuals, which is constrained much more significantly by economics, social traditions and political arrangements.

Keddie draws attention to a range of factors which have played a role in producing the situation of women in the Middle East, pointing to the inter-related significance of class, the impact of the West, and the transition to a modern and Western-influenced way of life, as well as historical tradition. Reading Islam as the inexorable source of equality discounts the many other reasons that might exist for positive improvements in the conditions of women, which may have very little to do with religion and its re-interpretation and much more to do with political expediency, economic changes or social dynamics. The focus here is mostly on potential explanations other than religion for the marginal role that women play in Middle Eastern societies.

Without a doubt, the marginalization of women in the political and economic spheres in the MENA region is easy to illustrate. Women participate unequally in the political sphere in most, if not all, countries in the region. While, as has been noted, the right of Turkish women to vote was recognized in 1930, for most other women of the Middle East, recognition of this right came much later, with independence. In some cases, however, the right is still denied. In Lebanon, women got the vote in 1952, Syria in 1953, Egypt in 1956, in Tunisia in 1959, Morocco 1963, Libya and Sudan in 1964. Jordanian women became entitled to vote only in 1970. While Bahraini women won the vote in 1973, elsewhere in the Gulf this happened much more recently – 2003 in Oman, 2005 in Kuwait and 2006 in the UAE. Women in Saudi Arabia still do not have either voting or candidacy rights, but have been promised both for local elections to be held in 2015.

Women in the MENA region also occupy fewer seats in parliament than in any other region of the world. For example, in 2000, women occupied 21 out of 524 seats in Algeria's parliament, 26 out of 250 in Syria, 9 out of 454 in Egypt, 16 out of 250 in Iraq, 5 out of 88 in Palestine, 4 out of 595 in Morocco, 2 out of 301 in Yemen, and 0 out of 760 in Libya. By the end of 2012, this had improved considerably in some countries. In Algeria, in the elections of 2012, women took 31 per cent of the seats in the National Assembly following the introduction of a quota for women's representation in parliament. In neighbouring Morocco, women won 17 per cent of the seats in parliament in elections held in 2011 under a quota system. In Iraq, women are guaranteed 25 per cent of the total seats in parliament by a law introduced in 2005. Elsewhere, and in the absence of quotas, the situation is different. Yemen has 1 female member out of a 301-seat parliament, while the 2012 elections in Egypt saw the level of women's representation fall from 9 to just 2.

It is clear that political life – and the public sphere, more generally – are dominated by men but, then again, this is the reality of most countries in the world. While the level of public participation by women is increasing in most states, it remains at low levels, both as compared with that of Middle Eastern men, and to other regions of the developing world. Israel and Turkey are the exceptions in this regard. Indeed, both have had women prime ministers in the past.

In the economic sphere, also, the role of women is marginal. Women's participation in the formal labour force is still limited compared with that of other world regions. However, it has been steadily rising since the 1960s. Factors such as the tremendous expansion in state bureaucracies and related services, economic development, falling fertility levels, the rising age of first marriage, rapid urbanization, increased educational levels for women and male labour migration from poor to oil-rich states have all played a part in the increase in rates of female employment. However, the pattern varies from country to country. Economic activity rates for women over the age of 15, between the years 1995 and 2001, range from below 30 per cent in Oman, Libya, Saudi Arabia, Lebanon, Syria and Jordan to 35 per cent in Sudan and Egypt, to 41 per cent in Qatar, to 48 per cent in Israel and 50 per cent in Turkey. There is a high concentration of women in public services (such as teaching), reinforcing stereotypes of certain occupations as the preserve of women. Women from well-off families are more likely to be formally employed, especially in the Gulf States.

However, it is not merely in the context of the formal political or economic spheres that women seem to labour under conditions that are unequal and discriminatory. In several countries, women face imprisonment, cruel punishments and even death under discriminatory laws. They can be prosecuted for their choices of clothing. They can be imprisoned for driving a car, as in Saudi Arabia. They can be subject to severe punishment, including death, for their sexual behaviour. In some states, including, Iran, Saudi Arabia and the UAE, women and men face sentences of flogging and stoning to death for sexual offences. Stoning to death, which is prescribed by Iran's Islamic Penal Code for *hudud* offences such as adultery, has been used to execute dozens of women since 1979. Iranian law outlines in some detail the manner in which the execution should take place. In Yemen, women imprisoned for offences against the moral code can be kept in jail indefinitely if they have no male relatives to go to, or if their relatives disown them because of their offences. Men imprisoned for the same offences are usually released on completion of their sentence. Furthermore, honour killings are implicitly or explicitly protected by law in several states in the region, including Jordan. One could enumerate other such examples.

Family matters in a number of countries including Iran, Egypt, Israel, Lebanon, and Saudi Arabia are governed by religion-based personal status codes. Many of these laws treat women essentially as legal minors under the guardianship of their male family members. Women are denied equal rights with men with respect to marriage, divorce, child custody and inheritance. Family decision-making is thought to be the exclusive domain of men, who enjoy by default the legal status of 'head of household'(Human Rights Watch, 2006). These notions are supported by family courts in the region that often reinforce the primacy of male decision-making power. These courts have rarely appointed women as judges, further denying women authority in family matters. As Lisa Taraki (2004) notes, this is not merely a feature of Arab societies: Israel is in line with its Arab neighbours in the area of family status. It has not adopted secular laws and the religious establishment exerts considerable influence. For instance, marriages can be contracted and dissolved only in religious courts. Women are not allowed to become judges in the orthodox rabbinical state courts and, as a rule, their evidence is not accepted, especially if there are male witnesses.

As mentioned, other factors besides Islam need to be brought into the analysis to explain this state of affairs. As Keddie (1979) argues, it is important to recognize that the transition to a modern and Western-influenced life structure has not been a simple progressive one for Middle Eastern women. Too many scholars have assumed, however, that modernization is essentially a progressive process, which improves everyone's way of life sooner or later. Yet, for many male workers and peasants this was often untrue, and was similarly untrue for several classes of women. For women in Europe, the rise of capitalism had negative impacts, too, removing many women from sources of productive income, while also prompting the advance of the first feminist ideas. The influence of Western and indigenous capitalism in the Middle East has had a similar two-sided influence. Women who did have a source of income – for example, female peasants, nomads and urban craft workers – increasingly lost their productive role, as the goods they made were purchased from distant producers. Many male workers faced similar difficulties. But, while working urban, rural and tribal women suffered a loss in their productive role and status with the growth of a market economy, the position of the top urban groups was improved. Upper- and middle-class men tied to Western businessmen and politicians began to acquire Western or Western-style educations, and to qualify as modern professionals, businessmen and bureaucrats. Such men were usually the first to respond to, or even encourage, women's demands for liberation, for modern education, for unveiling and for professional lives. This led to an exacerbation of differences in lifestyles between urban and middle-class women – who increasingly adopted Western or 'modern' ways, and lower-class women – whose families clung to the old ways, and whose men tended to see danger, rather than advantage, in the abandonment of customs sanctioned by tradition, law and religious leaders. The extremely skewed income distribution of nearly all Middle Eastern countries adds to this phenomenon of 'two cultures'. One prominent Algerian commentator, Sid Ahmed Semiane (2005), even suggested that there are two countries in one across the Middle East. Keddie (1979) concludes that constant attention to differences in class is vital to the study of women in the Middle East. This includes both the division among village, nomadic tribe and urban areas, as well as the numerous differences between classes within each of these. But, until recently, class, unlike religion, has scarcely been discussed in this context.

Similar points are made by Lisa Taraki (2004) when she argues that 'as in all societies a multiplicity of social, economic, political and cultural forces have shaped the statuses, experiences and living conditions of Middle Eastern women. For Taraki, an ahistoric conception of Islamic values as determinants of practice does not advance our understanding of complex historical practices, while the use of the unitary concept of the 'Middle Eastern' woman obscures the rich diversity in women's lives across region.

Asad Abu-Khalil (2000) has also offered an alternative perspective on gender relations in the Muslim world. While he acknowledges that the problems of Middle Eastern women remain acute, this is not something that has its origins uniquely in Islam. Islamic, Christian and Jewish jurists and theologians – all of them males – have provided Middle Eastern society with the most exclusivist and conservative interpretations of religious laws, which have burdened women in the family, the society and the state. In any case, while religion has played a role, Abu-Khalil suggests that culture is even more significant. Finally, he suggests that the role of the West in relation to gender-based inequality is itself questionable. As mentioned, historically, Western colonial powers shed crocodile tears over the plight of Muslim women and vilified Islam for its role in this oppression. Ironically, in medieval times Islam was actually attacked by Christian polemicists for being too permissive and tolerant in social and sexual matters. Western treatment of Muslim women has been hypocritical at best. In her study of women and gender in the Islamic world, Leila Ahmed dubs the Western attitude 'colonial feminism'. In the present-day Middle East, the responsibility of Western powers (and that of the United States, in particular) for the current state of affairs cannot be denied. Ever since the 1950s, successive American governments have supported Saudi Arabian Islam, and have often funded and armed Islamist groups, which have tormented Middle Eastern women and frustrated their efforts at emancipation. Furthermore, many of the oppressive governments in the Middle East survive only because of Western military and/or economic support. His conclusion is clear: the responsibility for local oppression has external dimensions also.

This discussion of factors other than religion, which might contribute to an explanation of the weak position of women in society and the degree of gender inequality that exists in the region, opens up the possibility of problematizing not only mainstream accounts of inequality, but also of the kinds of activism that exist to eliminate it. Women's rights activism is usually framed through the lenses of traditional liberal feminism because this is often seen as the only one that is normatively acceptable. Thus, there is a strong focus on Western-funded civil society women's organizations and on prominent secular women activists, who are usually members of political parties or associations. Taraki (2004: 350–2) proposes a number of 'forms and modes of women's political participation'. These include participation in national liberation struggles and movements, including the Algerian war of independence, the Palestinian resistance to occupation and the Iranian revolution. Second, women are involved in women's branches of political parties. Third, women participate in political parties as members. Fourth, women participate in women's organizations created by ruling parties and states such as the women's federations. Fifth, women may be involved in a wide range of independent, but not necessarily apolitical, organizations whose agendas vary in terms of their engagement with gender related issues and causes. Finally, women may participate in political life as voters and candidates in the electoral process.

However, while each of these is important, there is an implicit assumption that the only acceptable type of activism is that which is in line with Western values and with liberal feminism. This excludes from analysis the activism of many women within Islamist parties or associations and, as Box 8.3 illustrates, such exclusion would render justice to the complexity of women's activism. In fact, an examination and an explanation of women's activism in what can be defined as 'conservative politics' are necessary for two reasons. On the one hand, it seems to indicate a false consciousness on the part of many women who are active in parties and movements that are believed to be inherently opposed to women's rights and full equality. On the other hand, it may be suggested that, in reality, women's activism in Islamist parties and movements has very little to do with gender equality, being based instead on other variables, such as class or morality.

Women in Islamist parties and movements

There is no doubt that a degree of suspicion exists when it comes to explanation and analysis of the role of women in Islamist parties and movements. For critics, there is an inherent contradiction in the choice of a woman to join a political or social movement whose *ethos* is based on a

---

Box 8.3 Politics of piety

In a seminal study of how gender activism from an Islamic perspective can be understood and related to broader issues of political engagement on the part of women, Mahmood demonstrates the way in which secular-liberal principles are questioned in practice. Following the work and activism of a group of women intent on what can be labelled as moral reform of their surroundings according to religious precepts, Mahmood examines how such activism does not need to be liberal or secular to promote positive change. The point is that the agency of Islamist women should be taken into full consideration and looked at through the prism of their own values and cultural references.

Many analyses about gender relations and women's activism across the region assume that activism itself, to be even worthy of the name, has to be about the promotion of liberal and secular values. When this is not the case, either false consciousness or 'choosing the wrong path' is often invoked as an explanation for this behaviour. The argument here is that women who are 'activated' in society against the principles of secularism and liberalism are unwitting agents of patriarchy. A more nuanced approach is necessary, however; one which rests on the assumption that agency and autonomy can, and should, be presumed for Islamist women whether engaged politically or in moral reform campaigns.

Source: Saba Mahmood (2004). *Politics of Piety: Islamic Revival and the Feminist Subject*, Princeton: Princeton University Press.

---

perceived discriminatory reading of religious precepts that confine women to traditional gender roles. As Abdellatif and Ottaway (2007: 3) put it, 'secular entities jump to the conclusion that Islamism or even Islam itself makes use of religion to perpetuate discriminatory laws and practices'. This attitude of suspicion applies to liberal and secular women both in the West and in the Arab world, and is usually blamed on 'false consciousness' – meaning the misplaced conviction of many women that they should enjoy a lower status in order to maintain the social stability necessary to fulfil their traditional roles. Across the Arab world, the phenomenon of women in Islamist parties is looked on with the highest degree of suspicion, especially on the part of secular women who are politically engaged on a platform of gender equality and cannot comprehend the attraction that Islamist movements hold for other women.

The question is simple: why would any woman decide to become active in a movement or party that advocates strict traditional gender roles? In addition, critics see the phenomenon as undermining the progress they have achieved over decades of activism and struggles. This has increasingly become the case in the aftermath of the Arab Uprisings, with the accession of Islamists to power in Tunisia and Egypt. The military coup in Egypt, which overthrew the Islamist government in June 2013, was greeted with enthusiasm by many because it seemed to prevent the relegation of women to the private sphere, as the Muslim Brotherhood was perceived to be intent on doing. The reality is, however, much more complex than a simple dichotomy between Islamists who want to relegate women to the private sphere, and secularists striving for liberation and equality, because there are other divisions that matter in the understanding of the role of women in society; for instance, class divisions. Taking the example of Egypt, the discourse of President al-Sisi with regards to women is both paternalistic and patronizing, although not couched in religious language.

Nonetheless, the fundamental issue as to why so many women join, are active in and vote for Islamist parties remains a burning one for many more 'traditional' Arab feminists and for Western audiences as well. Skalli (2011) discusses the problems that the Moroccan women's movement – traditionally the domain of secular leftist women – is experiencing due to its inability to attract a new generation of activists, as many young women do not seem to be interested in working on and for women's rights. This reluctance to engage with feminist issues is highlighted in Kolman's work (2013) on young Salafi activists in Tunisia. Rather than shying away from civil or political engagement, these young activists see themselves as 'modern feminists' operating within a strict Islamic framework, and do not see any contradiction between the two. Skalli elaborates on the paradox of a younger generation that has more freedom, more access to information and enjoys greater democratic openings, yet which chooses to be disengaged from political activism in favour of gender equality, preferring instead to join the ranks of Islamism. Skalli's analysis points, in fact, to the confrontation that exists between secular and Islamist women when it comes to the way in which the state should legislate on matters regarding gender, as Box 8.4 discusses in detail. The scepticism of the secular and liberal sectors of Arab society with regard to women who join Islamist movements appears legitimate when one examines how the role of women has been traditionally conceived within Islamist movements. Clark and Schwedler (2003: 293) observe that 'at the onset of political liberalization in Jordan and Yemen in 1989 and 1990, respectively, the largest Islamist group in each country expressed strong views opposing women's full and equal political participation'. The leader of the Yemeni *Islah* party justified this by arguing that to allow women to vote would mean permitting them to be photographed for identity purposes, which was unacceptable because they would have to show their faces to strangers. As recently as the early 2000s, the more moderate Party of Justice and Development (PJD) in Morocco opposed changes to the personal status legislation that were meant to guarantee a greater degree of equality to women in the spheres of marriage, divorce and the custody of children (Dalmasso and

> ## Box 8.4 Islamist women and the state
>
> One of the most interesting aspects of gender relations in the MENA is the often harsh confrontation between secular and Islamist women activists. While there have been times when women on both sides collaborated on specific issues – for example, they came together in Algeria to pressure the state into releasing details about the fate of those that disappeared during the 1990s civil war – they have generally tended to remain on opposite sides of the fence. This is largely due to their profound ideological differences and, in the context of ideological divisions, gender does not matter much. However, as a recent study by Doris Gray (2012) demonstrates, there is also a disputed historical legacy at play, which is slowly emerging as a bone of contention in the aftermath of the collapse or weakening of authoritarianism since the Arab Awakening.
>
> There is little doubt that in many Arab countries,'state feminism' has generally favoured secular and liberal groups. The rapprochement between the state and feminist women activists had little to do with genuine political convergence but, rather, was the product of expediency. For the regimes, promoting women's rights and gender equality meant gaining international praise from the international community while, at the same time, strengthening a coalition against Islamists. For the women's movements, accepting the support of the state on gender equality meant that controversial legislation – for the majority of society, at least – could be passed without much interference. Thus, 'despite individual persecution, secular groups generally benefited from state support for women's rights, while most Islamists were jailed, went underground or were in exile abroad for decades'. The plight of Islamist women was often ignored or minimized in many liberal and secular circles and this has further exacerbated the confrontation between the two sets of activists across the region.
>
> *Source*: Doris Gray (2012). 'Tunisia after the uprising: Islamist and secular quests for women's rights', *Mediterranean Politics*, 17(3): 285–302.

Cavatorta, 2009). While the party eventually came around to accept the changes the King intended to push through, the change of heart appeared to be due more to political expediency than genuine conversion to the idea of equality.

But, it would be unfair to judge the position of Islamist movements on women today by referring solely to their past, as they have gone through a period of rapid ideological and institutional transformation (Cavatorta, 2012a, b), including significantly changed rhetoric and internal practice when it comes to gender equality. However, remnants of previous attitudes are still present and not all Islamist movements have 'progressed' on the issues, as the example of Hamas demonstrates (Milton-Edwards and Farrell, 2010). Despite the transformation of Islamism over time, the track record of some Islamists, and still-lingering suspicions about their doublespeak, continue provoke heated debate concerning their commitment to democracy and equality. The problem is also one of language in which equality and equity are confused and confusing. For Islamist women, the notion of equality is problematic because men and women are obviously not equal – and not only because the Qur'an is believed to state so. Islamist women strive for equity, in terms of which their public engagement should be valued as much as that of men, even if they stand for what, in liberal societies, might appear as patriarchal 'family values'.

Given all this, it is not surprising that over the last decade a number of studies have sought to explain the role of women in Islamist parties and their rise within them. One set of studies emphasizes internal party dynamics and proposes four different reasons for the prominent role of women. First, it is argued that the increased presence of women in Islamist movements is due to the realization on the part of the leadership that having women onboard would help to get women's votes out once suffrage was made universal. According to this argument, Islamist parties and movements actively recruit women so that they can then attract the support of other women. This is an argument based on the theory of rational decision-making on the part of political parties that wish to attract a different segment of the electorate. However, it does not seem very convincing. Islamist parties hardly need to attract new constituencies, as they are catch-all parties that perform well electorally across all sectors of society. Furthermore, women have been active in Islamist parties since times when electoral competition was neither free nor fair – or, indeed, did not take place at all. Second, it is argued that increased women's participation in Islamist parties and movements is due to the need to present a more moderate and modern image. This argument possesses greater validity, but discounts the fact that Islamist parties might not ever have been anti-women. In addition, it neglects the possibility that women in Islamist parties might be more radical and conservative than their male counterparts. We have examples from the region of prominent Islamist women taking a harder line on issues of individual choice – concerning women directly, as in the case of abortion – than male colleagues in the same party. Third, it is suggested that different factions co-exist within Islamist parties and, once more progressive elements control the party, women become more visible, because they fit with the ideological framework of the 'progressives'. Finally, some writers focus on 'changing opportunity structures: women within these parties have seized windows of opportunity unrelated to shifts in strategy and/or ideology' (Clark and Schwedler, 2003: 294).

A different set of explanations places emphasis on the profile of women joining Islamist parties. Some see rising levels of education of women across the Arab world as crucial and argue that increased education leads to heightened political activism. Others concentrate their attention on the family ties that seem to characterize women activists. Here, the suggestion is that they join Islamist parties because other family members are involved. Therefore, Islamist activism, whether political or social, becomes something akin to a family duty. But, these explanations have only limited validity, as they fail to explore the motivations of women for joining.

The first set of explanations treats women as if they had limited agency, since they are simply seen as 'chess pieces' utilized by factions within male-dominated parties for internal struggles or external consumption. This is dismissive of the agency of women, falling back on trite stereotypes about the domination of men over women in pious circles. It is problematic because it does not take into account the reality that individual choices can be, and often are, made on the basis of autonomous beliefs and experiences.

The second set of explanations, while moving closer to an examination of women's motivations, remains too general. Focusing on increased education might explain why women become more politicized in the sense that they are frustrated at the lack of opportunities after they complete their studies, but it still does not tell us why, specifically, they join Islamist movements, particularly when the latter tend to see women in traditional roles and not necessarily as full members of the workforce. Emphasizing family ties is certainly important, because there is some evidence that having male family members in Islamist movements might have an impact on the decision to join, as the cases of Rachid Ghannouchi's daughter in Tunisia or Sheikh Yassine's daughter in Morocco demonstrate. However, given the number of women activists, it is certainly difficult to argue that it constitutes the main reason for joining. In addition, men and women tend to meet when they become activists and form families following their decision to join.

A more fruitful line of inquiry as to why Islamist movements have become attractive to women who want to be politically and/or socially engaged is offered in the broad discussion of Islamist feminism mentioned earlier. A history of the phenomenon and the acceptance of its validity on the part of traditional feminism are beyond the scope of this chapter. Here, it suffices to say that, over the last three decades, dissatisfaction with traditional liberal feminism, the intellectual framework of which was imported from the West, gave rise to an attempt to construct an Islamic-specific alternative. Focusing their criticism on pre-Islamic patriarchal structures rather than on the religion of Islam, women activists began to make the argument that Islam was very much an egalitarian religion and, by returning to the concept of gender equality inscribed in the sacred texts and specific to Islam, women's rights could be advanced (Ahmed, 1992). This intellectual intuition spurred a significant amount of work on how traditional feminist goals and concerns could be claimed through a re-interpretation of key Islamic texts. A new feminist discourse began to emerge in the late 1980s and early 1990s that saw itself as alternative to that promoted by secular activists, who were accused of seeking to undermine Arab societies by importing values and traditions from the imperialist West. It is precisely the rise of anti-Western sentiment that allowed Islamist feminism to expand considerably. Within what is broadly called 'Islamist feminism' are different understandings and practices. There are, for instance, secular activists who have understood that the promotion of policies aimed at promoting gender equality have a better chance of success when couched and justified in religious language. Then, there are Islamist activists who claim that there is no need to link feminism and Islam, because Islam on its own provides for gender equality. Finally, there are Muslim women intellectuals who strive for the goal of gender equality without falling into the trap of assuming that secularization is a precondition of its achievement (Badran, 1995, 2009). The framework of Islamist feminism provides the necessary theoretical tools for explaining women's engagement in Islamist parties, and, as Halverson and Kay (2011: 522) state, 'while we may perceive these women as victims of false consciousness, we may also note that they embody a spirit of activism and the "Islamist feminist" perspective positions these women as agents in the construction of their own realities'. This was already borne out in a limited empirical study from the mid-1990s by Tessler and Jesse (1996) which suggested that women in Islamist movements saw their political engagement as a vehicle to assert their autonomy outside the home. This notion of challenging patriarchy through engagement in Islamist politics is also present to some extent among Palestinian women in Israel (Boulby, 2004). Islamist feminism, however, does not offer an answer to the question of what makes women join Islamist movements. It simply offers a way to understand the choice ex post facto. Just as Islam may not be the central explanation for gender inequality in the region, it can be postulated that women's activism might not have much to do with the desire for gender equality per se, as understood in the liberal feminist tradition. Thus, women's engagement in Islamist movements might be de-linked from any attempt to promote gender equality. In fact, it may be that the modernizing effect of the political activism of Islamist women is simply the by-product of a choice that has very little to do with the goal of reinventing the role of women in Arab societies through religion.

It is necessary, therefore, to look at other variables for explanation. From this point of view, it is their policy positions on a vast array of issues that drive women to support and become active in Islamist movements, and such policy positions do not necessarily have to do with gender-related questions. These policy positions find reinforcement in identity politics, with Arab–Muslim identity becoming a crucial factor in the decision to become involved. Islamist movements attract members and command significant support from the population because of what they stand for and represent. Conversely, political projects that are secular and liberal in nature are no longer as convincing or appealing as they used to be in the past, when leftist thinking was dominant across the region from Iraq to Tunisia. For some time, Islamist movements, of different ideological convictions and with different political strategies, have attracted a large female cohort of members and supporters who defy the expectation that women activists should follow in the footsteps of the previous generation when swathes of women joined the ranks of leftist parties and militated for the introduction of French-style *laicité*, secularism based on the separation between church and state, particularly in North Africa. More interestingly, the Arab Awakening may have strengthened the hand of Islamist parties and movements, rather than weakening them. In any case, what emerges from the picture of Islamist women is the way in which the specific type of 'feminism' they embody and promote is affecting how one thinks of women's rights in the Arab world. The dichotomy between traditional feminism as inherently progressive and liberating, and Islamist women's engagement in politics as inherently backward-looking and treasonous to women, is no longer tenable. The interactions between Islamist and secular women over the meaning of feminism and women's rights have led to the inter-penetration of boundaries, suggesting that the claims of conservative Islamist women, whether on women's rights or on any other issues, have to be taken seriously (Selime, 2011).

Problematizing the nature, causes and manifestations of gender inequality in the Middle East requires us to analyse a multiplicity of social, political and economic dynamics that go beyond simplistic linkages with the perceived essential nature of Islam. In addition, such analysis calls on scholars to eliminate normative bias and take into account the many forms of women's activism, even when such activism is of a conservative nature.

Key questions

- How do we conceive of the paradox of state feminism?
- What is the influence of liberal feminism in the Arab world?
- How do we explain Islamist women's activism?
- What does the politics of piety tell us about women's agency?

Further reading

Ahmed, Leila (1992). *Women and Gender in Islam: Historical Roots of a Modern Debate*, Yale University Press.

Clark, Janine and Jillian Schwedler (2003). 'Who opened the window? Women's activism in Islamist parties,' *Comparative Politics*, 35(3): 293–312.

Gualtieri, Sarah (2006). '"Should a woman demand all the rights of a man?" From the Cairo periodical, *Al-Hilal*, 1894', in Camron Michael Amin, Benjamin C. Fortna and Elizabeth B. Frierson (eds), *The Modern Middle East: A Sourcebook for History*, Oxford: Oxford University Press.

Keddie, Nikki R. (1979). 'Problems in the Study of Middle Eastern Women', *International Journal of Middle East Studies*, 10(2): 225: 240.

Seferdjeli, Ryme (2006). 'Two views of women fighters during the Algerian War of liberation', in Camron Michael Amin, Benjamin C. Fortna and Elizabeth B. Frierson (eds), *The Modern Middle East: A Sourcebook for History*, Oxford: Oxford University Press.

Tessler, Mark and Jolene Jesse (1996). 'Gender and support for Islamist movements: evidence from Egypt, Kuwait and Palestine', *Muslim World*, 86, (2): 200–28.

Online resources

Abu-Khalil, As'ad (2005). 'Women in the Middle East', *Foreign Policy in Focus*. Available at http://fpif.org/women_in_the_middle_east/.

Human Rights Watch (2006). 'Women's rights in Middle East and North Africa', *Human Rights Watch*. Available at: http://www.hrw.org/women/overview-mena.html.

United Nations (2010). 'Directory of UN Resources on gender and women's issues: North Africa and the Middle East' Available at http://www.un.org/womenwatch/directory/north_africa_and_the_middle_east_10476.htm.

World Bank (2004). 'Gender and development in the Middle East and North Africa: women in the public sphere' Available at http://web.worldbank.org/WBSITE/EXTERNAL/COUNTRIES/MENAEXT/0,,contentMDK:20261828~piPk:146830~the SitePK:256299,00.html.

Chapter 9

The Military, Security and Conflict

In a seminal article in 2004, Eva Bellin provided what seemed a perfectly simple and plausible explanation for the survival of authoritarianism in the Arab world (and Iran, it might be added): the robustness of the security apparatus. Rather than looking for complex structural explanations or actor-led models, when accounting for the global singularity and exceptionalism of the region in regard to authoritarian survival, Bellin concentrated her attention on the ability of regimes to maintain a cohesive and effective security apparatus that acted to repress dissent, silence opposition voices and, thus, prevent any change. Bellin identified a number of variables that fuelled the continuing strength of the security apparatus, and argued convincingly that, ultimately, what prevents democratic change in the region is the use, or the threat, of physical violence. Taken to its logical conclusion, Bellin's argument identified fear of physical violence, meted out by the state against dissidents, as the real obstacle to transitions to democracy.

Other scholars (Albrecht and Schlumberger, 2004; Cavatorta, 2007) partially disagree with this explanation and argue that regimes, even the most repressive, cannot survive for long on repression alone, and need other sources of legitimacy, be they economic, ideological, or other. However, there is no disputing that Bellin's argument had the merit of placing the role of the military and the security services centre-stage once more. The centrality of these actors to the politics of the region should not have been neglected to the extent that it has been. Since independence, both the military and, to a lesser degree, internal security services, have been major protagonists of Arab, Iranian, Turkish and, also, Israeli politics. In this chapter, we first highlight the role of the military in shaping the political, social and economic institutions of a number of countries in region, which make it almost impossible for the military to avoid 'playing politics'. This does not mean that the military is, or has been, a unitary actor. Far from it, the military in the MENA region has gone through profound change over time and has been characterized by purges, splits, professionalization and gradual, if variable, subordination to civilian control.

The chapter analyses these changes in some detail, as they have culminated, during the Arab Awakening, with the refusal of some military commanders to back incumbent leaders, when orders were given to shoot demonstrators (Geisser and Krefa, 2011). In fact, some suggest that the role of the military during the Arab Awakening is not particularly surprising

212 Politics and Governance in the Middle East

because, over time, and at least since the 1980s, it has been the internal security services that have assumed the dominant role in repressing domestic dissent. The infamous *mukhabarat* (intelligence services) was charged with monitoring and repressing dissent in society, as Arab states (and Iran) became progressively more authoritarian, with leaders almost completely cut off from their populations and insulated from popular and opposition demands. In some countries, such as Syria, the number of security services multiplied over time, constituting a network of repressive and spying agencies that led to the creation of East German-style police states (Ziadeh, 2010). Thus, military and domestic security agencies were often at odds politically, and in competition with one another for resources. Furthermore, in countries where the military used to govern directly, a shift occurred whereby they continued to 'rule, but not to govern' (Cook, 2007).

After analysing the domestic influence of military and security services, the chapter turns to the international impact of such large apparatuses. Regional politics has been profoundly affected by ever-increasing military budgets, expanding armies and the proliferation of security services. The chapter will also analyse some of the civil and intra-state conflicts that have characterized the region over time. All-out wars and minor confrontations have been a constant feature in the region since independence, with notions of pan-Arab brotherhood often cast aside in the name of national interest. In this mix, attention must be paid to the creation of the state of Israel and the regional tensions that it generated. On the one hand, the confrontation with Israel permitted many Arab rulers to justify the strengthening of their military and security services in the name of the battle against Zionism. On the other hand, it led Israel to build up its own military capabilities, which have been often displayed with great success over the course of the country's existence. No analysis of the MENA can ignore the Arab–Israeli conflict, which remains a crucial issue in the politics of the region.

The rise of the military

The importance of the military in the Arab world is both an outcome of the historical conditions present at independence and a process through which the military subsequently developed and changed over time. There are a number of reasons that help to explain why the military held – and, in many ways, continues to hold – considerable power. In countries where the process of decolonization was particularly violent, or in countries where state-formation has been heavily contested, 'men with guns' acquired both a military and a political role. In Algeria, for instance, the long war against the French empowered the military commanders from the border areas who had led the war effort, to the detriment of the political leadership and the fighters of the interior (Ruedy, 2005). Within three years of independence, Ben Bella, the political leader of the National Liberation Front (FLN), was ousted in a coup by Houari Boumediène, who took advantage of his military standing to chart a course for Algeria that was quite different from that which Ben Bella had in mind. The influence of the Algerian military did not diminish over time. It has always been considered the real power-holder in the country, leading one commentator to suggest that while 'countries possess militaries, the Algerian military possesses a country'. Therefore, it is no surprise that, at another crucial stage in the country's history, the military again intervened in political life, carrying out a coup in January 1992. In the late 1980s and the early 1990s, the Algerian process of democratization ultimately failed because the army decided to act to prevent the Islamist party, the Islamic Salvation Front (FIS), from winning power through the ballot box. The civil war which followed further empowered the military. Indeed, it was not until 1999 that a man with no military background, Abdelaziz Bouteflika, was elected to the presidency. But, in order to be elected, Bouteflika had to have the backing of the highest-ranking officers in the military because, as Volpi (2006) makes clear, the entire Algerian political system continues to be based around the decision-making power of the military and its intelligence services. This level of power has diminished in more recent times, due to increased professionalization, and the delegation of security duties to other agencies – but it remains important. Two important broader points emerge from this brief summary of the role of the military in Algeria.

First, the belief amongst the officer corps of the military that they are the custodians of the country's sovereignty against external enemies – a reasonable assumption – was accompanied by the much more problematic one – that the military had to guard the nation against domestic actors, even if they had been elected, when they were suspected of undermining the unity of the country and its foundational ideals. A number of armies in the region operated on a similar assumption that they were entrusted with the protection of the country's ideals and ideology. This provided the rationale for intervention in political and civilian matters. Since independence, most countries in the region have witnessed a number of successful military coups, in addition to numerous failed attempts. This is not simply a trait of Arab countries, as the case of Turkey amply demonstrates. Military coups were carried out three times during that country's history, when civilian rule was deemed to have 'deviated' from the prescriptions of Kemalist nationalist ideology, or when such rule was believed to be corrupt or ineffectual. Furthermore, the Turkish military kept watch on elected politicians, often pressuring them into courses of action preferred by the military. It is only since the election of the AKP government in 2002 that Turkish politics has seen the progressive marginalization of the military from political life and the dominance of elected representatives over security matters, both domestic and international.

Second, the military has tended, over time, to fade into the background, leaving the political scene to former military commanders who assumed civilian institutional roles. Thus, despite repeated and forceful earlier interventions, the militaries of both Algeria and Turkey progressively began to use their influence more subtly, operating behind the scenes to appoint – or, at least, guide the appointment of – leaders they could trust and rely on. In the final instance, both have remained important actors. But they have also had to cede some power to other social and political forces. However, the Arab Awakening, with its accompanying political and social volatility, seems to have drawn the military out of the barracks once again, as the Egyptian military coup of July 2013 against the democratically elected Islamist president, Muhammed Mursi, demonstrates.

In countries where the process of decolonization was less violent, armies did not immediately become as influential and interventionist as in Algeria and Turkey. However, the process of nation- and state-building soon provided an incentive for the military to take a leading role. In most cases, colonial powers generally left behind countries that had new and contested borders, unpopular leaderships interested in maintaining strong linkages with the former 'motherland', and desperate socioeconomic conditions. Initially set up to secure the new countries and their leaders from internal challenges, the military began to accumulate the resources and capabilities to carry out a number of other tasks connected to socioeconomic development. With the increasing appeal in the region of ideologies that carried strong socialist and anti-imperialist undertones, a cohort of officers within a number of Arab armies – the 'Free Officers' – began to see themselves as the solution to the problems their countries were experiencing. In Egypt, Iraq, Syria and Libya, these Free Officers came to power through military coups and with a radical agenda of social, economic and political transformation. The ideals of socialist-led development, together with a heavy emphasis on pan-Arabism and anti-imperialism – directed primarily at the United States, the United Kingdom and Israel – informed their domestic and international policies, as the military became directly involved in policy areas of all kinds, employing the civilian state bureaucracy, and, at times, replacing it, to pursue out their agenda. As Pratt (2007) makes clear, in these socialist radical republics, a degree of social and economic development occurred under the guidance of the army or of the coup leader turned president. The new rulers set about marginalizing other social and political actors – the wealthy bourgeoisie and the clerics in

Box 9.1   Nasserism

When Gamal Abdel Nasser rose to power in the early 1950s, he embodied the hopes of many Arabs for a successful process of de-colonization that would bring about much more than nominal independence. Nasser interpreted this desire for a radical break with a past of Arab subjugation to outside forces by combining a number of different and often controversial ideological elements into what seemed, at the time, a coherent framework for social, economic and political development in the Arab world. What came to be known as 'Nasserism' was a very powerful ideological force for a number of decades in the Arab world and, although its relevance has waned over the years, a number of political actors and parties claiming its legacy and advocating a return to its political practices can still be found today across the region. The ideological polarization of the Cold War fundamentally shaped Naasserism. On the one hand, Nasser and his followers were hard-core pan-Arab nationalists who wished to be free of what they considered the imperialist influences of the United States and the former colonial powers of Britain and France. This anti-Western stance translated into several attempts at undermining the West's allies in the region, fighting Israel – considered an imperialist and colonial power in its own right, and supporting Third World nationalist movements in their struggle for emancipation. In this respect, Nasserism was also very much concerned to implement socialist policies at home that would lead Egypt to sustained economic development outside the capitalist model that the West was accused of attempting to impose.

On the other hand, Nasserism was also opposed to communism and what can be thought of as Soviet expansionism. While there was a degree of cooperation with the Soviet Union on economic matters, Nasserists refused to become Soviet satellites and strived for non-alignment in the context of the Cold War. This balancing act between East and West was reasonably successful for a number of years. But, ultimately, it did not pay off because Cold War pressure eventually became too strong and Nasser's heirs in Egypt abandoned it in favour of an increasingly close alliance with the United States. Domestically, Nasserism would ultimately also prove to be a disappointment, as the socialist agenda implemented not only in Egypt, but also in other Arab countries whose leaders were influenced by Nasserism, failed to deliver long-term economic and social benefits. Finally, the pan-Arab dream of Nasserism did not materialize either, as narrower national interests prevailed over pan-Arab solidarity and brotherhood.

particular – in order to carry out their developmental agenda and become more forceful anti-imperialist actors abroad. However, Pratt also underlines how this strategy had the consequence of turning these countries into increasingly authoritarian states in which, in the name of national unity, no dissent was permitted.

The 'Free Officers' movement was created in Egypt, under the effective leadership of Gamal Abdel Nasser – whose ideological programme is discussed in Box 9.1 – with the goal of taking power in order to set the country on a very different course from that which King Farouk had charted from independence. In particular, the Free Officers wanted to assert genuine Egyptian independence by ridding the country of British influence and by making much bolder choices in terms of wealth redistribution and social programmes. The Free Officers were successful in their endeavor: in 1952, they took control of the country. While Nasser did not officially lead the military coup, there is no doubt he was the main decision-maker within the group. By 1953, the monarchy was abolished, and, by 1956, Nasser was president, a position which he held until his death in 1970. During his time in power, Egypt freed itself from the tutelage of the West, built closer ties with the Soviet Union – although he kept the Soviets at a reasonable distance and Egypt never became a Soviet satellite, fought wars with Israel to assert his anti-Zionist credentials, and attempted to modernize both the economy and society through the adoption of socialism, which led him to nationalize the Suez Canal. Nasser was also a strong proponent of Arab unity and promoted pan-Arabism across the region, finding other military officers willing to listen to him and prepared to follow in his footsteps. In many ways, during the 1950s and 1960s Nasser was the most admired Arab leader and a source of inspiration for other Free Officers movements elsewhere in the region.

The role of the military in Nasser's Egypt, as in many other Arab countries, is quite paradigmatic of the ways in which they changed and developed. Although every country in which military men came to power is obviously different, there are some common trends.

First, as the leaders of military coups solidified their power, they took on 'civilian' roles and began to distance themselves, at least superficially, from their military background. As they became presidents, or prime ministers, or 'guides' – as in Gaddafi's case – they needed to demonstrate that their prestige and appeal went beyond the uniform. While never severing their ties with the military they had come from, they began increasingly to rely on a plethora of other 'civilian' security agencies to remain in power, on the state bureaucracy to carry out policy decisions, and on a single party – or 'revolutionary councils' in Gaddafi's Libya – to mobilize support for the leader within society. This was rendered necessary because they needed to build alliances with sectors of society other than the military in order to carry out the sorts of policies they wanted to implement and to secure their position of power. Thus, while the military was an engine of change, a locus of ideological indoctrination and remained, in many ways, the guardian of the nation, over time a degree of distance emerged between it and the political leadership.

Second, as the years passed from the initial seizure of power, the interest of the military in promoting radical change waned. There were several reasons for this: diminished ideological enthusiasm; the achievement of important goals; generational change; or, more controversially, the marginalization of the military by the revolutionary leader who had come from its ranks, as in Libya's case (Haddad, 2012). Whatever the reason, the 'new blood' within the ranks became less ideological. This meant that increasing attention was paid to the professionalization of military service, and, while the military certainly continued to play an important role in securing the regime and acting as the guardian of a specific national self-image, ideology became less important. Acquiring new skills abroad, building links with powerful foreign militaries, obtaining new weaponry and setting up clear and more meritocratic career paths for promotion became the most important objectives of the new officer corps. The military was transformed from an engine of political change to the guarantor of the political status quo, in which it occupied a privileged position. In 'exchange' for this, the military required that political decision-makers tended to the professionalization of its members, while allocating a considerable part of the state budget to procurement, training and subsidized living standards for the military.

Third, military life, for an increasing number of officers, became a means to acquire social status and economic advantage. Military life guaranteed access to state benefits that few other sectors of the population enjoyed, such as specialized health care, housing and schooling. This persisted even when the economic crisis of the late 1970s and 1980s began to hit the rest of the population. Also, their connections with the upper-echelons of the regime, together with the dependence of many civilian decision-makers on the positive sanction of the army for their economic policies, meant that the military became an important economic actor. This is most evident in Egypt. But military officers played, and still play, a significant role in the economic life of Syria, Libya, Iraq and Algeria.

Finally, the divisions within the small groups of officers who initially carried out the military coup became increasingly apparent, leading to purges and assassinations. These divisions were due to increasing ideological differences over the direction of the country, as well as personal rivalries. This, in turn, led to the concentration of power in the hands of the most important figures within the group. In the Egyptian case, the original goals of the Free Officers were to marginalize the King, and initiate significant social and economic transformation – but also, for some, to lead the country to some form of democratic rule and pluralism. When, in 1953, Nasser instead opted for the abolition of all political parties except the one he set up (the Liberation Rally), dissent within the movement grew, but was quickly put down. Gaddafi was probably the worst offender in this respect, as he turned on his former allies frequently, setting up a campaign of assassination of dissenters that had global as well as domestic reach (Ougartchinska and Priore, 2013).

The role of the military in these formerly socialist radical republics countries is best summed up in this description of the Egyptian military by Albrecht and Bishara:

> although the Egyptian military has previously disengaged from direct polit-ical control, it was an indispensable part of the *ancien regime*. It served as the ultimate coercive backbone that political incumbents would employ in the case of immediate threats; it maintained significant influence on core issues in foreign policy ... and it was a pool for the recruitment for political positions ... Most importantly, the military had been given the opportunity to establish its own vast economic complex. (2011: 14)

These four trends, combined with the pressures of an unstable regional system which remained so even after the end of the Cold War – as will be highlighted in Chapter 10 – have had powerful consequences for the role of the military in the Arab republics. The increasing professionali-zation, and internal divisions among the earlier 'revolutionaries' within the military, over time led rulers to rely on a plethora of security services and agencies for internal dissent and repression. To a significant extent, these security services ended up competing with the military in terms of resources and political patronage, even if they were connected in one form or another to the military establishment. Being much more strongly linked to the patronage networks that rulers had put in place, these security serv-ices were entrusted with the domestic security of the regime. But, when serious domestic unrest threatened the very survival of the regime, the military was employed to deal with the challenge, as the case of Syria in the early 1980s illustrates (Lefévre, 2013). A further consequence of mili-tary purges was the increasing reliance of rulers on clan, tribal and family affiliations to maintain control of the military machine. While, in some cases, reliance on non-institutional types of affiliation was clear from the beginning, this development accelerated from the 1980s onwards, as support for regimes shrank and their survival was more acutely pinned on smaller, and more reliable, constituencies. For example, on coming to power in 1970, Syrian president and military man Hafez al-Asad began staffing the officer corps of the military with an increasing number of members of his own religious sect – the Alawites – in order to ensure the loyalty of the armed officers and to avoid coups. In addition to that, members of his own family were groomed to take leading positions in the security apparatus, which allowed for repression to be more effective by tying it to both family and Alawite community survival, as Box 9.2 explains. The structuring of the armed forces along sectarian and family

Box 9.2   The Ashes of Hama

Beginning in the late 1970s, the Syrian Muslim Brotherhood became the most powerful opposition force to the rule of Hafez al-Asad who had seized power in 1970 through a military coup which installed the secular *Baath* party as the engine of social and economic development of the country in a context of an anti-imperialist and anti-Israel foreign policy. Asad's rule, however, was not based only on ideology, but on sectarianism as well. The president hailed from the minority Alawite sect, which had a long tradition of being discriminated against by the Sunni majority. This sectarian factor became increasingly important as significant material resources were directed towards the social and economic improvement of the Alawite community.

Over time, the Alawites became the backbone of the state bureaucracy and the military. Along with the secularism of the policies Asad had begun to implement, sectarianism played an important role in the rise of the Muslim Brotherhood and its challenge to the regime. By the early 1980s, the challenge had assumed a military character. Asad responded by using the full power of the military to quell a Muslim Brotherhood-led rebellion. At this time, the Syrian special forces were under the command of Asad's brother, Rifaat, who was charged with putting down the rebellion. The decisive battle took place at Hama, where the Muslim Brotherhood fighters were comprehensively defeated and the city centre completely destroyed. The destruction of Hama remained for decades a powerful reminder of how the Asad-led regime would deal with opponents.

The events surrounding the confrontation between the Syrian Muslim Brotherhood and the Syrian regime are paradigmatic for a number of reasons. First, they highlighted the changing nature of the military, whereby leaders increasingly relied on extra-institutional linkages such as family and tribal ties to secure the regime. Second, rather than fighting external enemies, the military or, at least, special forces within them – were charged with repressing internal dissent. Third, any attempt to challenge the regime came to be perceived as a terrorist plot, usually carried out with external support, whether this was actually true or not. This pattern recurred during the Syrian uprising of 2011. Special forces led by Bashar al-Asad's brother are largely in charge of repression, together with an officer corps almost entirely made up of Alawites and with the support of Alawites militias. In addition, the regime refers to the rebellion as terrorists working for outside powers, notably the United States and Saudi Arabia, as if the rebels had no legitimate domestic grievances and support.

Source: Raphael Levéfre (2013). *Ashes of Hama*, Oxford: Oxford University Press.

lines survived the death of Hafez al-Asad. When his son, Bashar, took power in 2000, he could count on similar loyalty. During the uprising that began in 2011, a number of analysts predicted that the regime would collapse quickly in the face of determined and widespread opposition. But the regular army, together with a number of pro-regime militias, held fast. Part of the explanation for this resides in 'sectarian' safeguards that were put in place. However, where sectarian and tribal linkages were tenuous, other stratagems were chosen to ensure that the military would remain in the service of the leader. In Libya, Gaddafi's military was heavily manned by mercenaries from Eastern Europe and sub-Saharan Africa, as well as loyal tribal members, because on coming to power he had to face a number of attempted coups and did not want to empower any institution that might ultimately pose a threat to his regime.

While the military was a primary actor in the post-independence, socialist, anti-imperialist republics, its role, at least to begin with, was different in the conservative monarchies. Rather than being an engine for social and economic change, the military apparatus in the monarchies served regimes loyally and ensured that the 'revolutionary' ideas that toppled kings in Egypt, Iraq and Libya did not 'contaminate' the kingdoms. For instance, 'the Hashemite Jordanian monarchy has relied on the armed forces as its main pillar of support since the emergence of the regime itself' (Ryan, 2012: 8). Such loyalty to the monarchy held for a number of reasons. First, monarchs ensured that prominent members of the ruling family held important position in the armed forces in order to ensure control, while tribal alliances also played a crucial role. This has been the case particularly in Saudi Arabia. Second, international alliances with Western capitals during the Cold War led to a form of external tutelage of the armed forces that worked well, ensuring that revolutionary tendencies that might have emerged within the officer corps did not actually arise. A significant investment of money also ensured that there would be a higher degree of military professionalization. Most importantly however, was the relatively small number of men in arms. An exception to this, among the conservative monarchies, was Morocco. Muhammad V, the first post-independence king of Morocco, built up a large military in the aftermath of independence and was believed to have ensured its loyalty. However, his son Hassan II escaped two attempted military coups in a short space of time in the early 1970s. A group of leading army officers had decided that Morocco needed a profound change in direction, moving away from the 'imperialist' camp towards a closer embrace of the pan-Arab and anti-imperialist cause. The officers also had grievances regarding domestic policies, which they believed were not tackling the socioeconomic problems of the country. Finally, there was unease about the King's friendly diplomacy towards Israel. Both failed coup attempts were organized to eliminate the King – the first, in 1971, during a reception at one of his palaces; the second, in 1972, while he was on a flight back to the country – in the expectation that his removal would be the starting point of revolutionary change. Through a combination of luck and quick thinking, the King survived both attempts and set about purging the military, imprisoning or executing those who were held responsible for the attempts on his life. However, purges were not the only instrument that he employed to secure his reign. In 1975, he launched the 'Green March' – a nationwide campaign to take possession of the contested area of Western Sahara, a large territory previously under Spanish control, that the local indigenous population hoped to transform into an independent state. Morocco claimed that the territory was part of 'historical Morocco' and launched an invasion, taking possession of it and at the same time provoking an insurrection. While the question of the sovereignty of Western Sahara has yet to be determined, very large numbers of Moroccan troops are stationed there, keeping them away from Morocco proper and giving them something meaningful to do. The Western Sahara 'distraction' has permitted both Hassan II, and his son Mohammed VI, the current ruler, to manage the military in such a way as to remove it from any significant political role.

Irrespective of the nature of the set-up of the military or the significance of its domestic political role, the growth of the armed forces in such a strategic region led to two developments that would influence the international politics of the MENA. First, the armed forces required massive budgets to sustain them. The Cold War fuelled the growth of militaries across the region as the two superpowers battled it out for supremacy. Initially, the Soviet Union could count on the support of Nasser-led Egypt in the region and the Soviets made significant inroads in building links with other prominent regional actors such as Algeria, Syria and Iraq, while providing significant amounts of weaponry. The United States, for its part, developed very close relations with the Gulf monarchies, Jordan and Morocco. Increasing levels of oil wealth facilitated arms acquisition on an enormous scale, further militarizing the MENA. The astronomical figures that Gaddafi spent on weaponry on coming to power in 1969 remain legendary, particularly if one considers how small the population of Libya actually is (according to one report, between 1970 and 2009, he spent US$30 billion on weapons). Nevertheless, both Western powers (particularly France and Italy) and countries of the then Eastern bloc were more than happy to acquire market shares in Libya, given the size of the orders that Gaddafi put in. It should be noted that Libya was by no means the only country to spend very large amounts of money in weapons, as Saudi Arabia, Syria, Algeria, Turkey and Egypt all invested considerably in their armed forces. The end of the Cold War did not halt military spending; neither did it curb the influence of the armed forces when it came to securing a privileged position in the allocation of budgetary resources. The continued instability of the region, together with the presence of both international and civil conflicts, meant that countries would continue spending large amounts of money on military hardware. In addition, the competition for increasing market share, at a time when big powers were cutting down on their own military spending, meant that the MENA countries were specifically targeted by arms exporters. The instability that the 2003 war in Iraq created, coupled with the outbreak of civil conflicts in Libya and Syria, has done very little to curb expenditure on the military. On the contrary, the rebuilding of the Iraqi military after its dissolution by the US administration in 2003 required a significant amount of income from oil revenues being spent on weaponry procured in the United States. The scale of resources spent on military and security budgets has been a constant source of criticism in opposition circles in all Arab countries, particularly in more recent decades, not least because of declining living standards and the poor quality of public services. Critics suggest that, if at least part of the resources allocated to military and security agencies were redirected towards social spending, some of the most significant problems countries faced could more easily be tackled. This applies in particular to non-oil exporting countries. But all states in the region spend enormously on arms, generating negative political repercussions. For instance, Usama bin Laden highlighted irresponsible and inefficient military spending as one of the reasons for his opposition to the Saudi rulers (Burgat, 2005).

The second, and far more important, consequence of the significance of the military concerns the number of conflicts that seem to be an unalterable trait of political life in the MENA. Both internal and external security concerns dominated politics in the past, and, to a large extent, still do. Kerr proposed in 1971 that an Arab Cold War was taking place. This notion has recently been revived (Valbjørn and Bank, 2012) to explain the regional rivalries currently plaguing the region and driving conflict in a number of countries, while placing security, both domestic and international, very high on the agenda. The military has, therefore, been employed in a number of conflicts. On the domestic level, for example, there has been military involvement in civil conflicts in Syria during the 1980s, in Algeria during the 1990s, and in Turkey during the 1980s and 1990s. These were large-scale conflicts against armed Islamists (Algeria and Syria) and ethnic and linguistic minorities (the Kurds, in the case of Turkey). In each of these conflicts the military prevailed, although the price paid in terms of loss of lives was extremely high, with estimates of over 150,000 dead in the course of the Algerian civil war. Saddam-led Iraq also relied on the military to put down rebellions against the Kurds of Iraq in the north of the country in the 1980s, again in the early 1990s, and also against the Iraqi Shias in the south, who had taken up arms against the regime in 1991. While not on the same scale, both the Egyptian and Moroccan military have been called upon to put down civil unrest and 'terrorism', with the Egyptian military particularly involved in an anti-Islamist campaign in the 1990s which led to the death of thousands of people. The pattern recurred in August 2013 when the security forces were called in to suppress protests against the removal of Islamist president Mursi from office by the military. The result was the deaths of over 600 people.

While the military has been relied upon frequently in the domestic setting, it is obviously not their primary role. Soon after independence and with the creation of the State of Israel, many Arab countries identified the struggle against it as the most important one, because they deemed Israel an illegitimate creation that had taken away Arab land. Thus, since 1948 a number of wars have opposed Israel and its neighbours, with devastating consequences for the region in terms of stability.

The Arab–Israeli conflict

The establishment of the State of Israel in 1948 is, without doubt, one of the most significant events in the history of the MENA, quickly becoming a source of multiple conflicts that have yet to find a solution. The state of Israel was the outcome of a 50-year long campaign by European Jews to have a land of their own where they could create their own state institutions free from the anti-Semitism that had been a constant feature of European societies for centuries. In the late 1880s, under the leadership of Theodore Herzl, the Zionist movement developed into a potent force to convince European leaders of the need for a homeland for the Jews of Europe (see p. 52). The basic idea behind Zionism was that the establishment of a state for the Jews would solve two problems European societies were facing. First, it would resolve the problem of European anti-Semitism, which had led to enormous suffering for Jewish communities across the continent. If the Jews of Europe could be provided with a land of their own in which they could live, they would no longer suffer from anti-Semitism. Second, European states, which were building their own national identities, would be favoured by the departure of the Jews because this would create more homogenous societies. Herzl's political project built on a yearning for a return to Zion that is central to Judaism and this made the connection with the land of Palestine all but inevitable. Initially though, the Zionist movement was not particularly successful. European decision-makers were not keen to commit to the creation of a state for the Jews and many within European Jewry were unconvinced of the merits of Zionism, and were not enthused by the idea of leaving Europe to settle in Palestine, the land identified by Zionists as their future homeland. Many religious Jews, for instance, saw this project as usurping divine prerogative, insofar as the return of Zion should be an event initiated by God and not by humans. They viewed it, therefore, with a degree of suspicion. Furthermore, many secular European Jews were still determined to integrate fully within European nation-states, to which, having lived in them for centuries, they felt they naturally belonged.

Despite such opposition, Zionist efforts paid off in 1917, when Britain effectively sanctioned the creation of a Jewish state in today's Palestine. The Balfour Declaration was the first significant victory of the Zionist movement, but it did not do much in terms of encouraging European Jews actually to migrate. For decades, from the beginning of propaganda efforts to get European Jews to settle in Palestine, the numbers moving remained quite small, amounting to no more than a few thousand. Jews represented the majority population in Jerusalem by the middle of the nineteenth century, but their total number remained limited, compared with the Arab population. In the early 1930s, more Jews began to arrive, following a further rise in anti-Semitism in Europe. When the early settlers arrived in Palestine they did not encounter major hostility from the indigenous population, with some of the locals benefiting economically from the arrival of European settlers. The European Jews brought with them capital and new skills, which could contribute to the prosperity of the area, leading some prominent Palestinian families to welcome their arrival and acknowledge that they had rights to the land. As the numbers grew, however, and as the mandatory power, Britain, seemed unable or unwilling to stem the flow, Arab opposition intensified, leading to riots and general strikes to prevent further settlers from arriving. To local Arabs, the influx of Jews from Europe began to look and feel like colonization and they began to mobilize politically.

The events of World War II and the near annihilation of European Jews in the Holocaust made the Zionist project seem prophetic and many survivors elected to go to Palestine in order to escape their ordeal and construct a place where Jews would be forever safe because they would always be the majority population. With Britain quickly losing its empire and seeking to withdraw from the region as quickly as possible, a partition plan was devised by the United Nations which envisaged the creation of a Jewish state and a new Arab state in the land of Palestine. In the meantime, a violent three-way confrontation between Jews, Arabs and British forces had begun. Jewish and Palestinian militias fought both each other, as well as the British, in an attempt to obtain the best possible position on the ground, in the knowledge that a showdown would become inevitable once the British left for good. The UN-sponsored partition plan suited the Jewish community, but the Palestinians refused even to contemplate partition, as they felt that they should not give up any of the territory they deemed was being usurped. War became inevitable. When, in 1948, the independence of the new state of Israel was proclaimed, the armies of neighbouring Arab states joined the Palestinian Arabs in the fight. The war was relatively short and ended with a clear Israeli victory, which secured the survival of the new state, whose existence was quickly recognized by the two superpowers that had emerged from World War II: the United States and the Soviet Union.

However, no state, not even a diminished one, was created for Palestinian Arabs, and the remaining territory they lived on was annexed by Jordan (the West Bank and Jerusalem) and Egypt (Gaza). A Palestinian state was not created for three intertwined reasons. First, the political representatives of the Palestinians refused to contemplate the idea that partition was a forgone conclusion and that they should have accepted what was on offer. In hindsight, this might have been the wrong choice to make but, in the late 1940s, there was little or no support for partition among Palestinians, who felt that their land was being taken away and their rights denied. Second, the Palestinian and the Arab armies lost the war on the battlefield. As in many other, if not all, international conflicts, the winner is in a privileged position. Therefore, the leadership of the new state of Israel saw no reason to be magnanimous, particularly because no one had been particularly magnanimous to it. In addition, it should be noted that the Zionist project was partly based on the premise that the wishes of the indigenous non-Jewish population should not be taken into account. Finally, once the conflict was over, both Jordan and Egypt opted to annex parts of what should have become a Palestinian state, with little regard for the rights of their fellow Arabs.

The war of 1948 had a number of important regional and global consequences. First, it led to the creation of a state, Israel, which faced the hostility of all its neighbours, leaving it isolated in the region, and needing to prioritize security over all other matters. Over time, this led to the creation of a very powerful military apparatus, which, with the help of key international supporters – notably the United States from the late 1960s – has become the dominant military force in the region. Second, the war created the conditions for the emergence of a lasting Palestinian resistance. Despite the initial defeat, the difficulties in sustaining a Palestinian identity and meddling in Palestinian affairs by their 'Arab brothers', Palestinians are still battling – at times through violent means, at others through diplomacy or civil disobedience – to secure their own state. In any case, Palestinian identity is now fully established and, despite its internal divisions, Palestinian nationalism is a considerable mobilizing force. Third, the war of 1948 led to the creation of the Palestinian refugee problem. Whether 'by war or by design' (Morris, 1989), when hostilities broke out hundreds of thousands of Palestinians fled their homes to find refuge in neighbouring states – with profound consequences for host soci-

Box 9.3   Palestinian refugees and neighbouring states

Palestinian refugees have fared very differently, depending on where they ended up. Two characteristics informed the response of neighbouring Arab states to the arrival of Palestinian refugees – at least, in principle. The first was solidarity with their fellow Arabs; the second was the need to preserve Palestinian identity. Their responses were shaped by the view that the refugee issue was temporary. The presence of the refugees needed to be temporary, if it were to be in line with the doctrine of the 'right to return', a core claim of the Palestinians.

The reality is that the treatment of Palestinian refugees varies considerably from state to state. Egypt, which hosts 50,000 to 70,000 refugees, phased out privileges that had been accorded to them before the 1970s. Lebanon, which hosts several hundred thousand Palestinians, has been described as the worst example of how refugees are treated by a host country. In Lebanon, repression and discrimination against Palestinians was rampant, largely because the refugees were, and still are, seen as upsetting the precarious sectarian balance of the country.

The first wave of refugees in Jordan found it difficult to integrate in their host society. Anti-Palestinian discrimination existed and 'original' trans-Jordanians enjoyed privileged access to the highest positions of the state bureaucracy and the military. In both Lebanon and Syria, the political representative of the Palestinians – the Palestinian Liberation Organization – was central to conflicts that occurred in the 1970s and 1980s.

Syria took a very different approach. In 1948, Syria did not suffer from unemployment or limited natural resources. Therefore, the arrival of 90,000–100,000 Palestinian refugees, whose numbers never rose above 2–3 per cent of the population, did not threaten either economic or social stability. Syria accorded Palestinian refugees the same legal status as Syrian nationals.

Source: Asem Khalil (2009). 'Palestinian refugees in arab states: a rights-based approach', Robert Schuman Centre for Advanced Studies. Available at http://cadmus.eui.eu/handle/1814/10792.

eties, as Box 9.3 discusses. It is in refugee camps across Jordan, Lebanon and Syria that Palestinian resistance first emerged. The plight of the refugees is particularly important because their fate is still very much a crucial aspect of the Arab–Israeli conflict.

Finally, the 1948 war was perceived by all sides as only the first round of the fight. Israel began to perceive any threat to its security as a vital one, leading to pre-emptive strikes, notably the Six Day War in 1967, and conflicts that continuously destabilized the region. At the same time, Arab countries refused to accept the legitimacy of the existence of the State of Israel, building up their military capabilities in order to challenge it.

Over the decades a number of conflicts broke out. The war against Egypt in 1956 – in which Israel joined with Britain and France against Nasser – was quickly ended when the USA and the Soviet Union both placed pressure on all parties to stand down. In 1967, Israel launched a pre-emptive strike against Egypt, Jordan and Syria in anticipation of being attacked, given the hostile and war-mongering messages that had been coming out of Cairo and Damascus for some time. The 'Six Day War', as it has come to be known, saw Israeli troops make significant territorial gains and its legacy is still very much at the heart of the wider Arab–Israeli conflict. Following the short war, Israel took control of Gaza and the Sinai (from Egypt), the West Bank and Jerusalem (from Jordan) and the Golan Heights (from Syria). As a result, for the first time, millions of Palestinians in Gaza, Jerusalem and the West Bank found themselves under direct Israeli occupation. Israel eventually annexed the Golan Heights and gave the Sinai back to Egypt. But it maintained direct control of all the other territories and, most controversially, began to settle them. While initial Israeli policy regarding the newly acquired territories did not necessarily envisage large-scale settlements, the absence of a political solution to the conflict meant that, over time, and with the rise of the Israeli right, an increasing number of Israelis settled in the West Bank. The issue of Israeli settlements in what should constitute the future Palestinian state is one of the most complex problems to solve, and peace negotiations often stall on this sensitive point. Palestinians denounce Israeli occupation as the single-most significant obstacle to peace, although it appears that not much can be done about it, given the almost unconditional support of the United States for Israel. For its part, Israel argues, convincingly, that as long as terrorism is employed by Palestinian nationalists to make political claims, no peaceful solution can be envisaged.

In 1973, a further conflict broke out when Egypt launched a surprise attack on Israel, with Syria joining in soon after. Early Arab gains were quickly overturned by the Israeli counter-offensive and a return to the status quo. The 'Yom Kippur' war remains the last all-out conflict between Israel and its neighbours, although Israeli troops invaded Lebanon a number of times during the 1980s, 1990s and 2000s in order to secure its northern borders from Palestinian and Hizbollah incursions. The 1973 war convinced even the most belligerent Arab leaders that they were not able to defeat Israel though military means. The Tunisian and Moroccan leaders had always contended that fighting Israel was a waste of time and resources, and effectively maintained a neutral stance on the issue. Indeed, Morocco built friendly ties with Israel over time. The Gulf States were too weak and too beholden to the United States to join the fight and, while their anti-Israel rhetoric remained strong, took no direct action. By the mid-1970s, the new leader of Egypt, Anwar Sadat, had decided that peace with Israel was necessary in order to stabilize the country and focus on economic development. In addition, US pressure – together with the potential rewards – was a factor in Sadat's historic visit to Jerusalem in 1977, where he addressed the Israeli parliament. The peace treaty which followed, the Camp David Accords between Israel and Egypt, stabilized relations between the two countries and was not challenged either when Mubarak replaced Sadat, or even when Muhammad Mursi, a leading member of the Muslim Brotherhood, became president in 2012.

A decade after the Camp David Accords, it was the turn of the Palestinian Liberation Organization (PLO), and its leader Yasser Arafat, to choose the path of negotiations. The PLO had failed to achieve the liberation of Palestine and the annihilation of Israel through armed violence, while the Israelis had failed to end Palestinian resistance either in the occupied territories or outside of its borders. After the first *intifada* (from the Arabic word for 'shaking off' – usually translated as 'uprising' or 'rebellion') in 1987–8, which had shown both the injustice of the occupation and the poor leadership of the PLO, both the Israelis and Arafat became convinced of the need to do a deal, particularly because they both wanted to avoid the growth of the Palestinian Hamas, which had decided to abandon its quietist political stance and had become a nationalist-religious movement of resistance to Israel, employing terrorism to achive its objectives. International circumstances, too, were favourable to such a deal and, in 1994, the Oslo Accords were signed. The solution to the Arab–Israeli conflict had been clear to all actors since 1967: Israel would disengage from Gaza and the West Bank, the Palestinians would build an independent state there and guarantee Israeli security by not making further territorial claims. The 'land for peace' deal had a number of corollaries: Israel would recognize in some form that it had been responsible for the refugee problem, but would not take them back, and the refugees would instead be compensated; Jerusalem would become the capital city of both states; settlements would be dismantled (with some mutually agreed exceptions); the new Palestinian state would guarantee peace to Israel. The ultimate benefit for Israel would be the recognition of its legitimacy and right to exist by all Arab countries. Such recognition would not only ensure peace, but might lead in time to the building of ties to enhance regional cooperation.

Under the auspices of the international community, a number of Arab countries that had criticized Egypt for its choices in the late 1970s decided that they would also attempt to improve relations with Israel in support of the Oslo Accords. Jordan officially recognized the West Bank and Gaza as the territory upon which Palestinians would build their state and signed a peace treaty with Israel in 1994. Syria also came close to signing a deal with Israel to solve their long-standing territorial dispute. But the agreement never materialized and when the Oslo Accords began to unravel, Syria became the leader of the 'axis of resistance', although it never considered going to war against Israel, due to the imbalance of military capabilities between the two countries. Instead, Syria became one of the main sponsors of the two leading non-state actors intent on disrupting the peace process – the Palestinian Hamas and the Lebanese Hizbollah – both of which considered Oslo a sell-out.

Enthusiasm for the Oslo Accords of the early and mid-1990s was soon dashed, as the reality on the ground undermined the peace efforts that had led to the Accords in the first place. Much has been written in policy-making and academic circles about the failure of the peace process, with profound divisions as to which side should be blamed for it. More recently, however, a consensus has emerged pointing to two factors that largely explain the reason for the failure and for the continued inability and unwillingness of both sides seriously to negotiate a solution. First, as a number of Israeli commentators have suggested (e.g. Shlaim, 2005), successive Israeli governments have tended to negotiate in bad faith. While rhetorically committed to a peaceful solution in the longer term, short-term gains seemed to matter most. Chief among these was the expansion of territorial gains, while discussions with Palestinian negotiators were taking place. Specifically, rather than preventing further settlements, Israeli governments encouraged residential build-ups in the West Bank and Jerusalem, set up military posts, and generally changed the geography of the territories. The Israeli government only rarely gives official approval to the creation of new settlements. However, it is undeniable that the number of settlers has increased considerably during the 'peace process' and that a significant amount of land has been taken away from Palestinians to make room for Israeli security infrastructure. Palestinians perceived this as further colonization and as evidence that Israel was not genuinely committed to a viable two-state solution, simply wanting to create some sort of autonomous entity in the remainder of the territories that would be administered by the PLO. Second, Yasser Arafat was responsible for negotiating a poor deal for the Palestinians and, as Palestinian analyst Said Aburish (1999) has argued, seemed more interested in preventing dissent within Palestine, and tightening his control over the areas under PLO control, than securing a clear commitment to a two-state solution. In addition, when Arafat's negotiating incompetence threatened his authority and he was outflanked by the critics of Oslo, he talked up violence against Israelis, undermining his own position and, in the process, convincing many in Israel that he was not a genuine partner for peace. This ambivalence played into the hands of Palestinian spoilers such as Hamas, which, through its suicide-bombing campaigns in Israel, alienated the support of many ordinary Israelis for Oslo and led to counter-terror policies that, in turn, antagonized ordinary Palestinians.

In any case, the Oslo Accords failed quite early and quite spectacularly. Rather than providing the comprehensive solution to the Palestinian issue and to the Arab–Israeli conflict as intended, the failure of Oslo further destabilized the region. It created the conditions for the emergence and success of radical Palestinian groups such as Hamas, without whose inclusion a solution is currently impossible, but whose hardline stance and track record inspire little Israeli confidence. In turn, Israeli governments and citizens alike have hardened their positions on the Palestinian issue. This has led not only to increased daily violence in the territories, but also to the one-sided withdrawal from Gaza in 2005, which was subsequently cut off from its surrounding territory. The Hamas-controlled Gaza Strip represents a significant security challenge for Israel and makes it harder for Israeli policy-makers to relinquish control of the West Bank, because of fears that the territory would be used – as Gaza has been – to launch rockets into Israel.

This fear highlights a further paradoxical aspect of the policies pursued by both actors. The construction of a much contested and illegal 'separation' wall is seen as a fundamental security measure in Israel. Since the wall has gone up, suicide-bombings have ceased and the daily security of Israelis improved. But, for Palestinians, the wall represents further isolation from each other and an instrument for Israel to take more of their land away, reducing the size of any potential future state. This has led to greater frustration and resentment among Palestinians. The inability and unwillingness on both sides to design and implement a mutually beneficial negotiated solution is likely to lead, at some stage, to a renewed conflict. When that occurs, the wall will prevent suicide bombers from coming into Israel, but it is possible that the rockets Hamas now launches from Gaza will be launched from the West Bank as well. Without a political solution, all Israeli security measures are efficient only in the short term, just as Palestinian violence will not lead to long-term satisfactory results for the nationalist cause. The repeated rounds of fighting in Gaza between the Israeli armed forces and Hamas simply reinforce entrenched mutual mistrust and render the life of ordinary Gazans increasingly difficult.

Finally, the failure of the Oslo process means that the plight of the Palestinians is once again centre-stage, not only in the Arab world, but globally. This has led to a radicalization of views on Israel, which plays into the hands of its regional adversaries such as Syria and Iran. The bombing campaigns undertaken by Israel since 2006, to undermine the military capacities of Hamas and Hizbullah in Gaza and Lebanon, might look like efforts at winning the war on terror from an Israeli perspective, but they are also perceived by some in terms of Israeli extremism and imperialism, which fuels anger and resentment. Thus, 20 years after the Oslo Accords, Israel is increasingly seen as a pariah state by its domestic and international critics, which would be facing a hostile international community almost alone, if it were not for the unwavering support of the United States. Even Turkey, a long-time partner in the region, has distanced itself from many Israeli policies and actions in recent years, and openly criticized it for its militarism.

The Arab Awakening has not been about Israel – protesters were demanding changes at home, be they political or economic, and the Palestinian issue did not feature much. But, this should not obscure its importance for many in the Arab world and further afield, because the issue is also used instrumentally in a number of states to increase support for ruling regimes. Many Arab states are contending with profound domestic challenges at home while Syria, a traditional enemy of Israel, is engulfed in a civil war that will leave a terrible and long-term legacy. However, this does not mean that the Arab–Israeli conflict will become any less significant in the future. This is particularly the case with the emergence of non-state actors as significant players in regional politics. Hamas and, to a greater extent, Hizbullah have autonomous and independent diplomatic and military capabilities that can be put to use to serve the interests and ideological projects not of states, but of non-state entities. In addition, the proliferation of armed groups of all kinds in Syria, Lebanon and Iraq increases the number of armed groups and weapons in the region surrounding Israel, with potentially negative repercussions for its security.

While the Arab–Israeli conflict is central to the region and has structured both the domestic and foreign policies of its Arab neighbours, it would be a mistake to focus exclusively on it, as numerous other conflicts have shaped the MENA, and have led to a profound questioning of notions of pan-Arabism and Arab solidarity. Furthermore, intra-Arab conflicts were not the only ones to characterize the region. The Iran–Iraq war, which lasted eight years (1980–8), was, for example, a conflict of great brutality and with significant implications.

Inter-Arab and other conflicts in the MENA

The struggle against the colonial and mandatory powers in the Arab world often relied on a rhetoric of pan-Arabism in which language, ethnicity and common history – together with important religious commonalities – were the factors that united all Arabs, no matter where. The logic of pan-Arabism suggested that the struggle for independence was geared towards the creation of a single political authority under which all Arabs would live. This was clearly in contradiction to the reality on the ground. Many parts of the Arab world had, as a matter of fact, very little in common with each other. Not only had they been ruled by very different colonial masters, but their historical development had diverged, long before the arrival of colonial powers in the region. However, this did not diminish popular enthusiasm for pan-Arabism; neither did it prevent Arab leaders, in the aftermath of independence, from subscribing to it in one form or another.

The rulers of the radical republics were more committed to pan-Arabism because it carried with it a message of anti-imperialism that they espoused. But, even in the conservative monarchies, rulers had to accommodate popular sentiment regarding Arab unity, to some degree. However, the reality did not match the rhetoric, and, from the early days of independence, it became clear that the nation-states that had been created, no matter how artificial in origin, would behave according to narrow national interests rather than shared Arab goals. Indeed, it became noticeable that pan-Arabism was used in countries such as Syria, Egypt, Libya, Iraq and even Algeria simply as a device to advance specifically national interests and compete with fellow Arab states on the regional level. Pressure from the international system combined with personal rivalries to drive Arab states apart on a range of issues, including, but not limited to, territorial disputes, their stance on Palestine, and the role of religion in public policy. The growth of the military apparatus across the region almost inevitably led to the settling of differences through conflict. The point here is not to summarize all the inter-Arab state wars that occurred since countries in the region achieved independence, it is simply to underline the fact that regional competition for power and supremacy trumped notions of Arab solidarity and pan-Arabism more often than not in the post-independence era.

A few examples should suffice to highlight how regional leadership was contested. Soon after independence, for example, Algeria found itself involved in a border war against Morocco. The conflict, also known as the 'Sand War', broke out, ostensibly, because of uncertainty over the borders between the two countries, which had been poorly delineated by the French when they left. In fact, when Morocco was granted independence in 1956, France purposefully incorporated into Algeria, which they still controlled, a sizable territory rich in natural resources. When Algeria achieved independence, Morocco claimed that territory for itself and attacked Algeria. The war did not last for very long – just three weeks in October 1963 – and ended with an Algerian victory. But the conflict sowed the seeds of regional rivalry between Algeria and Morocco – a rivalry that is very much alive today. The continuation of the conflict in Western Sahara, which Morocco claims as an integral part of its territory, can be explained in part through the military, political and diplomatic support that the Algerian regime has provided for the Saharaouis who claim that Morocco is illegally occupying their land.

The Sand War was in many ways paradigmatic of the ideological battle lines in the Arab world during the Cold War. It pitted a socialist radical republic – Algeria – against a conservative monarchy – Morocco. A similar pattern can be detected in the inter-Arab wars in which Egypt was involved. Between the early 1960s and 1970, Egypt intervened in the Yemeni civil war, when the Yemeni republican government faced an armed opposition supported by Saudi Arabia. Nasser's Egypt perceived the Saudi kingdom as its main rival for regional supremacy and the Saudi alliance with the United States was deemed highly problematic in pan-Arab circles. The Yemeni civil war served as pretext to challenge Saudi Arabia in its own backyard. In the late 1970s, Egypt was again involved in conflict with a fellow Arab state: Gaddafi-led Libya. In his early days, Gaddafi had been an enthusiastic follower of Nasser and Nasserism. Indeed, at one point, he made the Egyptian president the offer of unification with Libya. By the late 1970s, though, Egypt had joined the US-led camp, while Libya remained solidly anti-imperialist and worked to disrupt US interests in the region. Egypt did not take too well to the Libyan challenge and conflict was inevitable. The border war between the two countries in 1977 was short-lived, but it was not the last Arab conflict. Immediately after the end of the Cold War, Iraq, under the leadership of Saddam Hussein, invaded Kuwait, claiming that the territory of the small oil-rich emirate had been cut out of Iraq by the British colonizers and rightfully belonged to Iraq. The invasion of Kuwait led to the first US intervention in the Gulf under the auspices of the United Nations, but, crucially, it also saw the participation of a number of Arab states, notably Syria, in the international coalition to drive Iraqi troops out of Kuwait and restore the sovereignty of the emirate. Iraq and Syria enjoyed very poor relations and Syria took advantage of the US-led intervention to weaken an old foe, with which it had been vying for regional supremacy for over a decade. Finally, it should be noted that Lebanon has often been the setting where proxy wars between Arab states were fought, leaving the country in a perennial state of political instability (Fisk, 2001).

The struggle for regional supremacy prevented Arab states from achieving a number of what had been considered shared objectives. First, a genuine collective front to resolve the Palestinian issue never emerged. Instead, the plight of the Palestinians has more often been used to advance national interests with different Arab states supporting rival Palestinian

---

Box 9.4   The Iran–Iraq War, 1980–8 (the First Gulf War?)

Territory was the major issue for dispute between Iran and Iraq from the early 1960s. There was an ongoing dispute over the Shatt al-Arab waterway, which, according to a treaty of 1937 was under Iraqi control but which the Iranians claimed the right to navigate. There was also the issue of Iranian assistance to Kurdish groups in revolt against Baghdad, which almost led to an all out military confrontation a number of times. The 1975 Algiers Agreement between Iran and Iraq demarcated the border along the Shatt al-Arab in favour of Iranian claims, in return for which they ceased their support for the Kurds.

But, the Iranian revolution of 1979 altered the status quo once more. The downfall of the Shah more or less coincided with the emergence of Saddam Hussein as President of Iraq. Relations between Iraq and the Islamic state of Iran deteriorated rapidly. The Sunni and secular leadership of Iraq feared that the new Iranian regime would seek to export its revolutionary Shiite ideology to the Shiite population of Iraq, some 55 per cent of the total, who regarded themselves as second-class citizens. There was a series of accusations and counter-accusations between the two states centred on territorial claims. Saddam almost certainly believed that post-Shah Iran was in such turmoil – its army weakened by purges – that it would not be able to resist a massive attack that would secure for Iraq the territorial gains it sought.

On 22 September 1980, Iraq invaded along a 300-mile front. Despite initial Iraqi gains, the Iranian resistance was much fiercer than expected. Indeed by 1982, the Iranians had regained most of the territory they had lost and for the next eight years or so, both sides fought out a long and bloody war of attrition. As the Iranians began to get the better of land engagements, they stuck to their demands that there could be no peace negotiations without massive reparations, an Iraqi admission of guilt and the removal of Saddam Hussein.

In response, Saddam sought to 'internationalize' the conflict and attract as much international support as possible. Before the war, he had courted backers among the Gulf States, such as Kuwait and Saudi Arabia, proposing that Iraq

---

factions. Second, attempts at political unity and unification failed spectacularly. The union between Syria and Egypt collapsed when Syrians complained that Egypt wanted to annex Syria, rather than unify the two states. Similarly, the unification of Sudan with Libya failed due to Gaddafi's inability and unwillingness to share power. Third, the regional organizations that Arab states created, such as the Arab League, the Union for the Maghreb and the Gulf Cooperation Council (GCC), did not develop into truly multilateral forums where shared political concerns could be discussed and economic growth effectively pursued, although the GCC has known a degree of success in economic integration more recently. The divisions that plague the Arab world have become visible once again in the context of the Arab Awakening, most notably on the issue of the Syrian civil war, as Chapter 11 will discuss in detail.

would act as a first line of defence against any threat posed by Iran. Both states, aware of their uneasy relations with their local Shiite populations, were prepared to be generous with financial support. Kuwait offered loans of over US$6 billion; Saudi Arabia even more. By some estimates, Iraq owed Kuwait US$15 billion and Saudi Arabia US$34 billion after the war. Other Gulf states also helped and most Arab states supported Iraq (with the exception of Libya and Syria).

As the conflict continued, both superpowers were also sympathetic towards Iraq, although the USA attempted to remain aloof from two regimes it considered repugnant. For the Soviet Union, Iraq was a long-standing client, notwithstanding its repression of the Iraqi Communist Party. Both superpowers had a common concern – the impact of Iranian victory on regional stability. Any attempt to export revolutionary Islamic ideology might not only destabilize Shiite populations in neighbouring states, but also might also inflame tensions in the Muslim communities of many regions of the Soviet Union. The USSR once more became the principal arms supplier for Iraq. France and Britain also traded substantially in arms, as did the People's Republic of China (which also supplied Iran). The war remained at stalemate for long periods. Indeed, it has been suggested that it suited Western – and, in particular, US – interests to have Iran and Iraq at each other's throats so as to counter any threat they might pose elsewhere.

Finally, in 1988, as the war began to go in Iraq's favour once more, (not least because of Iraqi use of chemical weapons against the Iranians and the Kurds who sought to exploit the war for their own advantage), Iran unexpectedly announced their acceptance of UN Security Council Resolution 598 which had called for an immediate ceasefire and withdrawal of all forces to international borders. (For Ayatollah Khomeini, it was a personal as well as a military catastrophe – according to Fisk, in *The Great War for Civilisation*, Khomeini said 'Woe upon me that I am still alive and have drunk the poisoned chalice of the resolution').

Sources: Beverley Milton-Edwards and Peter Hinchcliffe (2004). *Conflicts in the Middle East Since 1945*, London: Routledge; F. Gregory Gause (2005). 'The international politics of the Gulf', in Louise Fawcett (ed.), *International Relations of the Middle East*, Oxford: Oxford University Press.

Finally, inter-Arab rivalries should not obscure the conflicts in which Iran has played a central role with the massive destruction of the war against Iraq in the 1980s standing out, as detailed in Box 9.4. The Iranian revolution of 1979, as mentioned earlier, was notable not only because its domestic consequences and the ideological influence it had on Islamism, but also because it also changed regional dynamics. Rather than accepting the status quo, revolutionary Iran was bent, particularly under the guidance of Ayatollah Khomeini, on destabilizing its neighbours. With a combination of religious and sectarian rhetoric, Iran set about challenging Saudi Arabia, in particular, but also Iraq, Lebanon and the Gulf Emirates, relying specifically on the Shia connection. As a result, the Sunni world found one of its rare moments of unity when all of the Gulf countries backed the Iraqi invasion of Iran in 1980. The Iran–

236 Politics and Governance in the Middle East

Iraq war was of rare brutality, polarizing the region for a decade and fuelling foreign meddling. Neither country emerged as a clear winner, but the conflict shaped the way in which Iran has been perceived in the region ever since.

Taking on the mantles of anti-imperialism and anti-Zionism, Iran has become a central element in the 'axis of resistance', together with Syria, and, by virtue of its links to Shia communities elsewhere in the region, today it represents a powerful actor vying for regional supremacy, notably with Saudi Arabia. It is, in part, due to lingering suspicion of Iran's intentions in the region that its nuclear programme has become so controversial. The recent acceleration of the programme, in the quest for nuclear power, makes sense from an Iranian perspective for three reasons, although it should be emphasized that Iran denies that it is trying to produce nuclear weapons. First, nuclear capacity would ensure that Western-led attempts at regime change would not occur. Second, the bomb would allow Iran to achieve some sort of parity with Israel, the sole power in the region to possess nuclear weapons. Third, Iran would be able to contend with the potential unity of the Sunni world against it. The same reasons explain why so many global and regional actors are opposed to Iran's nuclear programme. The United States and other Western countries want to avoid nuclear proliferation because it contributes to instability and increases the chances of nuclear confrontation in already unstable regions. Israel has legitimate concerns about the Iranian nuclear programme precisely because it would lose the strategic advantage it now has in a region where it has no loyal allies or friends. Saudi Arabia and its allies are worried about Iranian expansionism and therefore fear the possibility of Iran acquiring nuclear weapons with which it could threaten its neighbours. In addition, there is the concern that if Iran gets the bomb, Saudi Arabia, Egypt and, possibly, Algeria would want to do the same, leading to the nightmare scenario, from a Western and Israeli perspective, of almost unlimited nuclear proliferation in the region. As mentioned, Iran claims it wants to pursue nuclear energy for civilian purposes only, but its assurances have not had much effect in allaying the fears of others.

In conclusion, the recent history of conflict in the MENA region demonstrates that a shared language, shared ethnicity and largely shared religion have not been sufficient to insulate states in the region from the imperatives of operating within a state-system where national interests are paramount and seem to trump all else.

Key questions

- What accounts for the high levels of military intervention in the politics of the MENA region?
- What are the core issues in the conflict between Israel and the Palestinians?
- Why caused inter-Arab conflict in the post-independence period?
- How have external actors impacted on conflict within the MENA region?

Further reading

Albrecht, Holger and Dina Bishara (2011). 'Back on horseback: the military and political transformation in Egypt', *Middle East Law and Governance*, 3(2): 13–23.

Bellin, Eva (2004). 'The robustness of authoritarianism in the Middle East', *Comparative Politics*, 36(2): 139–57.

Cook, Steven (2007). *Ruling, but not Governing: The Military and Political Development in Egypt, Algeria and Turkey*, Washington, DC: Johns Hopkins University Press.

Dowty, Alan (2012). *Israel/Palestine*, Cambridge: Polity.

Geisser, Vincent and Abir Krefa (2011). 'L'uniforme ne fait plus le régime, les militaires arabes face aux révolutions', *Revue Internationale et Strategique*, 83(3): 93–102.

Pratt, Nicola (2007). *Democracy and Authoritarianism in the Arab World*, Boulder, CO: Lynne Rienner.

Shlaim, Avi (2005). 'The rise and fall of the Oslo Peace process', in Louise Fawcett (ed.), *International Relations of the Middle East*, Oxford: Oxford University Press.

Online resources

Beinin, J. and L. Hajjar (20014). 'Palestine, Israel and the Arab–Israeli conflict: a primer', *Middle East Report*. Available online at http://www.merip.org/primer-palestine-israel-arab-israeli-conflict-new.

British Broadcasting Corporation (BBC) (2010). *The Iran–Iraq War*, radio documentary made to mark the 30th anniversary of the outbreak of the Iran–Iraq war Available at http://www.bbc.co.uk/programmes/p00zc0c5.

Draper, T. (1992). 'The true history of the Gulf War', *New York Review of Books*, 30 January. Available at http://www.nybooks.com/articles/archives/1992/jan/30/the-true-history-of-the-gulf-war/.

Chapter 10

The Middle East and the Wider World

The Middle East and North Africa have been a focal point of international relations for some time and, since the launch of the 'war on terror' by the US administration after the September 11 attacks on New York and Washington, DC, the importance of the region has only increased. There are a number of reasons that make the MENA such a significant strategic region, ranging from the presence of vast energy resources to the prominence of clearly anti-Western ideologies, and from the prevalence of civil and intra-regional conflicts, as highlighted in Chapter 9, to the international spillover of political violence and terrorism, which has affected countries all over the globe from Argentina to Indonesia and from the United Kingdom to Australia. Finally, the seeming intractability of the Arab–Israeli conflict, with all of the international diplomatic repercussions and divisions it generates, looms large in global politics because it can be easily construed as global struggle between monotheistic religions with all the consequences that this has in terms of popular mobilization.

This chapter focuses on the ways in which countries in the region interact with the international system and how they are affected by international politics. We will demonstrate how events occurring in the MENA have profound impacts globally. In turn, we will illustrate how global politics helps shape what takes place in the region. It should, however, be borne in mind that the interaction of the region with the rest of the world also has repercussions for how individual countries in the MENA relate to each other. This means that there are multiple levels of interaction and multiple playing fields, as Chapter 9 also illustrated when outlining regional rivalries and alliances. In short, this chapter highlights how external dynamics and powers influence the states of the MENA and their relations with each other, and how developments at the domestic level in MENA states affect world politics. There is a particular focus on the role of the United States in the region since the end of the Cold War, because the unipolarity of the international system has meant increased regional activism on the part of the United States. This is considered, together with the increasing influence of the European Union as an external actor in its immediate neighbourhood, as is the rise in influence of Russia and China, whose prominent role in the Syrian crisis demonstrates their renewed interest in the region, if only to challenge the position of the USA in international politics.

The US and the MENA at the end of the Cold War

During the Cold War, the MENA was a central arena for the global confrontation between the United States and the Soviet Union for the reasons highlighted above, and countries in the region were effectively forced to side with one or other superpower. The prevailing international political dynamics required that states should choose a camp in order to be afforded 'protection' and extract advantages. Broadly speaking, the post-colonial conservative monarchies fell within the sphere of influence of the United States, while the radical republics tended to gravitate towards the Soviet Union, although all maintained a certain distance from Moscow. This provoked a number of military and political conflicts between Arab states and further deepened regional rivalries, as discussed in Chapter 9, making the Middle East and North Africa a very 'hot' area during the Cold War. It should also be noted that relations between the two super-powers and their allies in the region were not unidirectional. Many of the MENA countries sought to keep their powerful patrons at arm's length on many occasions, and, at times, attempted to play one superpower against the other, in order to maximize benefits. There was the realization on the part of many Arab leaders that they could try to secure their power by 'playing' both sides while projecting an image internally of autonomy from international constraints. Despite this, the politics of the Cold War had a significant influence on the region, as the superpowers invested considerable resources in the effort to sustain their allies and attract new ones. For example, Egypt left the Soviet sphere in the 1970s to become a linchpin of the US strategy in the region. Algeria, for its part, claimed to be a fiercely autonomous country promoting third-worldism (Malley, 1996) while relying significantly on Soviet weaponry and standing firmly in what was the anti-imperialist camp. Although some scholars have suggested that the end of the Cold War did not greatly change the regional landscape (Karsh, 1997), the end of the rivalry between the USA and the Soviet Union had a profound effect on both regional relations and on the internal politics of individual countries. However, as Karsh notes, this is not the case when applied to the case of Israel. For Israeli policy-makers, in fact, the end of the Cold War did not change much in strategic terms because the enmity and hostility of the vast majority of Arab states did not subside with the fall of the Soviet Union. If anything, the regional game became more complex for Israel, insofar as it had to deal with emerging and powerful non-state actors threatening its security, in addition to its traditional enemies. In any case, the constraining role of Cold War politics should not suggest that countries and leaders in the region had no agency and simply reacted to what was taking place globally. However, the impact of the end of the Cold War should not be underestimated.

The MENA in a unipolar world

The USA emerged from the confrontation with the Soviet Union as the sole remaining superpower. In this privileged position, the USA, and its traditional Western allies, wished to remake the world according to their strategic interests – access to oil resources and expansion of markets first among them, and to promote their constitutive values of liberalism, democracy and economic openness (Krauthammer, 1990). As a result, the power of ideas and values began to feature strongly in the foreign policies of Western actors. This had significant repercussions in a region where authoritarian rule was the norm. Throughout the Cold War, the USA and the West more broadly had supported authoritarian regimes in the developing world in the name of anti-communism and Soviet expansionism. As a consequence, concern for human rights abuses, international law, and democratic accountability on the part of their international partners and allies was not a high priority for successive US administrations or for leading Western governments. It is important to note that nationalist causes were often equated with communist expansion and therefore became 'illegitimate' and dangerous for the US government. In order to avoid any risk of 'losing' precious allies in the war against communism, ethical concerns about supporting authoritarian regimes were usually set aside. The Carter administration in the late 1970s seemed to take such concerns more seriously, but having lost Iran to Shiia clerics and Nicaragua to the socialist Sandinistas, the USA quickly reverted to almost unconditional support for loyal dictators under the Reagan administration. This was true in the MENA as it was in Latin American, sub-Saharan Africa and Asia. A degree of 'ideological' and moral unease remained about disregard for the values of democracy and human rights throughout this period, but realpolitik imperatives prevailed. The end of the Cold War seemed to offer the opportunity to attenuate realist imperatives and re-introduce an ethical dimension in foreign policy. In addition, it became quite popular in Western foreign policy-thinking to assume that the expansion of the democratic zone across the globe could serve both ethical and material interests, particularly stability and economic openness. Thus, the aggressive promotion of democracy and liberalism could replace the ethical approach of the past. The ethical parameters of the permissible in international politics changed. In the Arab world, one of the very first countries to 'suffer' from the introduction of ethical parameters was Morocco. In 1990, French journalist Gilles Perrault published a book detailing the authoritarian nature and widespread human rights abuses of the Moroccan regime, a strong and loyal ally of the USA and France. Under Hassan II, the Kingdom of Morocco had become a very repressive and brutal police state with political opponents being eliminated, imprisoned or exiled. Bread riots were put down with considerable violence. The Moroccan regime, however, projected a different image abroad; a stable country with an enlightened king attempting to lead its country out of underdevelopment while remaining close to the West. French President Mitterrand put pressure on France's Moroccan ally to change the way he governed and 'encouraged' him to open up the political system, putting an end to the most blatant human rights abuses as well. This would have been inconceivable before the collapse of the Soviet Union. In much the same way, other Western countries seemed to take seriously the promotion of democracy and human rights across the globe. Together with the promotion of neo-liberal economic reforms, which were perceived to be conducive to liberalizing political reforms, democratic values became the mainstay of post-Cold War international politics for the United States and its Western partners. Indeed, there was a conflation between US strategic interests – unquestioned leadership in global affairs and international peace (Jervis, 2002), and its ethical position – liberal democracy as a universal good that all should enjoy. This is crucial to understanding the way in which US foreign policy, in particular, began to function after the end of the Cold War. Global leadership on the part of the USA meant both the advancement of all humankind towards a model of governance and behaviour that also secured US primacy in the international system.

US support for, and encouragement of, wide-ranging political and economic changes was crucial in the profound transformations of Eastern Europe and Latin America in the early 1990s (Huntington, 1993b) with successful processes of democratization occurring in Asia and sub-Saharan Africa as well. In the MENA, these global changes were felt as well. Countries that had enjoyed extensive ties with the Soviet Union found themselves in a double bind. On the international level, they lost a very powerful patron that could sustain their foreign policy stances and interests, and provide a considerable amount of material resources in the forms of economic and military aid. This was the case, for instance, for Syria and Algeria, which relied heavily on Soviet arms' transfers. On the domestic front, the legitimacy of the economic system based around socialist principles came under massive pressure from within the ruling élite, and from the population. Increasing calls for radical reforms of an economic system that was no longer performing economically and that was closed off politically began to be heard. The victory of the USA in the Cold War seemed to suggest that more pluralistic political systems and a market economy integrated into the global economic system would be able to deliver both material and political benefits. Countries such as Algeria and Syria, and socialist Yemen to an extent, had no choice but to adapt to the new international environment, leading them to abandon their more radical anti-imperialist positions. In short, they had to find a way to be more accommodating to Western interests in the region, without wholly undermining their own legitimacy and national narrative of resistance.

Algeria had already begun to 'court' the USA towards the end of the 1980s and quickly became an important interlocutor for it in the region, playing an important role in failed negotiations to avoid the 1991 Gulf War, using its considerable diplomatic weight and know-how to find an Arab solution to an Arab problem after Iraq invaded Kuwait in 1990 (Cavatorta, 2009b). In addition, the socialist model of economic development that Algeria had pursued was no longer working. The under-performing economy, too dependent on oil and gas revenues, needed to be restructured and, during the 1980s, market-oriented reforms were introduced in line with the Washington consensus on economic policy-making. Algeria's one party-rule also came in for both domestic and international criticism. This led the ruling élites to open up the political system and initiate a process of transition to multi-party democracy. Syria also quickly recognized the changes that had taken place internationally, and began to undertake partial reforms in the domestic sphere. These changes were cosmetic for the most part but, nevertheless, they began slowly to alter the bases of regime support away from the working class and the peasantry. But, in the foreign policy arena, Syria had to adapt faster to the changed international environment, acknowledging the increasingly preponderant role of the USA in the region. Hafez al-Asad, Syria's president, took decisions that would have been almost unthinkable during the Cold War. For instance, he acceded to US demands that he participate in the peace conference on the Arab–Israeli conflict in Madrid in 1991. More importantly, Syria was part of the UN-mandated and US-led international coalition that liberated Kuwait in the 1990–1 Gulf War that had been initiated by Saddam Hussein. In exchange for its participation in the coalition, Syria was able to secure both its hold on Lebanese politics and the gratitude of US policy-makers.

Such a dramatic turn-around on foreign policy matters, on the part of countries that had been at the forefront of anti-US agitation in the region, should not obscure the fact that traditional regional US allies also came under pressure to change their ways. Countries such as Morocco, Tunisia,

Egypt and the Gulf States, that had already been aligned to US and Western interests in the region on foreign policy issues, were now asked to become less 'problematic' partners through the introduction of proto-democratic reforms. Thus, in both Egypt (Kassem, 2004) and Jordan (Joffé, 2002), a number of liberalizing political and economic reforms were introduced in line with the new international spirit of the time. King Hussein of Jordan repealed emergency legislation and permitted reasonably free and fair elections, while president Mubarak of Egypt eased off domestic repression of opponents and began to introduce market-oriented reforms at a rapid pace. Even Saudi Arabia, the closest ally of the USA in the region, with the exception of Israel, and notoriously resistant to any type of reform, saw the setting up of a council to advise the king, a bold move in such a conservative political system (Basbous, 2004). Tunisia and Morocco also witnessed liberalizing initiatives in the late 1980s and 1990s, respectively, in an effort to inject renewed legitimacy into their respective political systems and ailing economies. In Tunisia, Zine al-Abidine Ben Ali became president in November 1987 and promised to transform the country into a democratic state by introducing multi-party politics (Anderson, 1991), and by overhauling the economy in favour of the market and international free trade (Sfeir, 2006). The Tunisian regime had a reasonable degree of success in modernizing the economy, attracting foreign investment and building stronger trade linkes with Europe; this resulted in rapid growth and decreasing unemployment. For a while, the Tunisian miracle seemed to work for the benefit of the vast majority of ordinary citizens. This in part explains why the facade reforms the regime implemented in the institutional realm were not opposed more strongly. Partly in response to pressure from its international partners, Morocco also initiated a process of controlled democratization, managed by the monarchy (Cavatorta, 2005). Finally, even in Libya, Gaddafi introduced institutional reforms to increase popular involvement in decision-making (Vandewalle, 2006).

Only Iran and Iraq failed to undertake any significant move to follow the spirit of the time and explicitly refused to recognize the unipolarity of the global system. Iran had always maintained a degree of equidistance from the Soviets and the USA since the advent of the Islamic Republic in 1979. Therefore, the collapse of the Soviet Union did not have a massive impact on the foreign policy or domestic politics of the country. Iran had become accustomed to isolation at the regional level and, for the most part, continued to be ostracized by its neighbours and the United States, although relations with Europe did improve in the late 1990s when the Iranian reformist scholar Khatami was elected president. It is for this reason that Iran simply reinforced its ties with its only genuine regional partner, Syria, and with a host of non-state actors that were becoming prominent actors on the regional scene, such as the Lebanese Hizbullah. While the religious dimension of these alliances should not be neglected – Shiism being the apparent glue of such ties, there are also dynamics of strategic convergence and similar world views that bound, and still bind, such actors together. For his part, Iraq's president, Saddam Hussein sought to take advantage of what he believed to be the uncertainty and volatility of the post-Cold War to promote an aggressive regional foreign policy that would 'rectify' the stalemate of the war against Iran during the 1980s. Arguing that Iraq had a historical claim on Kuwait, he ordered the invasion of the small kingdom, triggering the first post-Cold War conflict and, in the process, defying the 'new world order' the USA was seeking to build. The international community swiftly punished Iraq's invasion of Kuwait and, following its military defeat at the hands of a very broad US-led coalition operating under UN mandate, the country was placed under a very severe sanctions regime, which lasted until the USA invaded the country again in 2003. But the sanctions regime that was in place against Iraq in the 1990s merely prevented any political change from occurring, as Saddam held on to power as tightly as he could, stifling political activism and encouraging both tribalism and sectarianism.

When Iraq invaded Kuwait in 1990, it became an example of what would occur if international legality were so flagrantly flouted. The USA could not tolerate Saddam's challenge and opted for a demonstration of force. The invasion of Kuwait represented a security threat to the USA, insofar as one of its regional allies had been attacked and secure access to oil resources threatened. In addition, other US allies in the region, notably Saudi Arabia, were worried that Iraq's expansionism would eventually threaten their security as well. The USA could not let this challenge pass. Rolling Iraqi forces back from Kuwait was the perfect opportunity for the USA to flex its military muscle and to demonstrate its dominance of the international system. Crucially, this show of force could be conflated with the defence of international legality, highlighting that the UN Charter could be disregarded no longer.

The formation of a broad international coalition to defeat Saddam, liberate Kuwait, and restore international legality had something to do with the view that the war was just, but more to do with a perfect coincidence of interests and political opportunism that a host of countries seized on. For the USA, and a number of its Western European allies, it was the opportunity to conduct a military operation that combined elements of self-interest and ethics, 'selling' the war at home as a just cause that would secure the stability of the international system for the future, as well as through the notion of collective security on which UN founders had pinned so much hope. The international coalition restored Kuwaiti

Box 10.1   The 1990–1 Gulf War and its aftermath: a short summary

Iraqi aggression against Kuwait links to another significant aspect of the changes ushered in by the end of the Cold War; respect for international legal norms, as decisions taken by the United Nations Security Council now assumed real importance. The work of the UN in persuading members of the international community to respect international norms and law had been hampered in the context of Cold War politics, because of the veto power held by the superpowers in the Security Council. In the aftermath of the fall of the Soviet Union, Russia, the heir to the USSR seat at the UN, was too weak and dependent on US benevolence to prevent the UN from operating with less restraint. China, meantime, was too focused on internal growth to challenge US dominance at the UN. This meant that the USA, through the UN, could uphold international norms and legislation, in an effort to promote a workable collective security regime. In the new world order envisaged by George Bush Senior, who was US President between 1988 and 1992, effective multilateralism, led by the United States, would ensure both security and stability in the face of any aggressive authoritarian state which refused to conform to the requirements of international law.

The easy victory in Iraq left Saddam's regime in place, though. Despite encouraging a revolt in the south of the country, the USA did not support it militarily, allowing Saddam to reassert its power. In the north of the country, events took a different direction as a protected area for the Kurds was set up, encouraging hopes of potential independence of Kurds from Iraq. At a broader level, the war against Saddam mobilized a number of Islamist groups against their Saudi patrons and constituted an important weapon in the armoury of anti-Saudi regime sentiment across the region.

sovereignty – the ethical motive. It also restored the pre-invasion balance of power in the region – the realpolitik motive. For many other countries that participated in the war effort, particularly Arab states, it was largely about opportunism, insofar as they had to be seen to sanction the primacy of the United States in regional affairs, and were anxious to make a good impression. The example of Syrian participation is the most relevant one in this regard. With the exceptions of Jordan and Yemen – each of which, for a time, paid a harsh price for siding with Saddam Hussein – all Arab countries contributed to the war effort, definitively burying any remaining notion of Arab solidarity if it had ever existed in the first place. Securing a degree of favourable treatment from the remaining superpower was the major motivation for Arab countries to take part, even when it became clear the bulk of Arab public opinion was opposed to the war and viewed the efforts Saddam made to drag Israel and the Palestinian cause into the conflict with some sympathy – however self-serving this may have been. As a consequence, the war expanded the wedge between Arab rulers and their citizens. This occurred most notably in Algeria, where the opening up of the political system coincided with the US-led invasion. While the Algerian ruling élites attempted to play the role of mediators between Iraq and the USA, ordinary citizens sided overwhelmingly with Saddam and rewarded the Islamist party for its anti-imperialist tough stance. Kuwaitis were, and remain, grateful for Western intervention, as were the royals of the Gulf States, because they felt the United States would be a credible ally if they ever found themselves in a situation similar to that faced by Kuwait.

However, large sectors of the population across the Arab world were not persuaded by the rhetoric of international law as deployed against Saddam. First, sympathy for Kuwait's rulers was in short supply on the Arab street. Second, the use of international law demonstrated what, to many Arabs, were the double standards of the international community. Why would aggression and occupation be punished in the Iraqi case, but not in the Israeli situation? Finally, seeing Western armies on Arab soil to fight against an Iraqi leader who had portrayed himself as the last bastion against anti-imperialism rankled with many – both on the left, and in Islamist circles. The aftershocks of the Gulf war became clearer later in the decade, particularly in the Arabian Peninsula, with the emergence of extremists such as Usama Bin Laden who were scathing in their condemnation of the Saudi regime for allowing Saudi soil to be used by American troops. In any case, the war was a military success and:

> following the war, Iraq was placed under severe economic sanctions to weaken it militarily and teach a lesson to others who might have the intent of defying the rules of the New World Order. (Cavatorta, 2010)

The war demonstrated to all regional actors that the world had changed, and that toeing the US line was a requirement for traditional allies, as well as former rivals. The 1991 Madrid Peace Conference mentioned earlier also illustrates the extent to which the United States hoped to reshape the post-Cold War MENA, as the USA effectively compelled its reluctant ally, Israel, and its former foe, Syria, to attend the talks. The motivations for Syria and Israel to participate were obviously different, as were the inducements or threats deployed by the USA, but the participation of both testifies to the unipolarity of world politics at the time.

Thus, in the late 1980s and early 1990s, US attempts to reshape the region were successful and effective. Israel and Syria came very close to a peace deal, for example, which was brokered by the United States in the hope this would also have positive effects on the Israeli–Palestinian peace track. But, enthusiasm for unipolarity did not last for very long because it was based on the mistaken assumptions that all actors in the global system would accept a new world order with the USA at its helm, and that no challengers would emerge for a long time. Both assumptions proved to be mistaken. First, the conflation of US material interests and ethical values with their global equivalents proved to be very problematic. Some countries willingly accepted US economic, military, political and cultural dominance. But others began to proffer radically different alternatives and ideologies, while pointing at major inconsistencies and hypocrisies in US behaviour. This was particularly true in the Arab world where the tension between the universal values espoused and promoted by the USA, and the imperatives of realpolitik quickly became evident, setting off a long period of heavy and conflictual involvement of the USA in the region. Second, a number of regional and international actors became more assertive over time on the international stage, challenging the vision of the USA and its Western partners. Iran attempted to break out of its isolation to create a regional climate that would be less favourable to the USA and its main ally, Israel. Thus, despite geographical distance and religious differences, Iran became increasingly involved in Palestinian politics, through its connections with Hamas. At the same time, a resurgent Russia attempted to win back some of the diplomatic ground it had lost after the collapse of the Soviet Union. China's impressive economic growth also made it impossible to ignore as a potential global challenger. It is no coincidence that these three countries are at the heart of the ongoing Syrian crisis, using it as a means to undermine Washington and its allies. In short, the reconciliation of ethical stances with realist imperatives became too difficult for the USA to sustain for long under the weight of internal contradictions and external challenges from an increasingly hostile environment.

Democracy promotion and its limits

First and foremost, the sincerity of democracy promotion in the region on the part of the USA and its European allies was severely tested and, eventually, found wanting. The logic of democracy promotion was the assumption that democracies would solve their disputes peacefully, contribute to international stability, cooperate more closely on economic matters and, ultimately, produce better living conditions for citizens. The problem with this is that democracy's strength also rests on the uncertainty that surrounds elections. Thus, the outcome of genuinely democratic elections can be 'counter-productive', from the perspective of the West, if those who are elected do not wish to conform to Western requirements, in terms of foreign policy behaviour.

When Algeria began its process of democratization in the late 1980s, it attracted a considerable degree of political support in the United States, particularly in Congress. However, the process demonstrated that political movements that were opposed to many of the policies and values that the USA embodied would be the main beneficiaries of political opening. When the Algerian Islamist movement, FIS (*Front Islamique du Salut* – Islamic Salvation Front), with its anti-Western rhetoric, won both the local elections in 1990 and the first round of the legislative elections in December 1991, fear of Islamism began to grip US foreign policy circles once more. Since the Iranian Revolution of 1979, the USA had become wary of Islamist movements, despite sometimes relying on them for foreign policy purposes, against the Soviet Union, as was done during the Soviet occupation of Afghanistan in the 1980s. Such mistrust of Islamism had little to do with conflicting values or how Islamists might run the state. It was the product of the belief that Islamists in power would pursue an aggressive anti-Western foreign policy in a region where there are vast oil and gas resources where Israel, the most important US ally in the region, stands alone and where the proliferation of weapons is a genuine concern (Kepel, 2004).

The outcome of free and fair Algerian elections in 1991 saw the USA face-to-face with its own contradictions. The FIS stood for renewed anti-imperialism, opposition to Israel, refusal to support the United Nations on the Iraq issue and, finally, support for a new international economic pact, so that the proceeds of oil and gas wealth would be better redistributed. At the same time, FIS had come to power through the ballot box, and their popular support could not be disputed. As a result, it became clear that the promotion of democracy could facilitate the accession to power by democratic means of a political movement radically opposed to the policies of the USA. Eventually, the Algerian military intervened, carrying out a military coup to ensure that the Islamists would not come to power. The coup was greeted with relief in policy circles – US Secretary of State James Baker III claimed that he had been helpful in bringing it about. But, it is not merely the USA that can be accused of hypocrisy and double standards. In the case of Algeria, France was at the forefront of efforts to undermine the legitimacy of the FIS, encouraging the Algerian military, with which it had privileged relations, to carry out the coup. While the Algerian generals did not necessarily need to be prodded into action by France, it was made clear to them that no serious diplomatic consequences would issue from subversion of the democratic process. Quite the contrary: in the aftermath of the coup, Algeria began to benefit from French economic and military aid to help the new authorities to deal with the precarious situation in the country, which was rapidly descending into civil war. There are strong echoes of the Algerian crisis of the early 1990s in the coup that saw the removal of Egypt's elected Islamist president Mursi in the summer of 2013. However, thus far Egyptian Islamists have not responded with the sort of sustained political violence that was witnessed in Algeria.

Events in Algeria produced two outcomes that became mutually reinforcing. Arab rulers saw the opportunity to roll back on reforms – or, more precisely, to implement facade reforms that would ultimately strengthen their grip on power (Heydemann, 2007). If Islamists could be presented as an imminent danger to international stability, repression could be justified to an international audience. At the same time, the USA drew back from genuine democracy promotion across the Arab world, reassuring allies that processes of liberalization and reform would only continue at a pace dictated by Arab rulers. Indeed, the vision of Islamist-led regimes, and fear of the 'chaos' that might follow if they came to power, led the USA to strengthen its relations with Arab authoritarians. In many ways, the dilemma that characterized US policies in the region in the 1990s and 2000s is again on display in the aftermath of the Arab Awakening. After initially supporting the demands of demonstrators in Tunisia, Egypt, Yemen and Syria, and having intervening militarily in Libya to ensure the success of the anti-Gaddafi uprising, the USA saw Islamist movements reap the benefits of regime change and, again, began to question the validity of democracy promotion if the winners are problematic political movements. As mentioned, the support given to the Egyptian military for the anti-Mursi coup – leaving aside the mistakes, arrogance and incompetence of the Muslim Brotherhood while in power – is yet another indication of US uneasiness with Islamism.

Second, as mentioned, the aftermath of the war against Iraq in 1991 was much more problematic than first appeared. The USA and its Western allies presented the war against Iraq in terms of an ethical stand against aggression, but many Arabs perceived the war as a self-serving enterprise. Of course, a number of Arab countries joined the war effort, as we have seen. But, this was done for opportunistic reasons and against the wishes of many of their citizens. Being authoritarian states, they did not need any real form of popular sanction, but they generally underestimated the strength of popular feelings across the region in favour of Saddam Hussein and his invasion of Kuwait (Piscatori, 1991). Their decision to ally with the United States – and, in the case of Saudi Arabia, to call for US assistance and permit the presence of US troops on Saudi soil – was a slap in the face for many Arabs. Once again, Islamists were at the forefront of protests and demonstrations against the US invasion of Iraq, enabling them to strengthen their foreign policy credentials. When the war ended, opposition to US policies did not end or diminish – the plight of ordinary

Iraqis, whose country had been placed under crippling sanctions, was seen as another US stratagem to control the region and bring into line those rulers who challenged US policies. Popular opposition to US domination of international affairs sharpened the focus on the dilemma facing US administrations – namely, that stability and security in the region might not, after all, be the products of democratization. Instead, they came to be equated with continued support for authoritarian leaders across the region who could keep a lid on popular resentment towards the USA. In many ways, throughout the 1990s and the early 2000s, the Arab world became the exceptional case in US foreign policy. While, in the rest of the world, the USA genuinely promoted democracy and supported processes of political and economic liberalization, in the Arab world it supported authoritarian rule through the delivery of weapons, diplomatic cover and economic aid.

Finally, the gamble the United States took under George Bush Senior in seeking to resolve the issue of Palestine did not pay off. In exchange for supporting the war in Iraq in 1991, Arab countries had demanded that, at least as a gesture of goodwill, the USA should seriously engage in resolving the Arab–Israeli conflict, and attempt to address the plight of the Palestinians, which had always been an open wound in the psyche of Arab public opinion. George Bush Senior, together with his secretary of state, James Baker III, made a genuine effort to kick-start peace talks and, as mentioned, organized the Madrid Peace Conference, forcing enemies to sit at the same table. The process proved to be a reasonable success in the medium-run and, as then president, Bill Clinton was able to build on that to get the Israelis and the Palestinians to sign a comprehensive peace deal, the Oslo Accords in 1993. The early 1990s were years of great hope for peace across the region. But, when the peace process encountered its first obstacles, it seemed to many in the Arab world that the USA was not the honest broker it had appeared to be, siding at every turn with the Israelis.

As the situation progressively worsened, the disappointment of ordinary Arabs with US policies in Palestine grew, and the rulers of the two countries that had signed peace deals with Israel – Jordan and Egypt – came under increased domestic pressure to renege on them in solidarity with the Palestinian cause. This did not happen, but it was clear that the unravelling of the peace process further undermined the image of the United States for two specific reasons. It became apparent that, in its effort to maintain the peace process, the USA was prepared to pressure only the weaker side – the Palestinians – directly, as well as through its special relationships with Jordan and Egypt. Its reliance on authoritarian leaders whose domestic legitimacy on the Palestine issue was low, demonstrated once more that US interests clashed with popular will in the region. Also, and perhaps more significantly, US talk about a new world order under-pinned by international legality and justice was exposed as cynical hypoc-risy. Saddam Hussein had already linked the war against Iraq in the name of upholding international law to the complete absence of international pressure on Israel to abide by international norms. The unravelling of the peace process during the course of the 1990s seemed to prove that he was correct in his self-serving analysis. Arab public opinion, over time, shifted from a degree of enthusiasm for the peace process to outright opposition.

The impact of September 11: democracy versus security

Given all this, it is unsurprising that anti-American sentiment has been on the rise across the MENA region for some time and, while many contend – probably correctly – that the September 11 attacks against the United States in 2001 changed the world, they would be mistaken in believing that the attacks made a difference to US policy in the Middle East. If anything, they entrenched and solidified US assumptions and policies in the region. Despite a change in rhetoric, the war on terror did not modify existing trends, even if, for a brief moment, George W. Bush and his advisers seemed to give thought to overhauling the US policy framework towards the Arab world and the Middle East more generally. US rhetoric certainly changed between 2003 and 2005, as a number of prominent US foreign policy-makers, including the president, began to talk about the necessity to move away from supporting authoritarianism, committing US resources to help a democratic local civil society grow, and stating in no uncertain terms that the USA was committed to the creation of two states in Israel/Palestine. Indeed, a number of US policy-makers suggested that, in part, the attacks on the country had been possible because the USA was perceived as the 'bad guy', due to its support for authoritarian rule in clear contrast to its constitutive values and 'one of the conclusions that emerged from this reflection was that the absence of democracy in the Middle East/ North Africa was now a primary concern of the United States' (Durac and Cavatorta, 2009). The rhetoric was certainly new in terms of Middle East policy. In 2003, President Bush proposed a 'forward strategy for freedom in the Middle East', stating firmly that 'sixty years of Western nations excusing and accommodating the lack of freedom in the Middle East did nothing to make us safe – because in the long run, stability cannot be purchased at the expense of liberty' (Bush, 2003). Earlier, in December 2002, US Secretary of State Colin Powell had launched the Middle East Partnership Initiative (MEPI), committing financial resources to growing democracy locally. This was accompanied some time later by the launch of the Broader Middle East and North Africa Initiative (BMENA), again

Box 10.2   Can democracy stop terrorism?

In 2005, in the middle of the war on terror, F. Gregory Gause explored a most pertinent question. One of the assumptions of the war on terror, and one of the crucial justifications for the invasion of Iraq in March 2003, was that the fight against violent non-state extremism could be won, in part, through a renewed push for democratization in the region. The core idea was that opening up political space at the domestic level would induce many to participate in institutional pluralistic politics given that channels to express dissent would now be open. Unfortunately, democratization as the solution to the problem of political violence does not actually have a very good track record, since it is not quite true that the more a country becomes democratic the less terrorism it produces.

Viewed from this perspective, the whole democracy-promotion enterprise, as a solution for the problem of violent extremism, does not seem to be a good strategy to follow, because in the vacuum that is inevitably created – as in the case of regime change, for example – there are ample opportunities for political violence to occur. This is not to suggest that democratization should not be pursued, or that authoritarian rule inevitably insures against terrorism – this is also not the case. Democracy-promotion is a worthwhile policy in itself if the objective is genuinely to improve governance, create popular attachment to a political institution and formalize dissent over policy choices. It is not, however, the panacea for terrorism. In the Middle East, in particular, this is linked to a set of factors that the democratization of domestic institutions would not hugely affect. Significant obstacles to decreasing the level and intensity of terrorism remain, including sectarianism, imperialist foreign policies, widening socioeconomic divides or the Palestinian problem.

Source: F. Gregory Gause III (2005). 'Can democracy stop terrorism?', *Foreign Affairs*, 84(5): 62–76.

designed to encourage Arab democrats and with the ambiguous assumption that democracy prevents terrorism, as detailed in Box 10.2

The problem with the rhetoric and the policy initiatives is they had very little credibility when contextualized within the broader strategy of the war on terror, and came to be seen as token gestures made to satisfy international public opinion, but which the administration had neither the willingness nor the resources to see through.

In the medium term, the imperatives of the war on terror led the USA to pursue the same policies of the past. To begin with, fighting the war on terror required the support of authoritarian regimes in the region since the enemy was perceived to be the same: Islamism. In the name of the war on terror, the United States cooperated even more closely with the security services of countries that had used such services extensively to repress domestic dissent, such as in Jordan and Morocco. The USA also began to rely on the help of traditional enemies, such as Syria. All this might not have mattered if the objectives of the war on terror had been more limited but, under its cover, local autocrats began a new wave of repression that included all sorts of dissenters, be they peaceful or violent, secular or Islamist. While this new wave of repression might not have been foreseen, there is no doubt that US policy contributed greatly to it. Furthermore, while conducting the war on terror with the help of autocratic leaders, the USA was finalizing the invasion of Iraq, which began in March 2003, leaving a legacy of instability that has affected regional politics ever since. The rhetoric of democratization accompanied the invasion also. But it was seen by many as yet another imperial war to quash the dissent of countries opposed to US policies in the region, as well as being a strategic war for the control of oil and the region more generally. Finally, the rhetoric of democracy was severely tested once more in the mid-2000s. In 2005, legislative elections took place in Egypt, close ally of the USA for three decades. The opposition Muslim Brotherhood enjoyed substantial success despite not being able to participate as a party but only through independent candidates. The victory of the Brotherhood expressed the unpopularity of President Mubarak and the extent to which his policies were contested. In January 2006, the Palestinians also went to the polls to elect representatives to the Palestinian Legislative Council. In elections deemed free and fair, the Islamist Hamas movement won a majority of seats and was therefore charged with forming a government. The electoral success of Hamas in Palestine threw the peace process with Israel into further disarray (Milton-Edwards, 2007). Both elections revived the dilemma that Bush's new pro-democracy rhetoric seemed to have resolved. According to that rhetoric, the USA should have welcomed both sets of results, since the newly elected representatives had a genuine democratic mandate. However, once more, the conflict between the realist imperative of security and the 'normative' commitment to democracy saw the 'securitizers' win out. In fact, in some circles it was argued that Mubarak favoured the 2005 electoral success of the Muslim Brotherhood precisely because it wanted to demonstrate to the USA that the Brotherhood would take over Egypt if democratic mechanisms were in place (Achcar, 2013). As a result, in Egypt Mubarak was allowed to inaugurate a robust campaign of repression, while in Palestine the elected representatives of Hamas were frozen out, with disastrous consequences for ordinary Palestinians and, ultimately, for the peace process. US foreign policy reverted to 'business as usual', with the MEPI and BMENA initiatives marginalized (Dalacoura, 2005). The accusation of hypocrisy reverberated across the region once again, leaving the USA in the same dilemma as before, except that it was now embroiled in an unwinnable war in Iraq, which provided many young Muslim radicals the opportunity to fight for a new pan-Arab cause, with considerable negative impacts on global peace and stability. In conclusion, according to scholars such as Kepel (2004), the real problem is that core US objectives of accessing oil resources and protecting Israel do not leave real alternatives to supporting friendly dictators, in spite of awareness that such policies might have dangerous long-term consequences.

Obama and the MENA

The Obama administration came to power with the firm intention of abandoning the rhetoric behind the war on terror and was opposed to the policy of remaking the Middle East. Obama did not share his predecessor's emphasis on US unitilateralism, or on externally driven democratization through war. His administration was more aware of the dilemma at the heart of US foreign policy in the region. But, rather than attempting to solve it, Obama spent his first years in power attempting to circumvent and work around it. It is for this reason that the Obama administration paid more attention to mending fences with Arab public opinion, focusing on cultural dialogue and shared values. However, despite extricating the USA from its adventure in Iraq, Obama did not challenge the authoritarian nature of US allies in the region in any meaningful way and was unable, or unwilling, to shift Israel from its hard-line positions with regard to the Palestinians. More covertly, and with fewer troops on Arab soil, Obama has continued with the war on terror, as the recurrent drone strikes in Yemen amply demonstrate. Finally, Obama has had to deal with the longer-term repercussions of the 2003 invasion of Iraq. The Iraqi political system has become heavily sectarian and, in response, some within the Sunni minority have embraced political radicalism to challenge the power of the Shia majority. US troops might have left the country, but the instability of Iraq has profound consequences for the United States, as large swathes of the country have come under the control of radical Sunni Islamists as hostile to the new government in Baghdad as they are to US designs in the region.

The Arab Awakening initially seemed to force a realization that the USA had backed the wrong horse for too long, as the picture of widespread political protest drawing on basic human rights, dignity and governmental accountability emerged from the streets of Tunis and many other Arab capitals, and appeared to suggest that liberal democracy was finally about to arrive in the region. The USA began to distance itself from its former friendly dictators and encouraged the protesters. In addition, Obama opted to intervene militarily, through NATO, to support the anti-Gaddafi rebellion in Libya, lending American weapons to the cause of freedom and democracy. This initial enthusiasm for the democratic wave did not last for very long. Islamist electoral victories in Tunisia and Egypt, chaos in

Libya, a near civil war in Yemen, a full-blown civil conflict in Syria with the presence of radical Islamist groups, trouble in the friendly state of Bahrain, and the collapse of Iraqi authority in its territory have all shifted the momentum from support for change to the quest for stability at almost any price. US support for the Egyptian military coup in July 2013 is the most dramatic example of that, as is the absence of any condemnation for the repression of protesters in Bahrain.

However, relations between the USA and the MENA are not simply about politics and security. There is also a very significant economic component to the relationship that should be briefly mentioned. The post-Cold War era provided the opportunity for reshaping local economies in order to integrate them into the neo-liberal economic system. While countries such as Morocco had already gone through a number of market-oriented economic reforms before the collapse of the Soviet Union, dramatic economic changes began to occur in its aftermath as the 'Washington Consensus' was being promoted. Many countries in the region, including Turkey and Israel, faced increasing economic difficulties despite, or perhaps because of, the presence of abundant oil and gas resources. The neo-liberal economic model was presented as the solution to long-term developmental problems. The USA, through its leadership in international financial institutions, and directly through its extensive contacts with ruling regimes, pushed for a series of economic reforms based on an end to price subsidies, privatization, strict fiscal policies and free commerce, as the free trade agreement with Morocco indicates (White, 2005). Reforming stagnant and under-performing economies was certainly necessary, particularly in the face of a growing educated population in need of jobs, but neo-liberal reforms have had a devastating social impact. In addition, the reforms that were pushed through were hijacked by the ruling élites, increasing income distribution gaps and corrupt practices of resource allocation (Dillman, 2001). Nonetheless, in two short decades, all countries in the MENA came to subscribe to a neoliberal and market-oriented logic, which, paradoxically, is at the heart of the popular uprisings of 2011.

While the United States can hardly be blamed for all the economic and social ills of the Arab world, part of the anti-Americanism emerging from the region, and not necessarily limited to Islamists, is a consequence of its continued support for rulers, whether democratically elected or not, who continue to implement economic policies that create significant inequalities. Supporters of free trade and neo-liberalism see them as the means to open up closed and authoritarian political systems with the added benefit that, in the long run, such countries will also become economic successes. However, the reality emerging from the region is that, by and large, economic liberalization has led to a powerful coincidence of interests between crucial US economic actors – notably in the energy sector – and corrupt, wasteful and authoritarian regimes, as free trade agreements have strengthened authoritarian rule.

Clearly, then, the US role in the MENA, particularly since the end of the Cold War, has had a very significant role in shaping both the international politics and the domestic arrangements of countries in the region. In turn, regional events have had dramatic effects on the way in which the USA sees itself in the world, and the way in which it pursues its material and strategic interests.

The European Union: projecting normative power in the Middle East?

The predominant role of the United States in the region and the impact of its policies on the domestic politics of MENA regimes should not obscure the role of the European Union (EU). Given that European nation-states operate externally at two levels – individually and as members of the EU – conflicts and contradictions develop when the EU seeks to articulate unified and coherent foreign policy positions. But, increasingly, a significant degree of coordination and power is delegated to EU institutions. Since the inception of the EU, member states have been reluctant to cede sovereignty on foreign policy matters, preferring to integrate in other domains, perceived to be less sensitive. However, over time, foreign policy became an arena where coordination was called for and, in many ways, appropriated by central European institutions. Thus, initially, 'aside from generic declarations of principles on a number of foreign and security policy matters, there was no EU external policy, although the Commission of the European Union had exclusive power to negotiate trade agreements with entities outside the Union' (Cavatorta, 2010).

After the Cold War, the process of integration of foreign policy accelerated. Central to this process was the idea that the EU would become an ethical actor in international politics, attempting to promote universal norms and human rights without the credibility problems and focus on material interests that were seen to characterize US policy. Thus, the EU would engage all other actors on the global scene without resorting to threats and bullying behaviour but, rather, through positive inducements and the power of example, pointing specifically to the way in which economic integration through liberalism is the instrument for achieving both domestic development and international peace. It is through this self-perception of what it is, and what it does on the international stage, that the EU is referred to as 'normative power Europe' (Manners, 2002).

'Constructive engagement' in EU policy

Given the ideals that the pursuit of external relations were built upon, it is no surprise to discover that, since the early 1990s, the EU has implemented a policy of what can be labelled 'constructive engagement' with regimes in the region, including traditionally hostile regimes such as Iran and Syria, by attempting to 'export' its norms through cooperation. Despite the enormous changes that took place over time in the MENA, the EU never deviated from this. Constructive engagement is based on the understanding that the domestic problems of MENA countries – such as authoritarian rule, underperforming economies, and rise of political radicalism – are the main reason for the absence of regional peace and stability. The Arab–Israeli conflict, the intra-regional tensions and the political violence spilling over from the region into both Europe and the United States are all problems that could be solved by 'treating' the domestic diseases of the Arab world and Iran. In short, threats to international peace and security are due to the absence of democracy and development. In this respect, the stabilizing regional role of Turkey and its economic success are perceived as the product of Europeanization. Within the framework of EU thinking, the continuous decades-long interaction between Turkey and the European Union, driven by Turkish desire to accede to the EU, has provoked an osmosis of good European norms – democracy, human rights and free market – that have not only transformed Turkey but, crucially, have radically altered the way in which Turkey behaves on the international stage, becoming a factor of stability and peace. If this could occur in Turkey, it could also occur in the Arab states and Iran, so the logic goes. Democracy-promotion – operationalized through a number of different policy instruments and revised, over time, to suit changed circumstances – was, and still is, the main framing 'ideology' behind the EU's engagement in the region. However, democracy would, and should, not be achieved through the use or the threat of military force; rather, it should be achieved through political cooperation with both regimes and their opponents, and progressive economic integration through free trade agreements.

The Euro-Mediterranean Partnership (EMP)

Three instruments have been put in place to deal with the region since the mid-1990s when, under pressure from France, Spain and Italy, the EU began to take its southern neighbourhood more seriously. The most significant was the Euro-Mediterranean Partnership (EMP), also known as the 'Barcelona Process'. This policy framework was launched as a response to the Algerian crisis, which brought home to European countries, particularly those in the Mediterranean, the need to engage more systematically with states in the region in order to avoid negative international spillovers from domestic events, such as migratory movements and arms proliferation.

The EMP, which is a formal governmental multilateral framework that links the European Union with countries on the southern bank of the Mediterranean, rests on three pillars. First, there is a political and security partnership, whereby European countries cooperate with local governments in the region to promote the rule of law, human rights, and political pluralism. Such political cooperation has the objective of making governmental institutions on the southern bank more responsive to citizens in order to avoid repression of dissent, as this might radicalize and pose a serious threat. It also has the objective of increasing security in the Mediterranean through the promotion of conflict-resolution measures. Second, there is an economic and financial partnership, with an emphasis on 'sustainable and balanced economic and social development, with a view to achieving the objective of creating an area of shared prosperity' (EMP, 1995). The central idea here is that only market-oriented economic reforms and progressive integration of the southern bank into the EU market, through bilateral free trade agreements, can deliver the development and jobs necessary to stem the rise of political radicalism, create a pro-democracy middle class, and contribute to the strengthening of mutual relations to solve shared problems such as environmental degradation. The rationale for this rests on the idea of progressive linear modernization, with neo-liberal economic development influencing political arrangements that would increasingly move away from authoritarian practice and towards democracy. Finally, the third dimension is a social, cultural and human affairs partnership, which envisages the creation of linkages between universities, civil society organizations and governmental institutions, on both banks of the Mediterranean, to challenge the notion of a clash of civilizations (Huntington, 1993a) and to promote mutual respect and tolerance, which would then feed into the construction of a common identity, based on the respect for universal values.

The European Neighbourhood Policy (ENP)

The second instrument is the European Neighbourhood Policy (ENP). The ENP was the successor to the EMP, which never fully delivered on its promises. Cooperation between governments on both banks of the Mediterranean did increase after the launch of the EMP, but the overall outcome of EMP-based policies was problematic. The delivery of aid packages and the free trade agreements boosted economic integration and

growth, but the distribution of the benefits of liberalization was uneven
– both between the EU and the MENA, and within MENA countries
– and democracy did not take hold. Rather, the opposite occurred with
the strengthening of authoritarian rule. A change in the overall policy of
engagement with the MENA was designed and, following the September
11 attacks on the USA in 2001, the European Union became more proac-
tive in the way in which it promoted democracy in the Arab world. The
ENP was thus developed in 2004 with the objective of:

> offer[ing] ... neighbours a privileged relationship, building upon a mutual
> commitment to common values (democracy and human rights, rule of law,
> good governance, market economy principles and sustainable develop-
> ment). The ENP goes beyond the Barcelona Process insofar as it offers
> deeper political relationship and economic integration.

The rhetoric of the ENP is very similar to that of the EMP, but the
framework of the policy is very different, since the ENP is specifically
targeted at individual countries, rather than conceived for the whole
region in the context of a multilateral forum. The basis for this is that each
individual country on the southern bank should be 'treated' differently,
because each domestic situation was different from that of its neighbours. The overarching objective is still the promotion of democracy and
shared universal values, but the way to go about it is to take into account
the specificities of each country in order to set out Bilateral Action Plans
that offer inducements adapted to the national context. Nonetheless, the
ENP was also perceived as something of a failure in EU circles because
it seemed to focus too strongly on the necessity for political change in
the MENA.

The Union for the Mediterranean (UM)

The third instrument, the Union for the Mediterranean (UM) was
conceived by French President Sarkozy in 2007 and constitutes an innovation, insofar as it toned down the rhetoric of democracy promotion and
human rights, focusing instead on depoliticizing relations with the region
in favour of cooperation on technical issues of shared interest, such as
the development of new energy sources, or cooperating on integrating
infrastructural projects. 'Technocratizing' the relations between the two
banks of the Mediterranean, it was believed, would have a positive influence on economic development, and only when decent standards of living
were achieved across the region would the time be right to think about
democratic political reforms. However, the UM never really took off, as
it was undermined immediately by perceived Western support for Israel

in its attack on Gaza in 2008, which led an Arab boycott of the meetings (Seeberg, 2010).

The policy structure described here, and the policy choices made by the European Union, seem to justify the 'normative' label that the EU has enjoyed. Rather than seeking forcefully to promote what it considers universal values, or to implement aggressive policies against hostile regimes such as Syria, Iran and Gaddafi-led Libya, it has attempted, through positive inducements, to get all countries on the Southern bank of the Mediterranean to come around to the way in which the EU believes it is best to govern, both domestically and internationally. Conversely, the EU's belief in non-confrontation makes it reluctant to punish through sanctions and certainly reluctant to engage in military intervention. For instance, the United States adopted the Syria Accountability Act in 2004 which set economic sanctions in place to punish the country for its behaviour in Lebanon, thus underscoring how the USA would punish foreign policy stances of which it did not approve. The EU not only refrained from involvement in this diplomatic dispute, but began negotiations with the Syrian regime to sign an Association Agreement that would see the EU offer significant help to Syria in reforming its economic and political institutions in exchange for the opening up of the Syrian market. The assumption here is that political change will not come about rapidly and that there is, therefore, little point in the use of force or the threat of it, when the political consequences of military action are unforeseeable and almost invariably negative. From an EU perspective, engaging with authoritarian regimes is, therefore, a better option than ostracizing them, particularly when their actions are not perceived to be too reprehensible. However, many questions remain as to the validity, legitimacy and underlying intentions of the EU policy approach to the MENA.

The limits of EU democracy promotion

Despite the implementation of three different policy frameworks, the adoption of Association Agreements with a number of Arab states, and a significant increase in bilateral relations on economic, security and political matters, the overarching objective of the EU – the promotion of democracy as the path to international peace and stability – has failed. How long does one have to wait for the results of Europeanization to show up in targeted countries on the southern bank? For critics of the EU, constructive engagement takes too long and requires too many compromises with unsavory regimes. Second, when change finally arrived with the Arab Awakening, very little of it could be ascribed to the actions of the EU over the course of two decades of engagement. In fact, critics would argue that the Arab Awakening is, in part, a response to EU policies in the region, notably the promotion of neo-liberal economics, which led to greater socioeconomic inequalities and, as a consequence, fuelled resentment towards the regimes responsible for adopting them. What are the reasons for this failure? There are a number that are set forth in the literature on EU–Middle East relations, but they can be brought together in two sets of explanations.

The first set of explanations accepts the assumption of normative power Europe and imputes the failure to promote democracy effectively to specific problems that an actor such as the EU has to face. These include the inability of the Union to be more coherent in the pursuit of its objectives, because member states undermine such coherence when their crucial material interests are affected; the multiplication and overlap of EU institutions and frameworks preventing a smooth implementation of the policy; and the ability of authoritarian governments to deflect Europeanization by adopting facade reforms, while holding on to power through informal institutions.

The second set of explanations refutes the idea of EU policy-making as inherently normative, proposing instead that, as with all actors in international politics, the EU has both normative and material interests to pursue and defend (Youngs, 2004; Hyde-Price, 2006). In this context, the main reason for not having achieved the promotion of democracy is because that was never the real intention in the first place. Much like the USA, the EU is concerned that the rise of political radicalism – political Islam – would undermine its material interests in the region, such as access to energy resources and favourable trading patterns. It was realized quite rapidly at EU level that procedural democracy would very likely bring Islamists to power and, with them, uncertainty. Like the USA, the EU faced, and still faces, an important dilemma where the region is concerned (Teti, 2012). On the one hand, there is the belief that regional and global stability can only be achieved through the expansion of the zone of democratic states, within which conflicts are solved peacefully and economic exchanges take place securely. On the other hand, the EU fears that democracy, particularly in the short and medium term, is going to be advantageous to Islamists, with whom it feels it cannot deal. This belief might be wholly misplaced, but the perception is stronger than any reality, and therefore, for over two decades, the EU purported to promote democracy, while, through its policies, it helped to solidify an authoritarian status quo that was seen largely to deliver on stability. In addition, the economic dimension of the relationship between the EU and the MENA should not be neglected. The EU is the most important economic partner for many of the countries in the region, including Israel. It is also important to note is that the relationship is more beneficial to the EU than to its MENA partners, in terms of the direction of trade. This positive outcome for the EU – and for selected domestic actors in the MENA invariably linked to ruling élites – might be thrown into question with new and unknown parties and movements in power, particularly if they were elected because of their promises to revisit the economic choices made by their predecessors. Thus, despite the rhetoric of the EU and its focus on democracy, the policy structure had more contradictions than can simply be attributed to the divided nature of EU foreign policy-making (Pace, 2009).

The example of the elections in Palestine in 2006 illustrates what some see as the underlying hypocrisy of the EU. Having encouraged and worked for the democratization of the Palestinian political system for a number of years, the EU 'punished' the Palestinian Authority as soon as Palestinian citizens expressed their democratic voice by electing Hamas to power. There is no doubt that Hamas is an extremely controversial movement and a highly problematic political actor due to the violence it has visited on Israel, its rejection of the Oslo Accords and the peace process – to which the EU is committed, as well as its views on individual liberties. However, it participated in democratic elections and won the majority of seats in the Palestinian Legislative Council. It can thus claim to have had a popularly sanctioned mandate. The EU could have reacted differently, and more in line with its normative stance of talking to everyone, no matter how problematic. Instead, it decided to follow the USA on the path of ostracizing Hamas. Therefore, the EU, instead of providing an alternative to hegemony of the USA in the region, simply strengthened it.

In the wake of the Arab Awakening, there was a re-evaluation of EU policies towards the region, which began with the admission that the policies of the past were mistaken since they did not pay sufficient attention to the democratic will of the people, despite the rhetoric employed. It was also admitted that promoting democracy through cooperation with the institutions of authoritarian governments was bound to fail, and that the EU had paid far more attention to economic and security issues than it did to social questions. In practice, the rhetorical shift, post-Arab Awakening, has translated into more material resources being injected into supporting processes of democratization, and in abandoning the pretence that engaging authoritarian rulers will deliver political change. It is for this reason that heavy sanctions were placed on Syria following the start of the civil war in the summer of 2011. However, as Hinnebusch (2012) argues, the EU is still caught between the rhetoric of post-colonialism and the practices of neo-colonialism. European suspicions about the rise of Islamists, together with an inability to conceive of an economic aid programme outside the framework of neo-liberalism, fundamentally undermine the assertion that the EU has changed course. This further weakens the legitimacy and credibility of its policies in the region.

For the majority of countries in the region, particularly in North Africa, but also elsewhere, the EU presents a significant opportunity in terms of aid and trade, in addition to a model for governance that could deliver pluralism and development. However, the authoritarian rulers of the region have had no genuine intention to engage with the European Union and have cynically exploited contradictions in EU policy to safeguard their privileges by introducing what are little more than sham reforms. In some cases, linkages dating back to colonial times have had a profound impact on international relations between countries on the two banks of the Mediterranean, undermining both the actions of the EU and of local actors opposing incumbent regimes.

New global powers and the Middle East

As we have seen in the previous sections of this chapter, the United States and the European Union have been the dominant actors in the MENA since the end of the Cold War. Given their coincidence of interests, despite their rhetorical differences (Durac and Cavatorta 2009), both actors have had a tremendous influence on the domestic politics of individual countries and on the way in which local actors interacted with each other. While it would be mistaken to argue that the USA and/or EU managed regional affairs simply by rewarding friends and punishing enemies, no matter what their domestic politics were, it is true nevertheless that MENA countries found it extremely difficult to build international links that would allow them to escape from or ignore the US–EU embrace. Local agency should not be neglected and there have been instances of MENA actors, particularly non-state entities, providing a challenge to this dominance, but there is no doubt that foreign interference in domestic affairs has been considerable. This was demonstrated very clearly in the lead up to the war against Iraq in 2003, arguably the most significant event in the region over the last decade. The war – conducted by the USA and its allies without UN mandate, and based on false pretences – illustrated how little the USA took multilateral institutions or international norms into account in the post September 11 period. In addition, and more significantly, it demonstrated the sheer power of the USA and its European allies, as the war proceeded with very little open political opposition from members of the international community. France, Germany, Russia and China expressed degrees of disquiet, but no country could prevent the war from taking place and no one wanted to challenge the USA openly. US military superiority confirmed that it could ignore other actors in the system and still get its way.

The war was possible also because the USA exploited the weakness of others. Arab countries, far from being bound by so-called 'Arab solidarity', have had diverging foreign policy agendas for decades, as we have already seen, with leading regional actors vying for supremacy since the departure of the colonial powers. Thus, some countries, such as the Gulf States, were quite happy to see the removal of Saddam Hussein who, despite the difficulties faced by Iraq, still remained a pole of attraction for those disenchanted with the way in which the USA dominated the region, with the support of wealthy oil kingdoms. In addition, he was still considered a credible security threat to the small Gulf states. Egypt, another powerful US ally, supported the USA in order to eliminate a rival in the quest for Arab leadership, while Syria opposed military action in an attempt to become the leader of the axis of resistance to US imperialism, by drawing on the disenchantment of ordinary Arabs opposed to US policies in the region.

Unsurprisingly, Iran was ambivalent about the war against Saddam Hussein. On the one hand, there was a degree of apprehension about US military intervention to replace the Iraqi regime because of fears that Iran was also on the list of countries where regime change might be forced through military action. In addition, the presence of hundreds of thousands of US troops on two of its borders – Iraq to the west and Afghanistan to the east – could not be seen as reassuring in Tehran. On the other hand, Iran was far from unhappy about the removal of its old rival Saddam Hussein, and the near destruction of Iraq, because the country would no longer represent a major threat to Iranian security. Furthermore, the Iranian leadership was convinced, correctly as it turned out, that the rise of Shia political parties and movements in the aftermath of Saddam's removal would allow Iran to exercise a significant degree of influence over Iraqi politics. These opposing goals and allegiances within the Arab world and Iran meant that no regional consensus on Iraq, as on so many other issues before, could force the USA to go back on its decision, or even challenge it.

For their part, China and Russia were not interested or sufficiently strong at the time to deter unilateral action by the USA – being, in many ways, merely emerging powers. However, they subsequently internalized the lesson of Iraq in a variety of ways. Thus, while both acquiesced to the attack on Libya in 2011 because they had no particularly strong attachment to Gaddafi and wanted to be attuned to large swathes of Arab public opinion, they drew the line when it came to Syria. The Syrian crisis began when the Asad regime violently repressed the peaceful opposition in the early weeks of the Arab Uprisings. The opposition eventually took up arms against the regime and civil war engulfed the country. The USA and its regional and European allies support the rebellion and promote regime change, although there are increasing doubts about the democratic credentials of the Syrian opposition. On the other hand, China and Russia (particularly the latter) support Bashar al-Asad. The strong stance of Russia suggests the emergence of new powers, since the war in Iraq, to challenge Western countries – and, notably, the USA – in the region. In many ways, the invasion of Iraq and its botched aftermath have strengthened the resolve of these new global powers to engage with the region in order to provide an alternative for local regimes and, in particular, a degree of security to regimes traditionally hostile to the United States and fearful of US regional dominance.

China has thus far stayed away from political and security issues, preferring to focus on building economic linkages, as it has done across Africa. The main priorities for China in the region are increasing access to the natural resources vital to its economic growth and finding untapped markets. This is quite evident, for instance, in its relations with Algeria, where China is providing the workforce and capital for new infrastructural projects, while gaining access to a country rich in natural resources and with an appetite for consumption. The official visits of Arab leaders to China are another indication of the weight that Beijing has in the region. China constitutes an attraction for many Arab leaders because it provides a model through which economic development can be achieved while maintaining the political status quo, although Chinese leaders are still reluctant to be perceived a regional alternative challenging the United States. It is, however, obvious that the 'strictly business' approach of the Chinese is particularly welcome. A more forceful approach from China in terms of political and security matters would certainly alter the dynamics and power relations in place at the moment, particularly if it decided to build more solid links with countries hostile to the United States, or if it decided to assume a position of leadership on the Palestinian question. This has not occurred yet and China, unlike Russia, is not even part of the Quartet mediating between Israelis and Palestinians – a further indication that, for the moment, China is interested only in doing profitable business, as its interest in Algerian oil and gas (Box 10.3) indicates. The consequence of this for Arab countries is that there still exists no real alternative to dealing with the USA as the primary regional mover.

While China concentrates on commerce and shies away from political and strategic concerns, the same cannot be said for Russia. Aside from having a historical involvement in the region, Russia appears to be more determined to become involved in the regional politics, in order to send out the message that the world not only needs to be multipolar, but that it

---

Box 10.3   China and Algeria

As part of its increasing diversification of trade and investment, it is not surprising that China identified Algeria, an important oil and natural gas producer, as a crucial partner in the region. While most of the oil and gas extracted in Algeria is destined for the European market, Chinese firms are involved in exploration of future sites, giving them a stake in whatever new discoveries will be made. In this respect, much like the rest of the Middle East, Algeria represents an investment for the future when it comes to energy resources. This does not mean that trade between the two countries is marginal – quite the opposite is true. China has filled the need for infrastructural projects – such as the coastal motorway, that Algeria needed – and sees the country as a growth market for its exports. This has brought a significant number of Chinese workers to Algeria.

What is interesting about the relationship, as is the case with the rest of the region, is how China is employing what Alterman refers to as soft power. China does not push or bully and is quite aware that countries in the region tend to use relations with China as a bargaining chip in their much more complex relationship with the United States. In addition, China does not want to upset the United States in the region for the moment, although a confrontation seems inevitable in the future.

Source: Jon Alterman (2009). 'China's soft power in the Middle East', in Kuchins *et al.* (eds), *Chinese Soft Power and Its Implications for the United States*, Centre for Strategic and International Studies. Available at http://csis.org/files/media/csis/pubs/090310_chinesesoftpower__chap5.pdf.

---

is becoming so. Building on renewed economic development thanks to its resource wealth, Russia has over the last decade or so sought to provide some sort of balance to the USA and the EU. In 2006, in contrast to the actions of the USA and European leaders, the Russian government invited a Hamas delegation to Moscow to discuss the Arab–Israeli conflict, explicitly recognizing the democratic mandate – and, therefore, the legitimacy – of the Hamas leadership to speak on behalf of the Palestinians. While this gesture did not have any immediate concrete consequences for the peace process, it testified to the renewed willingness of Russia to engage in the politics of the region according to its own values and interests, rather than simply acquiescing in what the USA wanted. This Russian engagement has, in many ways, strengthened the so-called 'axis of resistance' formed by Syria and Iran together with non-state actors such as the Lebanese Hizbullah, in opposition to the dominance of the USA and its Arab allies in regional politics. While no formal organic alliance exists between Syria and Russia or Iran and Russia, it is clear that the relations are quite solid and built on the shared understanding that a US-dominated Middle East is counterproductive for peace, stability and the interests of the three countries. The stubborn support of Russia for the Syrian president during the ongoing civil war is a strong indication that the Russians will not tolerate

Box 10.4   The international community and the Syrian crisis

The Syrian civil war constitutes an unmitigated political and humanitarian disaster for all parties involved. But, it also reflects the complex nature of the political and diplomatic relations that characterize the region today. When the repressive authoritarian regime of Basher al-Asad began to face significant and open opposition in the first few months of 2011, it was hardly a surprise for Syria experts that he reacted with the use of widespread violence. Numerous accounts have emerged as to how the decision to use violence against peaceful demonstrators was the product of strategy devised by the leadership to polarize Syrian society and, ultimately, justify repression. The heterogeneous and disorganized Syrian opposition took up arms in the belief that Western countries would intervene much more strongly and help in removing Asad, as they had promised to do. US President Obama talked about red lines that the regime could not cross without punishment. But, these red lines were crossed on a number of times, and there was no real punitive response.

The civil war has now escalated into a conflict with considerable sectarian undertones and Syria has become the theatre for a much larger geo-political game. While the inability of Western countries to adopt a credible position on Syria should be criticized, the role played by China, Russia and Iran is particularly abysmal. Rather than attempting to use their position of relative strength to try to influence Asad to work for a peaceful solution that would avoid the human tragedies that have affected Syrians since 2001, they have all helped to worsen the situation. Russian weapons, as well as diplomatic support, together with Iranian logistical help, and Chinese diplomatic cover have all contributed to the escalation of the conflict. The Syrian opposition is certainly responsible for the taking of lives and the destruction of infrastructure, in addition to presenting an ideological and political vision that is in sharp contrast with the values of Western countries. But the radicalization of the opposition can be explained, in large part, as a response to the perception of abandonment by the international community. Money and weapons are channelled through *jihadi* networks whose patrons are in the wealthy Gulf States – again, this is in line with the geo-strategic importance that Syria possesses for regional actors.

Russia and the USA are fighting a new Cold War in Syria which has global repercussions, while Saudi Arabia and Iran are fighting a regional war for supremacy by proxy. In addition to all this, sectarianism has increased, with Shia militias from Iraq and the Lebanese Shia Hizbollah, fighting for Asad, while Sunni extremists from all over the world have joined with radical Islamist groups to fight against the Syrian regime. All this has helped to radicalize both Sunnis and Shias in Iraq, leading to instability in the country as well. The rise of the Islamic State (IS) in the summer of 2014 is directly linked to the collapse of state structures and institutions in both Syria and Iraq. IS was able – through its coherent ideology, sectarian appeal, and military capabilities – to fill the vacuum in the areas that were 'abandoned' by the Syria and Iraqi central governments. The conquest of territory on the party of a heavily armed and well-organized terrorist organization is a break with the past practices of al-Qaeda and constitutes a new security challenge for both international and regional actors who, in part, had contributed to the rise of IS through funding and political support in the early days of the Syrian crisis as an opposition force to Asad. The necessity to deal with the blowback falls on all of them.

US direct interventionism in the region any longer unless it is cleared with Russia, and envisage an increasingly significant involvement in the affairs of the region if only as a spoiler of Western objectives, as discussed in Box 10.4. Russian support for al-Asad has been explained through the historical links that exist between the two countries dating back to the Cold War when Soviet weaponry and training were provided to Syria to shore up the anti-imperialist camp in the Middle East. It has also been argued that the access the Russian navy has to the Syrian port of Tartous in the Mediterranean has featured prominently in Russia's backing of al-Asad. The Russians are afraid that a different government might no longer accept Russian military ships, preventing the country's access to warm waters. This is not to say that Russia does not share some concerns in the region with Western countries. Chief among them is the rise of ideological, motivated and well-armed Islamist groups. The Syrian civil war has spawned very violent *jihadi* movements, which have attracted a considerable number of foreign fighters, including many from the Caucasus. Russia is worried that some of these fighters will eventually go back and use their military and political skills to destabilize the Muslim regions of the country where anti-Russian sentiment is already widespread. In this respect, there is a coincidence of interests with Western countries, as the rise of *jihadi* Islamism threatens not only regional stability, but also domestic security. It is, in part, for this reason that Russia claims al-Asad should be supported. For Russia, he represents a local leader faced with an Islamist revolt, which, if successful, would inevitably create a rogue state bound to spread havoc in the region. This interpretation of the Syrian civl war is rejected in Western circles where the argument is that it is the authoritarian nature and the violent repressive measures of the regime of Al-Asad against initially peaceful dissenters that created the conditions for the emergence of *jihadi* groups. Irrespective of this, it has become clear over the course of the civil war that the rise of non-state actors – such as the Islamic State in Iraq and Syria as the principal force in opposition to both al-Asad and the Iraqi regime – finds Russia and the West having to try to collaborate on how prevent its further entrenchment in the region.

Conclusion

The overarching objective of democracy promotion, whether a sham or a genuine enterprise, has dominated the international relations of the region since the end of the Cold War. Both the USA and the EU, the dominant actors in the system, built their foreign policies around this objective and helped to shape the politics of individual countries and of the region accordingly. However, the core dilemma central to democracy promotion has never been resolved and this has not changed in the aftermath of the Arab Awakening. While democratically sanctioned leaders might, over the long term, ensure greater regional stability and defuse radical political ideologies while pursuing economic development, in the short and medium terms, the defence and achievement of the West's interests depends largely on the survival of authoritarianism, particularly in key oil and gas exporting states. This is true, even in countries such as Syria where the regime change that the USA and the EU pushed for at the beginning of the civil war has more recently been pursued with far less vigour, because of fears of what a post-Asad Syria might bring. As a result, Syria constitutes a powerful deviation from the dominant narrative of the Arab uprisings. The emergence of new powers interested in the region has somewhat altered the situation, but the region is far from being the locus of a nascent global competition. China is not really interested in it yet and Russia might not have the means to sustain such a challenge, although its stand on Syria is reminiscent of a Cold War rivalry being played out by proxy. What remains is widespread unease in the region with the leadership of the United States, particularly at the level of public opinion, together with an acceptance that such leadership is likely to remain in place for some time. Arab countries are divided over this. The conservative monarchies are still solidly behind the USA. The axis of resistance remains opposed to it, while a number of countries are in the midst of such historic domestic changes that foreign policy choices might not be of primary concern for them yet. Finally, it is interesting to note that amidst the convulsions of the Arab world, both Turkey and Iran seem to have grown in influence, although Saudi Arabia and, surprisingly, Qatar have also become actors capable of influencing regional events and shaping domestic politics in the rest of region, thanks to their financial power. In any case, there is little doubt the Middle East is likely to remain central to international politics for the foreseeable future.

Key questions

- How does one explain the paradoxes affecting the Western policies of democracy promotion since the 1990s?
- What is the impact of the war on terror in the MENA region?
- How should we understand the role of China in the Middle East?
- How have regional and international actors responded to the crisis in Syria since 2011?

Further reading

Cavatorta, Francesco (2005). 'The international context of Morocco's stalled democratisation', *Democratization*, 12(4): 548–66.

Dalacoura, Katerina (2005). 'US democracy promotion in the Arab World since September 11, 2001: a critique', *International Affairs*, 81(5): 963–79.

Durac, Vincent and Francesco Cavatorta (2009), 'Strengthening authoritarian rule through democracy promotion? Examining the paradox of the US and EU security strategies: the case of Tunisia', *British Journal of Middle Eastern Studies*, 36(1): 3–19.

Hinnebusch, Ray (2012). 'Europe and the Middle East: from imperialism to liberal peace?', *Review of European Studies*, 4(3): 18–31.

Hyde-Price, Adrian (2006). 'Normative power Europe: a realist critique', *Journal of European Public Policy*, 13(2): 217–34.

Pace, Michelle (2009). 'Paradoxes and contradictions in EU democracy promotion in the Mediterranean: the limits on EU normative power', *Democratization*, 16(1): 39–58.

Teti, Andrea (2012). 'The EU's first response to the "Arab Spring": a critical discourse analysis of the partnership for democracy and shared prosperity', *Mediterranean Politics*, 17(3): 265–82.

Online resources

Lagon, Mark (2011). 'Promoting democracy: the whys and hows for the United States and the international community: a markets and democracy brief', *Council for Foreign Relations*. Available at http://www.cfr.org/democratization/promoting-democracy-whys-hows-united-states-international-community/p24090.

Naumkin, Vitaly (2013). 'Understanding Russia's role in the Middle East', *Russia Today*. Available at http://www.russia-direct.org/qa/vitaly-naumkin-understanding-russia%E2%80%99s-interests-middle-east.

Youngs, Richard and Tamara Cofman Wittes (2009). 'Europe, the United States, and Middle Eastern democracy: repairing the breach', Brookings Institute. Available at http://www.brookings.edu/research/papers/2009/01/middle-eastern-democracy-wittes.

Chapter 11

After the Awakening

The events of 2011 clearly heralded a transformation in political dynamics across much of the MENA region, and constitute a profound shift in the ways in which scholars and policy-makers examine regional affairs, too often framed and explained through Orientalist stereotypes. Nevertheless, with the passage of time, it has become clear that initial enthusiastic expectations of a straightforward transition to democratic practice were misplaced or, at the very least, optimistic in terms of timing. By 2013, ongoing political instability in Tunisia seemed to threaten the most promising political transition in the region with the rise of conservative Salafi forces, the assassination of secular political leaders and the inability of the government to command widespread support – thereby provoking an increasing confrontation between Islamists and secular forces. However, the promulgation of a new Constitution in early 2014, with the consensus of the vast majority of the political class, appears to have set Tunisia, uniquely in the region, on the path of democratic consolidation. In Egypt, the appetite of the military to interfere in political life appeared to be undiminished, following the deposal of the elected Islamist president, Muhammad Mursi, in the summer of 2013. There, the losers were not only the Mubarak clan and the Muslim Brotherhood, but also the prospect of democracy in the medium term, insofar as what was effectively a military coup was heralded in many sectors of Egyptian society as the only plausible solution to political and economic crisis. The election of al-Sisi to the presidency in the spring of 2014, after he resigned his post in the military, seems to confirm the return of Egypt to old-style politics and the marginalization of aspirant revolutionaries. In Libya, rival militias contended for influence at the expense of stability, undermining attempts by the central government to assert its authority over the whole of the country. The instability in Libya has occurred despite reasonably free and fair legislative elections having taken place in the aftermath of Gaddafi's demise and, again, in the summer of 2014. The problem is that such elections appear to have further divided Libyans, rather than uniting them in the name of pluralistic politics. In Yemen, a fragile political balance held, but the country remains vulnerable to challenge from an array of quarters – secessionist movements and the presence of al-Qaeda-linked terrorists, to name but two of the most significant. In addition, the economy is unlikely to improve in the short and medium term, further undermining the new political structures. Thus, while to use Longley Alley's phrase, Yemen seems to have changed everything, nothing much seems to have actually changed (2013).

Syria, for its part, is torn apart by civil war that threatens to spiral out of control. It has also affected the neighbouring countries of Iraq and, to a lesser extent, Lebanon. As a result, another shift took place in responses to the region. The Arab 'Spring' was transformed into some sort of winter of instability, chaos and violence, leading to a renewed appreciation of the certainties of Arab autocracy, among Western policy-makers, and sectors of the Arab population tired and afraid after years of upheaval. Within scholarly circles, a belief in the inherent tension between democracy and the culture and dominant religion of the region was revived. For some, at least, what has taken place since the swift overthrow of some Arab tyrants in 2011 simply underlined the insights of the 'persistence of authoritarianism' paradigm.

This chapter examines some of the legacies of the Arab Awakening, focusing, in particular, on the characteristics of the protest movements and on the contexts within which they emerged. In addition, this chapter uses the legacy of the Arab Awakening to bring together the two central frameworks of this book, examining how the Arab Awakening has informed the interparadigm debate and how international–domestic linkages help to explain the different directions countries have taken following the uprisings.

Finally, the chapter is concerned with the broad theme of how we should make sense of political dynamics in the region since 2011. Too often, the cliché is trotted out that the Arab Awakening is a history-changing event that constitutes the '1989' moment of the Arab world. The objective here is not to downplay the significance of the momentous events that have taken place. But it should also be noted that, while great change has unfolded across the region, talk of revolution – let alone democratic revolution – is at best premature, if not simply erroneous. It is for this reason that it might be better to discuss in detail what has, in fact, changed, rather than making enthusiastic predictions that 'the end of history' – a notion that is problematic in itself – has arrived in the region.

The character of the protest movements

In order to understand the ways in which the uprisings have unfolded and why the possibility of democratic revolution was betrayed by subsequent events, it is necessary to focus on two key areas. The first concerns the nature of the 'revolutionary' movements themselves.

Revolutionary coalitions

It is commonplace that, on the eve of the Arab uprisings, formal political life across the region was stagnant. The controlled political systems of security (*mukhabarat*) states had succeeded in marginalizing opposition parties; cowing civil society; and co-opting, where they existed, official trade unions and other potential centres of dissent. What was most striking about the uprisings was that they were characterized by the entry of new political actors employing new tools for social mobilization and bypassing traditional means of organization, in the process, uniting – at least for a historic moment – a set of highly disparate forces around a common theme of regime change, expressed in now familiar demands of '*Irhal*' ('Go') and '*Al-shaab yurid isqat al-nizam*' ('the people want the fall of the regime').

In Tunisia, young people were at the forefront of the uprising. As the protests against the regime spread, the protagonists were 'young, unemployed, or informal workers; students; civil servants; itinerant peddlers; and marginalized or excluded individuals'. To begin with, they were on their own battling it out with the police and security forces. Some of the legally recognized political parties were close to the old regime, derived significant privileges from this and had little to gain from an anti-regime revolt – particularly one that had begun as another bread riot – with no clear political objectives. Others were more openly critical of Ben Ali's regime but, nonetheless, kept their distance from the protest movement; and others still had no real operational infrastructure in the country that could be easily and safely mobilized. The national leadership of the largest union in the country, the UGTT, had for decades developed a *modus vivendi* with the regime. On the eve of the president's departure from the country, the secretary-general of the union visited Ben Ali in his palace to reaffirm his support (Aleya-Sghaier, 2014). It is interesting to note that the early involvement of trade unionists in the revolution came from those local activists who had, for years, borne the brunt of the disastrous policy choices of the regime and who did not share the central leadership's conciliatory attitude towards it. The decisions of these local trade union activists to join forces with a disenfranchised youth, more interested in clashing with the police to affirm the illegitimacy of state authorities, constituted a powerful catalyst for the revolutionary movement as it brought different 'struggles' together. To this, bloggers, city-based activists and members of the increasingly disaffected middle class added their weight to the revolution, making it genuinely national. Naturally, conflicting narratives about the revolution emerged in its aftermath, and have also become embedded in the political struggles between different social and political actors, all of which claim revolutionary legitimacy. However, this does not invalidate the fact that unity and effective coalition building, however temporary, did occur, repoliticizing a population that had seemed devoid of any interest in political activity, due to the relentless authoritarian practices to which they had been subjected.

In Egypt, the protest movement was led by a disparate collection of youth movements, most of which mobilized online (Sika, 2012). The oldest was the April 6 Movement which was formed in 2008. More newly formed groups included the We Are All Khaled Said group, Youth for Justice and Freedom, the Youth of the Muslim Brotherhood, the Youth of Kifaya, young people of the Tomorrow Party, and young people of the Democratic Front Party. They were later joined by young people from a selection of political parties that spanned the political spectrum, including the leftist Tagammu Party, the Nasserite Party, the Popular Movement for Democratic Change, the Labour Party, the Wafd Party, and the Front of Coptic Youth. As in Tunisia, the legally recognized opposition parties were widely seen as ineffective and lacking in legitimacy, while the leadership of the Egyptian Trade Union Federation comprised Mubarak loyalists (notwithstanding the fact that Egypt had been the site of ongoing labour unrest in the years preceding the uprising). The Muslim Brotherhood was torn between a conservative older leadership that was wary of engaging too closely with the protest movement, and a younger generation that was prominent in anti-regime activism and sought to join in the struggle and spectacle taking place in Tahrir Square. In addition to overcoming ideological differences for a moment in history, the Egyptian revolution saw a temporary bridging of profound religious divisions as well, with Copts and Muslims sharing the same public space and briefly suspending the mutual suspicions that had characterized their relations since the 1970s (Brownlee, 2013). It is also important to note the class element in the Egyptian revolution. As in Tunisia, the dissatisfaction of swathes of the middle class led to the unitary cross-class marching to Tahrir Square (Kandil, 2012).

In Yemen, a similar pattern prevailed of established opposition parties with limited popular legitimacy, a civil society sector that was largely (although not exclusively) apolitical, and popular disenchantment with formal political structures and institutions. When anti-regime protests became widespread in 2011 following the departures from office elsewhere of Ben Ali and Mubarak, it was, once more, an array of youth-led organizations that were to the fore, consisting for the most part of those who had little or no previous experience of political life. An umbrella body emerged (the Civil Coalition of Revolutionary Youth) which brought together Yemen's four main youth organizations: the Alliance for the Youth's Revolution, the Alliance of the People's Youth Revolution, the Alliance of Youth and Students for a Peaceful Revolution, and the Coalition of Change Leaders.

In the square of Yemen's cities, the protesters were joined by members of Yemen's opposition parties, especially the Islamist, *Islah* Party, as well as elements of some of the country's very powerful tribes.

The pattern was similar elsewhere. Groups emerged – such as the National Campaign for Student Rights and the Jordanian Democratic Youth Union, the *Diplomés Chomeurs* (unemployed graduates) and the Moroccan Association of Youth, the Fifth Fence Group in Kuwait and the Bahrain Youth Society for Human Rights – to express the grievances and aspirations of youths who perceived their interests to be unrepresented by existing political structures and their needs to be unrecognized and unmet (Murphy, 2012). In Morocco, the February 20 movement contained a number of movements of different political persuasions and, in Syria, the demonstrators were drawn from different sectors of the population in terms of social class, place of residence and, significantly, religious affiliation. As in all the other cases, the young age of the organizers was a common trait.

What is particularly striking about the Tunisian, Egyptian and Yemeni cases is the speed with which youth movements succeeded in galvanizing popular and political opinion more broadly. In Tunisia, the protest movement was joined by lawyers and some of the judiciary who had earned the hostility of the regime, the rank and file of the UGTT, legal opposition political parties (including the Democratic Progressive Party), the formerly communist *Ettajdid*, as well as banned parties such as the Communist Labour Party of Tunisia, the Maoist *Al Watad* and a selection of Arab nationalist parties. After 14 January, Islamists became active in the anti-regime movement. In Egypt, the youth protesters were joined by union members – despite the fact that the official union leadership typically took a much more cautious approach, as well as the younger generation of the Muslim Brotherhood, the leadership of which also adopted a more cautious stance towards the protests. In Yemen, too, the established opposition parties were reluctant to endorse the anti-regime protests until government repression forced them to do so. However, as in other settings, the violence of the regime's response to the protests, especially after the killing of dozens of protesters on 18 March 2011, provoked the defection of key regime allies and broadened the base of the anti-regime movement.

'Leaderless' movements

However, while the achievements of the new youth-led protest movements are remarkable in the context of the political stasis of previous decades, their subsequent marginalization by longer-established political actors had much to do with their novel character. Volpi (2012: 2–3) argues that what characterizes the democratic revolutions of the 'Arab Spring' and differentiates them from 'traditional' democratic transitions and revolutions is that, unlike the former, they are 'unplanned, spontaneous political transitions' and, unlike the latter, they are not 'ideologically and politically organized'. The youth-led movements that were at the heart of the Arab uprisings were, for the most part, leaderless; relied on non-traditional forms of organization and communication (see Box 11.1, for a discussion of this point); and lacked a clear ideological platform, except for a focus on demands of regime change and political reform that had a resonance across most sectors of their societies. In Tunisia, Aleya-Sghaier (2014: 42) comments that the young people who participated in the revolution 'were not guided by ideology' and that 'the revolution was leaderless and spontaneous' at first, before established opposition parties, members of the legal profession and trade unionists came on board. Kaboub (2013) similarly writes of the emergence of a multi-class, leaderless movement when the collective experience of the Tunisian population with the oppression and corruption of the regime and the complete sense of humiliation that Tunisians were subjected to made the middle class realize that its socioeconomic status and interests were more aligned with those of the poor than with the regime and its élite class supporters.

In Egypt, the protesters 'came from different ideological backgrounds, religions, political orientations, and geographical areas' (El-Din Shahin, 2014: 55). Writing about Libya, Sawani notes that the 'February revolution' was 'spontaneous, without any prior planning or a unified leadership' (2014: 92). In Yemen, many of the youth groups at the heart of the protest movement rejected the old political parties almost as much as they did the regime. The protest movements eschewed formal structures and relied to a significant extent on social media, as well as on satellite television. These enabled the mobilization of collective action in ways that had previously been impossible, insofar as both significantly escaped the control and repression of the authoritarian state (Bellin, 2012: 138).

However, the novel, leaderless character of these movements, lacking either clear organizational structure or ideological platform, also limited their potential to take advantage of the political openings which followed the demise of autocratic rulers. Of the activists at the forefront of the 2011 uprising in Egypt, Roberts (2013) commented that they knew and could agree on what they did not want, but that was all. What happened, he suggests, was a popular uprising that lost the initiative because it had no positive agenda or demand:

> 'Bread, freedom, social justice' aren't political demands, just aspirations and slogans. A social movement might have made these slogans into

Box 11.1 Revolution 2.0

No analysis of the Arab Awakening would be complete without a discussion of the role of the internet – and, more specifically, that of social media. In some quarters, the uprisings have been described as 'Facebook' or 'Twitter' revolutions, as social media enabled protest movements to bypass real-life censorship and repression by mobilizing online instead to prepare the terrain for direct confrontation with the authorities. The enabling role of social media is beyond dispute, not least because many activists themselves have recognized and hailed their importance in organizing protests, side-stepping the police and linking up what used to be localized struggles into a more coherent set of demands, without necessarily meeting in person.

In addition, social media allowed protesters and opposition activists to relay what was happening in real-time both to fellow citizens and to an international audience, ensuring that, irrespective of the outcome of the protests, there would be a permanent record of events. Ultimately, many of the videos, and calls for mobilization and support, focused the attention of the world on Tunis and Cairo, in particular, rendering the adoption of repressive measures more difficult. However, acknowledging the importance of social media does not mean we should see them as the cause of the Arab uprisings – which, as we have seen, are rooted in much deeper socioeconomic and political factors.

Furthermore, the mobilizing power of social media should not be over-estimated, since a significant degree of mobilization occurred even when the internet was shut down, which suggests the relevance of face-to-face contacts and personal networks also. Additionally, the enabling role of social media should not obscure the fact that regimes also use social media to get their message out and to propagate alternative views while also censoring opponents. The propaganda war on social media between supporters of Bashar al-Asad and regime dissidents is an indication of this.

Finally, the widespread use of social media to link up with an international audience does not necessarily prevent public repression. While it is true that the world was watching events in Cairo, Tunis and elsewhere across the region, such that it seemed impossible for a harsh crackdown to take place in front of a global audience, it should be remembered that this is exactly what happened in Iran to the Green Movement in 2009, in the aftermath of the contested presidential election of Ahmadinejad to a second term in office.

In short, the role of social media deserves to be highlighted, but their effective contribution to the uprisings must also contextualized, particularly when the powerful role of more traditional and established media – such as satellite television, for example – tends to be neglected.

Source: Rikke Hostrup Haugbølle (2013). 'Rethinking the role of the media in the Tunisian uprising', in Nouri Gana (ed.), *The Making of the Tunisian Revolution*, Edinburgh: Edinburgh University Press.

demands by pressuring the government to take specific steps. But a movement that wants these desiderata and, at the same time, wants the government to clear off has a coherence problem. The only demand that mattered politically was '*Mubarak, irhal!*' (Roberts, 2013)

The incoherent character of the protest movements may have been exacerbated, in turn, by its reliance on social media. Bellin (2012) suggested that, even if social media can contribute to collective action designed to bring down an authoritarian regime, they might be less effective in building democracy afterwards. It may be precisely their anonymous, spontaneous and non-hierarchical nature that limits the capacity of social media to contribute to the institutionalization of democracy.

The marginalization of the youth movements

Thus, the youth-led protest movements, which drove four Arab autocrats from office, were innately vulnerable to marginalization in the post-uprising period. As Asef Bayat points out – revolutionaries stayed outside the structures of power precisely because they were not planning to take over the state. When they realized they needed to, they lacked the political resources – organization, leadership and strategic vision – that would be necessary to wrest control both from old regimes and from 'free-riders' who had played a limited role in the uprisings but were organizationally ready to take power (Bayat, 2013: 54) As a result, a key characteristic of the post-uprising politics of the region has been the marginalization of 'new actors' and the return to prominence of the 'old' (Durac, 2013). In Tunisia, post-Ben Ali political life is dominated by the Islamist *Ennahda* Party and political parties, together with their leaders, that predate the uprising. There is considerable evidence of the mistrust on the part of youth activists of the formal political arena. The first free and fair elections held in October 2011 saw a turnout of just over 50 per cent. The disengagement of youth from institutional politics is evident in the return to the scene of political debates from the 1970s and 1980s, with the same people engaging in those debates, as if the Ben Ali years had simply frozen them. In the words of one commentator:

> Young Tunisians despise party politics which they associate with corruption and abuse of power. Rather than establishing 'traditional' political parties, they conceive their political intervention through civil society associations and social movements that directly address their problems. (Honwana, 2011: 17)

In Egypt, the marginalization of the youth movements was at its clearest in the second round of presidential elections which saw the candidate of the Muslim Brotherhood, Muhammad Mursi, defeat the candidacy of Ahmed Shafiq, Mubarak's last appointee as prime minister. Subsequent events have revealed how little has changed in the politics of the country as the military has intervened to restore its 50-year dominance of political life (Stein, 2012), jailing or silencing both the Muslim Brothers and the young revolutionaries. In Yemen, the youth-led movement was marginalized in the design, execution and subsequent implementation of a deal for the departure of the president, Saleh, which was brokered by the Gulf Cooperation Council (GCC) and which saw the installation of his deputy as president, and a power-sharing government between the former ruling party and the opposition Joint Meeting Parties coalition. Party politics had such a bad reputation in post-uprising Libya that the 2014 legislative electoral rules required all candidates to stand as independents without affiliation to any political party.

But, a focus on youth, and its marginalization in countries where there has been political change, should not lead to the neglect of other important factors that influenced the development of the Arab Awakening. First, the widespread exclusion of the youth in Tunisia, Yemen, Egypt and Libya in favour of other social and political actors finds a parallel with the inability of the youth to mobilize significant sectors of the population in countries where there has been no apparent political change. This was not for want of trying, as the Algerian, Moroccan, Bahraini, Syria and even Saudi examples suggest. But, there are other social and political forces whose weight is necessary to instigate a revolutionary process and they are not so easy to mobilize. Second, both in countries where change has taken place and where it has not done so, the temporary and tenuous nature of coalition-building, that has characterized relationships between opposition actors in the Arab world for decades, has been significant. In revolutionary contexts – such as those of Egypt, Tunisia, and Libya and, to an extent, Yemen – the dismissal of the dictator was the high point of the revolutionary movement, but divisions emerged subsequently along traditional lines. These divisions have led to the stalling of the process of democratization and the return of authoritarian forms of rule, with the exception of Tunisia (Heydemann, 2013), where ties that had been forged, from the mid-2000s onwards, between the Islamist *Ennahda* party and a number of secular opposition parties somehow stood the test of democratic consolidation through what Stepan (2012) called 'twin tolerations'. This is not to say that ideological divergence, coupled with the return of mutual suspicions about each other's genuine intentions, has not undermined a difficult transition in Tunisia, particularly in relation to the 'culture wars' regarding individual liberties (Brody-Barre, 2013). The successful promulgation of the constitution in 2014 should not overshadow the very real divide between Islamists and secularists, which has deepened both at the institutional and social levels.

The Islamist–secular divide was also at the heart of the difficult process of change in Egypt, as the electorally legitimate rule of the Muslim

Brotherhood increasingly came under challenge from secular factions unhappy with the direction of the post-Mubarak transition. In addition to the traditional division between Islamists and secularists, which revolutionary movements had momentarily bridged, other temporary alliances have come crashing down. For instance, in both Tunisia and Egypt, the cross-class solidarity that had characterized the revolution faded away in the aftermath of political change. The Tunisian transition constitutes an essentially middle-class pact between a conservative bourgeoisie, close to *Ennahda*, and a more secular modernist one, close to the parties of the left and to the values of Bourguibism (Merone, 2015). This pact, however unsteady, has left out an important part of Tunisian society: a young disenfranchised urban and rural class that found itself materially and politically marginalized – and, therefore, increasingly attracted to radical ideologies of the extreme left or *jihadi* Salafism (Merone and Cavatorta, 2013). In the Egyptian case, there is a further problematic alliance that has not withstood the difficulties of the transition: that between Copts and Muslims. Despite the unity displayed in Tahrir Square, post-revolutionary Egypt has seen an increase in sectarian tensions, which has once more raised the debate about which political configuration best ensures the rights of religious minorities. The conclusion of many has been that authoritarianism does so. In other contexts, such as Libya and Yemen, where notions of social class division might be less applicable, we have seen the renewal of tribal and sectarian, as well as generational, divisions. In short, generational, sectarian, class and tribal divides, which served regimes so well in the past, have made a significant comeback and constitute an inescapable legacy of the Arab Awakening, even if they had faded into the background during its initial revolutionary days.

Similar divergences and divisions have affected countries where the awakening has not led to political change but, rather, to widespread civil conflict – as in Syria, or to a reconfiguration of authoritarian power – as in the Gulf states, Algeria, Morocco and Jordan. The early protests against Bashar al-Asad in Syria were far from sectarian. But, as soon as regime repression set in and the opposition became an armed one, sectarianism began to play an important role, with the regime attempting to project a self-image as defender of religious minorities – Alawis, Christians and Druze – and delegitimizing dissent on that count. In many ways, Syria is the ultimately self-fulfilling prophesy of sectarianism. Since the beginning of the fighting, the conflict has turned sectarian in many parts of the country, specifically pitting Alawis against Sunnis. However, this is far from being the only story of the Syrian conflict, and should not obscure the class dimension and the urban–rural divide. The problem, however, is that the more one highlights sectarianism, the more actors on the ground operate according to it, thereby reinforcing the validity of the argument. Thus, sectarianism does not necessarily explain the Syrian civil war, but it has become the lens through which many ordinary citizens see the situation, given the collapse of state authority and the necessity to 'pick a side' out of material necessity.

The capacity of the King of Morocco to fend off demands for genuine political change – by transforming the current executive monarchy into a constitutional one – stems from his control of political parties, but also from the weakness of the opposition, including the February 20 Movement. For instance, the decision of the opposition Islamist civil society association, the Justice and Charity Group, to leave the February 20 Movement weakened it – participation at demonstrations fell and the movement was inexorably marginalized.

While the traditional divisions in Jordanian society – ethnic, ideological and tribal – do not necessarily insulate the King from dissent, they did play a role in ensuring that demands for change never resulted in calls for an end to the monarchy, or for its diminished involvement in political affairs. Finally, as the case of Bahrain amply illustrates, the Arab Awakening in the Gulf has been tamed through a combination of the economic largesse available to incumbent regimes and the manipulation of sectarianism, pitting Shias against Sunnis. These practices and strategies have been temporarily successful because of genuine divisions within society that limit the likelihood of the formation of a common front opposed to authoritarian rule. This is even more so the case when change can be framed in terms of uncertainty and the difficulties neighbouring states are experiencing with pluralism. However, the success of some regimes in resisting pressure for change is also due to what can be labelled as 'authoritarian learning' (the concept is discussed in Box 11.2) whereby regimes learn from the errors and mistakes of their neighbours, putting in place strategies to avoid them (Heydemann and Leenders, 2011).

From this discussion, it emerges clearly that the character of the protest movements is crucial to an understanding of post-uprising political dynamics, especially in those countries in which a change of leadership took place. However, it is not the only set of variables of significance. In order to understand the turn of events in each of the countries in which there was significant mass mobilization for radical political change, it is necessary to take a number of other factors into account. These relate in particular to the strength or otherwise of regime-society relations, the role of the military, and the extent to which external actors have a stake in the outcome of events. Conversely, the absence of change should not simply be ignored, and the set of factors just mentioned played an important role there, too.

> ## Box 11.2   Authoritarian learning
>
> Many of the analyses of the Arab Awakening have emphasized the way in which Arab citizens and social movements across the region learned from the initial revolutionary experience of Tunisia in order to challenge the monopoly of power of Arab incumbents elsewhere. This type of learning – through the exchange of ideas, and the use of new social media and technologies – certainly favoured revolutionary contagion and it is striking how similar the techniques of action were. But, Heydemann and Leenders focus instead on a neglected aspect of this type of political learning that may ultimately have more relevance for our understanding of Arab politics. Specifically, they argue that, just as social movements and ordinary citizens learned new strategies and tactics of opposition from the experience of other countries, incumbent authoritarian regimes too have learned from each other, and from the mistakes made by the regimes that fell, in order to fend off challenges to their position. What also emerges from this study is the finding that already, by late 2011, authoritarian regimes in the region were converging on similar adaptive responses to challenge. Given the way in which the uprisings subsequently developed, with a number of revolutionary failures and the survival of many authoritarian regimes, the analysis proposed by Heydemann and Leenders deserves credit for highlighting processes that are often neglected. Just as shared language, symbolism and practices can, to a certain extent, facilitate learning between opposition actors in different countries, they can also enable the learning of ruling élites.
>
> *Source*: Steven Heydemann and Reinoud Leenders (2011). 'Authoritarian learning and authoritarian resilience: regime responses to the "Arab Awakening"', *Globalizations*, 8(5): 647–53.

Domestic, regional and international contexts

The second set of issues which must be taken into account in any explanation of the trajectory of the Arab uprisings concerns the specific contexts within which the uprisings took place – this includes the domestic political environment as well as regional and international linkages.

Regime-society relations

It is significant that in Tunisia, Egypt, Libya and Yemen, the regimes, respectively, of Ben Ali, Mubarak, Qadhdafi and Saleh had alienated a significant proportion of their populations. The impact of extended socio-economic distress, combined with political closure, repression of opposition and the widespread perception of corruption and nepotism, rendered the rulers of each of these countries vulnerable to challenge. It is important, for instance, to note that the revolts occurred at a time when the political succession of members of the presidents' families was widely anticipated, raising the prospect of turning these states into something like 'republican monarchies' (Sadiki, 2010). In Syria, by comparison, the regime of Bashar al-Asad was able to command much greater levels of popular support, and even legitimacy, among at least some minorities in that country – in particular, but not limited to, the Alawite community, to which many in the regime and in leadership positions in the security forces belong. Similarly, although the monarchy in Bahrain faced an opposition that drew on the country's 60 per cent Shiite population, it could also look for support among the significant 25 per cent of Bahraini nationals that were its Sunni co-religionists.

As mentioned in some detail earlier, specific types of state–society relations, related to profound sets of cross-cutting divides, explain both revolutionary failures and authoritarian survival in different ways. Among the latter, a number of countries stand out strongly. In Algeria, for instance, the experience of civil war in the 1990s, and the loss of hundreds of thousands of lives that followed that country's previous experiment with substantial political liberalization, led to an effective societal consensus that disturbing the status quo was fraught with danger. In Jordan also, the outcome of the protest movement had a great deal to do with the experience of instability in its neighbourhood, not least because of its location between Israel and Iraq. The 2003 invasion of Iraq posed challenges for the country's stability and security, as hundreds of thousands of Iraqi refugees crossed the border into Jordan. To the south, Jordan's neighbour Saudi Arabia was experiencing its own security challenges while to the north lay Syria, where the consequences of attempts to undo the status quo were plain to see. By the time the uprisings of 2011 broke out, the regional neighbourhood seemed less secure than ever. This led many Jordanians to support the ideal of reform but not the sort of regime change that was bringing violence to many countries in the region. The deteriorating situations in both Yemen and Libya further highlighted the dangers of radical change to many.

The role of the military

The role of the military has assumed renewed significance in analyses of Middle East politics, not least insofar as it has been crucial in determining the outcome of uprisings across the region (Coustillière, 2011). As Ryan (2012) notes, in every case where civilian pro-democracy and pro-reform protests were initially peaceful, the extent of any violence was determined by the response of soldiers and military officers. Bellin suggests that two factors have been important in determining the stance of the military. The first concerns the extent of social mobilization – if the numbers of protesters are high then the cost of repression will be high as well. The second concerns the extent to which the military has a stake in the survival of the regime (Bellin, 2012: 131–5). The military in Tunisia was small and had played no significant role in political life since independence; neither was it distinguished from the general population along ethnic or sectarian lines. Faced with large numbers of protesters, the Tunisian military had no strong stake in the survival of the Ben Ali regime (Brooks, 2013). Furthermore, the army, unlike the police and the intelligence services, played virtually no role in repressing dissent during the Ben Ali era. Finally, the stake of military officers in the survival of the regime was limited since the involvement of the Tunisian military in the economy was all but non-existent. However, this has not prevented some high-ranking officers, including Rachid Ammar, former Chief of Staff of the Armed Forces, from decrying the way in which the post-revolutionary authorities have dealt with security challenges and undermined the prestige of the security forces (International Crisis Group, 2013). This suggests that, even in contexts where the military refused to side with the authoritarian rulers and adopt a political role, post-revolutionary politics dynamics can still draw the military into the scene.

Egypt, as Tunisia, had a professional military that was not linked to the regime along ethnic or sectarian lines. But, unlike Tunisia, it was invested in the economic life of the country. Since 1952, all of the country's leaders before the uprising had been drawn from the military (Sayigh, 2012). It seems clear that the military in 2011, faced with large numbers of protesters, calculated that its interests would be better served by abandoning Mubarak, than by violent suppression of the protesters. The decision was facilitated by resentment of the fact that the President was grooming his son to succeed him, in a move seen by many as potentially threatening to the vested interests of the military.

Elsewhere, the reaction of the military to unrest was also crucial. In Bahrain, the army was linked to the ruling family by religion. The majority of the protesters were Shia, in contrast to the Sunni royal family and armed forces. In Libya, the military mirrored the country's tribal structure and fractured along tribal lines, thus prolonging the conflict there. In Yemen, also, splits in the military ultimately led to violence and a subsequent stand-off between pro- and anti-regime units which, in turn, motivated the intervention of external actors to prevent any escalation of violence and further destabilization of the country. Finally, in Syria, as in Bahrain, the military and the regime are divided along sectarian lines from the majority of the population. As we have seen in the previous section, these long-standing divisions have fed sectarianism which, in turn, has undermined efforts to arrive at any peaceful political accommodation between the regime and its opponents.

The role of external actors

The role of external actors has also been crucial to outcomes – if, at times, the opacity of external policies and interventions have been difficult to appraise. Some things, however, are clear. Neither Ben Ali nor Gaddafi had any influential friends left at either the regional or international levels when their respective regimes came under challenge. After temporarily offering help to Ben Ali to face down protestors, France performed a very rapid U-turn and indicated not only that they supported legitimate demands for change, but also that it would not accept Ben Ali's exile in France. The United States, already aghast at the vast corruption network of Ben Ali's entourage, and encouraged by the peaceful nature of the demonstrations, had very few qualms about letting Ben Ali go. The withdrawal of support from crucial allies diminished both the material and legitimacy resources of Ben Ali's regime, precipitating its fall. The case of Libya is even clearer in highlighting the relevance of the international dimension in determining domestic outcomes. Indeed, the coalition of forces arrayed against Gaddafi is exemplified in UN Security Council support for intervention to protect his opponents, which ultimately led to the demise of his regime (and, indeed, his own death/execution).

Egypt is, of course, different, as a number of regional and international players have sought to extract advantage from the dizzying twists and turns of events there over the past two years. The USA opted for a cautious path – only belatedly supporting calls for Mubarak's resignation, offering cooperation of a kind to the Muslim Brotherhood during its tenure in power, and, markedly reluctant to characterize the intervention of the military in the summer of 2013 to overthrow the elected Islamist government as a coup. The importance of Egypt on the geopolitical map of the region, and its crucial role in the Arab–Israeli conflict, render its domestic politics highly significant for the USA, which is anxious to support any political actor that guarantees a degree of stability and, more importantly, commits to the security of Israel.

Other international actors were less cautious. Qatar, with a population of some 200,000 nationals among a total of 1.7 million, has belied its size with an activist foreign policy across the region over the past two years. Whereas, in previous years, Qatari foreign policy interventions were typically in the form of conflict mediation, more recently it has supported Libya's rebels with weapons and equipment, and offered important support to the Muslim Brotherhood in Egypt, as well as to anti-regime rebels in Syria. Saudi Arabia, by contrast, and despite its self-styled Islamic character, was mistrustful of the Muslim Brotherhood (as it has been mistrustful of Islamist opposition at home) and offered support to the military-backed government that has replaced it. Saudi involvement has also been crucial elsewhere. In Bahrain, fear of a Shia government that might be sympathetic to Iran prompted military intervention in order to ensure the security of the Sunni Al-Khalifa monarchy. Further south in the Arabian Peninsula, Saudi concerns regarding potential instability in Yemen drove its role in the GCC deal, which ultimately brought an end to the uprising in that country, and inaugurated a process of political transition. In its policy towards the uprisings, which also included a proposal that the GCC should be expanded to include Morocco and Jordan, the Saudi regime was signalling to other GCC states that it was determined to take the lead in ensuring that the 'disruptive elements' of the effects of the uprisings would not reach the Arabian Peninsula (Kamrava, 2011). External intervention in Syria also prolonged the violence in that country as Iran, Saudi Arabia, Qatar, Turkey and a host of Western states sought to assert their influence over the outcome of its increasingly bloody civil war.

As was highlighted in Chapter 1, enthusiasm for the Arab Awakening diminished over time and it is not a coincidence that the absence of renewed protests and demonstrations across the region coincides with the renewed emphasis of international actors on stability and containment of conflict.

Conclusion: everything has changed/nothing has changed

Writing in the aftermath of the September 11 attacks, Fred Halliday noted that two typical responses emerged in relation to any great international upheaval: 'one is to say that everything has changed; the other is to say that nothing has changed'. Thus, there is an increasingly widespread view that 'when the dust settles the new Middle East will not be that different from the old one' (Valbjørn, 2012: 28). However, to assert that the uprisings have not led to revolution anywhere in the region is not to dismiss all that has happened as insignificant. There are a number of important lessons to be learned.

First, it is clear that a region that was marked by widespread de-politicization over the past several decades has witnessed a re-politicization of many sectors of society, the outcome of which is wholly unpredictable. Valbjørn suggests that one of the features of re-politicization is a revitalization of the formal political scene. Parliaments, elections and parties, previously considered empty shells and largely irrelevant to political analysis, have now become much more meaningful, making it important to understand the dynamics of these institutions and also to understand the impact of this on old and new players in the formal political scene. It is also important to note that this renewed politicization goes in many different directions with groups, parties and associations subscribing to widely divergent ideologies, promoting radically contrasting agendas and, often, finding very little common ground, aside from disdain for the status quo. This suggests that the flux within which the Arab world finds itself, in the aftermath of the Arab Awakening, is far from the globally dominant values and ideas of liberal democracy and neo-liberal economics. From Tunisian Maoists to Jordanian Salafists and from Yemeni jihadis fighting in Syria to Egyptian Copts calling for inter-religious dialogue, there is a very wide spectrum of political engagement that is both exciting and worrisome to observe, insofar as a shared view of the future does not quite exist.

Second, an emphasis on re-politicization in institutionalized contexts should not lead us to ignore other spheres and dimensions of politics – the various forms of mass social mobilization and street politics of recent years. Indeed, the degree of re-politicization invites us to re-examine whether the Arab world was, in fact, marked by a general de-politicization, or whether this was limited to the formal political scene, while other dynamics taking place below regime level were missed. Laryssa Chomiak has written of the 'spaces of political contention and resistance' that existed in Tunisia 'even under the increasingly authoritarian political conditions of Ben Ali's rule' but which were usually ignored because they existed outside the formal structures of politics. By way of example, she itemizes 'dodging mandatory elections, secretly mocking the president and his notoriously corrupt family, cultivating alternative identities in soccer stadiums, and subversively critiquing the regime in semi-independent and oppositional print publications' (Chomiak, 2011: 71). However, as Chomiak also points out:

> Rarely … is scholarly attention directed towards the space between official authoritarian narrative and the opposition and resistance that it breeds. Studies instead assume that authoritarian states succeed in obliterating oppositional politics. (2011: 76)

In this context, one should not forget the anti-neoliberal nature of the protests and uprisings, which have revived meaningful trade unionism, incentivized the insertion of many non-governmental organizations into the global networks of the alter-globalization movement and created space for alternative forms of economic organization.

Finally, Bayat makes the point – as obvious as it is overlooked – that our time frame for analysis of these extraordinary events is extremely circumscribed. He invokes Raymond Williams's notion of the 'long revolution' – a process that is complex and multifaceted, comprehending not only economic, but also social and cultural transformation, and involving the deepest structures of relationships and feeling:

> Consequently, rather than looking for quick results or worrying about set demands, we might view the Arab uprisings as 'long revolutions' that may bear fruit in ten or twenty years by establishing new ways of doing things, a new way of thinking about power. (Bayat, 2013: 60)

Key questions

- What were the key characteristics of the protest movements that led to the Arab Uprisings?
- What were their primary weaknesses?
- Why did the uprising in Syria fail?
- How have the Arab Uprisings changed the MENA region?

Further reading

Achcar, Gilbert (2013). *The People Want*, London: Saqi Books.
Brown, Nathan (2013). 'Egypt's failed transition', *Journal of Democracy*, 24(4): 45–58.
Gerges, Fawaz (2013). 'The Islamist moment: from Islamic state to civil Islam?' *Political Science Quarterly*, 128(3): 389–426.
Kamrava, Mehran (2014). *Beyond the Arab Spring*, London: Hurst & Co.
Matthiesen, Toby (2013). *Sectarian Gulf: Bahrain, Saudi Arabia and the Arab Spring that wasn't*, Stanford: Stanford University Press.
Tekdal Fildis, Ayse (2012). 'Roots of Alawite-Sunni Rivalry in Syria', *Middle East Policy*, 19(2): 148–56.
Wright, Robin (2012). *The Islamists Are Coming: Who They Really Are*, Washington, DC: US Institute of Peace.

Online resources

Aarts, P., P. van Dijke, I. Kolman, J. Statema and G. Dahhan (2012). *From Resilience to Revolt: Making Sense of the Arab Spring*, Amsterdam: Amsterdam Institute for Social Science Research. Available at http://aissr. uva.nl/publications/digital-library/content/from-resilience-to-revolt.-making-sense-of-the-arab-spring.html.

Hayes, David (2011). 'The Arab Spring: protest, power, prospect', *Open Democracy*, 11 April. Available at: http://www.opendemocracy.net/david-hayes/arab-spring-protest-power-prospect.

Hill, Ginny (2011). 'Yemen, Saudi Arabia and the Gulf States: elite politics, street protests and regional diplomacy', London: Chatham House. Available at http://www.chathamhouse.org/publications/papers/view/132823.

Honwana, Alcinda (2011). 'Youth and the Tunisian Revolution', *SSRC Conflict Prevention and Peace Forum*. Available at: http://webarchive.ssrc.org/pdfs/Alcinda_Honwana,_Youth_and_the_Tunisian_Revolution,_September_2011-CPPF_policy%20paper.pdf

Muasher, Marwan (2013). 'Year four of the Arab Awakening', Carnegie Endowment for International Peace. Available at http://carnegieendowment.org/2013/12/12/year-four-of-arab-awakening/gw1m.

References

Aarts, Paul and Francesco Cavatorta (eds) (2013). *Civil Society in Syria and Iran*. Boulder, CO: Lyne Rienner.

Abdellatif, Omayma and Marina Ottaway (2007). 'Women in Islamist movements: toward an Islamist model of women's activism', *Carnegie Papers*, 2: 1–13.

Abdelrahman, Maha (2002). 'The politics of "un-civil" society in Egypt', *Review of African Political Economy*, 29(91): 21–36.

Abdih, Y., A. Barajas, R. Chami and C. Ebeke (2012). 'Remittances channel and fiscal impact in the Middle East, North Africa and Central Asia – IMF Working Paper,' *International Monetary Fund*. Available at www.imf.org/external/pubs/ft/wp/2012/wp12104.pdf.

Abootalebi, Ali (1998). 'Civil society, democracy and the Middle East', *Middle East Review of International Affairs*, 2(1): 46–59.

Abootalebi, Ali (2001). 'State–society relations and prospects for democracy in Iran', *Middle East Review of International Affairs*, 5(3): 20–37.

Abrahamian, Ervand (1982). *Iran Between Two Revolutions*. Princeton: Princeton University Press.

Abu-Khalil, Asad (2000). 'Women in the Middle East', *Foreign Policy in Focus*, Available at http://www.fpif.org/briefs/vol5/v5n30women.html.

Abu-Lughod, Lila (2001). 'Orientalism and Middle East feminist studies', *Feminist Studies*, 27(1): 101–13.

Abu-Rabi, Ibrahim (1996). *Intellectual Origins of Islamic Resurgence in the Modern World*. Albany, NY: State University of New York Press.

Aburish, Said (1999). *Arafat. From Defender to Dictator*. London: Bloomsbury.

Achcar, Gilbert (2013). *The People Want*. London: Saqi Books.

Aghrout, Ahmed (2008). 'Policy reforms in Algeria: genuine change or Adjustment?', in Yahia Zoubir and Haizam Amirah-Fernandez (eds), *North Africa: Policies, Region and the Limits of Transformation*. London: Routledge.

Ahmed, Leila (1992). *Women and Gender in Islam: Historical Roots of a Modern Debate*. New Haven: Yale University Press.

Aita, Samir (2011). 'Abattre le pouvoir pour libérer l'Etat', *Le Monde Diplomatique*, 685, April.

Akhavi, Shahrough (2003). 'Islam and the West in world history,' *Third World Quarterly*, 24(3): 545–62.

Al-Anani, Khalil and Maszlee Malik (2013). 'Pious way to politics: the rise of Salafism in Post-Mubarak Egypt', *Digest of Middle East Studies*, 22(1): 57–73.

Al-Anani, Khalil (2012). 'Islamist parties post-Arab Spring', *Mediterranean Politics*, 17(3): 466–72.

Al-Awadi, Hesham (2014). 'Kuwait', in Ellen Lust (ed.), *The Middle East*. CQ Press.

Al-Azmeh, Aziz (1995). 'Nationalism and the Arabs,' *Arab Studies Quarterly*, 17(1–2): 1–17.

Al-Rasheed, Madawi (2010). *A History of Saudi Arabia*. Cambridge: Cambridge University Press.

Al-Tawi, Ayat (2013). 'New NGO law strikes fear in Egyptian civil society', *Al-Ahram Weekly*, 24 May. Available at http://english.ahram.org.eg/NewsContent/1/64/71987/Egypt/Politics-/New-NGO-draft-law-strikes-fear-in-Egyptian-civil-s.aspx.

Albrecht, Holger, (2005). 'How can opposition support authoritarianism? Lessons from Egypt', *Democratization*, 12(3): 378–97.

Albrecht, Holger and Dina Bishara (2011). 'Back on horseback: the military and political transformation in Egypt', *Middle East Law and Governance*, 3(2): 13–23.

Albrecht, Holger and Oliver Schlumberger (2004). 'Waiting for Godot: regime change without democratization in the Middle East', *International Political Science Review*, 25(4): 371–92.

Alexander, Christopher (1997), 'Authoritarianism and civil society in Tunisia: back from the democratic brink', *Middle East Report*, 205.

Aleya-Sghaier, Amira (2014). 'The Tunisian Revolution: the revolution of dignity', in Ricardo Laremont (ed.), *Revolution, Revolt and Reform in North Africa: The Arab Spring and Beyond*. London: Routledge.

Allal, Amin (2010). 'Ici ça ne bouge pas ça n'avance pas'. Les mobilisations protestataires dans la région minière de Gafsa en 2008', in Myriam Catusse, Blandine Destremau and Eric Verdier (eds), *L'Etat face aux débordements du social au Maghreb*. Paris: IREMAM/Khartala.

Alterman, Jon (2009). 'China's soft power in the Middle East', in Kuchins *et al.* (eds), *Chinese Soft Power and Its Implications for the United States*, Centre for Strategic and International Studies. Available at http://csis.org/files/media/csis/pubs/090310_chinesesoftpower__chap5.pdf.

Anderson, Lisa (1987). 'The state in the Middle East and North Africa', *Comparative Politics*, 20(1): 1–18.

Anderson, Lisa (1991). 'Political pacts, liberalism and democracy: the Tunisian national pact of 1988', *Government and Opposition*, 26(2): 244–60.

Ashraf, Ahmad (1996). 'From the White Revolution to the Islamic Revolution', in Saeed Rahnema and Sohrab Behdad (eds), *Iran After the Revolution: Crisis of an Islamic State*. London: IB Tauris.

Avnery, U. (1998). 'Israel's Declaration of Independence: squaring the circle', *Palestine-Israel Journal*, 5(2): 48–54.

Ayubi, Nazih (1991). *The State and Public Policies in Egypt since Sadat*. Reading, Berks: Ithaca Press.

Badran, Margot (1995). *Feminism, Islam and Nation: Gender and the Making of Modern Egypt*. Princeton University Press.

Badran, Margot (2009). *Feminism in Islam: Secular and Religious Convergences.* Oxford: Oneworld.

Baroudi, Sami and Paul Tabar (2009). 'Spiritual authority versus secular authority: relations between the Maronite Church and the state in postwar Lebanon: 1990–2005', *Middle East Critique*, 18(3): 195–230.

Basbous, Antoine (2004). *L'Arabie Saoudite en guerre.* Paris: Ed. Tempus.

Bayat, Asef (2009). *Life as Politics: How Ordinary People Change in the Middle East.* Stanford: Stanford University Press.

Bayat, Asef (2013). 'Revolution in bad time', *New Left Review*, 80: 47–60.

Beblawi, Hazem (1990). 'The rentier state in the Arab world', in Giacomo Luciani (ed.), *The Arab State.* Berkeley and Los Angeles: University of California Press.

Beinin, Joel and Lisa Hajjar (2014), 'Palestine, Israel and the Arab-Israeli conflict: a primer,' *Middle East Report*. Available online at http://www.merip.org/primer-palestine-israel-arab-israeli-conflict-new.

Beinin, Joel (1999). 'The working class and peasantry in the Middle East: from economic nationalism to neoliberalism', *Middle East Report*, Spring: 18–22.

Beinin, Joel and Joe Stork (1997). 'On modernity. historical specificity, and international context of political Islam', in Joel Beinin and Joe Stork (eds.), *Political Islam: Essays from Middle East Report.* Berkeley and Los Angeles: University of California Press..

Bellin, Eva (2004). 'The robustness of authoritarianism in the Middle East', *Comparative Politics*, 36(2): 139–57.

Bellin, Eva (2012). 'The robustness of authoritarianism reconsidered: lessons of the Arab Spring', *Comparative Politics*, 44(2): 127–49.

Benchemsi, Ahmed (2012). 'Morocco: outfoxing the opposition', *Journal of Democracy*, 23(1): 57–69.

Bensaad, Ali (2007). 'The Mediterranean divide and its echo in the Sahara: new migratory routes and new barriers on the path to the Mediterranean', in Thierry Fabre and Paul Sant Cassia (eds), *Between Europe and the Mediterranean: The Challenges and the Fears.* Basingstoke: Palgrave Macmillan.

Ben Yahmed, Béchir (2011). 'Jews de victoire...', *La Jeune Afrique*, 17, January.

Berman, Sheri (1997). 'Civil society and the collapse of the Weimar Republic', *World Politics*, 49(3): 401–29.

Berman, Sheri (2003). 'Islamism, revolution and civil society', *Perspectives on Politics*, 1(2): 257–72.

Black, Antony (2001). *The History of Islamic Political Thought.* Edinburgh: Edinburgh University Press.

Bogaert, Koenraad (2013). 'Contextualising the Arab revolts: the politics behind three decades of neo-liberalism in the Arab world', *Middle East Critique*, 22(3): 213–34.

Boulby, Marion (2004). 'Women and the Islamist movement in Israel: challenging patriarchy?', *Historical Reflections*, 30(3): 491–507.

Brody-Barre, Andrea (2013). 'The impact of political parties and coalition building on Tunisia's democratic future', *Journal of North African Studies*, 18(2): 211–30.

Bromley, Simon (2005). 'The United States and the control of world oil', *Government and Opposition*, 40(2): 225–55.

Brooks, Risa (2013). 'Abandoned at the palace: why the Tunisian military defected from the Ben Ali regime in January 2011', *Journal of Strategic Studies*, 36(2): 1–17.

Browers, Michaelle (2006). *Democracy and Civil Society in Arab Political Thought: Transcultural Possibilities*. Syracuse: Syracuse University Press.

Brown, Nathan (2012). *When Victory is not an Option. Islamist Movements in Arab Politics*. Ithaca: Cornell University Press.

Brown, Nathan (2013). 'Egypt's failed transition', *Journal of Democracy*, 24(4): 45–58.

Brownlee, Jason (2013). 'Violence against Copts in Egypt', *Carnegie Endowment for International Peace*, November: 1–26.

Brownlee, Jason, Tarek Masoud and Andrew Reynolds (2013). 'Tracking the Arab Spring: why the modest harvest?', *Journal of Democracy*, 24(4): 29–44.

Brumberg, Daniel (2002a). 'Islamists and the politics of consensus', *Journal of Democracy*, 13(3): 109–15.

Brumberg, Daniel (2002b). 'The trap of liberalized autocracy', *Journal of Democracy*, 13(4): 56–68.

Brumberg, Daniel (2003). 'Liberalization versus democracy: understanding Arab political reform', *Democracy and Rule of Law Project No. 37*, Carnegie Endowment for International Peace. Available at: http://carnegieendowment. org/2003/04/29/liberalization-versus-democracy-understanding-arab-political-reform/2bb8.

Burgat, François (2005). *L'Islamisme à l'heure de Al-Qaeda*. Paris: Editions La Découverte.

Bush, George W. (2003). 'Remarks by President George W. Bush at the 20th Anniversary of the National Endowment for Democracy' Available at http://www.ned.org/george-w-bush/remarks-by-president-george-w-bush-at-the-20th-anniversary.

Butko, Thomas (2004). 'Islam as an instrument of radical political change', *Middle East Review of International Affairs*, 8(4): 33–48.

Calandruccio, Giuseppe (2005). 'A review of recent research on human trafficking in the Middle East', *International Migration*, 43(1/2): 267–99.

Camau, Michel (2006). 'Globalization démocratique et exception autoritaire arabe', *Critique Internationale*, 30(1): 59–81.

Carapico, Sheila (2000). 'Passports and passages: tests of women's citizenship rights', in Joseph Suad (ed.), *Gender and Citizenship in the Middle East*. Syracuse: Syracuse University Press.

Cavatorta, Francesco (2005). 'The international context of Morocco's stalled democratisation', *Democratization*, 12(4): 548–66.

Cavatorta, Francesco (2006). 'Civil society, Islamism and democratisation: the case of Morocco', *Journal of Modern African Studies*, 44(4): 203–22.

Cavatorta, Francesco (2007). 'More than repression: strategies of regime survival. The significance of *divide et impera* in Morocco', *Journal of Contemporary African Studies*, 25(2): 187–203.

Cavatorta, Francesco (2009a). 'Divided they stand, divided they fail: opposition politics in Morocco', *Democratization*, 16(1): 137–56.

Cavatorta, Francesco (2009b). *The International Dimension of the Failed Algerian Transition*. Manchester: Manchester University Press.

Cavatorta, Francesco (2010). 'The international politics of the Middle East', in Ellen Lust (ed.), *The Middle East*. Washington, DC: CQ Press.

Cavatorta, Francesco (2012a). 'Introduction', in Francesco Cavatorta (ed.), *State-society Relations under Authoritarian Constraints*. London: Routledge.

Cavatorta, Francesco (2012b). 'The war on terror and the transformation of Political Islam', *Religion Compass*, 6(3): 185–94.

Cavatorta, Francesco and Vincent Durac (2010). *Civil Society and Democratization in the Arab World: The Dynamics of Activism*. London: Routledge.

Cavatorta, Francesco and Merone, Fabio (2013). 'Moderation through exclusion? The journey of the Tunisian *Ennahda* from fundamentalist to conservative party', *Democratization*, 20 (5): 857-75.

Cevik, Salim and Hakki Tas (2013). 'In between democracy and secularism: the case of Turkish civil society', *Middle East Critique*, 22(2): 129–47.

Challand, Benoit (2011). 'The counter-power of civil society in the Middle East'. Available at: http://www.deliberatelyconsidered.com/2011/03/the-counter-power-of-civil-society-in-the-middle-east-2/ (Accessed 12 March 2011).

Chomiak, Laryssa (2011). 'The making of a revolution in Tunisia', *Middle East Law and Governance*, 3(1): 68–83.

Chomiak, Laryssa and John Entelis (2011). 'The making of North Africa's intifadas', *Middle East Report*, 259: 8–15.

Chomiak, Laryssa and John Entelis (2013). 'Contesting order in Tunisia: crafting political identity' in Francesco Cavatorta (ed.), *Civil Society Activism under Authoritarian Rule*, London: Routledge.

Choudhry, Sujit and Richard Stacey (2013). 'Semi-presidentialism as a form of government: lessons for Tunisia', Center for Constitutional Transitions. Available at: http://www.yemenintransition.com/YetraCpanl/artImge/Semi-Presidentialism%20as%20a%20Form%20of%20Government%20-%20Lessons%20for%20Tunisia.pdf.

Clancy, Julia (2012). 'From Sidi Bou Zid to Sidi Bou Said: a longue durée approach to the Tunisian Revolutions', in Mark Haas and David Lesch (eds), *The Arab Spring: Change and Resistance in the Middle East*. Boulder, CO: Westview Press.

Clapham, Christopher (1985). *Third World Politics: An Introduction*. London: Routledge.

Clark, Janine (2004). 'Social movement theory and patron-clientelism: *Islamic* social institutions and the middle class in Egypt, Jordan and Yemen', *Comparative Political Studies*, 37(8): 941-968.

Clark, Janine and Jillian Schwedler (2003). 'Who opened the window? Women's activism in Islamist parties', *Comparative Politics*, 35(3): 293–312.

Coffman-Wittes, Tamara (2008). 'Three kinds of movements', *Journal of Democracy*, 19(3): 7–12.

Cohen, Sara and Larabi Jaidi (2006). *Morocco: Globalization and its Consequences*. London: Routledge.

Collyer, Michael (2008). 'Emigration, immigration and transit in the Maghreb: externalization of EU policy?', in Yahia Zoubir and Haizam Amirah-Fernandez (eds), *North Africa: Policies, Region and the Limits of Transformation*. London: Routledge.

Colton, Nora Ann (2010). 'Yemen: a collapsed economy', *Middle East Journal*, 64(3): 410–26.

Cook, Steven (2014). 'Legion and the limits of transformation of EU policy', *Foreign Affairs*, January 8, Availlable at http://www.foreignaffairs.com/articles/140640/steven-a-cook/turkeys-democratic-mirage.

Cook, Steven (2005). 'The right way to promote Arab reform', *Foreign Affairs*, 84(2): 91–102.

Cook, Steven (2007). *Ruling, but not Governing: The Military and Political Development in Egypt, Algeria and Turkey*. Washington, DC: Johns Hopkins University Press.

Corm, Georges (1993). 'La Reforme Economique Algérienne: Une Reforme Mal Aimée?', *Maghreb-Machrek*, 139: 8–27.

Corm, Georges (2008). 'Labor migration in the Middle East and North Africa: a view from the region', *The World Bank*. Available at http://siteresources.worldbank.org/INTMENA/Resources/SF_background-3.pdf.

Costello, V.F. (1976). *Urbanization in the Middle East*. Cambridge: Cambridge University Press.

Coustillière, Jean-Francois (2011). 'Les Forces Armées dans les révoltes Arabes', *Confluences Méditerranée*, 79(4): 67–80.

Curtis, Mark (2003). *Web of Deceit: Britain's Real Role in the World*. London: Vintage.

Dalacoura, Katerina (2005). 'U.S. democracy promotion in the Arab World since September 11, 2001: a critique', *International Affairs*, 81(5): 963–79.

Dalacoura, Katerina (2006). 'Islamist terrorism and the Middle East democratic deficit: political exclusion, repression and the causes of extremism', *Democratization*, 13(3): 508–25.

Dalmasso, Emanuela and Francesco Cavatorta (2009). 'Liberal outcomes through undemocratic means: the reform of the *Code du Statut Personnel* in Morocco', *Journal of Modern African Studies*, 47(4): 487–506.

Dalmasso, Emanuela (2012). 'Surfing the democratic tsunami in Morocco: apolitical society and the reconfiguration of an authoritarian regime', *Mediterranean Politics*, 17(2): 217–32.

Dalmasso, Emanuela and Francesco Cavatorta (2010). 'Reforming the family code in Tunisia and Morocco: the struggle between religion, globalisation and democracy', *Totalitarian Movements and Political Religions*, 11:2: 213–28.

Davidson, Christopher (2012). *After the Sheikhs: The Coming Collapse of the Gulf Monarchies*. London: Hurst.

Davis, Uri (2003). *Apartheid Israel: Possibilities for the Struggle Within*. London: Zed Books.

Dawisha, Adeed (2003). *Arab Nationalism in the Twentieth Century: From Triumph to Despair*. Princeton: Princeton University Press.

De Haas, Hein (2006). 'Trans-Saharan migration to North Africa and the EU: historical roots and current trends', *Migration Information Source*. Available at: http://www.migrationinformation.org/feature/display.cfm?id=484.

De Soto, Hernando (2011). 'The real Mohamed Bouazizi', *Foreign Policy*, 16 December. Available at http://www.foreignpolicy.com/articles/2011/12/16/the_real_mohamed_bouazizi?page=0,1.

Deeb, Mary-Jane (2012). 'The Arab Spring: Libya's Second Revolution', in Mark Haas and David Lesch (eds), *The Arab Spring: Change and Resistance in the Middle East*. Boulder, CO: Westview Press.

Dekmejian, R. Hrair (1988). 'Islamic revival: catalysts, categories and consequences', in Shireen Hunter (ed.), *The Politics of Islamic Revivalism*. Bloomington and Indianapolis: Indiana University Press.

Diamond, Larry (2002). 'Thinking about hybrid regimes', *Journal of Democracy*, 13(2): 21–35.

Dillman, Bradford (2001). 'Facing the market in North Africa', *Middle East Journal* 55(2): 198–215.

Dillman, Bradford (2002). 'International markets and partial economic reforms in North Africa: what impact on democratization?', *Democratization*, 9(1): 63–86.

Dowty, Alan (2012). *Israel/Palestine*. Cambridge: Polity.

Duelfer, Charles A. and Dyson, Stephen Benedict (2011). 'Chronic misperception and international conflict: the US–Iraq experience', *International Security*, 36(1): 73–100.

Durac, Vincent (2009a). 'Globalizing patterns of business, finance and migration in the Middle East and North Africa', *Mediterranean Politics*, 14(2): 255–66.

Durac, Vincent (2009b). 'The impact of external actors on the distribution of power in the Middle East: the case of Egypt', *Journal of North African Studies*, 14(1): 75–90.

Durac, Vincent (2013). 'Protest movements and political change: an analysis of the "Arab Uprisings" of 2013', *Journal of Contemporary African Studies*, 31(2): 175–93.

Durac, Vincent and Francesco Cavatorta (2009). 'Strengthening authoritarian rule through democracy promotion? Examining the paradox of the US and EU security strategies: the case of Tunisia', *British Journal of Middle Eastern Studies*, 36(1): 3–19.

Edwards, Michael (2004). *Civil Society*. Cambridge: Polity.

El-Din Shahin, Emad (2014). 'The Egyptian revolution: the power of mass mobilization and the spirit of Tahrir Square', in Ricardo Laremont (ed.), *Revolution, Revolt and Reform in North Africa: The Arab Spring and Beyond*. London: Routledge.

El-Erian, Mohammed, Sena Eken, Susan Fennell, and Jean-Pierre Chauffour, (2006). *Growth and Stability in the Middle East and North Africa*, Washington, DC: International Monetary Fund. Available at http://www.imf.org/external/pubs/ft/mena/04econ.htm.

El-Ghoneimy, M. Riad (1998). *Affluence and Poverty in the Middle East*. London: Routledge.

Enayat, Hamid (1982). *Modern Islamic Political Thought*. London and Basingstoke: Macmillan Press.

Encarnacion, Omar (2006). 'Civil society reconsidered', *Comparative Politics*, 38(3): 357–76.

Entelis, John (2008). 'Democratic desires and the authoritarian temptation in the Central Maghreb', in Yahia Zoubir and Haizam Amirah-Fernandez (eds), *North Africa: Politics, Religion and the Limits of Transformation*. London: Routledge.

Esposito, John (1998). *Islam: The Straight Path*, Oxford: Oxford University Press.

Esposito, John (2003). 'Islam and civil society', in John Esposito and Francois Burgat (eds), *Modernizing Islam: Religion and the Public Sphere in Europe and the Middle East*. London: Hurst.

European Commission (1995). *Barcelona Declaration*. Available at http://ec.europa.eu/research/iscp/pdf/policy/barcelona_declaration.pdf.

European External Action Service (EEAS) (1995). 'Barcelona Declaration and Euro-Mediterranean partnership', Available at http://www.eeas.europa.eu/euromed/docs/bd_en.pdf.

Faour, Muhammad (2007). 'Religion, demography, and politics in Lebanon,' *Middle Eastern Studies*, 43(6): 909–21.

Fargues, Philippe (2004). 'Arab migration to Europe: trends and policies', in *Arab Migration in a Globalized World*. Geneva: International Organization for Migration.

Farsoun, Samih (1988). 'Class Structure and Social Change in the Arab world', in H. Sharabi (ed.), *The Next Arab Decade*. Boulder, CO: Westview Press.

Fieldhouse, D.K. (2006). *Western Imperialism in the Middle East, 1914-1958*, Oxford: Oxford University Press.

Fisk, Robert (2001). *Pity the Nation: Lebanon at War*. Oxford: Oxford Paperbacks.

Fukuyama, Francis (1992). *The End of History and the Last Man*. New York: Free Press.

Fuller, Graham (2004). *The Future of Political Islam*. Basingstoke: Palgrave Macmillan.

Fumagalli, Matteo (2012). 'Voice, not democracy. civil society, ethnic politics and the search for political space in Central Asia', in Francesco Cavatorta (ed.), *State-society Relations under Authoritarian Constraints*. London: Routledge.

Gandhi, Jennifer. (2008). *Political Institutions under Dictatorship*. Cambridge: Cambridge University Press.

Garcia-Rivero, Carlos and Hennie Kotze (2007). 'Electoral support for Islamic parties in the Middle East and North Africa', *Party Politics* 13(5): 611–36.

Gause, F. Gregory (2005a), 'The international politics of the Gulf', in Louise Fawcett (ed.), *International Relations of the Middle East*. Oxford: Oxford University Press.

Gause, F. Gregory (2005b). 'Can democracy stop terrorism?,' *Foreign Affairs*, 84(5): 62–76.

Gause, F. Gregory and Sean L. Yom (2012). 'Resilient royals: how Arab monarchies hang on', *Journal of Democracy*, 23 (4): 74–88.

Geisser, Vincent and Abir Krefa (2011). 'L'uniforme ne fait plus le régime, les militaires arabes face aux révolutions', *Revue Internationale et Strategique*, 83(3): 93–102.

Gelvin, James (2008). *The Modern Middle East: A History*. Oxford: Oxford University Press.

Gerges, Fawaz (2013). 'The Islamist moment: from Islamic state to civil Islam?', *Political Science Quarterly*, 128(3): 389–426.

Gerges, Fawaz (2014). 'Introduction: a rupture', in Fawaz Gerges (ed.), *The New Middle East. Protest and Revolution in the Arab World*. Cambridge: Cambridge University Press.

Goldberg, Ellis (1992). 'Peasants in revolt: Egypt 1919', *International Journal Middle Eastern Studies*, 24(2): 261–80.

Goldberg, Giora (2006). 'The growing militarization of the Israeli political system', *Israel Affairs*, 12(3): 377–94.

Graciet, Catherine and Eric Laurent (2012). *Le Roi Prédateur*. Paris: Seuil.

Grami, Amel (2008). 'Gender equality in Tunisia', *British Journal of Middle Eastern Studies*, 35(3): 349–61.

Gray, Doris (2012). 'Tunisia after the uprising: Islamist and secular quests for women's rights', *Mediterranean Politics*, 17(3): 285–302.

Gray, Matthew (2013). *Qatar: Politics and the Challenges of Development*. Boulder, CO: Lynne Rienner.

Greenwood, Phoebe (2013), 'Victory for Israel's women of the wall after 25 year campaign', *The Guardian*, 9 June.

Gualtieri, Sarah (2006). '"Should a woman demand all the rights of a man?" From the Cairo periodical, *Al-Hilal*, 1894', in Camron Michael Amin, Benjamin C. Fortna and Elizabeth B. Frierson (eds), *The Modern Middle East: A Sourcebook for History*, Oxford: Oxford University Press.

Guazzone, Laura and Daniela Pioppi (2009). *The Arab State and Neo-liberal Globalization. The Restructuring of State Power in the Middle East*. New York: Ithaca Press.

Gubert, Flore and Christophe Nordman (2008). 'Migration from MENA to OECD countries: trends, determinants and prospects', World Bank. Available at: http://www.oecd-ilibrary.org/economics/migration-trends-in-north-africa_gen_papers-v2009-art11-en.

Gurses, Mehmet (2009). 'State-sponsored development, oil and democratization', *Democratization*, 16(3): 508–29.

Haas, Mark and David Lesch (2012). *The Arab Spring: Change and Resistance in the Middle East*. Boulder, CO: Westview Press.

Haber, Stephen and Victor Menaldo (2011). 'Do natural resources fuel authoritarianism? A reappraisal of the resource curse', *American Political Science Review*, 105(1): 1–26.

Haddad (1999). 'Les Algériennes dans le discours colonial', *Cahiers Berbères*, 20(1): 77–88.

Haddad, Bassam (2011). *Business Networks in Syria: The Political Economy of Authoritarian Resilience*. Stanford: Stanford University Press.

Haddad, Said (2012). 'Les forces armées libyennes de la proclamation de la Jamahiriya au lendemain de la chute de Tripoli: une marginalisation paradoxale', *Politique Africaine*, 125- (1): 65–82.

Haddad, Yvonne (1983). 'Sayyid Qutb: ideologue of Islamic revival', in John Esposito (ed.), *Voices of Resurgent Islam*. New York and Oxford: Oxford University Press.

Hafez, Mohammad (2003). *Why Muslims Rebel: Repression and Resistance in the Muslim World*. Boulder, CO: Lynn Rienner.

Haim, Sylvia (1962). *Arab Nationalism: An Anthology*. Berkeley, Los Angeles: University of California Press.

Haklai, Oded (2007). 'Religious-nationalist mobilization and state penetration: lessons from Jewish settlers' activism in Israel and the West Bank', *Comparative Politics*, 40(6): 713–39.

Halliday, Fred (1995). *Islam and the Myth of Confrontation: Religion and Politics in the Middle East*. London: I.B. Tauris.

Halliday, Fred (2002). 'A new global configuration' in Ken Booth and Timothy Dunne (eds), *Worlds in Collision: Terror and the Future of Global Order*. New York: Palgrave Macmillan.

Halliday, Fred (2005). *The Middle East in International Relations*. Cambridge: Cambridge University Press.

Halverson, Jeffry and Amy Kay (2011). 'Islamist feminism: constructing gender identities in post-colonial Muslim Societies', *Politics and Religion*, 4(4): 503–25.

Hamid, Shadi (2010). 'The myth of the democratizing monarchy', in Nathan Brown and Emad El-Din Shahin (eds), *The Struggle over Democracy in the Middle East: Regional Politics and External Policies*. London: Routledge.

Hanafi, Hassan (1982). 'The relevance of the Islamic alternative in Egypt', *Arab Studies Quarterly*, 4(1–2): 54–74.

Hardy, Roger (2010). *The Muslim Revolt: A Journey Through Political Islam*. London: Hurst.

Harrigan, Jane and Hamed El-Said (2010). 'The economic impact of IMF and World Bank programs in the Middle East and North Africa: a case study of Jordan, Egypt, Morocco and Tunisia, 1983–2004', *Review of Middle East Economies and Finance*, 6(2): 1–26.

Harrigan, Jane, Chengang Wang and Hamed El-Said (2005). 'The economic and political determinants of IMF and World Bank lending in the Middle East and North Africa', *World Development*, 34 (2): 247-70.

Hassan, Faysa (2001). 'Speaking for the other half', *Al-Ahram Weekly*, 523. Available at http://weekly.ahram.org.eg/2001/523/sc3.htm.

Hassan, Kawa (2012). 'Rethinking civic activism in the Middle East: agency without associations'. Available at: http://www.hivos.net/Hivos-Knowledge-Programme/Themes/Civil-Society-in-West-Asia/Publications/Policy-Papers/Re-thinking-Civic-Activism-in-the-Middle-East.

Haugbølle, Rikke Hostrup (2013). 'Rethinking the role of the media in the Tunisian uprising', in Nouri Gana (ed.), *The Making of the Tunisian Revolution*. Edinburgh: Edinburgh University Press.

Haynes, Jeffrey (2003). 'Comparative politics and globalisation', *European Political Science*, 2(3): 17-26.

Haynes, Jeff (2013). *An Introduction to International Relations and Religion*. Harlow: Pearson.

Henley, Alexander (2008). 'Politics of a church at war: Maronite catholicism in the Lebanese civil war', *Mediterranean Politics*, 13(3): 353-69.

Henry, Clement and Robert Springborg (2005). *Globalization and the Politics of Development in the Middle East*. Cambridge: Cambridge University Press.

Herb, Michael (1999). *All in the Family: Absolutism, Revolution and Democracy in the Middle Eastern Monarchies*. Albany: State University of New York Press.

Herb, Michael (2005). 'No representation without taxation? Rents, development and democracy', *Comparative Politics*, 37(3): 297-316.

Hertog, Steffan (2011). *Princes, Brokers and Bureaucrats: Oil and the State in Saudi Arabia*. Ithaca: Cornell University Press.

Heydemann, Steven (2007). 'Upgrading authoritarianism in the Arab world', Brookings Institution, Analysis Paper, 13: 1-37. Available at http://www.brookings.edu/,/media/Files/rc/papers/2007/10arabworld/10arabworld.pdf.

Heydemann, Steven (2013). 'Syria and the future of authoritarianism', *Journal of Democracy*, 24(4): 59-73.

Heydemann, Steven and Reinoud Leenders (2011). 'Authoritarian learning and authoritarian resilience: regime responses to the Arab Awakening', *Globalizations*, 8(5): 647-53.

Hibou, Beatrice (2011). *The Force of Obedience: The Political Economy of Repression in Tunisia*. Cambridge: Polity Press.

Hinnebusch, Ray (2003). *The International Politics of the Middle East*. Manchester: Manchester University Press.

Hinnebusch, Ray (2012). 'Europe and the Middle East: from imperialism to liberal peace?', *Review of European Studies*, 4(3): 18-31.

Hoffmann, Bert (2012). 'Civil society in the digital age: how the internet changes state–society relations in authoritarian regimes. the case of Cuba', in Francesco Cavatorta (ed.), *State-Society Relations Under Authoritarian Constraints*. London: Routledge.

Hoffman, Michael and Amaney Jamal (2012). 'The youth and the Arab Spring: cohort differences and similarities', *Middle East Law and Governance*, 4: 168-88.

Hoffmann, Anja and Christoph König (2013). 'Scratching the democratic façade: framing strategies of the 20th February Movement', *Mediterranean Politics*, 18(1): 1-22.

Hollis, Rosemary (2009). 'Europe in the Middle East', in Louise Fawcett (ed.), *International Relations of the Middle East*. Oxford: Oxford University Press.

Honwana, Alcinda (2011). 'Youth and the Tunisian Revolution', *SSRC Conflict Prevention and Peace Forum*. Available at: http://webarchive.ssrc.org/pdfs/

Alcinda_Honwana,_Youth_and_the_Tunisian_Revolution,_September_2011-CPPF_policy%20paper.pdf.

Hopwood, Derek (1991). *Egypt: Politics and Society – 1945–1990*. London: Harper Collins.

Hostrup, Rikke Haugbolle and Francesco Cavatorta (2012). 'Beyond Ghannouchi: Islamism and social change in Tunisia', *Middle East Report*, 262: 20–5.

Hourani, Albert (1962). *Arabic Political Thought in the Liberal Age 1798-1939*. Oxford: Oxford University Press.

Hourani, Albert (1991). *A History of the Arab Peoples*. London: Faber.

Howe, Marvine (2005). *Morocco. The Islamist Awakening and Other Challenges*. Oxford: Oxford University Press.

Human Rights Watch (2006). 'Women's rights in Middle East and North Africa', Human Rights Watch. Available at: http://www.hrw.org/women/overview-mena.html.

Humphreys, R. Stephen (1999). *Between Memory and Desire: The Middle East in a Troubled Age*. Berkeley: University of California Press.

Huntington, Samuel (1993a). 'The clash of civilizations?', *Foreign Affairs*, 72(3): 22–49.

Huntington, Samuel (1993b). *The Third Wave of Democratization*. Norman: Oklahoma University.

Hvidt, Martin (2009). 'The Dubai model: an outline of key development-process elements in Dubai', *International Journal of Middle East Studies*, 41(3): 397–418.

Hvidt, M. (2013), *Economic Diversification in the GCC Countries – Past Record and Future Trends: Research Paper No. 27: Kuwait Programme on Development, Governance and Globalization in the Gulf States*. The London School of Economics and Political Science, London. Research Paper. Kuwait Programme on Development, Governance and Globalization in the Gulf States, vol. 27.

Hyde-Price, Adrian (2006). 'Normative power Europe: a realist critique', *Journal of European Public Policy*, 13(2): 217–34.

Index Mundi (2014), 'Israel: foreign direct investment' Available at http://www.indexmundi.com/facts/israel/foreign-direct-investment.

Ingham, Barbara (1993). 'The meaning of development: interactions between "new" and "old" ideas', *World Development*, 21(11): 1803–21.

International Crisis Group (2013). 'La Tunisie de frontières: jihad et contrebande', Rapport 148, November: 1–39.

Iqbal, Farrukh and Mustapha Kamel Nabli (2004). 'Trade, foreign direct investment and development', Paper prepared for Conference entitled *The Middle East and North Africa Region: The Challenges of Growth and Globalization*, organized by the International Monetary Fund.

Ismael, Tarek and Jacqueline Ismael (2011). *Government and Politics of the Contemporary Middle East*. London: Routledge.

Israel Ministry of Foreign Affairs (MFA) (1948). *Declaration of Establishment of State of Israel*. Available at http://www.mfa.gov.il/mfa/foreignpolicy/peace/guide/pages/declaration%20of%20establishment%20of%20state%20of%20israel.aspx.

Issawi, Charles (1982). *An Economic History of the Middle East and North Africa*. New York: Columbia University Press.

Jamal, Amaney (2007). *Barriers to Democracy: The Other Side of Social Capital in Palestine and the Arab World*. Princeton: Princeton University Press.

Jansen, Godfrey (1979). *Militant Islam*. New York: Harper & Row.

Jervis, Robert (2002). 'Theories of war in an era of leading-power peace', *American Political Science Review*, 96(1): 1–14.

Jhaveri, Nayna J. (2004). 'Petroimperialism: US oil interests and the Iraq War', *Antipode*, 36(1): 2–11.

Joffé, George (ed.) (2002). *Jordan in Transition*. London: Macmillan.

Joya, Angela (2013). 'The Egyptian revolution: crisis of neo-liberalism and potential for democratic politics', *Review of African Political Economy*, 38(129): 367–86.

Judt, Tony (2010). *Postwar: A History of Europe Since 1945*. London: Vintage.

Kaboub, Fadhel (2013). 'The making of the Tunisian Revolution', *Middle East Development Journal*, 5(1): 1–21.

Kamrava, Mehran (2014). *Beyond the Arab Spring*. London: Hurst & Co.

Kamrava, Mehran (2011). 'The Arab Spring and the Saudi-led counterrevolution', *Orbis*, 56(4): 96–104.

Kamrava, Mehran and Frank Mora (1998). 'Civil society and democratisation in comparative perspective: Latin America and the Middle East', *Third World Quarterly*, 19(5): 893–916.

Kandil, Hazem (2012). 'Why did the Egyptian middle class march to Tahrir Square?', *Mediterranean Politics*, 17(2): 197–215.

Kandiyoti, Deniz (1997). 'Gendering the modern: on missing dimensions in the study of Turkish modernity', in Sibel Bozdoğan and Resat Kasaba (eds), *Rethinking Modernity and National Identity in Turkey*. Seattle and London: University of Washington Press.

Kaplan, Eben and Friedman, Caroline (2009). 'Israel's political system', *Council for Foreign Relations,* Available at: http://www.cfr.org/israel/israels-political-system/p8912.

Karam, Azza (1997). 'Islamist parties in the Arab world: ambiguities, contradictions and perseverance', *Democratization*, 4(4): 157–74.

Karsh, Efraim (1997). 'Cold War, post-Cold War: does it make a difference for the Middle East?', *Review of International Studies*, 23(2): 271–91.

Karshenas, Massoud and Valentine Moghadam (2009). 'Bringing social policy back in: a look at the Middle East and North Africa', *International Journal of Social Welfare*, 18(1): 52–61.

Kassem, Maye (2004). *Egyptian Politics: The Dynamics of Authoritarian Rule*. Boulder, CO: Lynne Rienner.

Kawakibi, Salam (2012). 'The paradox of government-organized civil society', in Paul Aarts and Francesco Cavatorta (eds), *Civil Society Activism in Syria and Iran*. Boulder, CO: Lynne Rienner.

Keddie, Nikki R. (1979). 'Problems in the study of Middle Eastern women', *International Journal of Middle East Studies*, 10(2): 225–40.

Keddie, Nikki R. (1981). *Roots of Revolution: An Interpretive History of Modern Iran*. New Haven and London: Yale University Press.

Keddie, Nikki R. (1991). 'Introduction: deciphering Middle Eastern women's history', in Nikki Keddie and Beth Baron (eds), *Women in Middle Eastern History*. New Haven and London: Yale University Press.

Keddie, Nikkie (1994). 'The revolt of Islam, 1790 to 1993: comparative considerations and relations to imperialism', *Comparative Studies in Society and History*, 36(3): 463–87.

Kenig, Ofer (2013). 'The 2013 Knesset Election results: a preliminary analysis of the upcoming Parliament', *Israeli Democracy Institute*. Available at http:// en.idi.org.il/analysis/articles/the-2013-knesset-election-results-a-preliminary-analysis-of-the-upcoming-parliament/.

Kepel, Gilles (1985). *The Prophet and Pharaoh: Muslim Extremism in Egypt*. London: Saqi.

Kepel, Gilles (2003). *The Trail of Political Islam*. London: Belknap Press.

Kepel, Gilles (2004). *Fitna: Guerre au coeur de l'Islam*. Paris: Gallimard.

Khalidi, Rashid (1997). *Palestinian Identity: The Construction of Modern National Consciousness*, New York: Columbia University Press.

Khalil, Asem (2009). 'Palestinian refugees in Arab States: a rights-based approach', Robert Schuman Centre for Advanced Studies. Available at http:// cadmus.eui.eu/handle/1814/10792.

Khazen, Farid El- (2003). 'Political parties in post-war Lebanon: parties in search of partisans', *Middle East Journal*, 57 (4): 605-24.

Kienle, Eberhard (1998). 'More than a response to Islamism: the political deliberalization of Egypt in the 1990s', *Middle East Journal*, 52(2): 219–35.

Kienle, Eberhard (2001). *A Grand Delusion: Democracy and Economic Reform in Egypt*. London: I.B. Tauris.

Kinsella, David (1994). 'Conflict in context: arms transfers and Third World rivalries during the Cold War', *American Journal of Political Science*, 38(3): 557–81.

Kinnimont, Jane (2012). ' "Bread, dignity and social justice": The Political Economy of Egypt's Transition', Available at http://www.chathamhouse. org/sites/files/chathamhouse/public/Research/Middle%20East/bp0412_ kinninmont.pdf.

Kolman, Iris (2015). 'Gender activism in Salafism: a case study of Salafi women in Tunis, Tunisia', in Francesco Cavatorta and Fabio Merone (eds), *Salaifsm After the Arab Awakening*, London: Hurst.

Kopecky, Petr and Cas Mudde (eds) (2003). *Uncivil Society? Contentious Politics in Post-Communist Europe*. London: Routledge.

Krauss, Clifford (2012). 'US reliance on oil from Saudi Arabia is growing again', *New York Times*, 16 August. Available at http://www.nytimes.com/2012/08/17/ business/energy-environment/us-reliance-on-saudi-oil-is-growing-again. html?pagewanted=all&_r=0.

Krauthammer, Charles (1990). 'The unipolar moment', *Foreign Affairs*, 70(1): 23–33.

Kubba, Laith (2000). 'The awakening of civil society', *Journal of Democracy*, 11(3): 84–90.

Laron, Guy (2010). 'Stepping back from the Third World', *Journal of Cold War Studies*, 12(4): 99–118.

Lefévre, Raphael (2013). *Ashes of Hama*. London: Hurst.

Lerner, Daniel (1958). *The Passing of Traditional Society: Modernizing the Middle East*. New York: Free Press.

Lewis, Bernard (1990), 'The roots of Muslim rage', *The Atlantic*, 1 September. Available at: http://www.theatlantic.com/magazine/archive/1990/09/the-roots-of-muslim-rage/304643/.

Little, Douglas (2004). 'Mission impossible: the CIA and the cult of covert action in the Middle East', *Diplomatic History*, 28(5): 663–701.

Liverani, Andrea (2008). *Civil Society in Algeria*. London: Routledge.

Longley Alley, April (2010). 'The rules of the game: unpacking patronage politics in Yemen', *Middle East Journal*, 64(3): 385–409.

Longley Alley, April (2013). 'Yemen changes everything...and nothing', *Journal of Democracy*, 24(4): 74–85.

Lust, Ellen (2006). 'Elections under authoritarianism: preliminary lessons from Jordan', *Democratization*, 13(3): 455–70.

Mahmood, Saba (2004). *Politics of Piety: Islamic Revival and the Feminist Subject*. Princeton: Princeton University Press.

Mainwaring, Scott and Matthew Shugart (eds) (1997). *Presidentialism and Democracy in Latin America*. Cambridge: Cambridge University Press.

Malley, Robert (1996). *The Call from Algeria*. Los Angeles: University of California Press.

Manners, Ian (2002). 'Normative power Europe: a contradiction in terms?', *Journal of Common Market Studies*, 40(2): 235–58.

Mansfield, Peter (1992). *The Arabs*. London: Penguin Books.

Marsot, Afaf Lufti (2007). *A History of Egypt from the Arab Conquest to the Present*. Cambridge: Cambridge University Press.

Martinez, Luis (2012). 'Lybie: les usages mafieux de la rente pétrolière', *Politique Africaine*, 125: 23–42.

Masoud, Tarek (2014). *Counting Islam*. Cambridge: Cambridge University Press.

Matthiesen, Toby (2013). *Sectarian Gulf: Bahrain, Saudi Arabia and the Arab Spring that wasn't*. Stanford: Stanford University Press.

McCallum, Fiona (2012). 'Christian political participation in the Arab world', *Islam and Christian–Muslim Relations*, 23(1): 3–18.

McKay, John (2012). 'Reassessing development theory', in Damien Kingsbury *et al.* (eds), *International Development: Issues and Challenges*. Basingstoke: Palgrave Macmillan.

McMeekin, Sean (2011). *The Berlin–Baghdad Express*. London: Penguin.

Menoret, Pascal (2005). *The Saudi Enigma*. London: Zed Books.

Merone, Fabio (2015). 'Enduring class struggle in Tunisia: the fight for identity beyond political Islam', *British Journal of Middle Eastern Studies*, 42(1): 74–87

Merone, Fabio and Francesco Cavatorta (2013). 'Salafist movement and sheikhism in the Tunisian democratic transition', *Middle East Law and Governance*, 5(2): 308–30.

Middle East Report (2013). 'Christians', *Middle East Report*, 43(267).

Milton-Edwards Beverley and Hinchcliffe, Peter (2004), *Conflicts in the Middle East Since 1945*. London: Routledge

Milton-Edwards, Beverley (2007). 'Hamas: victory with ballots and bullets', *Global Change, Peace and Security*, 19(3): 301–16.

Milton-Edwards, Beverley and Stephen Farrell (2010). *Hamas: The Islamic Resistance Movement*. Cambridge: Polity Press.

Mitchell, Timothy (1991). *Colonizing Egypt*. Berkeley: University of California Press.

Moghadam, Valentine (2004). 'Patriarchy in transition: women and the changing family in the Middle East', *Journal of Comparative Family Studies*, 35(2): 137-62.

Moghadam, Valentine (2010). 'Urbanization and women's citizenship in the Middle East', *Brown Journal of World Affairs*, 17(1): 19–34.

Mohammadi, Ali (2003). *Iran Encountering Globalization*. London: Routledge.

Molyneux, Maxine (1995). 'Women's rights and political contingency: the case of Yemen 1990–1994', *Middle East Journal*, 49(3): 418–31.

Morris, Benny (1989). *The Birth of the Palestinian Refugee Problem: 1947–1949*. Cambridge: Cambridge University Press.

Muasher, Marwan (2011), 'A decade of struggling Rreform efforts in Jordan: the resilience of the rentier system', Carnegie Endowment for International Peace, Washington, DC.

Mubarak, Jamil (1998). 'Middle East and North Africa: development policy in view of a narrow agricultural resource base', *World Development*, 26(5): 877–95.

Murphy, Emma (2012). 'Problematizing Arab youth: generational narratives of systemic Failure', *Mediterranean Politics*, 17(1): 5–22.

Najem, Tom (2012). *Lebanon. The Politics of a Penetrated Society*. London: Routledge.

Nasser, Gamal Abdel (1955). 'The Egyptian Revolution', *Foreign Affairs*, 33(2): 199–211.

National Security Archive (2013). 'CIA confirms role in 1953 Iran coup'. Available at http://www2.gwu.edu/~nsarchiv/NSAEBB/NSAEBB435/#_ftn1

Okruhlik, Gwen and Patrick Conge (1997). 'National autonomy, labour migration and political crisis: Yemen and Saudi Arabia', *Middle East Journal*, 51(4): 554–65.

Okruhlik, Gwen (1999). 'Rentier wealth, unruly law and the rise of opposition: the political economy of oil states', *Comparative Politics*, 31(3): 295–315.

Onley, James (2009). 'Britain and the Gulf shaikhdoms, 1820–1971: the politics of protection', CIRS Occasional Paper, Georgetown University 4: 1–44.

Ougartchinska, Roumiana and Rosario Priore (2013). *Pour la peau de Kadhafi*. Paris: Fayard.

Owen, Roger (2004). *State Power and Politics in the Making of the Modern Middle East*. London: Routledge.

Owen, Roger (2012). *The Rise and Fall of Arab Presidents For Life*. Cambridge: Harvard University Press.

Owen, Roger and Pamuk, Sevket (1998). *A History of Middle East Economies in the Twentieth Century*. London: IB Tauris.

Ozzano, Luca (2013). 'The many faces of the political god: a typology of religiously oriented parties', *Democratization* 20(5): 807–30.

Pace, Michelle (2009). 'Paradoxes and Contradictions in EU democracy promotion in the Mediterranean: the limits on EU normative power', *Democratization*, 16(1): 39–58.

Pace, Michelle and Cavatorta, Francesco (2010). 'The post-normative turn in European Union (EU)–Middle East and North Africa (MENA) relations: an introduction', *European Foreign Affairs Review*, 15(5): 581–8.

Pace, Michelle and Cavatorta, Francesco (2012). 'The Arab uprisings in theoretical perspective: an introduction', *Mediterranean Politics*, 17(2): 125–38.

Pamuk, Sevket (2000). *A Monetary History of the Ottoman Empire*. Cambridge: Cambridge University Press.

Pappé, Ilan (2005). *The Modern Middle East*. London: Routledge.

Perkins, Kenneth (2004). *A History of Modern Tunisia*. Cambridge: Cambridge University Press.

Park, Bill (2012). *Modern Turkey: People, State and Foreign Policy in a Globalized World*. London: Routledge.

Pellicer, Miquel and Eva Wegner (2012). 'Socio-economic voter profile and motives for Islamist support in Morocco', *Party Politics*, 20(1): 116–33.

Perrault, Gilles (1990). *Notre ami le roi*. Paris: Gallimard.

Perthes, Volker (1995). *The Political Economy of Syria under Asad*. London: I.B. Tauris.

Peters, Ann Mariel and Peter Moore (2009). 'Beyond boom and bust: external rents, durable authoritarianism and institutional adaptation in the Hashemite Kingdom of Jordan', *Studies in Comparative International Development*, 44(3): 256–85.

Pew Research Center (2012). 'Most Muslims want democracy, personal freedoms, and Islam in political life', *Pew Research Global Attitudes* Project. Available at http://www.pewglobal.org/2012/07/10/most-muslims-want-democracy-personal-freedoms-and-islam-in-political-life/.

Phillips, Sarah (2008). *Yemen's Democracy Experiment in Regional Perspective: Patronage and Pluralized Authoritarianism*. Basingstoke: Palgrave Macmillan.

Piscatori, James (1991). 'Religion and realpolitik: Islamic responses to the Gulf War', in James Piscatori (ed.), *Islamic Fundamentalisms and the Gulf Crisis*. Chicago: American Academy of Arts and Sciences.

Pollack, Josh (2002). 'Saudi Arabia and the United States, 1931–2002', *Middle East Review of International Affairs*, 6(3): 77–102.

Population Reference Bureau (PRB) (2001). 'Population trends and challenges in the Middle East and North Africa'. Available at: http://www.prb.org/About/InternationalPrograms/Projects-Programs/MENA.aspx.

Pratt, Nicola (2007). *Democracy and Authoritarianism in the Arab World*. Boulder, CO: Lynne Rienner.

Press, Eyal (2010). 'Israel's holy warriors', *New York Review of Books*, 29 April.

Pripstein Posusney, Martha (2004). 'Enduring authoritarianism: Middle East lessons for comparative theory', *Comparative Politics*, 36(2): 127–38.

Pripstein Posusney, Marsha (2005). 'Multiparty elections in the Arab World: election rules and opposition responses', in Marsha Pripstein Posusney and Michele Penner Angrist (eds), *Authoritarianism in the Middle East: Regimes and Resistance*. Boulder, CO: Lynn Rienner.

Project on Middle East Political Science (2012). 'The new Salafi politics', *POMEPS Briefings 14*. Available at http://pomeps.org/wp-content/uploads/2012/10/POMEPS_BriefBooklet14_Salafi_web.pdf.

Putnam Robert (1998). 'Diplomacy and domestic politics: the logic of two-level games', *International Organization* 42(3): 427-60.

Qutb, Sayyd (1978). *Milestones*. Beirut: Holy Koran Publishing House.

Rahman, Anisur (2011). 'Migration and human rights in the Gulf' in *Migration and the Gulf*, Washington, DC: Middle East Institute. Available at http://www.voltairenet.org/IMG/pdf/Migration_and_the_Gulf.pdf.

Richards, Alan and John Waterbury (1991). *A Political Economy of the Middle East*. Cairo: American University Press.

Rivetti, Paola (2013). 'Coopting civil society activism in Iran', in Paul Aarts and Francesco Cavatorta (eds), *Civil Society in Syria and Iran*. Boulder, CO: Lyne Rienner.

Roberts, Hugh (2013). 'The revolution that wasn't,' *London Review of Books*, 35(17). Available at http://www.lrb.co.uk/v35/n17/hugh-roberts/the-revolution-that-wasn't.

Rogan, Eugene (2010). *The Arabs: A History*. London: Penguin Books.

Ross, Michael (2012). *The Oil Curse: How Petroleum Wealth Shapes the Development of Nations*. Princeton: Princeton University Press.

Roudi, Farzaneh (2011). 'Youth population and employment in the Middle East and North Africa: opportunity or challenge?'. New York: United Nations. Available at www.un.org/esa/population/meetings/egm-adolescents/p06_roudi.pdf.

Rowe, Paul (2009). 'Building Coptic civil society: Christian groups and the state in Mubarak's Egypt', *Middle Eastern Studies*, 45(1): 111–26.

Ruedy, John (2005). *Modern Algeria*. Bloomington: Indiana University Press.

Rutherford, Bruce (2013). 'Egypt: the origins and conscquences of the January 25 uprising', in Mark Haas and David Lesch (2012). *The Arab Spring: Change and Resistance in the Middle East*. Boulder, CO: Westview Press.

Ruthven, M. (2006), *Islam in the World*, Oxford: Oxford University Press.

Ryan, Curtis (2012). 'The armed forces and the Arab uprisings: the case of Jordan', *Middle East Law and Governance*, 4: 153–67.

Sadiki, Larbi (2010). 'Whither Arab republicanism? The rise of family rule and the end of democratization in Egypt, Libya and Yemen', *Mediterranean Politics*, 15(1): 99–107.

Said, Edward (1978). *Orientalism*. London: Penguin

Salisbury, Peter (2011). 'Yemen's economy: oil, imports and élites'. Available at http://www.chathamhouse.org/publications/papers/view/179191.

Salloukh, Bassel F. (2010), 'Democracy in Lebanon: the primacy of the sectarian system', in Nathan Brown and Emad El-Din Shahin (eds), *The Struggle over*

Democracy in the Middle East: Regional Politics and External Policies. London: Routledge.

Sater, James (2010). *Morocco: Challenges to Tradition and Modernity.* London: Routledge.

Sawani, Youssef (2014). 'The February 17th *Intifada* in Libya: disposing of the regime and issues of state building', in Ricardo Laremont (ed.), *Revolution, Revolt and Reform in North Africa: The Arab Spring and Beyond.* London: Routledge.

Sayigh, Yezid (2012). 'Above the state: the officers' republic in Egypt', *Carnegie Endowment for International Peace*, August: 1–28.

Schlumberger, Oliver (2000). 'Arab political economy and the European Union's Mediterranean policy: what prospects for development?', *New Political Economy*, 5(2): 247–68.

Schlumberger, Oliver (2007). 'Debating the dynamics and durability of nondemocratic regimes' in Oliver Schlumberger (ed.), *Debating Arab Authoritarianism: Dynamics and Durability in Nondemocratic Regimes.* Stanford: Stanford University Press.

Schlumberger, Oliver (2007). *Debating Arab Authoritarianism: Dynamics and Durability in Nondemocratic Regimes.* Stanford: Stanford University Press.

Seeberg, Peter (2010). 'Union for the Mediterranean: pragmatic multilateralism and the depoliticization of European–Middle Eastern relations', *Middle East Critique*, 19(3): 287–302.

Seferdjeli, Ryme (2006). 'Two views of women fighters during the Algerian War of liberation', in Camron Michael Amin, Benjamin C. Fortna and Elizabeth B. Frierson (eds), *The Modern Middle East: A Sourcebook for History*, Oxford: Oxford University Press.

Selby, Jan (2005). 'The geopolitics of water in the Middle East: fantasies and realities', *Third World Quarterly*, 26(2): 329–49.

Selime, Zakia (2011). *Between Feminism and Islam: Human Rights and Shari'a Law in Morocco.* Minneapolis: University of Minnesota Press.

Sellam, Hesham (ed.) (2013). *Egypt's Parliamentary Elections. 2011–2012: A Critical Guide to a Changing Political Arena* (Washington: DC: Tadween Publishing).

Semiane, Sid Ahmed (2005). *Au refuge de balles perdues. Chronique des deux Algérie.* Paris: Ed. La Découverte.

Sfeir, Antoine (2006). *Tunisie Terre de Paradoxes.* Paris: Editions de l'Archipel.

Sharon, Jeremy (2012). 'CBS Report: Christian population in Israel is growing', *Jerusalem Post*, 25 December. Available at http://www.jpost.com/National-News/CBS-report-Christian-population-in-Israel-growing.

Shehata, Samer (2012). 'Introduction', in Samer Shehata (ed.), *Islamist Politics in the Middle East: Movements and Change.* London: Routledge.

Shehata, Samer (2012). *Islamist Politics in the Middle East: Movements and Change.* London: Routledge.

Shlaim, Avi (2005). 'The rise and fall of the Oslo peace process', in Louise Fawcett (ed.), *International Relations of the Middle East.* Oxford: Oxford University Press.

Sika, Nadine (2012). 'Youth political engagement in Egypt: from abstention to revolution', *British Journal of Middle Eastern Studies*, 39(2): 181–99.

Singerman, Daine (2004). 'The networked world of Islamist social movements', in Quintan Wiktorowicz (ed.), *Islamic Activism. A Social Movement Theory Approach*. Bloomington: Indiana University Press.

Skalli, Loubna (2011). 'Generational politics and renewal of leadership in the Moroccan women's movement', *International Feminist Journal of Politics*, 13(3): 329–48.

Smooha, Sammy (2002). 'The model of ethnic democracy: Israel as a Jewish and democratic state', *Nations and Nationalism*, 8(4): 475–503.

Springborg, Robert (2012). 'The political economy of the Arab Spring', *Mediterranean Politics*, 16(3): 427–33.

St John, Ronald Bruce (2011). *Libya: Continuity and Change*. London: Routledge.

Stein, Ewan (2012). 'Egypt's fraught transition. Revolution or coup?', *Survival*, 55(4): 45–66.

Stepan, Alfred (2012). 'Tunisia's transition and the twin tolerations', *Journal of Democracy*, 23(2): 89–103.

Stewart, Dona J. (2002). 'Middle East Urban Studies II: growth, environment and economic development', *Urban Studies*, 23(4): 388–94.

Storm, Lise (2013). *Party Politics and the Prospects for Democracy in North Africa*. Boulder, CO: Lynne Rienner.

Szymkowicz, Sarah (2013), 'Women in Israel: women of the Wall', *Jewish Virtual Library*. Available at https://www.jewishvirtuallibrary.org/jsource/Judaism/WOW.html.

Taraki, Lisa (2004). 'The role of women', in Jillian Schwedler and Deborah Gerner (eds), *Understanding the Contemporary Middle East*. Boulder, CO: Lynn Rienner.

Tank, Pinar (2005). 'Political Islam in Turkey: a state of controlled secularity', *Turkish Studies*, 6(1): 3–19.

Taspinar, Omer (2012). *Turkey: The New Model*, Brookings Institute. Available at http://www.brookings.edu/research/papers/2012/04/24-turkey-new-model-taspinar.

Tekdal Fildis, Ayse (2012). 'Roots of Alawite–Sunni rivalry in Syria', *Middle East Policy*, 19(2): 148–56.

Tempest, Clive (1997). 'Myths from Eastern Europe and the legends of the West', *Democratization*, 4(1):132–44.

Tessler, Mark, Amaney Jamal and Michael Robbins (2012). 'New findings on Arabs and democracy,' *Journal of Democracy*, 23(4): 89–103.

Tessler, Mark and Jolene Jesse (1996). 'Gender and support for Islamist movements: evidence from Egypt, Kuwait and Palestine', *Muslim World*, 86(2): 200–28.

Teti, Andrea (2012). 'The EU's first response to the "Arab Spring": a critical discourse analysis of the partnership for democracy and shared prosperity', *Mediterranean Politics*, 17(3): 265–82.

Tetreault, Mary-Ann (2011). 'The winter of the Arab Spring in the Gulf monarchies', *Globalizations*, 8(5): 629–37.

Tignor, Robert (1997). 'Introduction', in *Al-Jabarti's Chronicle of the French Occupation, 1798*. Princeton: Markus Wiener Publishers.

Trofimov, Yaroslav (2007). *The Siege of Mecca: The 1979 Uprising at Islam's Holiest Shrine*. New York: Anchor Books.

Trumbull, George (2010). 'Speaking of water', *Middle East Report*, 40 Available at: http://www.merip.org/mer/mer254/speaking-water

Tsourapas, Gerasimos (2013). 'The other side of a neo-liberal miracle: economic reform and political de-liberalization in Ben Ali's Tunisia', *Mediterranean Politics*, 18(1): 23–41.

Twomey, Michael (2006). 'Statistical tables and comments', in Camron Michael Amin, Benjamin C. Fortna and Elizabeth B. Frierson (eds), *The Modern Middle East: A Sourcebook for History*, Oxford: Oxford University Press.

Ulusoy, Kivanc (2014), 'Elections and regime change in Turkey: tenacious rise of political Islam', in Mahmoud Hamad and Khalil al-Anani (eds), *Elections and Democratization in the Middle East*. Basingstoke: Palgrave Macmillan.

United Nations (2010). 'Directory of UN resources on gender and women's Issues: North Africa and the Middle East'. Available at http://www.un.org/womenwatch/directory/north_africa_and_the_middle_east_10476.htm.

United Nations (2010). *The State of the World's Women: Trends and Statistics*. UN: New York.

UNDP (UN Development Programme) (2009). *Arab Human Development Report 2009: Challenges to Human Security in the Arab Countries*. Available at: http://www.unhcr.org/refworld/docid/4a6f0ad82.html.

US Energy Information Administration (2012). 'Top world oil producers – 2012'. Available at http://www.eia.gov/countries/index.cfm#.

US Library of Congress (2012).'Lebanon constitutional law and the political rights of religious communities', available at http://www.loc.gov/law/help/lebanon-constitutional-law.php.

Valbjørn, Morten (2012). 'Upgrading post-democratization studies: re-examining a repoliticized Arab world in a transition to somewhere', *Middle East Critique*, 21(1): 25–35.

Valbjørn, Morten and Andre Bank (2012). 'The new Arab Cold War: rediscovering the Arab dimension of Middle East regional politics', *Review of International Studies*, 38(1): 3–24.

Vandewalle, Dirk (2006). *A History of Modern Libya*. Cambridge: Cambridge University Press.

Volpi, Frédéric (2006). 'Algeria's pseudo-democratic politics', *Democratization*, 13(3): 442–55.

Volpi, Frédéric (2012). 'Explaining (and re-explaining) political change in the Middle East during the Arab Spring: trajectories of democratization and of authoritarianism in the Maghreb', *Democratization*, 20(6): 969–90.

Volpi, Frédéric (2013). 'Algeria versus the Arab Spring', *Journal of Democracy*, 24(3): 104–15.

Wall Street Journal (2011). 'Interview with Syrian President Bashar al-Asad'. Available at http://online.wsj.com/news/articles/SB10001424052748703833204576114712441122894.

White, Gregory (2005). 'Free trade as a strategic instrument in the war on terror? The 2004 US–Moroccan Free Trade Agreement', *Middle East Journal*, 59(4): 597–616.

Wiktorowicz, Quintan (2000). 'Civil society as social control: state power in Jordan,' *Comparative Politics*, 33(1): 43–61.

Willis, Michael (2002). 'Political parties in the Maghrib: the illusion of significance?', *Journal of North African Studies*, 7(2): 1–22.

Wilson, Chris (2007). 'Demographic transition in Europe and around the Mediterranean', in Thierry Fabre and Paul Sant-Cassia (eds), *Between Europe and the Mediterranean: The Challenge and the Fears*. Basingstoke: Palgrave Macmillan.

Wilson, Rodney (2013). *Economic Development in the Middle East*. London: Routledge.

Winckler, Onn (2011). 'Labor migration to the GCC States: patterns, scale, and Policies', in *Migration and the Gulf*, Washington, DC: Middle East Institute. Available at http://www.voltairenet.org/IMG/pdf/Migration_and_the_Gulf.pdf.

World Bank (2004). 'Gender and development in the Middle East and North Africa: women in the public sphere'. Available at https://open knowledge.worldbank.org/bitstream/handle/10986/15036/281150PAPER0 Gender010Development0in0MNA.pdf?sequence=1.

World Bank (2011a). *Middle East and North Africa: Migrants and Remittances Factbook*, Washington, DC: World Bank.

World Bank (2011b). 'The Middle East and North Africa and dependence on the capital-intensive hydrocarbon sector', *MENA Knowledge and Learning Quick Note Series*, No.38, March. Available at http://siteresources.worldbank. org/INTMENA/Resources/QN38_.pdf.

World Bank (2014). *Data: Middle East and North Africa*. Available at http://data. worldbank.org/region/middle-east-and-north-africa.

World Economic Forum (2010). 'Trade competitiveness and growth in the MENA region', in *The Arab World Competitiveness Review, 2010*, available at: http:// www3.weforum.org/docs/WEF_GCR_ArabWorldReview_2010_EN.pdf.

Wright, Quincy (1926). 'The bombardment of Damascus', *American Journal of International Law*, 20(2): 263–80.

Wright, Robin (2012). *The Islamists are Coming: Who They Really Are*. Washington, DC: US Institute of Peace.

Yemen Polling Centre (2010). 'Yemeni political parties: images, attitudes and societal demands'. Available at: http://www.yemenpolling.com/index. php?action=showNews&id=37.

Yergin, Daniel (1991). *The Prize: The Epic Quest for Oil, Money and Power*. London: Simon & Schuster.

Yilmaz, Hakan (2002). 'External–Internal linkages in democratization: developing an open model of democratic change', *Democratization*, 9(2): 67-84.

Yom, Sean (2005). 'Civil society and democratization in the Arab world', *Middle East Review of International Affairs*, 9(4): 14–33.

Yom, Sean and Mohammad al-Momani (2008). 'The international dimensions of authoritarian regime stability: Jordan in the post-Cold War era', *Arab Studies Quarterly*, 30(1): 39–60.

Yom, Sean and Gregory F. Gause (2012). 'Resilient royals: how Arab monarchies hang on', *Journal of Democracy*, 23(4): 74–88.

Youngs, Richard (2004). 'Normative dynamics and strategic interests in the EU's external identity', *Journal of Common Market Studies*, 42(2): 415–35.

Yousef, Tarik (2004). 'Development, growth and policy reform in the Middle East and North Africa since 1950', *Journal of Economic Perspectives*, 18(3): 91–116.

Zaccara, Luciano (2014). 'Elections and authoritarianism in the Islamic Republic of Iran', in Mahmoud Hamad and Khalil al-Anani (eds), *Elections and Democratization in the Middle East*. Basingstoke: Palgrave Macmillan.

Zakaria, Fareed (2004). 'Islam, democracy and constitutional liberalism', *Political Science Quarterly*, 119(1): 1–20.

Ziadeh, Radwah (2010). *Power and Policy in Syria: Intelligence Services, Foreign Relations and Democracy in the Modern Middle East*. London: I.B.Tauris.

Zoubir, Yahia and Ahmed Aghrout (2012). 'Algeria's path to reform: authentic change?', *Middle East Policy*, 19(2): 66–83.

Zoubir, Yahia and Louisa Dris Ait-Hamadouche (2013). *The Maghreb: Algeria, Libya, Morocco and Tunisia*. Praeger.

Zubaida, Sami (1993). *Islam, the People and the State: Political Ideas and Movements in the Middle East*. London: I.B. Tauris.

Index

Printed by Printforce, the Netherlands